The First Tithe

Memoirs and Edifying Discourses of the Hebrew War for Freedom

Dr. Israel Eldad

Translated with a Foreword and Notes
by Zev Golan

The Jabotinsky Institute in Israel
Tel-Aviv 2008

ISBN - 9789654160155

Originally published in Hebrew as *Maaser Rishon*

Distributed worldwide by:
Gefen Books
600 Broadway, Lynbrook, N.Y. 11563 USA
1-800-477-5257
orders@gefenpublishing.com
www.israelbooks.com

Printed and Designed by Hidekel Press Ltd.

Contents

Translator's Foreword

Eldad—one of the most controversial names in Israel for over five decades. A founder of the Jewish state whose story has, until now, been unavailable in English.

Eldad—arguing with Jabotinsky and defending a young, beleaguered Menachem Begin. Eldad—in the room when Begin is arrested by the Soviet police in 1940. Eldad—escaping from Europe and making his way to Eretz Israel (the Land of Israel). Eldad—the lonely nights in Tel Aviv with Underground commander Avraham Stern. Eldad—fiery leader of the Underground, sharing command with Yitzhak Shamir. Eldad—paralyzed while evading the police, directing the Underground from prison. Eldad—escaping from prison in a body cast. Eldad—ordering assassinations of enemies of Israel. Eldad—the most dangerous man in the new Jewish state, Ben Gurion's nemesis.

These memoirs follow him on his geographic and intellectual journeys: from Poland to Israel, from Schopenhauer to Stern, from philosophy to terrorism. Eldad provides English readers with an opportunity to know Stern, the man; Eldad introduces Uri Zvi Greenberg, the greatest Hebrew poet of the century; Eldad deals with the morality and motivation of the Jewish freedom fighters. In these memoirs, the man who fled the Nazi Holocaust together with Begin and who commanded Lehi, the Sternist underground, with Shamir, provides new, personal insights into these future prime ministers of Israel and new facts concerning the war for a Jewish state.

Readers of *The First Tithe* will accompany Eldad on his last-minute escape from the Nazis and on his perilous escape from prison, to the secret Command meetings with Shamir and the negotiations with Begin to unite the Underground, from the Holocaust to redemption.

The Hagana's story has been told; the Irgun's story, too. Now for the first time, the full story of the feared "Stern Gang" is available in English, told by the ideological force behind it. Eldad's recollections are honest and, when relating to the strange behavior of the Zionist establishment, especially controversial. His reflections are incisive, as befits one of Israel's great philosophers, the man who translated most of Nietzsche's works into Hebrew.

This book appears in translation at an especially urgent time, when world Jewry is trying to understand the baffling policies being followed by leaders of the Jewish state, policies which sometimes seem to contradict the purported commitment of these leaders to a safe and secure state. To try to understand what is happening in Israel today without knowledge of the facts and events described in *The First Tithe*, is like missing the first act of an opera or a Greek drama and expecting to understand the finale. These facts and events that preceded the creation of Israel are largely unknown, not only to English-language readers, but even to readers of Hebrew. Students in Israel are taught almost nothing of the history of modern Israel and absolutely nothing of what is described in this book. Historians and political scientists who try to explain Begin at Camp David, Shamir at Madrid, Rabin and Barak in their dealings with Arabs, without first understanding the roots of the behavior of these individuals and the movements they represent in Zionism, are writing blind. How can one explain Begin's far-reaching concessions without knowing of the rooftop conversations Eldad and Begin held in the 1940s? How can one understand Shamir's behavior as premier during the Gulf War without reading Eldad's analysis of the personality of his Underground co-commander? How can one account for the policies pursued by three different Labor Party prime ministers without putting their motives in the context of the Labor movement's goals before the creation of Israel, as described by Eldad?

My first encounter with Eldad was via a small booklet of his, *The Road to Full Redemption*. I'd had Jewish education from kindergarten through university and never anywhere heard the ideas expressed by Eldad. His inimitable prose put me on the Road of the booklet's title, and I have been on it ever since; I read it one spring and moved to Israel by summer. I immediately called Eldad and asked to meet him.

Eldad plopped with a deep, tired sigh into the chair opposite mine. I told him I could come back another time. "No," he sighed again, excusing his weariness. "It's just that I just finished translating Professor Walter Kaufmann's *Nietzsche* into Hebrew." The admiration I had for the author of *The Road to Full Redemption* turned now to awe. Having discovered this common affinity for the German philosopher, we discussed Nietzsche for a while. Eldad told me of a conversation he'd had with Kaufmann, Nietzsche's English translator. Eldad asked Kaufmann if he thought Dionysius, Nietzsche's free-spirited Greek ideal, were possible in Jerusalem. Kaufmann pondered this beautiful and deep question for a few seconds before replying: "Yes—King David dancing before the Ark of God's Covenant."

Eldad asked me what I was doing in Israel, and I answered that if I found a place to live and a good job, I was going to stay. "No!" he thundered, waving an accusative-parent's finger at me. The best answer he knew, he said, was given by Rachel Yanait Ben-Zvi when she was asked so many decades earlier why she had come. She answered with one Hebrew word: *Lihiot* (to live). This is your home and your country, continued Eldad, and you do not leave your country if you cannot live in a particular neighborhood, you move to another neighborhood or city. You do not leave your home if you cannot get a high-paying job, you take a different job. You need to make the decision to stay, after that all will be easy.

Years later I thanked Eldad for this advice, which worked for me. He told me then, on this later occasion, that the advice holds true for any decision. You need to make a decision and stick to it; all that follows is easy.

Over time I became one of Eldad's acolytes, often visiting his Rehavia apartment to run errands, help out, work on literary or political projects, or ask for advice. Eventually, following my first meeting, I had discovered Eldad's membership on the triumvirate that ran the Lehi Underground (officially named Fighters for the Freedom of Israel, and also known as the Stern Group) in the 1940's struggle for Hebrew independence, the Lehi being the most radical of all the movements fighting to expel the British from the Jewish homeland. Then I learned the story of Eldad's arrest, escape, and his chess games with Begin in war-torn Poland. Later I found out that Eldad had published a book telling his story of the Underground's fight for Israel. This is that book.

Eldad: Biographical Data

Israel Scheib (later, Eldad) was born November 11, 1910, in Eastern Galicia.[1] His mother was of Hasidic descent, his father an educated Zionist. Their home was what we would call traditional. The Scheibs took to the road as refugees during the First World War; Israel's father gave him daily Hebrew lessons. They played chess together in an attic apartment. One of Eldad's strongest memories from that time was his mother distraught at not having a candleholder for the Sabbath candles, and his father splitting a potato in two to hold the candles.

In 1918 the Scheibs moved to Lvov, in time for young Israel to witness a funeral procession for Jews murdered and Torah scrolls burned in a pogrom.

Israel was eight years old; his day began at 4 a.m. when he rose to buy bread, afterward rolling cigarettes with his brothers to help support the family. He was already reading Abraham Mapu's *Love of Zion* and stories of national renewal by Peretz Smolenskin, but also Daniel Defoe's individualistic *Robinson Crusoe*. No matter how poor they were, Israel's father always ensured there were plenty of books at home.

Israel attended a Jewish high school for classical, humanistic studies, then after school took private lessons in Hebrew and Judaism, and after these lessons went to night school for more Hebrew. At sixteen, he left home to study in Lodz, where the high school itself functioned in Hebrew.

Israel had two great encounters when he was eighteen: He read Micah Joseph Berdichevsky, who was heavily influenced by Nietzsche, and because of Berdichevsky, he decided to read Nietzsche's *Zarathustra*; and he heard Vladimir Jabotinsky lecture in Lodz.

That same year, having completed high school, Israel enrolled at the Rabbinical Seminary of Vienna, where every morning he studied Talmud, Bible, Ibn Ezra, Aramaic, Midrash, Jewish history and religious philosophy. In the afternoons, he studied aesthetics, Indian philosophy, logic, psychology, history and general philosophy at the University of Vienna. Six years later, he completed his university doctorate on "The Voluntarism of Eduard von Hartmann, with Its Basis in Schopenhauer," but he never took his rabbinical exams at the seminary.

Meanwhile, however, he had stepped onto the road of Zionist history. He attended, with his father, a protest demonstration at the local British consulate following the 1929 Arab riots in Eretz Israel. The next year, in what may have been the seminal event of his life, he read a poem by Uri Zvi Greenberg, "I'll Tell It to a Child," in the seminary library. The result was, as he put it, "an earthquake in my heart." He was attracted by the pessimism of the poem, which recalled to him the pessimism of Schopenhauer. In 1932 or 1933, Israel met Greenberg at a speech Greenberg was giving titled "The Land of Israel Is in Flames."

In the course of the 1930s, Israel attended Revisionist-Zionist (Jabotinsky's movement) student gatherings, lectured at Revisionist meetings, met Jabotinsky, learned of the first anti-British activist movement in Eretz Israel, the Brit Habirionim, and became friendly with Uri Zvi Greenberg. He also met his future wife, Batya Waschitz, in 1932. They were married in 1937. Most of Eldad's followers years later looked to him as a political leader and assumed his personal life was secondary. But Eldad was a romantic, and he and Batya shared a deep love that lasted over six decades.

Israel's first job after graduation was teaching high school in Volkovysk; he immediately fell in love with teaching, too. He published articles in Revisionist journals and became the commander of a local Betar (the Revisionist youth movement) chapter, though till then he had not even been a member of the organization. Natan Friedman, future co-commander of the Stern Group with Eldad and Shamir, at the time in charge of illegal aliya, first met Israel then.

Israel joined the staff of the Teachers Seminary in Vilna in 1937, where he stayed for two years. During that time, he rose in the Betar ranks to the position of regional staff officer. On September 10, 1938, Israel attended the Third Betar Conference in Warsaw; the rest, as they say, is history. In any case, the next ten tumultuous years will be found in these memoirs.

From the Conference, where he heard Jabotinsky, defended Begin, and met Friedman and Stern, Israel made his way to Warsaw, Vilna, Eretz Israel, the Underground, prison, the Latrun Detention Camp, and ultimately, the Lehi headquarters in Jerusalem and the assassination of United Nations negotiator Count Folke Bernadotte. Soon, Friedman was in Acco Prison ("broken," as Eldad describes him), Lehi members were arrested en masse by Ben Gurion, and some who escaped made their way to Israel Scheib's own hiding place to plan for the future.

Friedman, by then known by his nom de guerre, Gera, and fellow Lehi operative Matityahu (Matti) Shmuelevitz, were put on trial for terrorism. Scheib, by then known by his own code name, Eldad, spent the trial trying to round up witnesses to testify on their behalf. It didn't much matter, for Friedman was elected to Israel's first Knesset and that mooted the trial. Friedman and Shmuelevitz were running on the Fighters Party list, a group of Lehi veterans that also included Eldad.

At one party meeting, Eldad lectured on the *sulam*, Jacob's ladder (see Genesis 28: 10-17), thus beginning the next chapter in his life. The Lehi group split over the question of whether to adopt a pro-Soviet orientation. Shamir went leftward with Gera (though Shamir once asked me if I couldn't be sure it hadn't been Gera who had followed him), while Eldad remained true to what he saw as the legacy of Stern, Greenberg, and Lehi itself.

Following the split, Gera got the entire party apparatus and Eldad got an office in Jerusalem, from which he would publish his revolutionary journal *Sulam* over the next fourteen and a half years. Given that this journal produced no income, Eldad spent the spring and summer of 1949 writing *The First Tithe*. "The book was written in a trance, and with much pain," Eldad recalled.

Eldad eventually got a job teaching Bible and Hebrew literature in an Israeli high school, until Prime Minister Ben Gurion intervened and had him fired. Ben Gurion was afraid Eldad would imbue the students with his Lehi ideology. Eldad went to court and won, but it was a Pyrrhic victory, for no one would hire him after Ben Gurion had publicly fingered him as a danger to the state. Eldad turned to literary work, wrote "dime" histories of Underground battles, a biography of Mayor Avraham Krinitzi of Ramat Gan, a newspaper-style review of Jewish history called *Chronicles*, a Bible commentary (*Hegionot Mikra*), a polemic on the destruction of the Second Temple, weekly newspaper columns, and many more books, encyclopedia entries and other works. In 1962, Eldad was made a lecturer in Humanistic Studies at the Technion in Haifa. He taught there for twenty years, losing his job partly because he refused to strike for higher wages and criticized his fellow teachers for doing so. To Eldad, teaching was a privilege, for which he would gladly have paid rather than drawn a salary check. Plus, he felt, Israel had greater needs for its money than raising salaries.

Eldad died on the first day of the Hebrew month of Shevat, in January 1996. In the funeral parlor, in the hours before the funeral, one student sat alone with the body reciting Psalms; he said he wanted the poetry of King David to accompany Eldad heavenward.

The student kept returning to the Psalm, "Blessed is God my Rock, who trains my hands for battle."

Among the hundreds at the funeral, I found myself standing next to former prime minister Shamir, future prime minister Benjamin Netanyahu and former Knesset Speaker Dov Shilansky. Eldad was buried on the Mount of Olives, overlooking the Temple Mount, at the foot of the grave of his mentor and friend, Uri Zvi Greenberg.

In one of the last lectures I heard him deliver, before he fell ill, he spoke of the talmudic debate between the school of Hillel and the school of Shamai: Is it better for a man to be created or not to be created? After three years of arguing, the rabbis took a vote and decided man would have been better off not being created. But, the rabbis added, "Since he was created, let him examine his deeds." Eldad's enthusiasm was boundless: "This is all of existentialism!" he said. Everything is forced upon man, but since we are here—what is important is what we do.

In my last conversation with him, Eldad spoke of his failing health. I told him I was typing the manuscript of *The First Tithe*. He wistfully said he would give up the copyright to all his books, if only a publisher could be found to publish them.

*

Eldad generously allowed me to publish excerpts from this book in *Free Jerusalem*, my own history of all the Underground armies that fought for Jewish independence from 1920 to 1948.

A note on the translation: Eldad published *The First Tithe* without any index or footnotes, indicating that it was not meant to be an academic text. The book contains references to many people and events familiar to Israelis in 1950. Unfortunately, many of these heroes and villains are today forgotten, many of these historically pregnant events are today unknown. With Eldad's consent, I have when necessary for the understanding of the text added a minimal amount of explanatory data, but more often, and even then sparingly, I have appended endnotes with whatever information is important. None of the endnotes are Eldad's. I have also taken the liberty of occasionally inserting the Gregorian or solar calendar date in parentheses when Eldad indicates the Hebrew or lunar calendar date. If the text is therefore more readable and accessible, let this be my reward. If some readers find my assistance incomplete, let this be an impetus for further study of the period.[2]

Eldad was famous for his word play and his biblical exegesis, both of which were based on a rich knowledge of the Hebrew language and talmudic and midrashic sources. In some rare instances, for the sake of clarity, I have chosen to skip a passage rather than enter into an explanation of Hebrew etymology. My apologies to any short-changed readers.

Eldad appended an afterword to the third Hebrew edition of *The First Tithe*, which was dropped in the fourth edition and is not translated here.

I honestly do not believe one can have any understanding of current or future Israeli history without reading Eldad. I translated *The First Tithe* to afford understanding to those who are searching, and to help put readers, and certainly Israel, on the road to full redemption.

Zev Golan, Jerusalem

Introduction to the Second Edition

Thirteen years have passed since the appearance of the first edition of *The First Tithe*. The name and content of that book imply a second tithe; but there is none, not yet, at least not in any coherent way. Most of my spiritual energy has been invested in twelve volumes of *Sulam, LeMalkhut Israel* (The Ladder toward a Sovereign Israel); which was established together with my friends, carriers of the soul of Lehi,[3] carriers of the idea of complete Israeli liberation, of buttressing the concept of Jerusalem in the face of opposing concepts, in the face of empty concepts.

Unlike the years of the first tithe, these years have been without actual combat and without an official organization. And while this is not a positive development, still, we do not wish to be numbered among those who believe that what we do is important rather than what we say. We are descendants of a people who have at the beginning of their Bible and in the depths of their soul the declaration: "And God said let there be light and there was light," and we believe man was created in the image of God, and we believe—and know—from the experience of man and Israel and this generation, the great strength of words spoken truthfully and their power to induce deeds; for only light itself was created by God out of nothing, while since then man carries the light and flame, the light of clear thought that clarifies; and the flame of a burning soul that ignites, the eternal flame. The force of necessity below longs for this light and flame from above. This is the necessity of bodies who want redemption, who need redemption even if they do not consciously know it. And from this force and this necessity come the sure knowledge that redemption will come even if it is delayed, even if it has fallen with us into the coastal plain and the valley.

On this side of the mountains, of the Mountain, in the middle of the journey, it has fallen into the material. It may have fallen because of shortness of breath, or dammed-up soul, or weariness, or bounty—the body's satisfaction with its bounty or the soul's satisfaction with what has been so far achieved—or perhaps because of the natural limitations of the achievers. It has fallen under various and sundry kinds of inaction and non-fulfillment, of dropping the initiative, and even of an honestly felt and easily adopted attitude toward the State of Israel.

This state is an achievement only if it is viewed as a stage, meaning as a bridgehead toward *Malkhut Israel*, the Sovereign Kingdom of Israel, with all this entails in terms of strengthening its political position, especially in light of the hatred and plots surrounding it and the dark treason and plotting within, even among former Fighters for the Freedom of Israel, and with all this implies for the importance of maintaining the spiritual tension that desires the great things which are to come, things necessary and beautiful, which means raising high the idea of *Malkhut*.

We have come to the threshold of this *Malkhut* for which we are destined. That this is true can be seen in everything that surrounds us, from the confusion and continued desert and ruins in the geopolitical region waiting for Hebrew mastery, to our continuing social and spiritual oppression and servitude to both external and internal slavery—including the spiritual confusion within Israel on questions of Judah vs. Israel, Judaism vs. Israeli-ness, all of which are a sign that the process has come to a halt at its very beginning, a sign that the revolution is in its twilight and awaits renewal. The Almighty is signaling—with lights and with shadows, with all the colors and in all the directions of the historical and political and ideal traffic lights—what must come next in the process of redemption, and without which what has already been attained will not last, will become a modern version of Betar instead of a modern version of Modi'in.[4] And the fault lies not in the length of our arms, nor any inability, but in the fat that surrounds our heart and the fog in our brain.

For today, our arms are not short, and great is the physical power in the hands of the Jewish people in Israel and the Diaspora. This was not the case in those days that are the subject of this book. This was not the case of the Jewish people who were for the most part in cages and crematoria, slaughtered and shocked and shoveled and burned, and only a very few took their expansive souls in their little hands and set out to act, to begin the redeeming act. And though the deed was great and holy, this book will tell of the constant gap between the idea and song of the great Kingdom with their powerful desires and readiness, and the arms' inability to carry through, such that breath came up short and the soul turned asthmatic and the cannon, when it was forged, was given to those of little faith.

And so we have come this far, to the physical power of two millions in this little parcel of land, who are equal in ability and science and organization to all the surrounding states, who are equal in meaning and purpose to ten million Jews in Exile. In the land, we have the tremendous potential to manage our national and physical and spiritual powers in a wide expanse, yet we also see so many brains and hearts reduced to a lack of vision, or even an openly professed and exhibited anti-Vision of the type now expressed in what is called literature and art; a culture the content of which is abandon and which, in boredom and plenitude, mimics the wild and disturbed West which is actualizing the anthem of the East: No God, no king, no heroes.

Therefore let this second edition of *The First Tithe* come not only to meet the need of a first edition that long ago sold out, but also to fill the need to return to the great days of desire and action-which-flows-from-desire.

The Lehi movement published more material than other movements in the 1940s, and its publications have even been collected in two large volumes. This book does not purport to be the history of Lehi. It is a personal memoir. And if a baker may praise his own wares, let it be said that it speaks well of a book of this sort that after thirteen years, its author has nothing to change in its text, excepting minor inconsequential corrections. And though the words originally came close upon the organizational demise of Lehi, and though they came from the heart, a heart which was often burning and shaken, the author can sign off today on all the judgments and evaluations inside, which he judged the events, the movements and the people then and which—not this or that detail—are the stuff of this book.

From the perspective of thirteen years, from the permanency now attached to and the calm, for better or worse, attained regarding the past events, nothing stands out that obligates the author to say: I erred in assessing it. And the author is only able to take this view because he looks out from the *Sulam*, the Ladder. As he is neither prophet nor son of a prophet, and is unable to ascertain the end of things from their beginning, still he is able to see the beginning and what followed upon that beginning, the beginning of the ladder, the ladder toward which events moved, on which they climbed, even if they did not mount it; but all their value, and the means of judging them, is on this ladder, at the top of this ladder. From this ladder, the relative importance of what happened—and what may yet happen—is judged, and this is done so that it may happen again on the coming rungs, and this is my wish for those who continue to climb the ladder.

Israel Eldad

Introduction to the First Edition

The First Tithe

> Gaze from Your holy abode, from the heavens. We have done that which You have commanded us; do, You, that which You have promised us. Gaze from Your holy abode, from the heavens, and bless Your nation Israel with sons and daughters, and bless the land You have given us with dew and rainfall, with the offspring of cattle, as You have promised our forefathers: 'A land flowing with milk and honey,' so that You will give flavor to the fruit.
>
> Tractate *Maaser Sheni* (Second Tithe), Chap. 5, Mishna 13

Why a "tithe"? Because ten years are included in this book. Ten years beginning with the month of Mar Heshvan in the year 5699 according to the Hebrew calendar,[5] when I appeared for the first time before a conference of the leaders of the war for freedom, with inner certitude of and outer profession of the way to war. Ten years ending with Mar Heshvan 5709 (1949), underground in the State of Israel, underground for Jerusalem.

Why a "first" tithe? Because I have not fulfilled all my obligations with these first ten years. When the Temple stood, our forefathers used to bring three tithes. Their lives were regally sovereign; they labored and fought for their crops, and they were obligated to pay with these crops, bring tithes from them. We, whose lives hang in the balance, must pay with our lives.

After the "first tithe" comes the second tithe, that tithe which during ancient Temple times was eaten in Jerusalem, and that which belongs today to Jerusalem. Heavenly Jerusalem and earthly Jerusalem. Jerusalem, over which the second stage of the war for freedom is still being fought.

The third tithe obligatory upon the people of Israel is the tithe set aside for the needy. This, too, will come. Every vision has its time, like rungs on a ladder. Each year has its tithes, and sabbaticals and jubilees will yet be celebrated.

God grant me life that I may pay my tithes.

"Give flavor to the fruit," as it is written in the Mishna quoted above, about which the commentator *Tosafoth Yom Tov* says: "Give—even if milk and honey aren't flowing there." Not every year that tithes were brought was one of flowing milk and honey, yet it and its fruit still had flavor, meaning. For this flavor, for the meaning given life during this decade and for those to come, I recite a blessing: Blessed is He who gives meaning to life, without which it would be meaningless.

Part One

IN THE GENERATOR

Momma and Poppa

A tithe to my mother and father. I cannot even begin to understand myself without them. A father does not set his son in the backyard as he might set a pot, to be filled with heaven-sent water. A mother does not leave her son as she might a pot, to be filled with earth-grown vegetables. No, Father himself is water from heaven; Mother, fruit of the earth. Father is a pipeline, drawing his son from the springs of history, and Mother is nature's breast. Their spirit flows, as our blood. A person who writes the truth writes of his mother and father even if he does not mention them, even if he thinks he does not.

A tombstone, too, for my mother and father. I must erect a tombstone for them, for their bones are scattered or burned. Momma wanted her son to be a rabbi and preacher, famous and respected. Poppa wanted his son to be an author. Neither Momma nor Poppa had a chance to see what became of their son. They will at least have this tombstone at my book's beginning.

*

They walk among us always, those we call the dead, and they want so much for us to know that they walk among us (this may be all they want now). But many barriers stand between us. They get through only occasionally, when we come near their form of existence—in dreams, for instance. We cannot summon them at will, not in séances and not by charm. We can descend to the depths but we cannot raise those depths. Momma and Poppa are in my depths, and occasionally I see them there.

Life's greatest dialectic, the model, perhaps, for all dialectics: how two dissimilar (and even opposite, sexually) people are united in one person's flesh and blood and character.

When did I last see them together, Momma and Poppa?

The last time, while my father was alive, was on my twenty-fourth birthday, the ninth day of Heshvan 5694 (1933), the day I left Lvov to study in Vienna. My father was already two months into his illness and six months before his death, paralyzed on his right side. I will never know whether his mind was affected or whether we only thought it was, since we made out only one word for every ten his misshapen mouth mumbled. I could not figure out his answer when I asked if I should go and study or stay by his side. Once he tried elaborating on one of his favorite passages from the biblical commentator Ibn Ezra;[6] with his wise eyes he realized that though I nodded, I did not understand, and he began to cry. I had never seen him cry, just as I had never seen him ill before. The night before I left for Vienna, he understood and he wept, aloud, like he had never done. He knew . . . And Momma, leaning against the wall, she wept silently, as she had never done before. She knew, too . . . father and son would not meet again.

I did see them together again, after Poppa's death. On the night of the twentieth day of Iyar 5701 (1941), five weeks after my arrival in our land (me, in *Jerusalem*!!), in that form of reality we call a dream, I saw one of my younger brothers (but where was the youngest of all?) and myself standing a short distance from a hill. Momma was on the hill, saying: "Look, Leib, your children are all dressed up and they have completely forgotten you." And then I saw the coffin with Poppa inside. I woke and realized this was the first time I had forgotten the anniversary of my father's death, his *yahrzeit*, the twentieth day of Iyar. I blamed my forgetfulness on the long journey and the excitement of my first days in the country, but somewhere in the recesses of my mind I thought: All his life he longed to make aliya, to move to Eretz Israel (the Land of Israel). As a youth he had been the first Zionist in his village. His mother, brothers and sisters emigrated to the United States and sent him money and a visa so that he, the oldest child, could join them. He refused, his only wish to go to Eretz Israel, but he never made it. I lived under this banner of love and hope. The date of Poppa's death weighed heavily upon me; it was marked on the calendar of my heart; it hung always before my eyes. Only now, with my arrival in Eretz Israel, was Poppa appeased, did he find rest, his lifelong desire realized in me. Momma, however, could not rest. Women are influenced more by biology than history. Momma was a Zionist because she loved Poppa, who was a Zionist. Later she became a Zionist Revisionist because I, her oldest son, was a flaming Revisionist.[7] Momma remained a mother and a wife, though her son was far away and her husband dead, and now she had come to remind me: *Even in Israel you must remember the death of your father*, my son.

I saw Momma and Poppa together one more time, on the day of my arrest, the third day of Iyar 5704 (1944). By then Momma, too, was no longer alive, for the goyim had killed her in Lvov.[8]

Both of them came to show me their love, she in her way and he in his.

That story—the story of my escape from school, the jump from the fourth story window, the arrest—rightfully belongs to a later chapter of my life and book. Of course, in life everything is connected. Body and soul and past and future and the individual and the masses and life and death and "reality" and the imagination. But literature begets analysis. Mixing stories can be dangerous. What would people say if I were to include my vision of Momma and Poppa as part of the "realistic" story of my arrest? That I am "confused"? Better I should tell that story now.

She stood above me, leaning out of the window through which I had climbed, passionate and excited and urging: "Hurry! Hurry!" As I descended, I saw her mouth open, ready to shout in despair—a shout I knew well, or to laugh wholeheartedly—a laugh I knew equally well. She would laugh like that when Poppa read from Shalom Aleichem, or when she "fixed" (as she used to say) someone but good, or when she won at an inconsequential card game, or when someone complained that one of her sons had abandoned this or that girl (none of her three sons, actually, married a woman to her liking). And I am sure she laughed so, with all her soul, when she herself rebelled against her elderly, Hasidic, upper-class family and married, at seventeen, my free-thinking, enlightened, Zionist father who milled grits during the day and studied Ibn Ezra, Smolenskin and Friedrich Schiller at night. I heard her laugh like that during World War I, upon her return from a silk-smuggling mission to Vienna, as she told how she had fooled the tax officials. She was the family's breadwinner. Poppa refused to serve in the army of Ephraim Yossel (the Jews' nickname for the good emperor Franz Joseph) and he refused to inflict an injury upon himself to dodge the draft. So he sat at home, reading *Robinson Crusoe* and *Love of Zion* with me and teaching me chess. And Momma, the woman of valor, remained calm while sweating, and alive while laughing.

This time she did not laugh. Oh, the pain endured at the hands of the goyim who had killed her had probably ebbed by now and, in any case, she knew how to laugh even when in pain. No—she was not held back by pain, but by her inability to ascertain whether I was going to survive the course she was advising, as I flew from the fourth floor. In the last picture I have of her, her mouth is open, ready to shout in despair or laugh triumphantly. The "last picture"? Not precisely. I saw her for the very last time in the detention camp at Latrun; she was charred, all charred. I did not recognize her, I just knew it was her. At the time, I was not aware that one year had already passed since the final Nazi "action" in Lvov. She probably laughed then, too, even when they took her, laughed and said: "But you will not take my Israel in any 'action,' he is in the Land of Israel. He lives."

But there, leaning from a fourth floor window on the corner of Frishman and Hayarkon Streets in Tel Aviv, the shout and the laughter were both visible in her expression. Her mouth was poised, as she herself was poised all her life between suffering and love of life, between tears and laughter, between total innocence and complete understanding, between poverty and royal bearing (inherited from a line of Chertkov Hasidim); dynamism, constant dynamism. As I scurried down a shaky pipe, fleeing from the British detectives, I was ordered from the window above: "Fly!"

The pipe was broken or bent at one point—everything spun and quickly vanished. Apparently I went deaf—otherwise, why didn't I hear her shout of despair? But before I lost consciousness I saw him.

My father stood below. He was not shouting (he did not know how), but he self-assuredly spread his arms to catch my falling body.

With a laugh he advised: Take it easy, take it easy, my son. Escaping? It's okay, even necessary. But to get killed or maimed? God forbid, it's not worth it. "A macca di goyim!"

My father hated all the Gentiles, very much. A calm hatred. An intellectual hatred, for he was an intellectual. He loved Schiller, quoted his poetry by heart. Goethe, however, was anathema to him. He once told me of a young woman who moved in intellectual circles who was always quoting Goethe. There was nothing by or about Goethe with which she was not familiar. But when the conversation turned to Schiller—silence, not a word from her. Her friends asked her to explain and she replied that she was reading from Meyer's *Lexicon*; she had finished the letter "G" but had not yet gotten to "S."

"With you it's the opposite," I asked my father. "You know everything about

Schiller but I've never heard you quote Goethe. Why not?"

He smiled. "Me, I'm a Hebrew and I read as Hebrews do, right to left, so Schiller is closer to me than Goethe."

Poppa's smiles and humor always filled our room. "Room," for the five members of our family never had more than one room. Troubles, too, we had—but never sadness. Not even on that summer day in the month of Av 5689 (1929), when Poppa returned from a demonstration at the British consulate. He had been struck in the face by the horse of a mounted policeman who was charging at the protestors. Poppa had been in the front row.

Music, too, filled our room. Poppa knew by heart all of Goldfadden's historical operettas and he sang them all. The first song he taught me was Bialik's Zionist "El Hatsipor."

Poppa referred to himself as a "plain Zionist," without stipulations. He stopped reading the Warsaw paper *Der Haint* the day it refused to print Ben Zion Katz's article in defense of Avraham Stavsky.[9] At about the same time, coincidentally, my life was hanging somewhere between heaven and earth because of Stavsky.

Stavsky was one of three members of the Zionist-Revisionist movement accused of murdering Chaim Arlosoroff, a rising star in the Zionist labor movement, on a beach in Tel Aviv. I was attending the Rabbinical Seminary in Vienna. One of the students declared vociferously that the Revisionists had murdered Arlosoroff. I took the stage and announced: "Friend, if by this time tomorrow you have not recanted, then be prepared to fight." A commotion ensued but laughter prevailed; the other student was quite a bit larger than I. The following day I asked him, "Friend, do you recant your remarks?" When he answered that he did not, I stood on my tiptoes and, to everyone's surprise, slapped him. He wasted no time, grabbed me by the waist and ran to the window (second floor) and dangled me in the air, ready to let go. My fellow students miraculously rescued me.

But now I return to my father standing in the yard of that house on the corner of Frishman and Hayarkon, his arms spread to save me from a fatal crash landing. "Take it easy, take it easy."

My two brothers walked this moderate path, joined the "Zionist Youth" movement, married, furnished their apartments well, and were murdered by the Nazis. "Take it easy, take it easy." And I—my mother's Hasidic blood overpowering my father's—I climbed higher and higher and, since the "easy" doors of my father shut behind me, I jumped from Momma's window. The key is not to wait. Just do not wait. The homes of the wealthy have space enough for waiting rooms. The homes of the poor do not have much separating the inside from the out.

Thus I saw them together for the last time, the two who make me complete, in that critical moment when I swung between heaven and earth, when I freed myself from the constricting Tel Aviv building (and mind-set), when I leapt into a new order of things, a higher order, a deeper order. I was weakest and strongest then, and the two of them stood with me. I realized then that a person never really leaves them.

When did I last see my mother alive? After Poppa's death I bought her a silk dress, black with white dots. These two colors, interspersed, are my favorites. And in these two colors—since then even dearer to me—I saw her last. On a very black Tevet night in 5701 (1941), Momma came to a village near Vilna to bid me farewell as I set out for the Land of Israel. A thick snow, a black night. A long black train, Momma in a window, her hair white, bright white, blowing like a flag. The train moving farther and farther away and Momma shouting, shouting bitterly: "Israel!!!"

October 1938, Poland

1. Youth between Abyss and Vision

I open my memoirs with the October 1938 Betar World Conference in Warsaw. Not because this conference was Betar's turning point on the road to the Irgun Zvai Leumi (IZL, the underground Irgun),[10] for I am not writing a history book, but because it was the first historically important event in which I took part, and where I contributed to what happened.

Betar (short for Brit Trumpeldor) was the Revisionist Zionist youth movement founded by Vladimir Zev Jabotinsky[11] and Aaron Propes in 1923. Betar was named for Joseph Trumpeldor, the Russian war hero who moved to Eretz Israel and who died defending the Galilean settlement of Tel Hai against Arab marauders. By the late 1930s Betar was the largest youth movement in Poland, with over 90,000 members.

Betar had until now seen in me a "mere" educator. True, I had been the commander of a Betar chapter and later of the Volkovysk region. I had even worn—not without hesitation—the commander's uniform. But basically I was ignorant of the movement as a whole. Even after I moved to Vilna and worked in the large and wonderful Betar chapter there, I participated mostly in the same work that in Betar, no less than in other movements, was and is disparagingly called "cultural." In Vilna the chapter at least operated in Hebrew, since it was under the command of the very capable Israel Epstein. But the military-minded IZL cells that were sprouting up in Poland chose—the blame for this lying with certain IZL leaders and emissaries from Eretz Israel—to denigrate cultural education. The boys and girls who received IZL military training sometimes saw themselves as aristocrats, scornfully looking down at, and sometimes mistreating, those whom I "merely" taught the Bible and songs of Uri Zvi Greenberg. Notwithstanding my own "extremist" and "militant" views, I was left with a bitter aftertaste, one that resurfaced when in the headquarters of Polish Betar, Menachem Begin[12] and I were told to snap to attention before the Polish representative of the Irgun.

Not that I was, or we were, anarchists or anti-militarists, Heaven forbid. I would stand at attention before Jabotinsky, I would come to attention without an order and without any snapping. To stand otherwise before Jabotinsky was impossible. The soul came to attention and went taut, the body followed involuntarily. I do not know the fate or paths of the many people who stood before Jabotinsky or whomever else, with their bodies more rigid than their souls. But for some reason I felt—and maybe Menachem Begin felt the same, I did not ask—offended when we were ordered to attention not before a man, but before a position. The man may have been worthy, but we jumped only for his title.

In any case, I was not one of the members of Betar ("Betarim," as we were called) who opposed the Irgun. I supported its politics and its organization—though Jabotinsky himself did not, at that time. But my support was emotional and ideological since I knew nothing of what was actually happening in the national and world Betar movements, or who was in the Irgun or what its relationship was to Betar and the Revisionists. I was immersed in the world of literature and education and first grasped the organizational and political problems at this conference. Till now I had participated only in small committee meetings. One in Vienna, the Revisionist Council, shortly after Jabotinsky returned, sorely depressed, from America. He had failed to strike a chord in the hearts of the masses there and he told us he had just about decided to retreat to the literary world (Jabotinsky was a well known poet, playwright and novelist). His contact with Polish Jewry rekindled his desire to fight. As he talked of Poland's Jews and the young Betarim there, new hope crept into his sorrowful voice and his blank eyes.

I also attended a Betar committee meeting in Grodno in 1936, with Samuel Katz representing the leadership. I delivered a "nice" speech, educational and literary, and we went home.

A third meeting was of the "Maximalists," with Abba Ahimeir, in a narrow room in Warsaw. (Ahimeir was the leader of the maximalist, or most nationalist and activist, faction of Betar in Eretz Israel. He, together with the poet Uri Zvi Greenberg and the publicist Y. H. Yevin, organized the "Brit Habirionim," the forerunner of the future Underground in Eretz Israel.)[13] The tension was high at this Warsaw meeting; much bitterness, much rattling of swords. But no flag was raised; and God was equally absent. The meeting left no impression on me.

I might as well add that I was not even an official delegate. I had been invited at the suggestion of Isaac Remba as an expert on education.

What lay above me, then, I knew not; but what lay below I knew well. My opinions were not born of organizational squabbles, but of probing the perplexities of my soul, Hebrew history, Uri Zvi's songs, and the perplexity that abounded in the grass-roots Betar chapters that were my turf, which I visited, whose frustration I breathed.

I knew only two or three of the hundreds of delegates. Israel Epstein, who was one of my students in the Vilna Teachers Seminary and a commander of Vilna Betar. And Natan Friedman,[14] whom I had met before, if briefly. Six months earlier, in Volkovysk, I received an urgent letter instructing me to be at the Bialystock Betar chapter at nine o'clock the following Sabbath morning. Natan Friedman was waiting there and he spoke with me alone, though others had been invited, of an organized secret immigration to Eretz Israel. He asked that I find suitable candidates from Volkovysk for this important but illegal project. (Later, too, Natan was to be my first organizational contact with the Underground.)

I was not even aware, at this point, that Natan Friedman and Menachem Begin were part of an organized opposition within Betar, a group which had left the Betar Commission to protest the stagnant policies of Aaron Propes. (I wonder, is this a law of our Nationalist Movement, that our leaders reach a certain apex and are then daunted?)

And one more person was there with me, though he was not there. Uri Zvi was with me.

I first heard his name in 1927 from a friend my age, a Communist and a Yiddishist, who lived not far from me in Lvov. This friend asked if I had read *Mephisto* and proceeded to quote whole chapters from memory. My friend's name was Sinkover, his brother was a Yiddish poet. If not for those chapters he recited, I would have long ago forgotten his name.

Even so, I myself did not read Uri Zvi for several years.

In 1932, I visited the Vienna Jewish Library and asked for the magazine *Maaznayim* (Scales). The issue they handed me included the poem "B'Aznei Yeled Asaper" ("I'll Tell It to a Child").

At the time, my scales were equally balanced between devotion (for me, devotion means total devotion) to philosophy and literature and devotion to Zionist activity (I had been a supporter of Jabotinsky's movement ever since the Arab riots of 1929, when the Jews of Lvov took to the streets shouting: Jabotinsky! Jabotinsky!)

"I'll Tell It to a Child" tipped the scales. No longer were there two worlds, a world of thought and literature and a world of politics, with an either/or choice to be made. A bridge rose in my blood between these two worlds, between poem and messiah. I ascended the bridge and on it I march to this day, with no inner conflict or second thoughts. A friend, Dr. M. Kurtz, was witness to the trauma that passed over me then. From that time, he read every newspaper with me; but I went my way and he did not, which proves that something within me was ready and waiting for that encounter with the poem. The soil had been tilled by my father and watered by the visionary and majestic *Love of Zion*. The sprouts waited for the great teacher and that teacher came. He came in the raw power and good melancholy of "I'll Tell It to a Child."

Later, I saw and heard Uri Zvi at a public assembly in Lvov, lecturing on "The Land of Israel in Flames." (He saw them though the flames then were still beneath the surface, hidden in British offices and Arab hands and a "prosperous" Jewish "Yishuv" community!) He came alone, simply climbed atop the stage without a presidium, without a chairman, without an introduction. He began:

"No one invited me. No one introduced me. By myself I come, by myself I call to you, by myself I rent an auditorium and advertise."

Years later I went to his parents' home in Lvov when I heard he was visiting. I found his mother in the kitchen. His father sat on a couch in the next room. The kitchen and the room were quiet and pure in their simplicity. Uri Zvi was in the next room. I entered but could not explain why I had come. If Uri Zvi had not already been aflame, and able to take hold of flammable material, I would surely have left as confused as I had come, rather than as flaming as I did leave.

Since then, I am nothing more than a thorn in a burning bush.

And he burned in me as I traveled to the Conference.

He burned and they—thousands of youth, and especially Betar youth, scattered throughout the cities and villages—they cried within me.

In the Land of Israel, Arab riots against Jews. Over Europe, a blackening shadow spreads, grows more despicable, screams and screams; not the aesthetic, mournful scream of the tragic "Raven," but a guttural, choking scream.

In the many cities and villages, the youth loiter, forces moving but doing nothing. Strength just withering. Or spending itself on the nonsense of collecting pennies for Jewish National Fund (JNF) charity boxes or breaking JNF boxes in protest, or participating in old Zionist Congresses and then a New Zionist one, or organizing petitions and then again holding Congressional elections. Young men and women walk the streets of Zelva and Peski and Volkovysk and Vilna, fires burning within and gnawing at their own flesh, for the flesh of real enemies is kept from them.

In the Latrun Detention Camp (much later, in Eretz Israel) we used the word *casedra* to refer to a walk around the prison camp, a walk that was rich and full in comparison to the endless *casedra*s walked by the Jewish youth in countless cities, walks around the various competing youth movements, walks between bridges and churches, markets and streets, stations and movie theaters. Tens of thousands of young people walk and walk, the blood still in their veins, not yet spilled in the wars in Poland and Russia; the muscles still strong, not yet thinned by hunger and disease; the breaths they draw still deep and the lungs still stout, not yet filled with gas. They walk and walk, thousands of them, thousands of hands waving meaninglessly, groping each other in love born of boredom, arguing out of hatred born of emptiness.

The Betar chapters have reached their peak. How long can one maintain the revolutionary fervor of the soul, can one fence with sticks, can one write petitions? And the hunger and poverty in the cities presses, too. If not for the miracle of the Russian trials of Trotskyites thousands upon thousands of the best Jewish youth, hungry as they were for action and redemption, would undoubtedly have joined the fighting and much-persecuted Communists. The persecution of the Trotskyites and the anti-Semitic tone of the trials deterred many. A Jewish youth, revolutionary and extra-territorial in character, was ready to join either an extra-territorial world revolution or a revolution to territorialize the Hebrew people. A revolution for Russia or Poland is, for the Jew, ultimately no more than assimilation within a different social system. The Dreyfus trial, though it was more than just a symptom, destroyed the illusion of a White assimilation, and the Trotskyite trials were the symptom which destroyed the illusion of an extra-territorial revolution, in other words: of a Red assimilation. Actually, by this time even the Communist revolution had become more connected to land and nationhood, and the young Jew was no longer able to be a pioneer on that front. As it was, the best of the Communist movement was Jewish, but if not for these trials, the boredom and frustration within the Jewish community would have pushed many more thousands into the arms of this foreigner's revolution.

Betar became the alternative for the revolutionary, dynamic spirit of the youth, and Betar grew tremendously in the mid-1930s.

The 1938 Betar Conference was an expression of the dense atmosphere of the Hebrew revolution as well as of this revolution's necessity, and it gave expression to the great dynamic forces which had collected in the cities of Poland, forces for which Betar was no longer able to be an outlet. Intimations of the Irgun were a cool breeze in this dense air and an anchor of salvation. Ordinary Betar members still wondered why a new structure (the Irgun's) was necessary to fulfill the promise of the old. Meanwhile, young Betarim were still lowering their heads in shame when I told them that all they needed to participate in the illegal immigration was 400 zlotys—and they knew that in their parents' homes there was nothing left to sell. And the local chapters were still immersed in inertia. In

Eretz Israel, the British had just hanged Shlomo Ben Yosef, the first Jew to be martyred for Hebrew independence in Eretz Israel since the Bar Kochba revolt 1,800 years earlier. Ben Yosef had gone to the gallows in his Betar uniform, with Jabotinsky's name on his lips. But even his image was already losing its freshness and becoming passé, shorn of the magic of a one-time act of redemption—redemption from the troubles of the nation as well as personal troubles, from the hunger and emptiness and boredom and depression appearing in every eye, on every street, in every chapter, on the drawn and resigned faces of all the mommas and poppas who no longer knew how to provide meaning for their children, for all the gates to meaning were blocked.

I bore in my blood the poetry of Uri Zvi, I bore in my soul the silent cry of these frustrated faces, and I bore in my mind the cold cruel thoughts that radiated from the coldness and the cruelty that were descending as lead from the skies of Europe and rising as an iceberg from its ground. I went to the Conference to listen, and did not know whether I would speak. I did not know for whom it was worthwhile to fight, or against whom; but I knew what must be dethroned and what must be enthroned. Between Abyss and Vision dangled our movement, dangled the youth, dangled an entire people.

For some reason, I reached Warsaw only on the second day of the Conference. I entered the Academic Building and sat, as was my wont since my university days, in a corner, able to see all and everyone. In this auditorium among the hundreds of delegates, I found myself a stranger. On the dais of the presidium, one or two faces were recognizable. *I was unable to see who was on the balcony.*

2. Soaring with Jabotinsky, the "Rosh Betar"

Rarely are we fortunate enough to reach the heights, the towering levels of holiness and purity, to which the Rosh Betar[15] raised us in his sublime elegy for Shlomo Ben Yosef. Even though we realized that his love and admiration for Ben Yosef's heroic martyrdom did not yet contain the signal to continue onwards, still—the sanctifying force was so powerful, the holy water so holy, that we felt the shells peeling off, the souls being cleansed, all impurity being banished. He made us, our weaknesses and our sins white—not with burning coals or scalding irons, but by virtue of his own glow. I am certain that the auditorium was wrapped in darkness; but I am equally certain that the air was a soft velvet blue, and into this blue flowed his fluorescent words, and not one of us discerned his own soul anymore.

I had felt this way only a handful of times before: when reading the final chapters of Nietzsche's *Thus Spake Zarathustra*; at Vienna's Royal Theater production of *Peer Gynt,* during the final scene as Solveig sits white among the white mountains singing her eternal love song, and the old, very old Peer Gynt returns after his years of wandering and tribulations and searching and bows at the feet of the loving, pure singing whiteness; and when Alexander Moissi sang the final words of *Ghosts* in his magical voice: "Mother, give me the sun, give me the sun." And after this speech of the Rosh Betar, I again felt this way whenever Rabbi Arye Levin[16] intoned the "Av Harachamim" memorial prayer for us in the cell of the Jerusalem Central Prison (each time he intoned it, as if it were the first). He recited and we, all of us, repeated—the Sternists in Cell 18, the Irgunists in Cell 19, the Hagana's self-proclaimed non-believers in Cell 23 and the criminals, thieves, murderers, forgers, et al. in Cell 29, the same room used every Sabbath as a synagogue. He recites and we all repeat and the Merciful Father who will avenge our spilled blood descends to us and there are no more bars and no more walls and no more pigs and mules guarding us and we are swift and strong and free, so free.

At the Conference, though, the walls and flags were draped in mourner's black, our uniforms were as brown as the soil around Ben Yosef's body, the air was deep blue and the song was white as snow-white doves, joyous and gay, soaring higher and higher.

Jabotinsky was able to rise above the many moments of awful personal pain caused him by the Ben Yosef affair; he was able to overcome, to see the tragic beauty, and he was able to raise us with him. He revealed the mythic in a singular heroic act, and all the details, performed as they were in naive simplicity, became symbols and signposts. We had all read and re-read the details of the final night and final morning in the life of the first man to ascend the gallows in the war for Hebrew liberation. Not a single particular from the life of that normal boy had escaped us; he wrote or spoke not one word which we had not already heard. And now the master magician proves to us that we had seen nothing, heard nothing—we had been blind and deaf. We had not absorbed the ultraviolet rays, the ultra-high frequency waves; we had been searching in the rhetoric and politics, while they were in the so-human, the very simple, Ben Yosef's request for soap and a comb on the morning of his hanging, his complete awareness of the value of his action and his complete unawareness of his own value. We had seen and been inspired by the Betar uniform on the body ascending the gallows and Jabotinsky, the great tragedian, had seen the pure man, far more pure and far more holy than the uniform.

And now he sang his song, Rosh Betar! There was no melody, yet it was music, there were no rhymes, yet it was compact and interwoven and measured and free, as only Jabotinsky knew how to compact and weave and measure and even bind yet free.

This was his Song of Ascension, like the Songs of Ascension sung by the Priests in Temple times. A song that uplifts.

That night we were overcome, we were defeated, we were totally purified.

3. The Squeaky Door Wins

The following day we, the defeated, won a victory over him, the angel.

We whose youth had not beaten to the pulse of Pushkin and Lermontov, whose hearts had not bled as his had over the cruelty of the Russian Revolution, we who had not had the interlude he had between the First and Second World Wars to enjoy Italian skies and melodies—we did not understand his political analysis, nor why he refused to meet Mussolini. We were not of the generation that had fought for freedom, liberalism and parliamentary democracy, and we were unable to comprehend the basis of his support for the parliamentary British government and the freedom and respect accorded the individual in England.

This was the psychological background to the argument and the struggle that took place the following day.

Menachem Begin rises to speak.

The *enfant terrible* of Polish Betar. A rare blend of lawyer and romantic. He is to Jabotinsky as a Roman student is to a Greek teacher. He tries to follow in his teacher's path but his very nature prevents him from reaching the latter's true gentility and nobility. Begin is closer to drama, farther from tragedy. Jabotinsky is the refined tragedian, his student is simpler in thought and expression. Jabotinsky often closed his eyes in order to see, sealed his lips in order to think. His student does not. The teacher surpasses the student in beauty, but reality overtakes both of them in its ugliness and we must act within reality.

Menachem becomes the spokesman for the activist opposition in Betar. If he does not succeed in pulling Betar out of the mire in which the establishment has placed it, then no doubt remains that the more-active Irgun will swallow Betar whole, with or without a formal agreement between the two organizations. The youth is fed up with sitting in groups, writing petitions and booing the politics of the Jewish Agency. Ben Yosef was the first overt expression of rebellion in Eretz Israel. He acted without being ordered to, either by Betar or by the Irgun. Now, in Poland, the great center of Betar's strength, the number of Ben Yosefs is growing. Jabotinsky made a wonderful gesture in his elegy. He said: "I give you *now*, Ben Yosef, the order to do what you did." This sentence, however, was lost in the magical song, and the ambiguity remained: was it or was it not a political commitment for the future, indicating that from now on Jabotinsky will be giving the orders we want so much, to end the Jewish self-restraint we are so tired of in the face of repeated Arab attacks in Eretz Israel?

The Betar chapters are in a state of crisis. The members openly scorn their commanders. Boredom is pushing them outside Betar. The secrecy surrounding the Irgun, its training courses and the echo of activity in Eretz Israel are drawing them to the increasingly numerous Irgun cells. The choice facing Betar is to fall apart or to adopt an activist policy.

Menachem is the spokesman for the activist opposition.

As is often the case in polemics, the opposing sides turn to formulas.

Menachem chooses for his the Betar oath, an oath written by Jabotinsky himself. The relevant portion declares that "I will raise my arm only in defense." Menachem says that he opposes this restraint and he calls for a change in the oath: "I will raise my arm to defend my people and conquer my homeland."

Of course, the formula is significant in practical terms. The formula commands. And yes, claims Begin, the time has come that it command. We can no longer look to the world for help, not this world of wolves. Now Begin plays his last and best card: A few months ago the Munich Agreement was signed and Czechoslovakia abandoned. The good, liberal Western democracies abandoned Czechoslovakia without mercy and without conscience just as Czechoslovakia turned to them for help. The world is cruel and understands only force and *faits accomplis*. The time has come to call for Rebellion in Eretz Israel.

Thus Begin's speech.

After all the irrelevancies of the past, finally someone has said what needs to be said. Wild applause, absolutely wild, especially from one corner where, I am told, are seated the delegates from Eretz Israel. *I am still unable to see who is on the balcony.*

Jabotinsky asks for the floor. Unlike the previous evening, he cannot now respond poetically, not to Begin's challenge, not to all that Begin has whipped up in this auditorium. So he must respond in prose and he does. His prose is cutting. His knife is ever sharp and it pierces.

He opens with the parable of squeaking. He hates three types of squeaks: Calves that squeak in the morning when a man is yet asleep, but we must forgive them for, after all, they do provide milk. So, too, the squeaking of machinery in a factory or of railroad trains on their tracks is unpleasant, but they do, after all, benefit society. One squeak, however, he hates with all his heart and there can be no forgiveness, for it serves no purpose: the squeaking of a door on its hinges. "And your speech, Mr. Begin, is just such a squeaky door." The sharp parable is followed by tragic political prose:

We must consider the mathematics, the relative strengths. Our forces are not yet enough, therefore there is no point in mumbling about a Revolt.

Then, another of his classic parables: Tragedy strikes an area, a terrible fire. Many victims, many orphaned children. Help is extended to them—at first they are sent to different homes. But as time passes, the good people grow tired of the stranger-children. Tension and animosity poison the air. Finally a wise man realizes that even the best of men does not a want a stranger in his home. This does not mean that he is cruel; rather, his charitable instincts must be harmonized with normal self-interest. The solution: Everyone contributes to the establishment of an orphanage. The children leave the private homes to the satisfaction of the owners but they are not abandoned, for they have their orphanage.

In other words: The world is not so charitable that its states—even the most democratic of them—will permit all the Jewish refugees to enter their borders. But the world is not so cruel that it will refuse all help. The good among the nations will wholeheartedly support the idea of a Hebrew state, which can be compared to the parable's orphanage.

And finally: If you, Mr. Begin, do not believe the world still has a conscience, then you have no alternative but to drown yourself in the Vistula River.

In the course of Jabotinsky's speech, someone asked a question and mentioned the Irgun newspaper *Di Tat* (*Hama'as*, meaning: The Deed), to which Jabotinsky thundered, motioning violently: "There is no connection and can be no bridge!"

I, the newcomer, was again puzzled. Was this evidence of a major split in the movement, or simply a tactical maneuver on Jabotinsky's part? I felt as I had the previous night when I could not tell whether the posthumous order Jabotinsky gave Ben Yosef was a mere gesture, or an actual change of policy induced in him by, as he said, "My master and teacher, Shlomo Ben Yosef." And deep inside of me, I found the idea of an orphanage offensive. It was embarrassing. We do not want to be orphans and we do not want charitable people to build us an orphanage. Yesterday's elegiac-oration had uplifted me; now this oratory depressed me.

I had my name added to the list of speakers. As I was upset, I paid no attention to the speeches which followed Jabotinsky's. I think there were four or five.

As I was being handed the floor, Jabotinsky took advantage of the pause to get his briefcase and rise to leave.

Then (so I later learned) Isaac Remba whispered to him that so-and-so was about to speak, and apparently Remba added some complimentary words concerning my literary ability, etc. Had he known what I was about to say he probably would not have done me this favor. In any case I am indebted to him for turning Jabotinsky's attention toward me, which made it easier for me to speak, mostly because I intended to criticize him.

To my right, below, sat Jabotinsky, the Rosh Betar. To my left, above, sat Menachem Begin. We had not met previously, and I do not know whether he realized I was about to come to his defense after Jabotinsky's terrible attack. But I certainly did not believe in the world's conscience and I had no intention of heading for the Vistula.

I am not overly fond of nobility or good manners when it comes to polemics, but the presence of Rosh Betar dictated politeness, not for any ironic effect, but out of a genuine desire not to hurt him. I began by apologizing that I, too, would sound to him like a squeaky door but—and again I apologized—something once happened to me that proved that even a squeaky door can be useful. A door's squeaking once awakened me from my sleep and saved me from the thieves who had opened it (I made up this story, but from a historical point of view this is unimportant, for it *could* have happened). And when thieves break into our home, a squeaky door is to be welcomed. And "thieves" *have* broken into the Nationalist Movement: surrender and opportunism.

My opening met with applause and with gales of laughter, though not because of its humor. The audience's reaction was only a symptom. A heaviness had weighed on the hearts of most of the delegates since Jabotinsky had spoken. Menachem had spoken from the heart—from their hearts—and had been angrily rebuked. My opening dispersed the heaviness. The score was evened.

Long afterward, Jabotinsky's son Eri told me that his father had applauded louder than anyone else, exclaiming: "He got me!" But he was undoubtedly reacting to the aesthetics, to my returning his blow. Jabotinsky was one of the last great aesthetes, therefore he always preferred humor to violence, and he was truly noble—unlike us.

After I had deflected the attack on Begin—which is to say, on us, all of us, all the squeakers of doors—I mounted a counterattack, choosing just that point that had hypnotized us, subdued us: Jabotinsky's ode to Ben Yosef.

I envy the honorable Rosh Betar, I said, his ability to soar to such heights and see the Shlomo Ben Yosef affair as he does. Great strength is needed to reach those heights. We, the younger generation, are too weak, too nervous. We are unable to focus our complete selves on the miracle that most moved Rosh Betar: Shlomo Ben Yosef asking for a comb to straighten his hair on the morning of his hanging. We, with our faults and weaknesses, instead focus our attention on the fact of Ben Yosef's neck having been broken by the British. Our vision is wide enough only for this disgusting crime and the murderers, and we are unable to gaze silently at the tragic majesty of the victim's heroism. In any case, we cannot give all our energy to this silent admiration.

Next, I moved to the mathematics. I have never enjoyed, nor been very proficient at, math; sometimes, of course, numbers are important but sometimes they are not decisive. I spoke of the danger facing us if we choose to constantly harp on the mathematical odds. I mentioned, not very originally, the victory of the numerically inferior Maccabees.

At some point, I do not recall exactly when, I exploited my being on the rostrum to suggest that the Conference send its greetings to the Prophet of Sovereignty and Revolt, Uri Zvi Greenberg. I took the thunderous applause that followed to be another indication of the direction in which the Conference was moving.

By the way, from the speaker's rostrum I was finally able to see the balcony, from which frequent applause was coming. *But who was there, I did not know.*

I most infuriated Rosh Betar when I referred to the huge gap between the mentalities of the nineteenth and twentieth centuries.

He left in the middle of my speech. There were those who later tried to comfort me by telling me he had another meeting. I have my doubts. I think his ability to tolerate the squeaks had its limits, which I crossed. May the God of the long-suffering—on behalf of whose suffering souls and longing for action I spoke—forgive me if I did offend his gentle ear, so fond of music. We are the generation of dissonant music.

The Conference climaxed with the victory of this dissonant music. The Hebrew nation could not wait for better odds, did not have time for the conscience of the world to awaken. Future developments, unfortunately, would make this all too clear.

The Conference voted by a vast majority to approve Menachem Begin's proposal to change the oath, despite Jabotinsky's objections. Then Jabotinsky was unanimously and enthusiastically elected Rosh Betar, Supreme Leader of all Betar. In appreciation, Rosh Betar gave us yet another Song of Ascension, the most beautiful of all his poems: "Min Hayom Bo Nikreti Lefeleh." Not a door squeaked, no one breathed.

The Conference's decisions were to serve as the connection and bridge between Betar and the Irgun. I will, however, reserve comment on whether, in the long run, I think this was beneficial for the struggle for liberation.

4. Epilogue and Prologue

Secretly, on the sly:

Natan Friedman approached me as soon as I had finished speaking and told me someone wanted to talk to me on the fourth floor in room number so-and-so.

I went upstairs and entered the long, narrow, calm room—strikingly calm in contrast to the noisy auditorium.

Seated at a small table was a man, also calm. Dressed, unlike everyone else at the Conference, in a dark civilian suit. His face thin, calm. His fingers long, thin, calm. Even the calm was long, thin.

Calmest of all: his voice. Dark gray.

He told me he had listened to my speech from the balcony. It was a good speech, but one that imposed obligations. What did I think should be done? Should Betar continue its own restraint, its purely verbal opposition to the Jewish establishment's policy of restraint? Should we remain loyal to Betar come what may?

I answered that we should make one more attempt. If Betar can be won over to the activist side, then why break up an organization with so many valuable people in it?

Natan Friedman was present during this conversation but said nothing.

The conversation was calm and noncommittal. Questions were left hanging, or so I thought. I understood later, of course, that my partner in conversation considered a split in Betar unavoidable. He asked my opinion merely to feel my pulse, to learn how far I was willing to go.

Only after I reached Eretz Israel did I learn that I had spoken to *Yair*.[17]

The Blade of Time

Time is not a tunnel, equally wide its entire length, an apathetic instrument allowing events to flow through. Time lives and spins, widens and narrows, an active participant in all that flows through her. She resembles a dagger. Your finger toys with it, you know that only one edge is sharp and dangerous, but as you approach the end the blade becomes thinner and soon only the tip remains, nothing left to take hold of, no place to stand, no room to play. You run or are impaled.

Now, were you the sole owner of this knife you would know how to treat it, to control it. Alas, many are the masters of dagger-like time, and in their hands it is transformed into a living, unpredictable creature. Before you can recoil you are trapped on its edge, its tip, between heaven and earth.

1. Yes, There Is a Spiritual Center

People can be exiled, or in exile, even in their own homeland; there is, indeed, much of the Diaspora even in the State of Israel. A structure called "state," army officers and government cabinet ministers are not enough to uproot the thought processes of Exile, the inferiority complexes, the internecine hatred, the inability to feel sovereign.

The other side of this coin is the influence of Eretz Israel, the atmosphere of the settled Jewish community (the "Yishuv") in Eretz Israel, on the Diaspora. Even before the state was established in 1948, the Land of Israel already served as a spiritual and moral center for world Jewry. This, however, was not necessarily for the best.

When in the summer of 1949 the principal of one of Tel Aviv's more respectable high schools explained to me that he was unable to employ me because of my past politics—which I certainly never recanted and which I continued to profess in publications such as *Sulam*—I heard echoes of an event that occurred in Vilna several months before the Holocaust. The Tel Aviv principal, however, was not imitating the earlier ways of the Diaspora. Rather, he was acting in the best tradition of the old Yishuv, having not been affected in the least by such things as the establishment of the state and the acquisition of Israeli citizenship. And that which had been done to me in a Vilna school ten years earlier was part of the same Yishuv-"Zionist" tradition.

For two years preceding the World War, I served as the head teacher of Hebrew studies at the Teachers Seminary in Vilna, the only institution in Poland then training Hebrew teachers. The students were on a high level and I enjoyed my work. In the course of my first year the principal discovered that I was a Betar member (he was close to the left-wing Hashomer Hatzair) and I was notified that I was to be fired without explanation.

The students, by and large also members of Hashomer Hatzair, nonetheless protested my dismissal. Apparently I had not made it a habit to offend the majority, with which my views were at odds, since now the students were defending me. The administration had no pedagogic rationale for letting me go, for though I had never read even one pedagogic manual I was not such a bad teacher. So I stayed.

A year later the political situation in faraway Eretz Israel took a turn for the worse. The first Irgun counterattacks shocked those Jews who continued to espouse restraint in the face of Arab provocations. In the Betar journals being published in Warsaw, I knew no limits in my criticism of Hashomer Hatzair. Still, my lessons were not affected. No one ever accused me of discrimination in the treatment of my students. Only once did I display any favoritism in the classroom, and then not on the basis of political loyalty but of . . . familial loyalty. The student I favored was my wife who, it seems, excelled in all her studies except Hebrew. I should have failed her. At the grading conference the principal asked what grade I wished to recommend for Batya Scheib. I said simply: "Unsatisfactory."

The poor, confused principal knew this meant failure and could only stutter: "And so . . . and so what happens . . . ?"

Again I said simply: "She passes to the upper class."

"Yes, but . . . but . . . for what reason?"

I ended his confusion and drew laughter from the teachers: "Family reasons." This was the first and last time I favored a student, and the Lord who watches over peace in the home will plead my cause on Judgment Day. But even this happened only at that critical moment. In the class, I treated her as I treated everyone else. Once I even ejected her for eating during class. What happened at home that night is another story.

The atmosphere at work was good. I worked enthusiastically; I loved my work and my students. This love led me—then and also later in Eretz Israel—to sin against the cause of Freedom. I was an "accomplice" in the struggle for freedom, I assisted, but I held back from committing my whole self and all my time until external forces finally pulled me from the classroom. In Vilna, I was pulled by Jews, in Tel Aviv by British. If this turned out to be for the best, I must thank those who did me these favors, though their intentions were surely for the worst.

I erred in Vilna, and later I repeated the error in our homeland (eternal recurrence!). I believed there was one base, a common ground, in the roots of Israel's culture, literature and history. I sought to reveal the deepest roots from which all the branches have sprouted, from which we draw our vitality, our reason for being in the world as "a people that dwelleth alone" (and how strong must we be, physically and spiritually, to be faithful to this ancient edict!). I was prepared for any material sacrifice. Regardless of the total wealth of the Jewish people, I was prepared for an unjust division of this wealth amongst ourselves, as long as it provided for our security. But I was not prepared for any spiritual sacrifice or compromise. I tried to show and prove how deep is our world, are our wells. We may learn from others, but this is never *necessary*, because almost nothing of theirs is not to be found already in the culture of Israel, beginning with "In the beginning . . . ."

Naturally, when I say "material" I give it a wide definition. Material is land, money, population, science and also arms, which protect all the other forms of material. Of this, I refrained from speaking in the Teachers Seminary, to avoid arguments. My conscience was not overly at ease about this self-imposed silence, but I told myself: You can speak of this from other platforms.

And so I did, and then I was punished—in the very area I shied from touching. This, too, is an eternal law and a moral lesson. Witness: A play by the murdered poet Yitzhak Katznelson, may God avenge his blood, appeared in the Kislev 5699 (December 1938) edition of a school newspaper published by the Tarbut Association (sponsor of the Teachers Seminary) in Warsaw. The subject: the Hasmoneans. The message: a defense of the policy of restraint. Judah Maccabee and his brothers appear armed with *megillah* scrolls instead of swords and they deliver speeches in praise of *megillot* and against swords.

This, in Kislev *5699*, the third year of the bloody Arab massacres in Eretz Israel! Nine months before the outbreak of World War II! Four years before the Warsaw Ghetto Uprising that came too late, ten years before the creation of the Israeli army.

Perhaps, in some library in Israel or elsewhere, a copy of this newspaper and this play has survived. It would be an important historical document.

My blood, which had no desire to be spilled in a Gentile slaughterhouse, boiled. I published in the Betar weekly *Hamedina* (The State), on the front page, under the headline, "What is Hanukkah?" an open letter to the Tarbut movement in Poland.

I wrote that I was not going to take the playwright to task. Perhaps he has the right to get lost on the roads of his imagination, though one would hope he would confine himself to unplowed areas instead of threshing a field already claimed and owned by the heroism of the Maccabees. No, my complaint is lodged against Tarbut. You, I wrote, are not poets and should not roam so freely in the wild fields of the imagination. Why must you present the students of Israel with this falsification of history? You wish to advocate restraint? Please. Find yourselves some "heroes" in our history—and there were some—who favored restraint. But why must you maul the Maccabees and Matityahu the "terrorist," the murderer of assimilationist Jews, and his sons the aggressor-soldiers? Why must *they* be the ones to hold scrolls and preach against the sword?

Two or three months later an answer arrived: a letter of dismissal. As this was already the second year of my employment I could not be fired without cause, and an explanation was indeed attached: because of an article published against the Tarbut institutions.

A struggle ensued involving the Teachers Union and much public pressure. The students again rose to defend me, but when the national leadership of Hashomer Hatzair distributed a pamphlet ordering its members to demand my dismissal, they fell silent. (I wonder if those residents of Israel today—one in Haifa, one in the Knesset—who were responsible for my being fired remember this incident.)

Here we have a fine example of moral and cultural influence emanating from the Yishuv to the Diaspora.

As I had meanwhile been asked to join the Betar Commission headed by Menachem Begin, and had been asked by Uri Zvi Greenberg to work for the paper *The Moment*, I chose not to press the issue and agreed to leave with six months' severance pay. I was given promissory notes, not one of which was ever paid. The war came. The notes became worthless paper, together with all the educational and political notes of Tarbut and Hashomer Hatzair.

And another tragi-comic epilogue. The principal scheduled a meeting of the teachers for the anniversary of Ben Yosef's hanging; perhaps he did so unintentionally. A commemorative ceremony was set for 5 p.m. at the Betar chapter, so I asked that the meeting be postponed. Without me, the head teacher, there could be no meeting. The principal refused. I appeared at the 4 p.m. meeting in my Betar uniform, with a tag of mourning. At 4:45 I rose, apologized and said I had to go. The principal, Dr. Shmuel Amarnet (he surely will not mind that I mention his name; with the state of the educational system in Israel today, it can only help his career), angrily ordered me to stay.

I repeated: "For me, today is a day of mourning."

He replied: I do not recognize days of mourning for murderers.

The teachers grabbed me, as I lunged with all my strength toward the abusive blasphemer. Several days later, on the seminary steps, two Betarim did what I could not and left the principal covered in blood. I had not sent them, but I praised them then and I do so today. That principal roused more and hotter blood in my heart than his own body shed on those steps.

The teachers' meeting had of course ended, but the Betar memorial for Ben Yosef came to pass and so did all that it roused in the mourners' hearts. And therefore Ben Yosef's name lives and breathes in a Jewish state today.

2. Inside the Generator

The last six months before the war were terrifying, awesome. Great masses of Jews bursting with fear and bursting with desire mobbed the streets. I do not think that even the war of partition and the establishment of the Jewish state in 1948 saw such a wave of messianic desire. Maybe because in the interval, six million flames had been extinguished, maybe because the Underground's war in Eretz Israel had released, little by little, the desires and energies that had accumulated. But in the spring and summer of 5699 (1939), every Betar chapter and every Irgun Zvai Leumi (IZL) cell was a powerhouse; and together, they erupted, stirred, and were stretched to the limits awaiting the great release that would, that must, come.

After years of empty discussions, the Zionist movement and the Mapai (Workers or Labor) Party and the Jewish Agency and the Histadrut Labor Union were suddenly as irrelevant as if they had never even existed. No more Jewish National Fund, no more immigration certificates, no more of their endless negotiations in London, no more of their restraint. These disappeared, slowly but surely, from the hearts and minds of all. Independent strength, made ready to act by recognition of historical responsibility, was accumulating. We ceased to be an opposition, within or outside the Zionist Organization. We began to breathe the air of a legitimate liberation movement. The military courses, the independent aliya,[18] the great plans for large-scale action, the first steps toward an independent foreign policy—all these at last put the Nationalist Movement on the right course . . . one or two years too late.

Courses in weaponry and preparation for the "Aliya Bet" immigration, courses in arms and turning illegal aliya into the "national sport" of our youth! God in heaven! If only we had acted sooner!

Jabotinsky says there will be no war! Jabotinsky explains why there will be no war! He uses logic! He has never been wrong!

Why is he wrong this time? Because with all his heart, he does not want this war at this time, when we are not yet prepared. At this hour of great progress, to be suddenly stopped? No, no, there will be no war. And his logic bowed to his will and to this necessity. War would spell total destruction.

These were the last, tense months of the Freedom Movement in the Diaspora.

Jabotinsky is scheduled to arrive in Poland; from Riga or Kovno he is coming to Vilna. He will be here for urgent consultations.

Uri Zvi Greenberg and Dr. Arye Altman come from Warsaw to receive him. Sunday, the eighteenth day of Iyar 5699 (1939). I have arranged a festive reception at the Betar chapter. Jabotinsky has not yet arrived. I take the two visitors from the Warsaw train station straight to the Betar chapter. The two visitors? In truth, I hardly know Dr. Altman and he does not interest me in the least. Not that I have ever heard anything disparaging about him; no, he just does not interest me. Only two things exist for me: At the chapter, five hundred Betarim are standing in line, five hundred match-sticks ready to be struck, five hundred ready to be lit, five hundred bodies ready for action, five hundred throats thirsty for a Sovereign Kingdom. And Uri Zvi, here he comes, the man I see as the Burning Bush. He will strike the matches. Seven days ago Uri Zvi had set aflame the pages of *The Moment*: "Aza-Acco!" he wrote. Acco symbolizing Ben Yosef who was hanged there,[19] Aza symbolizing a would-be immigrant who drowned off the shores of Eretz Israel and whose body washed ashore in Aza (Gaza). I decide that in our chapter we will greet Uri Zvi not with the time-worn slogan "Tel Hai!" but with "Aza-Acco!"

Tel Hai: The Galilean fort in which the one-armed Joseph Trumpeldor and his friends died in defense of Jewish homes and lives. "It is good to die for our country," gasped the dying Trumpeldor. But the adoption of "Tel Hai" as Betar's slogan is responsible for much of the recent educational and ideological stagnation. "Tel Hai" was appropriate and great for its time, but not for twenty years after the event. The problem it addressed is not our problem. The issue is no longer the formal aspect of heroism. "It is good to die for our country" is beautiful and holy, but does not tell us how to act. The idea can lead, as it did in the Hagana, to heroic defense. But is this the purpose of Betar? The tie to Joseph

Trumpeldor and the "Tel Hai" slogan brought about this dissonance between that which was demanded by reality and that which was implied by the slogan, between the tremendous spiritual energy and the intellectual poverty.

I was never inspired by the "Tel Hai" slogan. So I allowed myself to break the Betar tradition. Uri Zvi had conceived a slogan for our time: "Aza-Acco."

I whisk him straight from the station to the chapter. Dr. Altman tags along; I have forgotten about him.

Later, I was told that he had been very hurt that I had not mentioned him, not introduced him, not invited him to enter the flaming circle of five hundred Vilna Betarim. I had not excluded him intentionally. I had heard neither good nor bad of him. But for me he was simply outside the circle. (The thought never occurred to me that afterward, during the war in Eretz Israel, he would remain pretty much outside the circle.)

The circle of bodies was ablaze. And Uri Zvi was ablaze. He was set ablaze when five hundred uniformed torches wrote in flame across the air: "Aza-Acco." Uri Zvi was moved and said what he said. I do not remember what he said. I do not know whether I discerned his words then, whether anyone did. A fire was raging in the chapter, in our hearts, in our blood. I do not know the name of everyone who stood in line that day. One was Mike (Simcha) Ashbel, that I do know. He managed. He managed to get out. He managed to fight in an IZL unit and he was captured in the south, on the road to Aza, and he was sentenced to death and he had his sentence commuted and he fell in the IZL attack on Acco Prison. And if the five hundred from Vilna had managed to come, and the five thousand from the Vilna Region, and the fifty thousand who stood ready in Poland, their blood roaring: "Aza-Acco"; if they had managed to come, then surely we would today be sitting not in our shrunken state, between Aza and Acco, but between the Nile and the Euphrates as destined, as necessary.

We met in a hotel room the following day. About ten of the movement's leaders in Vilna were there. Israel Epstein and I represented Betar. Uri Zvi sat to my right.

Jabotinsky unveiled two plans. Actually, he "unveiled" only one; the second could only be sketched in general terms.

The first plan: Zion-Sejm. "Sejm" means parliament. We must appear before the world as the true representatives of the Hebrew people. If we succeed in attracting two million voters—and considering the current dissatisfaction with the Zionist establishment this is entirely possible—then our views will carry much import. He, Jabotinsky, will know he has tremendous support behind him.

The voting itself and the convening of a parliament will propel the Freedom Movement forward. And this plan will be much more effective if carried out in tandem with the second: the organization and training of one hundred thousand Jewish soldiers for aliya and conquest.

How Uri Zvi knew what was going on inside of me, I do not know. Maybe my anger appeared on my face, or maybe he understood I would naturally be angry, or maybe he transferred his feelings to me empathetically. In any case, when Jabotinsky stopped and left the room for a minute, Uri Zvi whispered to me (the room remained silent even in the president's absence, for his presence remained): "Don't take the floor, don't say anything, you won't convince him anyway, it's not worth upsetting him."

Only rarely do I reject the advice of a prophet, but now I did. I had to. I spoke not from my heart but from the hearts of tens of thousands of Betarim—though they had not appointed me an official spokesman, our blood pulsed in unison. Of course, I spoke quietly and politely. My anger was channeled into the trembling in my voice and hands: I think I speak in the name of the youth here when I say that we choose the second plan but not the first. The youth does not wish to devote its time and energy to more petitions and elections and polls. We no longer believe that millions of votes can shake the world's conscience. The first plan will distract us, our minds and our strength, and bring nothing. For the second plan we will give everything.

This time Jabotinsky did not get angry. Apparently he knew this would be the activist reply. He must have received the same answer in other places. Perhaps he thought the second plan would pacify the youth. Undoubtedly he also considered it a serious alternative were the political plan to fail. Perhaps he also viewed it as a pressure tactic. He was indeed the Father of the Revolt, but he was also the great artist, the greatest theatrical genius of his generation; and he was not ready to sacrifice any life, to spill one drop of blood, unless forced to do so by the necessity of there being no other choice, and unless he was sure of victory. He now wanted by the sheer force of his will to postpone the collapse of the world and the military option in Eretz Israel, in order to use the time to prepare our people and our allies.

In principle, he was right. He would have been right had we been masters of time, but by then we were already standing on the razor's edge, the knife's point.

That same day or night, Uri Zvi sat in my home and read to me and to Eliahu Slotsky (whose soul was beautiful and who often said Hebrew grammar was itself poetry) his ballad about the funeral of Slermeyer, a Jewish student murdered by Polish students in Lvov. The terrifying ballad contained in its darkness all the darkness that was to descend on everyone, on everyone there. The ballad has been lost. The poet left it with his mother; she and it were lost together.

While we were sitting in my home, Rosh Betar Jabotinsky—accompanied only by Israel Epstein—was entering the Vilna Cemetery to visit, as he said, a few friends, including the wonderful Dr. Rimini who had recently passed away. (He had been a zealous Zionist-Revisionist, his wife a Bundist, his daughter a Betaria, and his son between the Bund and Communism. Their house was a dove's nest of honor, love and respect, and always beautifully calm.)

Israel returned from the cemetery extremely depressed. Rosh Betar had said to him: "It's important to visit friends, for perhaps I'll be meeting them soon."

3. The Last Days of the Rotary Press

I moved to Warsaw in August 1939.

Uri Zvi took me from the editorial offices of *The Moment* to its rotary room. Uri Zvi, the lover of myth, the "irrationalist," revealed himself to be a lover of technology, with a particular fondness for printing presses. How the spirit of the words dons flesh and becomes print! I have little interest in machines. I prefer watching the man standing next to the machine. Uri Zvi says that the machine, too, is a miracle of humanity, an arm of man, the fruit of his creative mind.

I stand for the first time facing the most modern rotary machine in the world, imported just now for the most widely read Jewish newspaper in Poland, a machine which has become the property of the Nationalist Movement.

Back upstairs in the narrow editorial office, Uri Zvi burns. The flame gushes as from a volcano. As is natural for a flame, it consumes and destroys. Naturally, it leaves in its wake ashes fertile with life and riches and power. The newspaper assumes a new form and a new spirit.

What has *The Moment* been until now? A popular, broad-based-national-non-party newspaper. A vehicle for Prylucki. And for Hillel Zeitlin, who spreads his holy prayer shawl wide, wide enough for all of Israel—but all of Israel no longer wants to live completely underneath a prayer shawl, no longer wants only the holy Sabbath. And for dozens of writers and reporters who supply readers with their daily worries. And here comes the guiding hand. Under Uri Zvi's hand the divisions and splinters drop off, flow away to the horizon, and single, single is the current flowing toward Redemption. The ground is burning underneath everyone's feet in the Diaspora. Jabotinsky explains, justifies, analyzes in the pages of *The Moment*. Uri Zvi marches as a pillar of fire at the head of the paper, across the wide burning columns. I am invited to edit the literary section, a lantern beside the fire.

And Jews are standing in the streets of Warsaw, gathering, their own sparks gathering around this pillar of fire.

The streets of Warsaw—

I saw them, too, for the first time as I watched the rotary motion. The streets are also rotating. They suck in, they spew out, suck in, spew out countless tens of thousands. Each cog rushing to perform its function. Some with beards, some without. Some with canes, some without. Some with covered heads, some bareheaded. With briefcases or packages, in work clothes or frock coats. They run, the cogs run, they are alive—though somewhere out there knives are already waiting for their white necks. Somewhere out there the bricks are already being laid for the crematoria. And they are rushing, rushing still. One feels like shouting into the ears of those running: Stop! For God's sake, stop! You are running on the precipice!

No one stops. The present is devouring the future, in every mouth. You cannot worry about life when you must worry about bread. The cog cannot contemplate the fate of the machine, nor of what rolls from the presses, even if he is alive, even if he is a Jew who by virtue of being a Jew must think in universal terms. Stores in small villages yawn without customers, the young yawn without work. The brain experiences a boring, a boring into the brain. In Warsaw, this boring mosquito is not heard. The wheel rotates above the din which is not heard. And now the fiery flame leaps from the pages of *The Moment* and sweeps all in its path—it cannot be withstood. Soon everyone will be looking toward the same redeeming horizon, soon. The rotation is being steered, direction has come.

I lose my way in the streets of Warsaw, as one confused by the rotation. Vienna is larger than Warsaw and I was there for six years but Vienna is a village compared to Warsaw, a mere village. The Jews, too, were quieter there, mellower. In Vienna, apparently, the news is still being printed with hand-operated presses. In Vienna, traffic is still brought to a halt to rescue a dove caught in electrical wires. In Warsaw, the twentieth century is erupting. Whether I like it or not. Vilna is quainter, more spiritual, but Warsaw is reality. Rotation is reality. You adjust to it, learn to control it—or you stay somewhere off to the side stammering about ideals and liberalism and conscience and "the world will never allow it." In Warsaw you feel: The world will indeed allow it. There is nothing that cannot be done by the rotary machines, quickly and precisely. If you grasp it, it will build you a grand kingdom, measured and drawn and fine and proper. If it grasps you, it will slice your flesh piece by piece with the same precision and speed.

This was Warsaw in August 1939. This was the state of our people in August 1939. The entire Old World, all of yesterday's politics, all the little blue JNF boxes that amounted to one big yawn, all the empty words of the Zionist organizations—all these were as if they had never been. On one side: Hitler. On the other: the British White Paper making escape to Eretz Israel impossible.[20] Between them: one path only, the path of the rotary machine, the one-time Movement for Liberation, the act of conquest. And the Revolt has a song, it has commanders, it has tens of thousands of soldiers, and an entire nation floating upon the waters.

If only time, time, time will not wrap itself around our necks too tightly. To breathe, breathe, breathe. This is the load on our hearts.

And behold, from the rotary-wheel, news: An act of reprisal by the Irgun Zvai Leumi against Arab rioters. Hundreds of Arabs killed. Arabs stricken with fear.

The hand-operated presses of the men of yesterday's Zionism, the men of the shekel and the charity boxes, tap out their condemnation of the avengers. But the public is glad, is relieved. The heart is glad. No longer will the blood of Israel be cheap.

And headlining *The Moment* is an article by Zev Jabotinsky: "Amen!" Not everyone realizes how heavy was Jabotinsky's heart as he wrote this Amen. Uri Zvi practically pulled it from him, and he edited it, too (what courage, editing Jabotinsky!): taking out all the softer material, all the gentler passages which would not have passed through the steel, which were inappropriate to a rotary machine. The rotation of the twentieth century cannot digest softness. It lacks mercy. "Amen" said every Jewish soul in its depths, deep down, even if the mouth was mumbling disavowals.

In contrast, there are no such internal struggles of the soul in the editorial offices of the IZL newspaper. The bosses there are Samuel Merlin and Natan Friedman. Seventy percent of the material is supplied by Dr. Y. H. Yevin. He sends his articles from Eretz Israel under seventy-seven different names. In the editorial offices of *Di Tat* the ground is being prepared for the future conquest of Dir Yassin; the laws of revenge—as good for our day as for the days of Joshua Bin Nun and King David—are being taught. And the youth, both its legs still in Poland but its thoughts and desires and emotions far from this Poland which it does not want and which certainly does not want it, this youth reads *Di Tat* and already sees itself among the orchards and mountains of Galilee and

Jerusalem, on the battlefields of freedom.

I find myself lost in the spinning streets of Warsaw and I attempt to adopt my Viennese-Vilnaese soul to the new pace.

The rotation has not yet reached the Betar Commission, only recently established by Menachem Begin, the object of all of his energy, which will yet be the bridge between the stagnant Betar and the conquering Irgun. It has been arranged for members of the Commission to receive high-level military training, enabling them to be both political *and* military leaders. My position is in the Cultural Section, I have the task of pushing meaningful words through the hollow educational pipes left over from the Tel Hai days of Betar. I have another unspoken goal: to save the movement from the leadership of those IZL commanders—I have discerned a few such types—who deride rather than honor intelligence. I have much hope that Menachem will extend me all the help I need.

Educationally and militarily we are still in the preparatory stages. But in one area we have already entered the rotary era: aliya. Thousands upon thousands are making aliya freely, an army of liberation in the making. One more month, one more month, one more month. Each Betari, each member of Brit Chayal, each member of an Irgun cell who reaches Eretz Israel is a great additional force worth dozens or even hundreds of "pioneers" trained in restraint who long with all their desire for a higher quota of immigration certificates. These so-called pioneers are healthy enough in body to repel Arabs and the British but they are sick, sick of soul, mumbling about revolution while gazing woefully at . . . Chaim Weizmann.

Jabotinsky's attempt to establish a rival World Zionist Organization was a failure. The New Zionist Organization did not make our movement independent, as hoped, but rather found itself competing with the Jewish Agency. Five valuable years wasted. Can we make up the lost time? Time, time, time is rushing toward the edge with terrifying speed. We must hurry the revolution.

A family update, but one that speaks of the times: My wife is whisked to Lvov. Her brother had disappeared. Seems he acted independently, crossed the Rumanian border alone and with no money. Caught in Czernowitz, he was beaten and returned. Ten days before the war.

With the signing of the Molotov-Ribbentrop Agreement the situation heats up. Depression spreads in the Commission offices when Menachem returns from the Rumanian border: The last transport was stopped and no one knows whether it will be permitted to cross into Rumania. More than one thousand people are on the border. It appears to be the border between Poland and Rumania; it is actually the border between salvation and destruction.

Menachem enters my room and asks how my work is progressing. I answer: "Not well, there is no proportion between what we are doing here and what is about to happen to the world." Menachem smiles, gives me his usual patron's slap on the shoulder and says, "It does not matter, Israel, we must continue."

The hand continues to pen plans, pamphlets, articles, but the heart is not in them.

When the war finally breaks, the situation at first seems clear. This is a war against Hitler; three days later the Jewish masses rejoice opposite the British Embassy celebrating England's entrance into the war. A heavy stone rests on our hearts.

We have lost the race with time.

Menachem attempts to continue with business as usual. The optimists are saying we will hold out, the British squadrons are already on the way. The pessimists are saying we will hold out for a year. Menachem prepares instructions on how to act in either case.

On the third day, Uri Zvi bursts inside. Israel Epstein and I are in Menachem's room.

"What are you doing here?!" shouts Uri Zvi. "Get out immediately. It's all over!"

We do not understand.

Uri Zvi points to a map of Poland, to the Bug River. "The Russians will move to this point. The Germans will come from the west. In two weeks it will all be over!"

He was off by one week.

Uri Zvi urged me to leave Warsaw with him. I, of course, would not leave the Commission without an order to do so. Had I left with Uri Zvi, I might have crossed the still-open Rumanian border and reached Eretz Israel two years earlier than I eventually did.

One day a bomb fell on the *Moment* building. The building collapsed on the modern, new rotation.

We left Warsaw on the seventh day.

We were scattered, on every road, by foot, by car, by train. We were scattered and so were the rotating cogs, the paper balloons, the lead geysers. We were scattered and so were the plans, the visions, the lives. We were scattered and so was the one great chance for a Majestic Realm of Israel established the easy way, in an act of tremendous liberation. We were scattered.

The result is no secret today. What happened to our people is no secret, nor what happened to the revolution. The revolution did not take place. Not the liberation from others, not the liberation within ourselves. We were too late.

The war came to the rescue of the Mapai-Weizmann regime in Zionism. The rotation was destroyed. The provincial, hand-operated "Zionist" machine remained.

The same regime that withheld immigration certificates from people like Dov Granek and Dov Gruner because they did not belong to "their" political party.

Look at the few who made it, look at Dov, tall and blond, the scourge of the British, look at Mike Ashbel, at Dov Gruner, at Avraham Amper.[21] Look at these few and know:

Tens of thousands like them remained there. Dovs for Israel. Lions, panthers for Israel. How can our blood not cry, when it knows what could have been done here in Israel if another ten thousand, another five thousand, like them were here! For they were there, they were ready, they longed to give their blood—here! Look at what the few have done, and know what could have been done if the many had made it, the many whose dear bodies were charcoaled into nothingness, into awful, barren nothingness.

Oh, we were very late.

Refuge in the Jerusalem of Lithuania

1. Bodies without Heads

Roads closed, expanses shrank. A ray of hope shone from Vilna. A final gesture on the part of the city known as the "Jerusalem of Lithuania," a final gesture on behalf of the last exiles for whom she is haven, a final gesture before her disappearance from the stage of Jewish history.

Vilna took us in, one by one. She was a window on the ark being tossed between the seas of Nazism and the ice of Siberia. She was a window left open for aliya.

She took us in one by one, then by the dozens, by the hundreds. Almost all the members of the Betar Commission found their way to Vilna. We organized, together with representatives of the IZL, the dispatch of emissaries to the borders of the Russian occupation and beyond, to the lands under German occupation. The watchword was: Come to Vilna, in tiny Lithuania; and the Betarim came by the hundreds, half-frozen in the harsh winter, some dying on arrival.

The Moment no longer exists. *Di Tat* no longer exists. We publish the weekly *Hamedina*. Everything in reduced form. Our energy, too. Depression.

The IZL commanders live in "splendid isolation," as full of secrets as always, but the training in the use of arms does continue. Even the plan to provide Betar officials with military training moves ahead, albeit on a smaller scale. In a kitchen belonging to Betar refugees, we take our first steps. Menachem Begin, Natan Friedman, Israel Epstein, David Yotan and I. First steps meaning, literally, first steps: Attention. At ease. Attention. At ease. Right face. Forward march. Afterward, the first lessons in light arms.

The instructor: Avraham Amper.

We spend our time devising various plans of escape from this surrounded corner of northeastern Europe. One fantastic plan involves the renting of small boats to set sail on the Baltic Sea. Someone was even sent to check out this possibility. Mordecai Oringel was sent; he disappeared. We knew he would never return. Twenty years later he arrived in Israel from Siberian exile.

Immigration certificates reached Lithuania. A total of twenty certificates have been allocated to Betar and the Revisionists. A few for Youth Aliya. And the remainder?

We have plenty of time to think, to argue. I publish in *Hamedina* a series of three articles titled "Hostile Neutrality," words meant to describe the attitude we should adopt toward the British in Eretz Israel. The articles are allowed to appear in the tradition of a free competition of ideas, since the editors disagree with most of my conclusions.

The Jabotinsky-Trumpeldor legacy of support for the Jewish Legion in World War I is unfortunate. People have an "automatic ideology." It is simple: they believe they must form a Jewish Legion to fight alongside the Allies, just as was done in the First World War. In my articles, I scrutinize the differences between 1917 and 1940. Then, our Land had been in Turkish hands; today, in British. British promises are worthless. Then, the units of the Legion had fought to capture Eretz Israel; today they will be no more than cannon fodder in the service of the power that enslaves Eretz Israel.

This new "legionism" is, therefore, a phrase empty of concrete political meaning for us.

Bits of news begin to reach us, news of a crisis within the IZL in Eretz Israel. Someone sends word: Yair has opened his own store. We have no details, are given no reasons for these occurrences.

The political confusion is overwhelming us, and Menachem is forced to call a board meeting to assess events. Attending are the members of the Lithuanian Commission, headed by Glazman, Betar chairman Dillion, Dr. Arye Koeppel and us. Natan Friedman is representing the Irgun. Three opinions are voiced: Y. Wirnick at one extreme advocates packing away our flags for the duration of the war. We should not be fighting British rule while there is a war going on against Hitler. I am at the other extreme: We should exploit Britain's weakness and attack. Politically, we should be guided by the principle that whoever offers a helping hand is our ally. Menachem says he is in general agreement with me, but we differ in style. Actually, it is a lot more than style: Menachem speaks of the need to act in Eretz Israel, but he sees such action merely as a form of pressure to encourage Britain to come around to our view.

These are the directions of the argument. We want to hear the IZL representative but he is silent. And the few words he does utter amount to silence. Of course, he is in a difficult position. Silence, in any case, has its advantages over speech.

We do not vote, but we send a protocol of the meeting to Eretz Israel, to voice the opinions of we who are in Lithuanian exile. (I do not know what became of this protocol.)

A letter from Uri Zvi. He asks that we rescue the manuscripts he left in Lvov. He writes nothing of the situation in Eretz Israel. Almost nothing—his closing words are a scream: "My heart—it's a miracle it doesn't burst."

On the twentieth day of the Hebrew month of Tamuz we organize a memorial ceremony for Bialik and Herzl. In Vilna, this is an emotional day, the first time that a Hebrew meeting is being permitted in the university auditorium. Much Jewish blood has been spilled here, much Jewish honor trampled, and this now is a political consolation. The hall is too small for the many who come.

First, Menachem speaks about Herzl, then I speak of Bialik. The third speaker is Dr. Shapira, the dean of Hebrew literature at Kovno University. A tumult outside, as he is speaking. The news spreads rapidly: Moscow charges Lithuania with a provocation. Moscow announces it has crossed into Lithuania. The Red Army is already entering Vilna.

Dr. Shapira is confused. He lacks the strength to continue speaking. Ten minutes more. He stops. He wants to close the meeting, but we remind him: We close with *Hatikva*.

By then, everyone knows. The Red Army is entering Vilna. The fate of each individual is unclear, but the fate of the *Hatikva* anthem is obvious. She will be strangled. Therefore, friends, let us sing, let us sing with all our breath, with our chest that still . . . still breathes.

And all of us know we are parting from her. And we sing in devotion, in love, in tears.

Outside in the street, people are already waiting for the Red tanks. The stores are shut.

2. We Cannot Cry, So Let's Play Chess

Twenty days later a young man—I think he was Gordon Mayashisky—entered the large kitchen of the Betar refugees. He had a black ribbon on his lapel and black words on his tongue:

Radio London announced this morning that Jabotinsky . . . is dead.

Our faces froze, white; disbelief was our first reaction. I slowly began to understand the words of our sages that the weeping of the Divine Spirit is done secretly. We all wept secretly.

On the seventh day of mourning, in the utmost secrecy, a small cluster of the most dedicated met at the graves of the Betarim who had frozen to death on their way to Vilna. We recited the Kaddish. Menachem recited—but did not sing—the Betar anthem, and we dispersed into the crowd of thousands who had come to pay their respects to Rabbi Chayim Ozer Grodzinski, who was buried that same day.

Nonetheless, rumors reached the Soviet police and some of us were interrogated about this counterrevolutionary weeping.

Sensing an "evil eye," we left the city.

Saying this hurts, and even shames, but there were many evil eyes. Eyes we knew, until now, as good eyes. Even the eyes of Betarim. . . .

One gentle boy, for example, few were as fine as he, the son of a Vilna judge. Suddenly, whispering: Watch out for him. What? Him? It cannot be!

I run to him and ask him, straight out: Listen, this is what they are saying about you. His head drops, tears fall on his soft cheeks:

"If they had ripped me to pieces I wouldn't have cared. But they threatened to send my elderly mother and father to Siberia. I couldn't risk it. But I . . . I am only working in the Economic Section, against hidden storehouses."

I had no reason to defend the storehouses of speculators. I had neither storehouses nor enough money to make purchases on the black market; still, the heart ached, ached very much.

We left the city.

I found an apartment in a town near Vilna. Till then, no Jews had set foot there. The old women who rented us the top floor of their house crossed themselves seven times before condescending to rent to Jews; they said so openly, the economic situation left them no choice. High Polish officials had lived in this town before the war. Men were almost unseen now. They ran, they were arrested, they were taken prisoner. One of our neighbors was a young woman, the wife of a pilot. Since the start of the war she had had no word of him. Night after night she neatly prepared his bed, should he choose *this* night to return.

Ironically, we were safer in these Gentile surroundings, away from evil eyes. Had the Germans come, though, the women would undoubtedly have turned us in.

Menachem and his wife Aliza, my wife Batya and I, and two other men of our circle lived there. Israel Epstein and Natan Friedman visited. The houses were in pine forests, on hills. We gathered wood in order to cook.

In the evenings, Menachem and I played chess.

Once, we organized into a "labor force" and worked widening the Russian railroad tracks. As with everything in Russia, they are wider than in the West. Everything is wider. The tanks are wider, the hearts are wider, and Siberia is very, very wide.

So we sat in this town called Pavilnis and we waited. Waited . . . for what? Menachem had a visa to Eretz Israel in his passport; he was waiting for permission to travel via Russia. We busied ourselves with the preparation of papers and visas and we hoped for permission to leave. We had heard that the Russians were going to do something in Vilna they had done nowhere else—for there is no explaining the Russian winds—they were going to let anyone with a visa leave. Suddenly, visas began appearing.

I can only add this tragicomic anecdote: We were traveling between Vilna and Kovno when we heard a Jew sigh. "And why do you sigh, Jewish friend?" "I want to be at home already, in the homeland." "Which home?" "What do you mean? In Curacao." For the Dutch Consulate had apparently decided that one did not need a visa to enter a certain rocky South American island under its sovereignty. With this in mind, Jews began to whisper that one could get a transit visa through Japan, which would be enough to get permission to leave Vilna. So the Jews sat, their souls longing for their homes in Curacao.

We played chess and we waited.

3. Menachem Begin, Gatherer of Wood

One hot summer morning between Yom Kippur and Succot (on the holidays themselves we had walked to Vilna for prayer services) when I was home alone, a short Lithuanian came by asking for Mr. Moses Begin.

"No, this is the residence of Menachem Begin."

"It doesn't matter. Mr. Begin will come Friday at eleven o'clock to the room indicated on this invitation."

What can I do? I am not a dog and I do not have a well-developed sense of smell.

Menachem did a little checking; the room seemed to be located in the municipality's Department of Engineering.

The smell became more noticeable.

The Lithuanian returned a few days later and demanded that Mr. Begin appear at that office. Near our house, and at the train station, we began to see people whom we did not recognize. In this town, we recognized everyone. They began following Menachem but, since his wife went everywhere with him, they refrained from approaching him. He enjoyed a form of "diplomatic" immunity . . . .

Friday at eleven o'clock the man appeared again. We were sitting on the lovely, glass-enclosed veranda. Menachem spoke first:

"Listen, young man, you seem pretty suspicious to me. This is an engineer's office at the municipality and I have nothing to do with engineering. You are a suspicious character. I'm going to call the police."

The poor *schlemiel* was overjoyed and exclaimed, "Good, good, let's go to the police."

"I'll not go anywhere with you."

The young novice stuttered a bit and left.

Well, Friday is Friday. The Sabbath meal needed to be cooked. The two women wanted to cook but we were out of wood. Menachem and I took a sack and went into the forest to gather wood. The law of Moses does permit the gathering of wood on Fridays.

But there is another law, one that decrees that Menachem Begin must be followed as he gathers wood on a Friday.

We stepped outside. The smell was stronger. All around us, as if these guys were all coincidentally milling about.

When they spotted us headed with a sack for the forest, they probably smiled wider than those railroad tracks. We were obviously on our way to do something counterrevolutionary.

We pretended we noticed nothing, entered the thick of the forest and collected our wood. Unintentionally, we happened to sing Hebrew songs a bit louder than usual. (A few weeks earlier we had actually buried some documents in the forest, but very deep, and the forest is very big.)

Apparently our gathering wood was not counterrevolutionary enough since they let us return home peacefully.

Our wives attended to the stove while we sat on the veranda in the autumnal Polish sun, golden and warm, and began a chess competition. The women were somewhat nervous, but when were they not?

The concert began at about twelve o'clock:

Three tall, elegant men entered. Our spirits lifted a little; at least it was not going to be some Lithuanian lout.

They stepped onto the veranda. Menachem invited them to sit. They declined. "In that case I, too, must rise," said Menachem.

I cannot remember the result of this dispute on etiquette, whether they sat or we stood. The women continued in the kitchen; at least their hands continued.

"Why did you fail to appear at the office to which you were invited, Mr. Begin?"

"Because I have nothing to do there. I have nothing to do with engineering and honestly, gentlemen, why are we bothering with this whole game? I am a lawyer and I know a little about papers, and the paper brought by that fellow was a rag, not a document."

"And what document would you like?"

"Speak clearly, have you come to arrest me?"

At this point one of the detectives committed the terrible faux pas for which he was later rebuked. He said: Yes.

(His "crime" related to the method: Arrest a man when he is alone, not when others are present. Do not tell him he is being arrested, so that during the interrogation he can be threatened with arrest. Menachem's unusual, calm conversation must have thrown the detective off balance, and he answered "yes" to what was obvious even without his reply.)

"And you have an arrest warrant, sir?" Menachem did not let up.

"No, but I do have identification," he answered, taking out and handing Menachem his NKVD identification which read "Ministry of Interior" and meant secret police.

Menachem capitulated. "If so, it is all right. I'll get dressed."

Another surprise:

Aliza Begin steps out and asks: "Will you gentlemen join us for lunch?"

"No, no, thank you," one of them quickly responds. "We are in a hurry; a car is waiting for us downstairs."

"Am I permitted to take books?" queries Menachem.

"Why? You'll be back shortly."

He took a Bible anyway.

Menachem carefully polished his shoes. The one who finally broke was my wife, not his.

"Don't cry, Batya," said Menachem as he took leave of us.

The last chord:

Menachem opened the door, stepped aside and let the three men step first.

"Here, you are my guests."

Aliza accompanied them. Later she told us that downstairs Menachem asked to be allowed to visit the lavatory, about one hundred meters away. The mesmerized gentlemen apparently forgot about security requirements and allowed him to go unaccompanied. Afterward they walked to the car and again promised Aliza that her husband would be back soon.

"Yes," Menachem said to Aliza, "about the interrupted game, tell Israel I lost, I give in."

For the record, he had not yet lost. We were only on the seventh or eighth move. The battle was still before us.

Only this needs to be added:

Years later when I met Menachem for the first time in Eretz Israel—and I had not believed we would ever meet again—he said: "Nu, Israel, they interrupted us in the middle. We will continue?"

"We will continue, Menachem."

And so we did.

4. "The Best of the Gentiles"

The day after Menachem's arrest, our Christian landlord's attitude toward us took a surprising turn for the better. They cursed the Bolsheviks and promised that from that day on they would pray in church that we successfully reach our destination, the Holy Land. Surrounded as we were by enemies: Nazis, British, Communists, we had not expected to find allies in elderly Polish-Christians.

A tall and very white Catholic church stood on a hilltop a few hundred meters from "our" house. Many white steps led to the square in which the white building stood framed by green pine trees. It was always quiet there, quiet like the surrounding forests, like the sadness that descended upon the town when its men and youth disappeared, and only the wishes and longings moved about. Anytime she wished to cry, a Christian soul was able to enter the church and worship in solitude, to kiss the feet of the statues, to weep for her son, her husband, her father, all of whom are gone, and for beloved Poland which is gone, and to beg Mary the "mother," the "one," the "beloved," the "endeared," to return her son, her husband, her father and beautiful Poland.

Occasionally, some envy would creep into my heart, at this ability to be alone with and submit to the "mother." We—whose Father is in heaven (I mean no comparison)—we do not go to Him except in a *minyan* (prayer quorum), in public. You may wish to say Kaddish when you are alone, but you cannot, for no one is there to answer "Amen."

Even more, that gold and blue autumn, I envied their bells. Why do we not have bells in our houses of prayer? No other sound rises as the sound of bells, no other sound settles into the soul as softly as a bell's. In the manic evenings of that wonderful Polish autumn, the sounds sprouted white wings, then pink ones, then red, then pink, and then blackest black, as they plunged into the depths of the air, the world, the valley and the spirit. The rustling of the golden yellow leaves which fell and fell and fell mixed with the sounds lapping at them, and together they plunged groundward into the darkness till death, till death, till silence.

At home, the air was heavy with loneliness and despair. Batya supported us by working in the city. Our problem was neither bread nor fear of more arrests, but rather: the purpose. This inactive life, what is its purpose?

The golden autumn gave way to rainstorms.

Despite the rain and mud, I wandered the streets of Vilna. Everything seemed muddy, gloomy. Familiar faces became unfamiliar. This man now peddled shoelaces; this wore a Communist pin and was accepted to the university; this refused to answer when addressed in Hebrew; this crossed to the other side of the street. "Don't trust your brothers." Suffocating.

One such stormy day, a ray of light struck me:

A gathering in the courtyard of the large synagogue—the funeral of a yeshiva student. I approached thinking that perhaps my soul, at least, will find some warmth.

A rabbi rose to deliver the eulogy; I had not seen him before among the rabbis of Vilna, maybe he headed the yeshiva. He opened with a question: Why was Moses buried opposite the idols of Bet Pe'or? The answer: Israel had sinned by idolatry, with Ba'al Pe'or, and Moses was buried there to serve as testimony that not all Israel had sinned, had worshiped false gods.

The eulogizer explained the symbol: "The yeshiva student who died has risen to heaven and is testifying: Not all of Israel is worshiping false gods."

Not satisfied with hinting, the speaker made things clear: Materialism has spread, become Torah and law among us, and it has its own commandments; our brothers are forsaking the spirit of Israel for materialism.

The listeners began exchanging glances, but the speaker had already risen in a pillar of fire, consuming but not consumed. His throat released all it had held back all these months. Many left, looked this way and that and left. Those who remained came closer and closer together in the courtyard, around the coffin, and I felt as I had in the cemetery when we marked the seventh day after the death of Rosh Betar. But here the robe of the Torah was that which spread itself in all its width and depth. The eulogizer's arm reached beyond the borders of the Russian occupation and the borders of time, beyond the Russian and French Revolutions, and it grasped the first Hebrew revolution at Mt. Sinai when we became a nation. We inched closer and closer together, the eulogizer still spitting flames. As he said, "You are called 'man' and the nations of the world are not called 'man,'" the Divine spirit entered anew the cloth that is our bodies and our barren bones.

Then I knew: I had seen a reincarnated Rabbi Shimon Bar Yochai. Then I believed the mystical Zohar really was written by the second-century Rabbi Shimon Bar Yochai, really did emerge from his dark cave. Our legs were still stuck in the mud of that courtyard in Vilna, in Russia, in Exile, in our hopeless situation, but our hearts were again sure, proud, beaming.

I was in contact with two students in one of the yeshivas, as part of a sort of underground we had set up to encourage the school-aged youth to learn Hebrew. From them I received talmudic excerpts and midrashic legends which I took with me to the Christian-Catholic town of our isolation, and from every page I gathered Rabbi Shimon's sparks.

From the time I took hold of that hand which was extended to me from those depths, I have not feared evil—neither from Ba'al Pe'or idols nor from good Gentiles.

Another acquisition from those days remains, from which I have never been weaned: the longing for bells. When many years later I stood with Eliahu Amikam on Jerusalem's lofty Mt. Herzl, as Theodor Herzl's body was being re-interred there, I asked Eliahu: Don't you feel that something is missing? He replied: Yes, the thunder of cannons. I answered: And I would prefer the glorious sound of bells leaping from here to the surrounding mountains, and farther, and farther, and deep. Heavy sounds, ringing, uplifting, filling the clean, clean air until they are actually visible, descending from above to the tops of the wild mountains and ascending again to the blue, carrying the heart with them. Bells—I want to hear bells, Eliahu, now.

Aliya

1. Beyond Logic

Too many Jews worked for the secret police, too many people knew about the forged visas and passports. The Soviets must have known. Yet the government feigned ignorance, allowed us to leave. One cannot seek logic here. Just as the arrests followed no logical pattern, with Menachem being arrested the same day as three minor Revisionist workers, while more prominent figures remained free. Nor can logic explain why many of those arrested and interrogated and released said they were questioned intensively about Natan Friedman, editor of the terrorist, fascist, etc., newspaper *Di Tat*—while Friedman himself enjoyed his peregrinations throughout Vilna in broad daylight. Then when the police were ultimately searching for him in the homes and cafés of Vilna, he was walking in and out of official offices fifty kilometers away in Kovno, handling the last formalities before his quiet and calm departure, under the very eyes of the same police.

My wife's mother and my mother came to bid us farewell, came forty kilometers in the deep winter snow; they had to steal across the border, for free passage between Lvov and Vilna was by now forbidden. My mother-in-law begged us to stay, to return to Lvov, and somehow we would get by. Her pleas notwithstanding, she had brought with her hundreds of precious dollars, without which travel was impossible (maybe dollars were the "logical" basis for our exit permits, too). She had sold whatever items from the house she had been able to, and had brought the money. She had also brought contraband chocolate, putting her life on the line as a smuggler to bring chocolate to her children.

Our brothers, too, came to bid us farewell, then went. They were "taken care of," thank God, working and making money. He who works—eats; equality for all, Jew and Gentile alike, he who works—eats; with the small difference that tomorrow the Jews will themselves be consumed in ovens. But meanwhile—that accursed "meanwhile"—they work and eat. I, the gypsy, am the only member of my family to stubbornly refuse to be taken care of; I continue wandering.

Try explaining to them, to two mothers, that I despise suffocation, any suffocation, that which strangles the body and that which strangles the soul. I did not hate Communism—I was neither a bourgeois nor an economic liberal, and I did not miss the butter and chocolate and luxury items which had disappeared from the markets. But I could not bear the guaranteed equality, just as I could not bear the charity of the old Catholics. Also I was jealous of those

Russians who donned Red Army uniforms and remained Russians, whose eyes sparkled when they said "Moscow," whose nostrils widened when they said "Volga," whose blood warmed when they said, "We rule all Siberia as far as Vladivostok." Try explaining to them, to our mothers, that our own Spiritual Empire demands a Territorial Empire. Try explaining that Jerusalem exists not only in prayer books but in us, as our mothers' bodies exist in ours, their children's. I think this is all very logical, but if someone were to prove to me that it is illogical, I would say: To hell with logic, we must atone for our logical sins.

Shlussberg, the Communist in charge of the Soviet office in Vilna, shook my hand—trembling as it held a Hanse travel permit—as I left his office, and he said, *auf wiedersehen*, and I do not know what he meant, whether he spoke as a representative of Soviet rule, whose scope of vision included the entire globe, or whether perhaps the Jewish spark in Shlussberg's soul spoke, as it, too, set its eyes on one precious corner of that globe.

We left Vilna, called the Jerusalem of Lithuania. Everything there which was comparable to Jerusalem—is now gone. It is terrible, but the message must be clear: It was not Jerusalem, it could not be Jerusalem. Jerusalem is not in Lithuania and Jerusalem is not in America, for Jerusalem is not one of the ephemeral spirits created at twilight just before the Sabbath, which are not bound to the ground. Not even the Spirit of God was able to hover above the depths forever; how much less able is the spirit of man, or the spirit of Israel.

2. Moscow

Three days in Moscow—our time is short, so are our tempers. Our departure was a miracle, our visas for Eretz Israel are forged—every hour counts. Every day in Moscow costs us ten dollars. Someone with a lot of money and a valid passport would do well to spend several weeks taking the pulse of the Russian and Communist capital from the elegant Intourist Hotel. Even with much time and money, though, I would still be unable to see Moscow objectively. The subjective obstacles are too overwhelming. First, my Western democratic experience, however little we had of it in Poland. The fear of constant police surveillance, the knowledge that this sturdy building is constructed to leave no wall without ears—one starts with a negative feeling. A man who is choking cannot savor even the good taste of air and food. We have not yet adjusted our breathing to the air of Moscow. Breathing is perhaps easier for one who has adjusted.

The second subjective obstacle is ours, and Jewish. You hear the Vilna official traveling with you say that his brothers and sisters in Moscow fear being seen with him, lest they be suspected of Zionist sympathies. You attend the government-supported Jewish theater and see all the posters in Russian. Not one Yiddish word in the entire building. During the play, whispering: The older generation is constantly translating for the younger. In ten years, who will translate for the children of these youth? Only in Odessa did we hear two young people speaking Yiddish. And the play: Goldfadden's *Two Kuni Lemels*. The National Theater of a nation of millions is still performing one of Goldfadden's shoddiest plays. Shalom Aleichem and Goldfadden, Goldfadden and Shalom Aleichem. Anything else? Anything new? Nothing new.

Despite my subjective restraints, I attempt to absorb. I refrain from commenting, as my traveling companions do, on the luxury of our hotel, the excellent food, the dancers, and so forth—all only a few hundred yards from bread lines. Our hotel brings dollars to the Russian treasury. The dollars serve the nation on the bread line. They do not provide colorful clothing or even boots for their feet—only tanks, tanks, huge tanks. And the drivers are Russians. When I later reached Eretz Israel, I breathed deeply and well. The people had meat and butter and clothing and the best of everything, without foreign currency and dollars; I choked, however, when I saw the streets of our capital filled with tanks, tanks . . . and the drivers were foreigners.

The gold domes of the church-crowned Kremlin are visible from our hotel. A red star shines above the Kremlin at night. Deep below, tunnels lead from the churches to the Kremlin. The Russian capital is not in Leningrad, not in Odessa, only in Moscow, in the heart of Moscow. Again you feel: Blessed is the people which destroys and builds, builds and destroys, changes clothes and changes regimes according to its concrete needs, but which is on its own land with its own language, and all its blood and thoughts are united in its heart, its one heart. The heart is irreplaceable, all else is mere skin. Skin peels and regenerates; that which is inside remains. Years will pass, few or many, and Marx will indeed be remembered as one of the world's geniuses, along with Newton and Einstein—but Peter the Great will be holy in Moscow. Lenin, too, will be holy in Moscow. For they increased the power of Russia. These are my thoughts as I pass Lenin's Tomb, church bells pealing in the distance.

I had first heard Lenin's name in the synagogue in which my father "worshipped" every Sabbath (he really went to win the Hasidic Belz synagogue over to Zionism, and to enjoy the weekly biblical portion, and to study with his friends the commentaries, beginning with Ibn Ezra). One of my father's circle was Yehiel, bearded and earlocked, who attended synagogue every day of the week, morning, afternoon and evening. He pored over the Talmud, the laws, Maimonides, the Midrash, discussing with all every apostrophe in the Law and in . . . Spinoza.

He was talking to me once—I was thirteen—of worldly affairs. Suddenly he asked: "Do you know who is the greatest man in the world, after Moses?" As a regular listener to his discussions I tried to decide whether to reply Maimonides or Spinoza. But he answered first: Lenin. Then he unraveled the greatness of the Revolution, and I probably would have accepted much of what he said so fervently, had he not made the obvious mistake of criticizing Zionism and Eretz Israel.

A worker in a box factory, he was a lover of Torah as few others I have known, and . . . a Communist. He Hebraized his name from Yehiel Reich to Yehiel Ani (Hebrew for "poor").

I thought him a strange man. But the name of Lenin stayed in my heart.

We soon reached Odessa, where we did not stay long. Our only thought was that there should be no trouble, no trouble. Uncertainty gnawed at us till the last minute. I have only one memory of Odessa: An old Jew shining shoes, speaking softly, asks what is new in the Jewish and Zionist world. We tell him Jabotinsky, the man from Odessa, is dead. He is visibly shaken. He knew him. He had lived on the same block as Vladimir. Two tears roll down his wrinkled cheeks. Had I been able to take them and pack them away, I would have donated them to the Betar Museum in Tel Aviv, but in the customs-room of Odessa Port even the soles of our shoes are ripped open and searched. I packed the tears in my heart, and now they are on my cheeks as I write this.

3. The Barlas Episode

I do not know where Mr. Barlas is today, I am only surprised that he has never been made Israel's minister of immigration. Then, he was the representative of the Jewish Agency in Istanbul; he sat in the Park Hotel and "took care of" aliya from the Eastern European countries, which were then burning or being strangled.

Several months before my departure from Vilna, we had sent two guinea pigs in order to test the forged visas we were producing. We needed to know if and how Mr. Sleptor of Cracow and Asher Sofer of Betar would make it. Several weeks passed and a telegram arrived informing us that they had failed and were going to be returned to Russia. A second telegram arrived from Mr. Barlas: "Do not travel on English papers." "English papers" meant the forged visas. We had printed letters from the British consulate in Kovno, to the effect that Mr. So-and-so had a Palestinian visa waiting for him in Turkey. The British consulate had actually sent some such letters in the days preceding its closure. Copying the letters was not difficult, though not all the imitations succeeded. The imprints of the two British lions resembled cats more than lions. Having no choice, we made do with cats. The open question was how the cats would fare in Turkey, after they had been favorably received by the Russian office responsible for exit visas.

Now, these two telegrams. Everything collapsed. What remained? The home in Curacao? The meaning "returned to Russia" was obvious: Siberia. We waited for more news. Nothing. Meanwhile, more "lions" and "cats" were moving. They had nothing to lose. Some despaired of this method and volunteered instead for the Czech army. Some did the impossible and paid two hundred dollars, to travel via Vladivostok.

Later, when we arrived in Istanbul, a German Jew named Max Brod boarded the boat. All the "cats" rushed to tell him the "secret." He tersely announced: *Everyone* will disembark. Who is spreading rumors about "English papers"? Everyone has good visas! I will let everyone off.

And he did. Our transport included about sixty Betarim and a group of twelve from Hashomer Hatzair, led by a member of their Governing Council, Mr. Diamont (he later Hebraized his name to Shamir). Once in the city we learned that the Sleptor-Sofer telegrams were nothing more than pressure being applied by Barlas. He had forced them to wire us, on pain of being refused their immigration certificates to Palestine, and he had threatened to have them arrested and returned to Russia. He tried playing the same game with us. He managed to foam at the mouth: We are causing him unpleasantness in Ankara. Without visas we cannot continue. We will be delayed in Turkey until the next quota of certificates comes through. What would happen if hundreds and thousands like us were to come? They would build detention camps for us.

That was it. Detention camps! *There*, tens of thousands of the best Zionist youth—from all movements and parties—stood between Nazi fire and Siberian ice and here, the danger is detention camps until the certificates arrive.

The Hashomer Hatzair Council member ranted and raved to us about Barlas. If not for those telegrams he, too, would have organized the departure of hundreds of his movement's members. As it was, he had not dared. Betar had been a little more daring.

Barlas attempted to convince us to send similar telegrams to Vilna to prevent more "cats" from coming. Of course, we refused. Two weeks later another boat arrived with hundreds of passengers, again mostly Betarim. Their entry was more difficult. Mr. Barlas sat in his hotel refusing to move or budge. The precious Jew Max Brod utilized all his connections, saying he "would not permit one Jew to be removed from these shores." And he did not permit it.

Our noses detected the odor of the "Organized Yishuv" for the first time in that Park Hotel room of Barlas. Maybe Barlas had a sense of smell, too—maybe the smell of these boys reached him as time went on. Many of them served in the ranks of the IZL and the Lehi. The "cats" became lions again in the homeland, but Hebrew lions, digging their nails into the necks of the British lions.

4. The First Englishman

Our first Englishman was captain of the small transport ship which brought twenty-five of us from Turkey to Haifa. The crew, twelve young men, was Jewish. In the Diaspora, we had received oranges from Eretz Israel wrapped in paper and men wrapped in the ideological garb of various political movements. This was my first direct encounter with men from Eretz Israel, without any wrappings. They were strong of body and good of heart.

The English gentleman sat below in the only cabin, and never even thought to offer the cabin to the four or five women who froze each night on the deck.

I first caught sight of him on the third day at sea, in early morning, as we prepared to enter the port of Alexandretta. He mounted the bridge and peered through his field glasses, searching. For Alexandretta.

Well, I was no expert, we were moving closer, closer to shore but no one saw Alexandretta. When we were close enough to see that not only was there no port, but there were not even any buildings on shore, the goy gave the order to return to sea. A bit further south, the ship again approached the shore. Again, when we were close, we saw nothing. Again, about-face.

Members of the crew are laughing. Why, we wonder? Among them are four who have been to Alexandretta several times and know exactly where it is. Why do they hold their tongues? Answer: Let the goy knock his head against the wall. As it is, the crew is pressuring the management to fire him, a Jew is already in line for the position, why should they help the goy?

He, our captain, stands serenely on the bridge, puffing his pipe, from time to time peeking through the glasses.

Four times he approached and four times he returned to sea. On the fifth try he found the port.

Then I recognized him.

He is David Hume, the greatest of English philosophers. He is Hume, though he has probably never heard the name.

Hume is on this little boat at sea, because Hume's method was: "You ask if the sun will shine tomorrow. I reply: We will see; almost certainly, but not for certain, for only a law is certain, and we cannot know if this is a law. The most I can say is that until today the sun has shone each morning, but we cannot conclude that this is a necessary law."

After Hume—and in response to his doubt and the principle of experience—came Kant the German, who said a priori laws do exist, which are pre-experiential. Kant sat and thought and investigated and formulated the various laws that he did but which do not concern us here, for we are dabbling not in philosophy but in character. The German is unable to move without law. He is unable to stage even a revolution without law. Nor can he murder without law. The law does not force him, but the law is his will.

Every once in a while somebody appears in Germany and decides it should be a world empire. Therefore—the world must be conquered. Therefore—the Germans establish a Command, draw plans, fight wars—and knock their heads against the wall.

The a priori method, the overall plan, is a great advantage. But also a disadvantage: One small error somewhere along the line, or one faulty screw, and the entire machine comes to a halt, or explodes.

Though England has been a parliamentary country from time immemorial, the decision was never made to become an empire. As Hume said, "We will see." First, some thief acted on his own. Then a missionary set forth, Bible in hand, to heal the soul of those hurt bodily by the thief. Then a merchant set out to alleviate the difficulties of the first two. And when three Englishmen happen to be in a land with tens of millions of savages, they sit around a table, drink a little, rest a little, and are the government of the new Crown Colony. Ultimately, all three are revealed to be agents of Intelligence—the left hand knew not what the right was doing, but miraculously the two hands did what needed to be done.

Thus, more or less, the Empire rose and fell, as an afterthought, with no—Heaven forbid—plans for conquest or self-interest.

Another difference: A whole philosophy rose in Germany, grounded in thick, scientific tomes, that the German nation is a superior nation. No such theory ever rose in England, though each and every Englishman sees his race as superior and looks down not only on the colored races but also on Europeans and even, deep inside, on Americans, though these he envies their wealth and power. But without theories, without a law.

When one Englishman sought to formulate an anti-Semitic theory, he left England, became a German, and wrote the book of anti-Semitic theory, *Foundations of the Nineteenth Century*. The author: Chamberlain, the German.

As the Empire rose—little by little, as if by coincidence—so it fell.

"Will the sun set on the Empire?" "I don't know," David Hume would answer, "until today empires have tended to fall, and this one shows signs that it may fall. But . . . we will see. We cannot consider it a law."

One accustomed to thinking in terms of laws and hindsight may ridicule the English, confused as they are, without order, without a priori thought, pushing forward toward the desired result. But again, Hume would ask: "Must the way of laws and plans be best? I do not know. Even if it has succeeded several times, we cannot infer that it is a law."

These thoughts entered my mind not in condemnation or in praise, but in order to "know before whom you stand." On the boat, I saw: Behind us, Germans are destroying according to plan. We are being carried by an English captain with plenty of time. Our sailors stand to the side and laugh at the ignorant, clumsy "goy." And we are hoping that when we reach the shore, God and the goy both willing, we will try to replace him. . . .

Well so be it. We still had a little time, we—the dozens of us—arrived. Exactly one year later the hundreds on the decks of the *Struma* did not arrive.[22] And two years later, millions arrived at the crematoria.

The young stood to the side and enjoyed themselves. The Englishman stood on the bridge and did not get excited, not even when on the fifth attempt the boat entered the port.

5. The Blessing of the Land

Two days later we approached Eretz Israel.

The first place to extend its arm to us was Acco.

I called to Batya, took her hand, and said to her:

"Look, Acco."

Part Two
THE WALL MOVES

Darkness

1. Within the Walls of Jerusalem

I stepped ashore in Haifa three days before the Passover holiday of 5701 (1941), and the next day I went to Jerusalem.

Coming ashore had not moved me, neither had reading the signs written in Hebrew, nor hearing a bus driver speak the holy tongue. At the entrance to Jerusalem I received my first jolt. My soul trembled when four of the Jewish bus passengers stood and rent their clothes in a display of mourning.

At that moment, my soul was rent; I felt it bleed. I knew I had arrived. I did not make the traditional tear in my clothing, because of an aversion to commandments imposed from outside oneself. The deeper I feel the command inside of me, the more I recoil from its external trappings. While I did not rend my garments, tears welled in my eyes. Only one time afterward did I experience something similar. When my daughter was born I was not overly emotional, but six or seven months later, alone in a room with her a few feet away, I suddenly felt eyes rolling over me, wave after wave. I felt warm inside, and with tears falling I approached her bed, noticing her for the first time as my daughter. As those four Jews stood and rent their clothes, the centuries of my soul opened and attached themselves to Jerusalem.

Three houses were already mine when I arrived in Jerusalem.

One mirrored my parent's home, belonging to my mother's family. Ida, the granddaughter of Reb Israel Laifer (whose fame and righteousness won me the friendship of the majestic Rebbe of Chertkov when I arrived in Vienna), had a pleasant house at 4 Rehov Ben Yehuda.[23] Aharon Meletz headed the family, a man of Torah and enlightenment, brilliant, soft hearted, with a gentle sense of humor, so much like my father, who had loved him deeply.

Here we lay our baggage, live our first weeks in Eretz Israel, relieve ourselves of childhood memories, sigh over the family we left there, begin talking of earning a living, of working, of practicalities. Three years hence, warm lunches will every day be sent from here to one whose being "practical" and whose work will have led him to the Jerusalem Central Prison. Every day kind Ida will spice the food with Momma's spices, and Aharon Meletz, had he still been alive, would certainly have every day added his good smile and a witticism about my "craziness" and this would have been to me like a good, forgiving greeting from my father himself.

This was my first home in Jerusalem, in place of my parent's home.

A second home mirrored the days of my youth, the season of shaking free of Momma and Poppa, the season of studies, the season of that motley crew of Nietzsche and Kant and *Yoreh De'ah* and the "Wiener Wald" girls and the *Pirkei deRabbi Eliezer* ethics and the Reinhardt Theater, my student days at the Rabbinical Seminary and at Vienna University. This was the home of my dear friend Dr. Moshe Leb Kurtz. Here we hold our first seder. Here our souls learn to walk in the realm of the restored Hebrew language, walking, running, spinning in the sounds and chords of the infant Hebrew nation. Here we relieve ourselves of more memories, not all of which impress the two women of the house. And here, too, we talk of earning a living, of work, of being "practical." Four years hence, Kurtz and I will again sit at a festive table, though without women—women were not allowed in the Latrun Detention Camp. I will then be a detainee and Kurtz a guest, the visiting rabbi. But at this earlier dinner in his home, we speak seriously about employment, about arranging something, about being practical. He is a member of the religious Hapoel Hamizrachi and works for the Youth Department of the Zionist Organization. We do not speak of politics. The address: 50 Rehov Ussishkin.

And my third house in Jerusalem mirrors the Third House of God, the Third Temple. In the third house we do not relieve ourselves of anything. There is no relief at all here. In this house there is only loading. Day and night, loading. We are loaded with complaints, loaded with cargo, very heavy cargo, cargo that blazes in our minds, our hearts, our bodies.

This is the home of Miriam and Yehoshua Heschel (Y. H.) Yevin. And the home of Uri Zvi. A house at a corner, an intersection. Always an intersection.

Here intersect Rehov Geula, Rehov Mea Shearim and Rehov Chancellor. Here intersect the new and the old, the Jewish and the foreign worlds.

At this intersection stands a house, and in the house a basement, and in the basement lives Uri Zvi.

*

Of course, one must descend, down the stairs, as one descends to the Kotel, the Western Wall.[24]

That first Passover in Eretz Israel, I descended to the Kotel. And there I learned to hate. At the entrance, four English goyim stood guard over the Kotel. Their laughing faces reflected our degradation. I began to hate them as I hated this despicable situation. Arab filth above, and the Kotel below, deep below and underneath the impudent, expansive, mocking mosque.

The cluster of confused, crushed, prayer-shawled Jews crouched against the stones, wailing; behind them—Arab pollution; to their side—four goyim from some distant island; above—a magnificent Ishmaelite temple. Here, all began to become real to me, and the feeling was unbearable, unbearable. This is the spot at which all will be decided. The roads of the world criss-cross, in Christian crosses or swastikaed crosses, in Moscow, London, Washington or Berlin. Our roads cross at this spot, as do our degradations, as all our shame comes together here. The Kotel absorbs the weeping of all the exiles, the weeping over all the blood, the human weeping and the Divine weeping. And within the wrinkles of its stony forehead are embedded magnificent memories of priestly blue, of splendid purple. How can the Kotel absorb all these? From where does it draw the strength? Perhaps the bones of the ancient Zealots and Birionim are gathered underneath, supporting the Wall. How does it stand? And not collapse, not melt? How?

Fear suddenly grips me as I stand at its side for the first time. What if the Kotel were to move?

Yes, suddenly—the Kotel will move.

And then? Then?

Then the river of tears that has been poured in will burst forth and swirl around us, we who stand at its side, and the river will flow above us, over our heads, and on, rolling in waves of anger over this whole Yishuv that endures the shame of the armed British and filthy Arabs so near the stones. And we will all of us drown, as the legendary Atlantis, or as the legendary bell that drowned leaving no trace other than a dreadful pealing at night.

Perhaps the Kotel will move otherwise, with mercy. Perhaps the purple from between its folds will spread itself at our feet, at the feet of our children, princes who bear fruit and gold for the glory of Jerusalem, for the kings of Jerusalem. The Kotel moves . . . goes to greet its kings and lovers. Behold, descending the steps . . . Judah Halevi, the Baal Shem Tov,[25] and there—Herzl. And there, among the throngs, there is Poppa. His lips are moving. What is Poppa saying? He is singing, singing the "Song of Shulamith" by Goldfadden, the pilgrim's song.

Perhaps it will move. Move already, Kotel! This way or that, to drown or to crown, anything but this shame, this repulsive position between goyim and mules. Anything but this!

*

Again I descend, to the living Kotel of our time, to Uri Zvi.

Like the Kotel, he is a massing of the sorrows of the centuries.

Like the Kotel, he retains the glory of days past.

Like the Kotel, he has the power to stand between those who hate and those who scorn. His are huge, ancient stones of song.

And like the Kotel, he is confined and alone.

I descend to the basement of prophecy.

In its poverty, it resembles the Lvov apartment of his parents. There in Exile, it was on the second floor and here in Eretz Israel it is in the basement. There the entrance was through a spacious kitchen, here almost nothing separates inside from out. One immediately enters the poverty, the purity. He, the so-called "fascist" poet, the "hater of the proletariat," lives in a poverty that not one of the "socialist," "revolutionary," "proletarian" poets in this Yishuv has ever tasted. The "bourgeoisie" has strangely forgotten to provide this "number-one enemy of socialism" with even a piece of bread. What strange socialism and strange "fascism" and strange "bourgeoisie" in this land!

As the apartment is below ground, the passers-by on the street seem to be walking on the heads of those inside. Naturally, the walls are damp. Two cells in the basement and many beds, like a prison.

In one wall—a window. Along two walls—beds. The wall opposite the window —books, books, books. Mostly holy books.

In this poverty, in this crowding, here is the living Kotel that moved and—he burns, or perhaps he is already black as if charred or gray from a shower of tears, and now—he again catches fire. And rarely does anyone remember to bring flowers to the basement for him to smell.

An Underground cell had operated in the apartment until a short while before my own arrival. Eliahu Amikam and Shlomo Trachtman had lived there, but as the net closed in, the house had to be evacuated. The residents were followed, called to the police, arrested. The feeling of solitude inside grew heavier.

"How did you escape?" asks Uri Zvi for the third time since I stepped inside.

Again and again, I relate the details of the story and the visas and the letters and the dollars—but Uri Zvi still does not understand and after he has heard everything he asks once more:

"How did you really escape?"

For I am talking in three dimensions and he is thinking in four, looking for the deeper meaning behind the chain of events, as every living or inanimate detail leaps from its place in existence into a world of symbols. Everything is a symbol, coming to tell not of itself but of something else. Uri Zvi's conversation is incomprehensible unless this key is understood. He appears to grasp at inconsequential points, to shy from the main ones. So, too, he uses this four-dimensional language to tell me of the split between Yair and David Raziel.[26] He does not cite any names; he mentions neither the event nor the reason. Occasionally Uri Zvi says "he" and one must guess from the context who "he" is. The only name he speaks outright is that of the late Jabotinsky, and he is emphatic, convinced that something about Jabotinsky's telegram "to him" (Yair) reinstating Raziel is phony. In any case, Uri Zvi believes, Jabotinsky was misled, given incorrect information about the situation here. Uri Zvi refers to those who purport to be Jabotinsky's heirs to the leadership of the Revisionists and the youth with the bitterest words in the political lexicon, but Jabotinsky himself is untouchable, and cannot be accused of treason or of deserting the front.

No waiting room, no hallway—I immediately enter the fire. Most of that to which he is referring is still unknown to me or, at best, clouded over. With the passage of time I will slowly learn to decipher his clues and codes. At this point I absorb all, that which is understood and that which is not.

When I tell him of the suffocation under the Soviet regime in Vilna, of the fear of informers—among even those closest to one—he chuckles: "The situation is no better here. On the contrary, it is worse."

I find this difficult to believe.

"Look," he warns, "meanwhile be careful, do not speak to anyone, not a word. You hear? Not a word!"

Natan Friedman comes to Jerusalem and arranges my first meeting with Yair in Tel Aviv.

2. The Stake in the Ground

I cannot recall the date, but it was at 10 p.m. on a Tuesday, and the rendezvous was set for the corner of Rothschild and Marmorek Boulevards.

Contact with the Underground had been made a few hours after my arrival, when Avraham Amper—tall, erect and calm in all that he did, in his manner of speaking and in his smile, the very model of a member of the Underground—met me at the Bat Galim Immigration Center. Amper told me, in general terms, of the split in the Irgun between Yair and David Raziel. Neither of us saw a need for me to be persuaded. From that day at the Betar Conference, through my articles in *Hamedina* advocating the continued struggle against the British despite the World War, to my speeches before the Betarim in Mersin, the Turkish port at which we waited to embark for Eretz Israel—my road led straight to Yair.

Amper was there to meet every boat arriving from Turkey, greeting the Betar survivors and drafting them into Yair's ranks. Most of the Betarim were former charges of Amper from the days of the Irgun courses in Poland. These survivors of Polish Betar became the organizational backbone of Lehi. In the years that followed, I often asked myself what would have happened if all the future leaders of the Underground had not succeeded in reaching Eretz Israel: Begin, Friedman, me, and the many others in high positions. A second question: Why did the leaders of the Underground come from abroad and not from the ranks of the Irgun in Eretz Israel? Can this be related to the awful curse: "A land devouring its inhabitants"?

Or perhaps the answer is in the Torah of our fathers which we brought with us, but which is weaker among the native "Sabras"?[27]

They came on the small transport boats, drop by drop, not as teardrops but as drops of iron. Avraham Amper was the contractor, steward and guardian of these iron drops. He addressed me as if I were already inside; as for me, the argument with Jabotinsky had not ended, I had not chosen to grease my doors with pure olive oil to stop the squeaking. Let them squeak, let them grate.

The World War, of course, descended on everyone as skies of steel. To measure pain and plenty in this world, however, is not simple. Even on a tossing boat, a man may still be able to enjoy the comforts of one cabin. The steel skies hanging over our heads descended rapidly; and, ironically, great weights were lifted from the hearts of many in the small cabin called the Hebrew Yishuv, weights which had lain on them since the issuance of the British White Paper in 1939.[28]

The White Paper had been a sort of Rubicon. Many stood at its banks and were forced to decide: to cross or not to cross. The "Restraint" vs. "Response" debate could not continue. The choice was now between being dragged along in the British game of Arab "riots" and "outbreaks" or crossing to the front, to war with the British regime. The Jewish Agency wished with all its soul to continue the game, with more Roundtable conferences, renewed bargaining, new MacDonald letters[29]—anything to avoid the waters of the Rubicon for which their entire spiritual, mental and organizational structure was unprepared. The White Paper afforded the Irgun Zvai Leumi great potential:

If the Organized Yishuv establishment does not declare war, the historical initiative will pass to the non-establishment IZL. Had that happened, all the developments which began in the years 5702-5703 (1942-1943) could have begun then, in 5699 (1939): the split—then a united rebellion—then the point of no retreat—and finally, victory. This process, had it only been started a few years earlier, would have benefited from the awesome rear-guard of the Underground, the reserves of tens of thousands of Betarim, the reserves of millions of Polish Jews, and the only possible result would of necessity have been a shining Kingdom in the entire homeland, instead of pieces of a people in pieces of a land in a shadow of a state.

We were, however, too late. The World War relieved many of the dilemmas they faced. Many jumped joyfully into the arms of the surprising solution: a war with Hitler. We must, they exclaimed, postpone settling our score with the British; it is so easy. No effort is necessary. Flow with the rest of the world. Plenty of rhetoric can carry you, and much hate that comes easy, and many hopes that come easy for an enlightened, free, democratic and just world of tomorrow. Thus we are relieved of the spiritual and physical efforts required to stand alone in battle. And the enlistment in the British army advocated by the Establishment and by the Irgun, in "Palestinian" or Jewish units or not, which all amounted to enlistment in an army, and for the front, this did not require a pioneering force of the spirit. Very many—and good people, mostly—enlisted and in doing so they took a load on their backs and off their hearts. The depression that weighed on the mind and blood along the banks of the Rubicon of a War of Freedom was lifted with this enlistment. The tension which had built since 5996 (1936), which peaked in 5699 (1939), should have and could have given birth to the fury of the Hebrew Revolution, propelled by an impetus rarely equaled in all of history. Instead this tension was relieved and the Hebrew Revolution delayed and when it came—in all its strength and beauty—it was only a shell of what it would have been had it come earlier.

And if, in spite of everything, it did come—instead of being delayed even longer—then this was thanks to those few who entrenched themselves deep within Hebrew independence, the last trenches dug in a front that soon collapsed.

The logic behind my Betar Conference speech, the logic behind my demand during the Vilna consultation to continue the war against the British despite the war against Hitler—this same logic operated when Yair's missionary, Avraham Amper, met me and found nothing to conquer. He merely informed me of the split, which at the time I had not yet heard of but which did not surprise me.

I may well be the only individual who entered the Underground then without any of the formalities and ceremonies long in practice. I entered not as a body entering a body, which demands something tangible, but as spirit entering body, without the clicking of heels and without the mumbling of an oath. I did not click heels but I stood tall. I did not mumble an oath with my mouth, but neither did I break the one in my heart. (Only once did I take the Betar oath in Poland. And that, I broke. I failed to obey the Betar authorities when ordered, upon my arrival in Eretz Israel, to join the Plugat Giyus, the Betar work corps; nor did I appear before the British army Enlistment Center operating in Metsudat Zev, the Revisionist and Betar headquarters. I did appear one last time with Israel Epstein before the Betar Commission to explain why we were not joining the Plugat Giyus. We had our say and went our ways. I continued, in a new framework. Israel waited for the old framework to change. Thus I broke with Betar, which had above its office door a sign urging enlistment in the British army.)

Much excitement in the air that Sabbath: The Hapoel (Labor)-Betar soccer game. The result: a 2-2 tie.

*

My first time in Tel Aviv and already I hate it. I have always had an aversion to flatness, which provides nothing for the eye or the soul to grasp. Haifa is, I think, beautiful. He who has eyes sees from Haifa far into the distance. More than coincidence led Herzl to prophesy such greatness for her. Much potential is hidden in the rock of the Haifa mountains. But Tel Aviv? Flat and light—and Vision does not emanate from plains; one does not lift light weights, the muscles of the soul do not tense, for one does not set out to conquer the light and easy. Nor does Tel Aviv contain sadness; where, then, will it find truth? Only when one nears Jaffa does he begin to sense real life. Perhaps the loaded-down trucks and porters in Jaffa give it weight and movement. In Tel Aviv—none of this. Tel Aviv is to the Land of Israel as lipstick to a woman's lips. Pleasant for a quick glance, but not for a close kiss. There is nothing here to get close to, no force to hug and no depth. When in her later years my mother began applying lipstick, I commented that the lipstick was not adding to her beauty: "Your white hair is your crown."

"Yes," she replied, "if all the men in the world were my sons, I would make do with the crown of age, but . . . ," and she blushed and her eyes watered, for only a few years had passed since my father's death and she was only flesh and blood, her blood as flaming red as her hair was flaming white.

And as I kissed my mother and forgave her, so will I kiss Eretz Israel and forgive it Tel Aviv, though Tel Aviv itself I cannot kiss, covered as it is with lipstick.

So I wander in the "first Hebrew city . . . ." Sometimes the sound of this description of Tel Aviv makes me sick, as if I were watching some kitsch at the theater. Such a cheap joke. Who first spoke this bit of "wisdom" about the "first Hebrew city"? Three other cities can compete amongst themselves, I believe, for this title: Hebron, Shchem and Beersheba. But Tel Aviv? Would not a more historical truth be to call it the "last Hebrew city as of now"? With what terms are we defining "first"? With what historical proportions?

I eventually learned that rather than being a single, isolated instance, the phraseology is a symptom. Lack of historical perspective is the root of the poison and the wormwood prevalent in the field of our literature as well as our politics. Anyone who can say "the first Hebrew city" with such ease will also be able to tolerate the main street of that city being named for some English general (Allenby), and will also agree, despite circumstances favorable to us, to an internationalized Jerusalem. And he will similarly be able to refer to Trans-Jordan as a neighboring state. This is the root of a-historical Zionism.

I wander the streets of the last Hebrew city, as of now.

I walk the artery of its life, Rehov General Allenby. I pass the Histadrut labor union and the employment offices, but though I am indeed unemployed, I have not come to Tel Aviv for work. I pass many—some magnificent—stores, but I am not yet established in Eretz Israel. Apparently, I will begin to establish myself on that Rothschild-Marmorek corner. I have not come to Tel Aviv for its days.

Tel Aviv has nights, too. I can smell the scent. The scent of an early summer night on Rothschild Boulevard. The boulevard is long, very long, from the Allenby corner to the far corner. I walk toward my corner. The whispers of this moment's (and all time's) fireflies rise from the benches. Couples, couples. Secrets "no ear has yet heard," looks "no eye has yet seen," and feelings and heartbeats "no heart has yet felt." Secrets and looks and feelings which at this very moment are being shared, seen and felt by hundreds of millions around the world, as they have been since Adam and Eve in the Garden of Eden on high, and down to the lowest rung of hell, from the beginning of time till its end, the one real "International" in the world, the secret of the trees above the couples, the secret of the blood in the veins. This is the moment, and this is eternity. But I have come neither for the moment nor for eternity. I have come for history. Therefore I do not linger on the benches, as I once lingered on the same type of benches on the long boulevards of Vienna, or on the hill of Lvov, in the days when I breathed the air of the moment and the air of eternity, when I was beyond history, when I lived the life which resembles writing on air—involving effort, movement, enjoyment, pleasure—but nothing real. Nothing remains of these letters written on air. Now that I am breathing the air of this boulevard, I take pleasure in the scents of the night—but as a passer-by. I do not close my nostrils, I do not shrink the size of my lungs, but I do not stop for the scents. I continue toward my corner. My hour, then, is drawing near. Many here are glancing at wrist watches, at pocket watches. And they decide: There is still time to tarry. We can sit a little longer, we will not be late. And many were late. They got stuck in the current of the Allenby crowd, or they fell asleep on the incubator benches of the boulevards and they missed the meeting. They were too late for history.

*

As the Yishuv stood in its past, its Allenby days and boulevard nights, Yair stood on the farthest corner and waited for me as he waited for the remaining few; for he was alone, very alone, all this time.

He reminded me of our first meeting in Warsaw; this second meeting was the personal and organizational conclusion to the premises he had heard me expound in the Conference debate with Jabotinsky. When Yair said to me, "I am happy to see you," he was not merely being polite but neither was he expressing feelings of personal friendship. Too many of his friends and of the people under his command failed to draw conclusions from the premises. "I am happy to see you" means: I am happy to see another who has not lost himself. And while some followed Yair because they believed in him personally or believed in other commanders, this "I am happy to see you" held more, and also held that happiness a man enjoys when he overcomes chance. Chance played no role in this meeting.

Ben Gurion had declared there would be a war with Hitler as if there were no

White Paper and a war with the White Paper as if there were no Hitler. In reality, the war with Hitler was fought even without a Hebrew army and, at first, without even a Hebrew Brigade. And, in reality, there was never any war with the White Paper. As for the nationalist wing of the Zionist movement, the Revisionists tried to found a Jewish Legion but meanwhile they enlisted in the British army, receiving nothing in return, not even promises; and they had meanwhile agreed to a truce with the British in Eretz Israel, and worse: They sent to serve the British the one man who under no circumstances should have been sent, the man who not long before had symbolized the rise of the Hebrew revolt, the Commander in Chief of the Irgun, David Raziel. Unconditional surrender. Nothing in return for the truce, the service, the surrender; no promises at all for the future. That which may have been permissible for individual Jews in Eretz Israel, or perhaps for Zionist movements which had negative ideological bases (for which Zionism was a means of saving endangered Jews) should certainly have been forbidden for the man who symbolized the fusion of all our physical and spiritual forces in the concrete national War for Freedom.

Tactical and political considerations could have played a role in deciding if and when to actively fight British rule during the World War—but on the principle of noncollaboration between the Movement for Freedom and the foreign regime there should have been no wavering. Historians of the Irgun will have to determine one day who was responsible for David Raziel's surrender, and for the consequent weakening and depletion of independent Hebrew strength. Notwithstanding the great love Yair once felt toward Raziel, he understood Raziel's death—in a British jeep in Iraq, on a faraway foreign battlefield, in a foreign battle—to be the decree of fate, a logical link in the chain of abandoning the War for Freedom.

As the others fell or broke, only he, Yair, remained a stake planted firmly in the War for Freedom. Nothing could budge him. He would not surrender.

In the throat of the British regime in Eretz Israel, this last bone remained. The White Paper was in force. The bones of the Irgun Commander in Chief lay far away. From Betar headquarters in Metsudat Zev, Jewish youths leave dressed in British army uniforms.

Such was the situation when Yair planted the stake of his will and belief and said: No. This veto was not heard, at first. A very few members of the Irgun heard. Then the sound of the pounding of the stake reverberated within the ranks of the Nationalist Movement. As the Hagana leadership and the British police and Intelligence of course knew of the split in the Irgun, they readied their nets.

The nets worked well. They caught our attempts to establish contacts abroad. They caught Yair's body, too. But the stake remained firmly in the ground. One by one, ropes caught hold of it, tied to each other, tied to the stake. Without that stake many more would have gone their separate ways, scattered themselves. Without it, others would not have been forced to make decisions.

We would have been even later.

3. A Language with No Alphabet

For three-quarters of a year my involvement with the Underground consisted of my meetings with Yair and the editorial work we did together. My "contact" was Avraham Amper; Natan Friedman had been sent on a sort of diplomatic mission—first to work privately in Syria and then to establish in Turkey, a neutral country, a political office to deal with the rest of the world. I did not meet any of the veteran members of the Underground, in accordance with Yair's wish to protect me as much as possible—though he was wont to say that "too many people in the 'Nationalist Movement' have heard you and read you, and there are too many chatterboxes, even unintentional ones, among them, for your support for us to remain a secret very long. But as of now, we are not prepared to integrate you into the Underground."

The Irgun, too, sent feelers my way, however half-heartedly, but they did not seem to crave an explicit and explained "no" from me personally. One who approached me honestly was Israel Epstein. Without asking, he knew in which direction I was pointing, and rather than attempt to lobby me, he always attempted to justify his own position. When we learned that Menachem Begin had been saved, he grabbed at the straw: He will wait for Begin to arrive.

The Revisionist-Betar newspaper *Hamashkif* was also a problem. I was asked by Isaac Remba to contribute material. Remba saw himself as my patron ever since he had published my first articles for the Nationalist Movement in London's *Hametsuda*. These were actually literary pieces relating to Bialik, Berdichevsky, Schopenhauer—and the Revisionist press never did shy from my literary pieces.

Yair's preliminary decision was in favor of my writing for *Hamashkif*, the paper of his ideological opponents, on the assumption that "it is a good disguise, a seal of approval."

Later Yair thought otherwise: Since I was known in Revisionist and Betar circles as an extremist, they want my articles to give their paper a seal of approval in the eyes of any who may be wavering between the Revisionists and Yair, or whose conscience may be unsure about remaining with the Revisionists and Betar. I should not provide this seal of approval.

I had meanwhile been hired for part-time work at the Hebrew Gymnasium (high school) in Tel Aviv, and I exploited this as an excuse to withdraw from the paper. Only once did I return, and rather dramatically: For the anniversary of David Raziel's death, I wrote a piece supposedly about the holiday of Shavuoth, "David's Sin." I wrote that King David's sin with Bat-sheba cannot be exaggerated from a national-political point of view. The wrongdoing centered on flesh and blood weakness, a matter of individual morality; but the real national, or political, sin of David was that while Saul was engaged in a life and death struggle with a foreign ruler in Eretz Israel, David was sitting in Ziklag.

Mr. Remba missed my point and informed me that the article would be published, as he hoped the censor would not object; Remba was wrong. The censor did block the article—not the British Censor but the *Hamashkif* self-censorship. Lubotzky and Levenberg of the editorial board opened Remba's eyes.[30] When I came to the office Remba told me the article was the work of a provocateur. "Go to Yair to write articles like this," he said, adding other comments best not repeated out of respect for he who was once secretary to Jabotinsky. After Lubotzky and Levenberg added some abuse of their own, I took my manuscript and left.

Left *Hamashkif*. In terms of maintaining my cover, I probably did not act wisely. Had Yair been alive, he would most certainly have forbidden me to act as I did. But this was a few months after his murder and I was very depressed, the days were black and bitter.

In truth, Yair did not let me inside any part of the Organization (at that time Stern's Lehi Underground was still called HaIrgun Hazvai Haleumi B'Israel, to distinguish it from the official Irgun Zvai Leumi, which ended its name with an additional word before "Israel": B'Eretz Israel [in the Land of Israel]). I knew nothing of Yair's conflict with his chief aides, who later turned themselves in to the British police and willingly went to jail. I knew nothing of the serious financial difficulties, and only by reading the newspapers did I learn of several of the operations carried out that tragic winter, of the explosion on Rehov Yael[31] and of the Rothschild Boulevard robbery. Yair offered to explain the operations and their failure only afterward: "When you clear forests, chips fly," he said on the dark stairway of an apartment we were leaving on Rehov King Solomon. Jews died because of a 1,000 lira robbery. Two boys were arrested. Today we can see that a forest of enemies has indeed fallen, but at that time the Hebrew public was furious: Two officers were killed on Rehov Yael and two innocent Jews were killed in the course of a robbery. No one saw a reason for these casualties. An ideological vacuum, an emotional vacuum. A few proclamations printed on unclear stencils, too lengthy in any case, and a few broadcasts, could not explain to the public the reason for the bloodshed. Yair's great mistake was that he wanted the Hebrew public to understand the grammatical laws of the War for Freedom, including the exceptions, at a time when the public did not yet know the alphabet. Yair assumed that the arguments taking place within the Betar leadership and the Irgun were taking place within the general public as well, whereas in reality the public did not even see the British regime as a foreign ruler, much less understand that a Jewish police officer was serving that foreign ruler. These concepts were foreign to the Yishuv's mode of thought, and to the Diaspora's, too. Few spoke in these terms. "Uproot the British regime from our land" sounded to the average Jew on the street like "Uproot the mountains from our land." Not only because of the difficulty involved—this excuse emerged only years later, after the idea had at last penetrated the brain. At the time the idea was still absurd, for the national consciousness was based on the Balfour Declaration and to many, many people we seemed to have gotten a land replete with dunes, mountains and British. Here and there, yes, we do have complaints, but "foreign regime"? How can this be? "Completely" nationalist newspapers were writing of "our government" without even doubting the simplicity of the matter.

Between Yair and even the best among his opponents there still lay this tremendous difference in approach: They admitted we must fight in order to be free, and he said we must fight because we are free. Because the others desired to be free they could for various reasons delay the decisive war. But whoever felt himself already free had to fight immediately.

This feeling of Yair's was the cause of the gap between him and public opinion. He spoke a language that was not comprehensible.

Yair's circle of acquaintances understood this language, to whatever degree. But as there were no middle-of-the-roaders to serve as intermediaries between Yair and the public, the circle remained in linguistic quarantine. To the dozens of people inside, the matter was most simple: The British are foreigners here; we will fight them without compromise. The loaded "piece" in the hand heightened an individual's feeling of freedom, of independence. Yair's faith in this fundamental feeling of freedom blinded him to the necessity of waiting for the appropriate moment to act. "Must the enemy commit an atrocity against me before I go to war against him? Is not his being here a provocative act?" This is true, but one must be conceptually and emotionally prepared to understand it.

The preparation came just two weeks after Yair's murder. The sinking of the *Struma*, the drowning of its hundreds of Jewish refugees. Had Yair not been compelled to act beforehand, by circumstances that were not in reality compelling, and if not for the shootings at Yael and the robbery and then the shootings at Rehov Dizengoff and Rehov Mizrachi Bet[32]—many doors and many hearts would have opened to Yair after the *Struma*. Many ears would have been ready to hear his broadcasts, many minds would have absorbed his albeit sloppily stenciled proclamations.

Yair, however, lived in his hermetic, pure world. Even in his poetry, two worlds always oppose each other. Yair saw no grays, no bridges.

Those last months, he was already walking above the abyss, without the benefit of any bridges underfoot. No strong organizational bridge, no comprehending home front. Solely by the force of his vision, his will and his sacrifice. The idea crossed over safely, but Yair's body was shattered in the abyss.

Those last months we spoke much about the fundamental problems of Hebrew history. Even today I tremble when I pass the bench in Dizengoff Circle on which we sat, Yair talking in his calm, measured voice: Moses and David are the different types of genius hovering above the events of our time. On one hand, the Exodus from Egypt; on the other, the establishment of the Kingdom. The role of Moses was played by Herzl and by Jabotinsky. We must play the role of David. Only Uri Zvi, in his poetry, brings these two worlds together, the world of the Jews and the world of the Hebrews.

We did not argue, therefore remembering if a particular sentence was spoken by him or by me is not easy. The single difference was my voice was less calm, my sentences less measured than his. Eventually he read me *Ikarei Hatechiya* (Principles of Rebirth) and handed it to me to prepare a commentary. I sat and wrote for a day or a week or a month—I do not know. I wrote without pausing for breath. But he paused while reading it, chapter by chapter, and he was not overly satisfied. Retaining his usual courteous manner, he said, "I would have written it differently, though I agree with all that you wrote."

He was a Lithuanian educated in the classics, combining the coldness of a *Mitnaged*[33] with the poetic balance of a Greek. How could he approve of the lava pouring from my Hasidic volcano?

And he—he casts this massive lava burning inside the both of us. I pour and he casts, one massive, measured and balanced, in both form and content, casting.

Others can surely relate more interesting details about struggles within the organization, or more information about Yair's foreign policy intentions in 5701-5702 (1941-1942). I am able to write of Yair's ideological thoughts for they were not new to me. They were long embedded in my soul, originating in chapters of the Bible and in legends of the messiah; and as a result of Uri Zvi's poetry, they were raging in my soul. The concepts of a Davidic Kingdom stretching from the Nile to the Euphrates, a sovereign Hebrew nation reigning in the Middle East, a Renaissance in body and spirit—are drawn from Abrahamic wells and carried by renewed prophecy. The newspaper founded by Yair in Poland, aimed at the assimilating Jewish-Polish intelligentsia, was called *Yeruzalema Vizvolena* (Liberated Jerusalem) and alongside its Polish name was the Hebrew *Malkhut Israel B'chayil* (The Kingdom of Israel through Strength). The concepts were not taught to me by Yair, though they were holiest to him. Yair's originality was in the casting of these concepts into cells. Cells of cadenced songs with rhymes in every line for weapons, and cells of freedom fighters with grenades and guns for weapons. Cells to bring about the conditions necessary for the fulfillment of the desire for the great kingdom. And he was entirely a song of this type, steel of this type, cast of desire.

4. Shevat 5702 (February 1942)

Events occurred at a maddening pace.

Failure on Rehov Yael. Undoubtedly even a more successful operation would have resulted in an uproar, even if the dead had been, as intended, British officers. Even then, such an operation at that time may not have been appropriate. Attacking the heads of the government would have been more justified than attacking its lower echelons, and to make matters worse, the echelons hit turned out to be two Jewish officers. The public was not in the least mollified by the claim that Officer Schiff was a scoundrel who had even assaulted demonstrating workers in Petach Tikva. Even those who believed this, could not—and rightly so—justify this maximum penalty at the hands of an underground political group. The eventual death of an injured Englishman provided, at first glance, a new rationale, as he was the man who had hanged Ben Yosef. But this was not convincing, either, for his death was obviously a coincidence. And Ben Yosef had died "long ago." Action against his hangman should have been immediate. As time passes, the score becomes political and not personal.

The skill with which the operation was executed (a minor explosion in a rooftop apartment, then the explosion of a mine on the threshold when the investigating officers arrived) did temporarily raise morale in the ranks, but this dissipated as the police resumed their pressure.

Failure leads to failure. The death of two Jewish bystanders and the capture of two of our boys during the theft of 1,000 lira were not encouraging. The circle of fate closed around us. The air on the streets was hostile. The British were aware of the mood and used it well: wanted posters on the walls, in newspapers. Prizes offered. The offer of money was worthless—a Jew will not inform for money. An atmosphere of terrible hate was created and this was far more dangerous to us than the lure of money.

Another blow. Some of those appearing on the wall posters turned themselves in. We were not surprised; most of these men were broken long ago. The public, however, took notice: a sign of crumbling.

Nerves of steel were needed.

Yes. Even *Hamashkif* published Yair's photograph. Along with a lead article that expressed the hope the police would find those who were to blame. "The police are urged to take measures": this sentence appeared in the "nationalist" paper, and only the black frame around the masthead "With the regular participation of Zev Jabotinsky," only that black frame separated his name from the remainder of the page and thereby saved the honor of the late fighter Jabotinsky, the first Zionist to be incarcerated in Acco Prison. Our hatred for the Irgun, born during the split, grew.

Number 30, Rehov Dizengoff. Amper and Jack were seriously injured, shot with their hands up by Wilkins. They were beaten in the car, again in the hospital; eventually they died. Svorai and Levstein were injured and arrested.[34]

We agonized over who was to blame for the discovery of the room at 30 Dizengoff. We raised many possibilities and ignored only the simplest, that we knew nothing about caution. That same day, I entered Natan Friedman's house in broad daylight to tell who had been injured. His wife was home, alone. A few days later she was arrested there. Obviously, the apartments were known to the secret police, and they chose when to play their cards.

We were fools; therefore we were criminals, guilty of criminal activity toward the war. The hatred surrounding us, the traitors surrounding us, the tragedies occurring, all these are insufficient to obscure the complete lack of caution with which we acted.

Walking out at night, people shone flashlights in one's face. (These were dark nights.)

Nonetheless, I continued to meet Yair. He was not depressed, just sad and knowing. A sure, calm knowledge. He was often silent. Occasionally he did not hear what I said. He spoke of his mother. He was glad she had found work; she would see his picture on the walls less often. A final farewell, near Zamenhoff and King Solomon. Someone approached and said, "I was already very worried. You are a little late."

Indeed, the hour was almost 11 p.m. The streets were empty. Perhaps he slept that night in one of the safe houses, or perhaps he was already trapped within the circle of fate that afforded no more freedom to think, that pulled everything inside with such awful necessity. Perhaps he already slept that night in the room belonging to the wife of one of those so recently arrested.

During those final days, matchmakers appeared. The Revisionists announced that they would save him if he surrendered. He would "only" be arrested. The Hagana was more "courteous," offering to protect him provided he remain on one of its kibbutzim. Needless to say, Yair rejected the first ridiculous suggestion, but he also rejected the second more clever and elegant suggestion. The question was not: to live or to die. The question was: how to live? As a slave or as a free man?

On the afternoon of the twenty-fifth day of Shevat (February 12) a Jewish police sergeant came to my house and brought me the news.

He did not know how they discovered the apartment or what had occurred inside. Only this: They wrapped him in a blanket, dragged him down the steps and threw him into a car. And the woman who had been in the room shouted: "They murdered Stern, they murdered Stern! You will pay dearly for this!"

The woman was Tova Svorai.[35] *She* paid dearly. With difficult years in Bethlehem Prison, years away from her daughter, and all the time very ill.

One of the murderers, Wilkins, also paid, later, with his blood.

Black banners were not hung in the city. The press, without exception, published the official version, that Yair was shot while attempting to escape. *Hamashkif* added, "He was known as a composer of extremely nationalist songs."

The following day I was in school as usual. I did not tell the students to rise in memory of a fallen leader of Israel. After class a teacher, Dr. Yom-Tov Levinsky, surprised me as we were walking: "It's a shame . . . it's a shame . . . he was so talented, a real genius. The university gave him a stipend and sent him abroad. He was a patriot, it is a terrible shame."

I still do not know why, in those black days, Yom-Tov Levinsky said this to me. Perhaps my silence had betrayed me, had aroused his suspicion. But why did he say this to me? To tempt a response, or to comfort me? Levinsky was a longtime member of the Mapai Party. On the other hand, he was steeped in Torah and love of Israel. Was it possible? Was it possible that not all the souls were sealed tight, that only their mouths were shut by fear?

There were some houses in which the words "Mazal tov! Congratulations!" were spoken. Houses in Israel . . . .

And the secret police and the government celebrated, as if the last stake had been uprooted.

At night, Hisia came.[36] She had been his secretary, had sat with him till four in the morning typing what he said. She was unable to say more; she was sobbing, rivers and streams of tears and moaning . . . . She did not shock me then. She shocked me seven years later when she voted at a Lehi conference against the concept of *Malkhut Israel*, the majestic Kingdom of Israel, and I asked her not with a sobbing voice but with a sobbing heart: Hisia, you were with him, and now this concept is foreign to you, it does not speak to your heart? And she was silent, and the eyes which once wept looked to the sides . . . .

A woman's weeping has never shocked me. Only the weeping of a boy or a man.

5. Empty Pits and Full Ones

Darkness is not in itself evil. If something is fashioned in it, if life is planted in it, if weapons for war move in it, then the darkness is good, the guardian of secrets. Blessed is the night that is full of secrets. Blessed is all that is full, only the empty is evil.

When I was doing my doctorate, I enjoyed Schopenhauer's writings but not his goal of nirvana, empty nothingness. As a child I was of course moved by the story of Joseph being tossed into an empty pit by his brothers, but the bow of my soul was drawn with hate and ready to act only when I read Rashi's commentary on the verse "The pit is empty, no water is in it," that "water is not in it but snakes and scorpions are." An empty pit is therefore more dangerous than one filled with snakes and scorpions; it induces apathy. Nature abhors a vacuum and so does man, but while nature cannot be fooled, man can.

The "pit" that was the Yishuv was empty. Pockets were not empty. The period was a prosperous one, both the private and the kibbutz sectors benefited from the war. Enlistment centers meanwhile handed the sons of Israel to the British and received nothing in return, while in cafés and houses of ill repute the daughters of Israel handed themselves to the soldiers of other races in return for money or nylon stockings. The former exchange was worse than the latter, for the latter was not at the nation's expense and did not adorn itself with the glitter of patriotism. The enlistment was of individuals, with individual motivations, and while those who fell in African and Italian battles in British uniforms will be listed in private or family ledgers—heroes no less but also no more than the children of Israel who fell in American or Russian uniforms—they will not be entered in the ledger of their own people's blood. There was no national-political return on this enlistment, these dead.

I have more respect for those who enlisted directly at British army centers rather than through the Yishuv's National Institutions or the nationalist centers. Direct enlistment was honest, not promising more than it really was. Enlistment via Jewish institutions was a political error, fostering the illusion that it would bring a national or political reward. Today Moshe Shertok (Sharett) glorifies his behavior and claims that those who enlisted learned how to fight a war and also lent a hand to Jewish emigration from Europe after the war. He is like one of Shalom Aleichem's characters, who sets out to buy a dairy cow and brings home a goat. Of course, a goat has some value and does no harm. The character appears ridiculous only because of the hopes he pins on the goat. The ridiculousness of the enlistment was in the singing of *Hatikva* around it.

The enlistment was covered in powder and lipstick, but whether it was honest could be judged by one criterion. In Tevet 5703 I wrote in the Underground newspaper *Bamachteret*: "They are prepared to take revenge upon the Germans because the British are of the same mind. But if Heaven forbid the British were to oppose it, they would fall silent, too. This is Jewish revenge à la Shushan—by permission of the king." Similarly, Communists felt free to fight in the war, once Russia was attacked.

Neither the Hebrew Yishuv nor the Zionist movement existed in any tangible sense during the first years of the war. An empty pit. Shedding crocodile tears in response to the "ravages" being suffered by Brother Joseph overseas, they hoped to do penance for their inactivity. But all the time that the Yishuv supported enlistment to help the British, no real effort was made to save our brothers.

Struma.

Struma came as no surprise. Her situation was known. The British were subjected to no serious pressure. There were strikes and hunger fasts and moaning like cattle, but not a fist was raised, because the only hands that were still acting on behalf of independent Hebrew thought had been cut off in the month of Shevat 5702. And the *Struma* ship, with all her desperate Jewish refugees, sank on 7 Adar 5702 (February 24,1942), seven days after Shevat, two weeks after

Stern's murder.

All the other hands were voluntarily chained. All the others willingly chained themselves to MacMichael and Shaw's British wagon. The IZL enlistment center continued operating for the British. Dr. Chaim Weizmann, then president of the World Zionist Organization (and later the first president of the State of Israel) writes in his book—with frankness that can only originate in a deep contempt for his own people—that during a visit to the United States (on personal scientific business) he agreed to the advice given him by London not to discuss the Jewish problem with Roosevelt—at all—and not to make any requests. Meanwhile, the Jewish Agency and Vaad Leumi (General Council) beat boys who did not want to enlist, kidnapped and tortured the remaining survivors of Lehi, and held strikes and hunger fasts . . . .

The pit was empty. The worst kind of pit. Darkness engulfed the Yishuv. Empty darkness. No thoughts of freedom, no actions to save others, nothing, emptiness.

Only our pit, the pit of the few Lehi fighters, was not empty. There was no water in it—only blood, snakes, scorpions.

We were stunned, ideas sank in only slowly, slowly, the few loners gathered slowly, slowly. As usual in a collapse, the crumbling had not yet ceased. But the black pit was not empty. It was full of pain and full of hate.

The days following the twenty-fifth of Shevat were filled with the desire for revenge. Called suddenly to Jerusalem, I met the new top man, Tselnick. He informed me that Yair—seeing his end near—asked that our revenge not be impetuous, but that we give the matter thought and consideration. And, indeed, a grand and extremely cruel plan has been formulated. Its success will mean the elimination of all the leading government officials in Eretz Israel in one operation. First, the Chief of Police in Eretz Israel will be assassinated. The road to the cemetery will be mined, and all the dogs coming to the funeral will be taken care of. One delicate problem remains—the Chief Rabbis will undoubtedly attend the large-scale funeral. How can we avoid injuring them? I suggest that we appear at their homes at the last minute and detain them there or elsewhere until after the attack. We prepare an announcement to be issued afterward.

Revenge for the blood of Yair. Revenge for the blood of the *Struma*.

And this type of revenge is worthwhile. Not only for emotional reasons, not only to fulfill our obligation, not only to lift the terrible weight from our hearts, not only to rejoice over the death of murderers. The revenge is also wise, considered and purposeful. Our blood is not cheap—says the revenge. The last stake has not been uprooted. The killer's hands will not be raised against us again.

I was called to Jerusalem for another meeting with Tselnick. My contact forgot to tell me the meeting place has been changed. I wander for hours in the alleys of the Bukharan Quarter, then along sad King David Street. I have no address, all the addresses have been changed, no safe houses remain. I return to Tel Aviv to wait.

Then Tselnick turns himself in to the police. The hard-pressed remaining few offered many explanations. Two years later we shared a barracks in Latrun Detention Camp for a few weeks. Tselnick spoke not a word to me. The riddle remains unsolved, even today.

The plan, nonetheless, is still in effect, we who remain will act come what may.

The plan failed: The Chief of Police miraculously survived the bomb planted in his car; his driver was killed but does not merit the grand funeral.

The pit into which we had been thrown deepened. No water, no air. Only more blood, more snakes, more scorpions and betrayals, betrayals. And each arrest leads to more arrests.

Who remains? Is there a man left in this wasteland? The twenty-fifth day of Shevat, the seventh day of Adar, and no reaction, nothing. The newspapers and public gatherings are full of chatter, endless talk, but not any real hate.

An independent-minded Revisionist, Tel Aviv Councilman Dr. Moshe Cohen, does not bother asking his party's permission, and at a city council meeting he raises the issue of Lehi members being murdered by the police. But the "Civilian Bloc" of non-socialist politicians is busy doing brave battle against taxes imposed by the Vaad Leumi's Jewish Redemption Fund ("Kofer Hayishuv"). The civilians are expending their little courage and energy on an internal Jewish front.

A few months earlier one of the prisoners in the Mizra Detention Camp had written: "We are confident that the year 5702 will put us on the path to the realization of our goals and the God of Israel will watch over and preserve his fighters."

For some reason, the God of Israel chose not to watch over and preserve his fighters. Perhaps He was right. Perhaps He, the God of Israel, is not obligated to protect those who do not protect themselves. Is the Lord to be a guardian of fools? Man has been given intelligence—this is a great privilege, and a greater obligation.

The year 5702 brought us to the verge of extinction.

I regularly met with the few who were still "outside," that is, not inside a prison or hospital. Among my visitors was one, a great gabber. According to his pointless prattle, he would have set fire to the entire Empire in one fell swoop; but the Empire was lucky, saved by a miracle, for he was arrested with seven others in Haifa. Then Frunin came by, arguing that by right of seniority and rank, he should be in charge. Rank notwithstanding, no one listens to him. He comes to see me, the ideologue, frequently, but has nothing to say. We print two lonely sheets against enlistment in a foreigner's army; a voice in the wilderness, but we have no alternative. Frunin, meanwhile, is hungry. We are all hungry. Each of us is allotted five grush per day. And if the stencil man forgets to give Drora her allocation, she goes for days without eating, thinking the funds must be exhausted. A few days later they remember and give her the money. She drinks several bowls of soup and faints.

Of our prisoners and detainees, I know only Natan Friedman. From Yair, however, I know that powerful forces are locked behind bars. They pace like caged lions. Each one is equal to a thousand from the Organized Yishuv that willingly offers itself to British Intelligence, a rag in its hands. Those in prison are the only free individuals in the country.

For now, though, they are enjoined from activity and remain only a moral—a mighty moral—force. Their presence in jail at this time is itself a political action, a sign of non-resignation, a sign that an autonomous Hebrew will survives, that an independent, political Hebrew intelligence functions. In prison, however, they are being consumed by the very fire burning within them, and they are further disheartened by the lack of activity outside.

The few yet outside are dedicated to the utmost, to the limits of the humanly possible. Partisans know that somewhere, a nation waits; scouts know they are walking ahead of the army. But the tiny group centered around Joshua Cohen,[37] Hisia Shapiro, Anshel Spielman, this group is more unfortunate than isolated partisans or scouts cut off from their army. Behind this group there is no nation, no support and no army, not even on the horizon. They are enveloped in a vacuum, in darkness. And if the darkness holds any surprises, these are only the flashlights of snakes, of people ready to turn the fighters in. The fighters' only support is faith. Their nation consists of several dozen detained prisoners in Mizra.

In the orchards lying outside the city, I meet Joshua Cohen, the first person I have met who exudes strength. He does not speak of having any formal authority. His character is his authority. We discuss our possible behavior should the Germans invade. Rommel is approaching and rumors are circulating that seventy airplanes have been readied to evacuate the leaders of the Yishuv. The

Revisionists supposedly want more seats, having been promised only two. Joshua Cohen cannot comprehend this nonsense. Our principle is war against any foreign regime here, period. What is there to discuss? Sure, difficulties lie ahead. We are without mountains, without forests (at the moment, Joshua's "forests" are undersized citrus trees, and the Sheikh Munis hills are "mountains" to this man who was so obviously born to be a partisan). I feel that in him I have finally found something to take hold of, though he lacks initiative and is in need of a commanding officer. I am encouraged as our meeting ends, and he escorts me to the city, the Hatikva neighborhood. His picture hangs everywhere, but his appearance is that which really endangers him: He is tall, black-bearded, his voice is a deep growl, and his eyes—two Bren machine guns.

High ranking and high quality commanders (yes, sometimes rank and quality went together) were sitting in the Jerusalem Central Prison, but a prison is tightly sealed, communication with those inside difficult, and escaping is many times more difficult. The trials had come one after the other, all set-ups. The accused made excuses, the lawyers argued and the verdicts were prepared before the trial had begun anyway. Only the trial of Moshe Svorai and Yaacov Levstein takes on political color. The attorney Guitein proves that the police had shot men who had their arms raised in surrender. This trial, therefore, becomes the only trial on weapons charges to be conducted behind closed doors. True, the attorney informed the directorate of the Jewish Agency, the Vaad Leumi, and the Hagana about this—but why would they respond? For at the very same time the Hagana kidnaps Ephraim Zetler and tortures him, learning from him the location of the arms storeroom for which he is responsible; then to show their "gratitude" for the information they throw him in the gutter for a British police van which "happens" to come by at just the right moment.

How many crowns rest today on the head of whoever was responsible for the torture and handing over of Ephraim Zetler? And Zetler was only one of many such instances. Where are all the "heroes" of Israel who participated? Why do they not admit and accept responsibility for these deeds? Today they are very powerful and would undoubtedly enjoy immunity; no harm would come to them. They would probably be given another honor, if room still remains on their shoulders. On the bones of Zetler, as on the body of the IZL fighter Yedidya Segal, who was kidnapped and murdered by the Hagana in January 1948, no spot remains that did not bleed at the hands of these "heroes."

The pit into which we fell in 5702 was very deep; inside was no organization, no bread, no weapons—but neither was the pit empty. There were the two Bren guns in the eyes of Joshua Cohen. There was my spirit, longing for the molds into which I could pour my molten thoughts and desires, longing to raise the banner of Yair. There were the few, the dozens of faithful whose eyes consumed the barbed wire surrounding the Mizra Detention Camp. And there was blood, and a score to even. And snakes, many snakes all around.

But other than this power that remained (and that was not very much of a power) there was only vacuum, a vacuum that existed under cover of shouts or sobs or even under cover of "underground secrets" that secreted nothing but deceit. Beyond our power-that-was-not-so-powerful the entire Yishuv collaborated before *Struma*, during *Struma* and after *Struma*.

Interludes

1. At Home

"And you promised that after we arrived you wouldn't get involved in politics!"

"And I'm really not involved in politics. What do you want from me?"

A woman's heart cannot be fooled. The school "meetings" were too frequent and too long into the night. She might at least suspect me of some other type of "involvement"! But some of the contacts come to the house; anyway, she knows me.

She truly, honestly, does not want me involved. She did not want me involved when it was not dangerous; and she certainly does not want me involved when I am liable to find myself sitting in jail, or wrapped in blood-soaked clothes, or in a shroud.

She does not want the involvement. She is tired of running and pained at having been torn from her mother and father and brothers who were left behind, and now she is also employed, despite the difficulties of a new language and environment (she is a social worker). When she comes home she wants quiet, security, warmth.

These, I do not give her.

"Understand me. I cannot live like that. I cannot. I take my political beliefs, which I have always held, to their ultimate conclusions. Some people believe exactly what I believe, but they like to wear ties. They knot their ties neatly around their necks, cutting the brain off from the flow of blood, and this solves the problem. The mind to one side, life to the other. I, you know, don't like ties, I don't like dividers, you know . . . .

"Understand me. My beliefs are nurtured not only from external wellsprings, from the songs of Uri Zvi, but also from my veins, and in my veins flows blood. Dynamics, you know.

"What would you have me do with my dynamics? Should I turn to a life of parties? Of cards? Of women?"

"That would be better," she says. "I consent."

I know she does not, but at the moment it seems preferable to her. At least then we could quickly separate and dissolve the problem. But over this . . . .

"Understand me. I've told you more than once. I lived differently once. I spread my energies in all directions and squandered them. Even on nationalist activity. Until I decided to concentrate everything on and for this great, beautiful thing called: the Vision of *Malkhut Israel*, the Majestic, Sovereign Kingdom of Israel. And then, just then, I decided to marry you—to consecrate one corner while freeing all my energy for the great goal. I don't want to be shut up within myself like all the rest, I can't live a carefree life with thousands of small pleasures and thousands—excuse me, tens of thousands—of small troubles. Night and morning and afternoon and salary and the theater, etc., etc., etc., swallowed in the great human yawn, living in order to live. I want all this to have a meaning. A meaning for all of life. Do you understand? And this is the meaning I have attached to my life: to make myself a link in this great, great chain; to be consciously and proudly a son to Father Abraham, to Shimon Bar Yochai, to all the great and beautiful Jews; and not only passively conscious, but to have the consciousness that obligates action; to channel the flow of all my spiritual energies, building dams where necessary and bursting through any dams erected by foreigners for their own benefit. So many strengths are sleeping within, embedded within us Jews. I want to see the symmetry of all these strengths heaving together in a tremendous, creative current. I want to see in my lifetime a mighty, beautiful and good Hebrew king in Jerusalem. And if not in my lifetime, then I want to die certain—at that last moment—that such a king will rise and that I played some role in his coming, in his beauty. I do not want to die, do you understand? You are all dead, dead, dead. Your lives evaporate into the void or into nature; it's all the same to me. I love man, history, the immediate. Eternity is as relevant to me as the void . . . ."

As this current fails to electrify her (as one subject to nature), I try "Zionism."

"I don't want us and our children to be slaughtered as our brothers are slaughtered over there. I don't want it. I prefer to slaughter others . . . ."

Afterward, years later, later, after her suffering while I sat in jail, and then during the British siege and then through the searches while I was in hiding underground, afterward she admitted once: "When I talk to others I stand up for you, I explain you, and I defend you. When I see how they mock you, I hate them. Being near them at work is difficult. But when I am alone at home and I see so many people living quiet, tranquil lives, I don't know why I must suffer for them. No one cares. For whom? For whom? I don't know, and I want a little rest . . . ."

To this deep pit in which we stood, surrounded by snakes, covered with scorpions, drenched in our own blood and alone, so alone—to this deep pit, on top of all our enemies, was added—not in malice—this. And this, too, we had to overcome.

2. Teaching by—and for—the Hour

I taught at the small Ben Yehuda Gymnasium (high school), 7 Rehov Mapu. The size was not a plus—not many students and not much pay. Nor was there any correlation between the effort and the results. A supervisor once remarked: It's a shame your abundant energy is expended on a small class of ten students; this amount of energy is enough for a class of fifty.

I, however, found consolation, too, in the small size, which meant a lighter workload and more time for other matters. Teaching not all the time but for all time.

Teaching mathematics would have presented me fewer problems. Mathematics is sexless, characterless. Any beauty it has is a formal beauty, which may bring pleasure but which will not burn. And I am the type who burns and sets afire. Teaching Bible and modern literature was therefore easier for me, for I set words, eyes, and souls afire. The difficulty was that I was forced to contain the fire within myself—these were the days of darkness, as ordered by the King of Britain and the Jewish National Institutions.

Alas, I had to remain within certain boundaries. Alas, I will not claim to have been too scrupulous about doing so. If I was not able to include Uri Zvi's poetry, I was at least able to remove Ahad Haam.[38] I retained only the minimum necessary for the graduation exams, and I lowered that minimum as Ahad Haam had lowered the level of Hebrew vitality. A thousand times I thanked the author Mendele Mocher Seforim for having said that "Ahad Haam, in his article 'Moses,' buried Moses." I did have an obligation to explain Mendele to my students, no? Mendele was not barred from the curriculum. I had, then, an opening to attack Ahad Haam's so-abstract and so-idle approach; I was prevented, though, from explaining how Ahad Haam had become the ideologue of Zionism, a movement whose mission was to infuse life into dry bones, to insert impulse, not to stifle it.

To my great joy and the obvious pleasure of Professor Frankl, who sat in on my lessons, I included the midrashic legends in my courses. Whether this gladdened my students—they were either born in Eretz Israel or immigrants from Germany and in either case, unacquainted with Midrash—I do not know. I tried to make my presentation enjoyable. I certainly enjoyed it.

To refrain from castigating the domestic Zionist institutions was most problematic. To talk of the Arabs and the British was permissible, and after *Struma* even fashionable, the more curses the merrier. But to dare to speak against the "national" institutions would be bringing politics into the schools and was therefore forbidden, as was, needless to say, mentioning an Underground.

The one time Dr. Levinson, the principal, called me was sufficient. He showed me a few "pearls" he had found in the compositions of my students. One had written, among other things, that: "We must simply corner the English in dark alleys and slaughter them." The topic was "Weapons, Weapons, Weapons." The principal did not get angry but politely asked why I had not responded to these sentences. I innocently replied: "Sir, I am a Hebrew teacher and I don't interfere with political views. This sentence is written in perfectly proper Hebrew, and I can only correct errors of style." The principal conceded the point and made do with the comment that in any case, fifteen-year-old students should not be given topics of this sort.

I had one quarrel, ironically with a member of Betar, Rephaela Erlichkeit. An intelligent and clever girl, yet slack in her studies and, if this were not enough, wild in her behavior. She particularly pestered an old, good-natured physics teacher. As I was class advisor I spoke to her, I tried everything, even contacting her mother. To no avail. Finally I resorted to the one argument I was convinced would win: Betar pride, self-bearing, *Hadar*. You are a Betaria. Does this not obligate you to behave with *Hadar*?

Rephaela came to class the following day carrying a stenciled volume of Jabotinsky's articles. In front of the entire class she leafed through all the articles and found the famous passage in which Jabotinsky writes that he never liked students who were well behaved, polite, outstanding, and so forth.

I answered whatever I did, a very forced answer, and my failure was obvious. Two years later Rephaela was arrested and sat in Bethlehem Prison. Released, she, the great rebel, was about to join Lehi when at the last moment she changed her mind because of . . . Lehi's actions against British soldiers on Rehov Hayarkon.

I did slip once more. A student one day told me he had read in some Underground newspaper called *Hehazit* (The Front) an article that could have been taped from one of my lectures on the poet Saul Tschernichovsky . . . .

All told, I remember the school lovingly. During the day it provided me with my first bread in Eretz Israel as well as the enjoyment of teaching, and during the night—it provided the ideal location for the first meetings of the Lehi Central Command.

3. Hulda

As the seventh-grade teacher, I was required to accompany my class on several weeks of farm work. Much of the public opposed this farm work, claiming that the students were being exploited for the benefit of the kibbutz economy. The Revisionists, too, opposed the work, claiming that it was a means of converting urban youth to socialism. I was not alarmed by the economic exploitation or by the danger of conversion. Obligatory work seemed to me to be good for the youth and good for the country. And the Revisionism of 5702-5703 (1942-1943) didn't seem much more patriotic than the socialism of those years. To me, the only question was: Will Hebrew rebels emerge from this or not?

We went to Hulda. The kibbutz did not get rich from our labor. And our students were not enthused with the kibbutz. Relations were good but lacked enthusiasm. No stormy debates were held, no horas were danced. Hulda . . . .

I gained from observation, conversation, quiet arguments, and one party.

I had long been familiar with their theories, their philosophical grounding in A. D. Gordon.[39] Gordon! The absurdity of transplanting Tolstoy to our land! Religion—we have one and it is good; labor—it is necessary. But to make a religion of labor—that is idolatry. The farmers of Zichron Yaacov are good and healthy without Gordon's ideology, which is the idol worship of individualism disguised as a utopian commune. It amounts to counterrevolution. Desertion. A stripping of all historical and political reality. I saw its reality in Hulda; I was least shocked by the socialism there. On the contrary, many families were living in separate homes. One of the members complained of the lack of social life. Outside of work, there was almost no cooperation. These matters have been written about—and more than enough—elsewhere, and I was far more interested in the human and group units and their relation to what was happening to the nation and the country. And I found good farmers. They love their patch of land. Inspired by Ephraim Chizik, they are as prepared as he was to defend their land. To defend. But tell them: "Be rebels! Come and let's drive the British from our land!" and confused, uncomprehending eyes will stare back. They are far from politics of any kind. Oh, they feel the pain of the Jews of the Diaspora—most have family there. Yes, they are angry at the British High Commissioner, "may his name be cursed" (the "extremists" among them adding: "May his name *and memory* be cursed"). But to rise, to leave the cowshed and crops, wife and child, to go fight? What? Everyone knows there are National Institutions and they are leading the struggle . . . .

Yes, they rely on the National Institutions. And the National Institutions can rely on them.

A few years later, in Latrun, I often looked to the south-west and wondered: If one of the escape plans should succeed and I were to reach Hulda, what would happen? I'll go to the cultural director with whom I became quite friendly and say: "I am Scheib. You remember. I escaped from Latrun and need shelter." What would happen?

I know what would happen. No, they would not turn me over to the British. They are less revolutionary and less "practical" than the members of Kibbutz Haartzi (the National Kibbutz Movement); they are actually very kind folk. They would stutter a little, consider a lot and conclude that the British would be likely to show up looking for me. No, they would not be able to shelter me but neither would they turn me over. I would be free to go my way. They would point me in the right direction. "You understand, this is most unpleasant, but we are responsible for the farm. They will search . . . and they will find our weapons . . . .You understand . . . ." As a matter of fact, several months after my school's visit, the British searched and discovered the arms, without recourse to any pretexts, and several men were sentenced to many years.

I attended the Harvest Festival. I remember that someone wept for an hour over . . . the wheat and the soil and the sunset. An elegy, an outpouring, as if reciting "Lamentations," not over the Destruction of a nation, and not over the Destruction of our Temple, but over wheat and corn. This, at the same time that a harvest of blood was taking place for millions in Europe, and ships of refugees were sinking at sea because the armies of an evil kingdom were occupying our shores.

Also addressing this festival was a Hulda resident who had been sent on a tour of the United States by the Hechalutz movement. He told of his failure and the failure of all the messengers sent to the United States. We showed them, he said, Jewish National Fund movies. And what did we show? Some farm in the Valley. We are excited by it; there is the clean cowshed, a tractor, a chicken coop. But those Americans yawned. Why? Haven't they seen nicer ranches in America? Cleaner, more orderly farms? What is so remarkable here? That a cow has a Hebrew name? No, this doesn't excite our brothers in the United States. This doesn't inspire them to join Hechalutz and move here. . . . Our propaganda is doomed from the start.

These were the messenger's honest words.

I recalled them a few years later, when news reached Eretz Israel of the huge success of the Underground's U.S.-based Peter Bergson group,[40] and the enthusiasm aroused in America by the Underground's operations in Eretz Israel. I recalled them again when this wave of enthusiasm crested during the actual war with the Arabs, when more American youths volunteered than in all the decades of “pioneering” and “kibbutz” propaganda. Our brothers in America have good hearts—give them Vision and give them deeds and momentum and they will come, they will give their money and they will give their blood. But for a provincial-utopian kibbutz—no.

And rightly so.

Yes, the Hulda farmers are good farmers. Their minimum: A. D. Gordon. Their maximum: Tel Hai.

Prehistory.

Stirrings

1. Michael Convenes the Central Command

Out with the accursed 5702.

With the escape from Mizra Detention Camp of Yitzhak Yizernitsky-Shamir,[41] whom I will refer to by his nom de guerre, Michael, the organization of Lehi began. I had not known him previously. Later, I learned that when the split occurred, he had not joined Yair; the men of the IZL unit under his command, despite his orders, did. He himself switched to Yair only several months afterward. He is short and wide. His speech is slow and considered. His will is strong and deep—in any case, stronger and deeper than his powers of theoretical thinking. The result is the unique character of his work. He draws something into the circle of his thought, concentrates on it with the entire force of his mind and body, the entire force of his will, and he acts. But he is unable to simultaneously deal equally effectively with another matter, as he does nothing without total concentration. This regimen is most advantageous for the first steps of Underground organization and operations. Growth then is literally man by man. And Michael relies on no one. He insists on knowing everyone personally. This requires much time, but he is able to form a direct impression of an individual's value. Michael uses this same method to win our first support from the population-at-large. He finds the first sympathizers who can help us with money, warehouses, apartments. The orchard "forests" do not provide enough protection. Rooms must be found. A press must be started. An engineer named Givon donates 1,000 lira with a strict condition: it must be used for a press. He adds: You'll pay me back when we have a state. Today in Tel Aviv there is an "Elisha Press" which is not the same press but which is named after Elisha (Yerachmiel Aharonson), who together with Zvi Schneiderman and Haim Dviri, "brought" us this supporter and many others like him. This is Michael's strength—working with individuals, in organizing and in acting.

But as the work expanded, this strong point contracted. Because Michael wishes to direct everything, down to the last detail, everything grinds to a halt. The regional commanders are grumbling about being fettered, lacking all freedom of action. Michael's strength does not mix well with speed.

This picture did not become clear to me until later, when I began to involve myself in the organizational problems, when I myself began to grumble about the slow pace of development, which was hardly equal to the needs of the hour, and the wrong proportions between the head that thinks and the body that acts.

In any case, I was not involved in organizational problems during the first stage, or even after the Central Command was established. Till then we were functioning without an establishment, without a legitimate authority. Michael escaped from Mizra in order to organize the surviving remnant. Only six months later did he inform me, briefly, as was his manner:

Someone was disturbing the organizational work. As of now he is okay and will not disturb us anymore. We must establish a Central Command. This Command will include the two of us and a third fellow whose talents are administrative and financial.

The first meeting of the Central Command of Lehi was held in the library of the Ben Yehuda Gymnasium. I was the librarian, so I had use of the room; I told the doorkeeper I was giving private lessons at night.

My Underground rendezvous is the "Bet Hamoreh" Teachers Club reading room. I play chess there every day; as with everything I do, I play chess temperamentally. Had I preserved some mathematical ability, I might have become an excellent player. As it is, I am only a not-bad amateur. As an encore to my chess playing career at the Teachers Club, I will take up a similar trade in the Latrun Detention Camp. Meanwhile, I play with the semi-teachers, those who teach between their vacations (provided there are no strikes then). During one game, between moves, my opponent asks if I heard about the Jewish chap killed on Rehov Mazah a few hours ago.

No, I haven't heard.

Another move and another. The game continues even after the arrival of my contact, and after I have gone to greet her and read the note with the information that Elisha Aharonson was killed, and even after the second note warning me not to loiter about the streets, as there will be a response. So I return to the table and the teacher and the game.

Another move and another. My situation is very good, yet I am losing the game. On a different battlefield my situation is very bad, losses are being incurred; but I will not lose, to lose is forbidden.

2. Between Bach and the IZL

"Bach" and "Bach-nik" were the nicknames given by Lehi members to members of the IZL. "Bach" was the abbreviation of David Raziel's Underground appellation, Ben Chananel. In our mouths, Bach was a stinging curse usually accompanied by frothing, or at least disassociation and disparagement.

I never used this word, for the poisonous hatred felt by almost all of Yair's men toward the IZL was not within me. I had not been in the Irgun before the split and had not been torn from it during the split. Psychologically, the hatred was logical: Friend had been torn from friend, brother from brother, the war was over every soul and every piece of property, every commander and every arms cache. Years later I was shown a note from one IZL leader actually threatening civil war if Yair's organization did not change its name (when Lehi still used the name Irgun Zvai Leumi B'Israel). Dozens of other little and some not-so-little factors deepened the chasm of the bitter political differences. I understood the differences but was free of their emotional implications.

Some tried to explain the split to me in terms of the personal incompatibilities of the two commanders: Yair, the man of political theory and poetry; and Raziel, the man of organization and military order. But to scramble after such explanations was superfluous. The essential difference between their deaths is the surest sign that they were arguing not over titles and honor but over fundamental problems, or the fundamental problem: an unconditional truce with the British regime or unconditional war against it.

Were *The First Tithe* a history book, I would be forced to determine whether David Raziel's activities were treasonous. As this is not an official history of the War for Liberation, let this comment suffice: Those who announced a halt to their war without receiving any commitments in return for this halt, those who enlisted in the British army—not as individuals, Jewish citizens of the world who felt obligated to enlist, but as members of a Hebrew Military Organization —these men definitely appeared to be traitors in the eyes of the others, the few who bitterly watched these events.

Arriving after the split, I saw only the political issues. "IZL" was a political term. For my friends, its veterans, it was also a bitter emotional term; and this bitterness was expressed in the name Bach. The IZL members, in turn, called us the "faction," symbolizing for them that we had taken apart their structure. I fought in conversation and in ink against this emotional aspect, against the hatred. Especially after the IZL abandoned the ways of Bach and became the fighting IZL of the mid-1940s. Even when political considerations demanded unity, both parties remained with deep wounds not easily forgotten.

The hatred for the "traitors," for "those who surrendered," was embedded in our men. For many of the old-timers, this hatred would become one of several reasons to discover socialism. When the IZL did join in the war against the British, the differences between us were less obvious and these men were confused; their hatred demanded they somehow distance themselves from the IZL. They sought to build a new house on the same foundation of hatred, and this led to their opposing the IZL by moving toward socialism. They had other reasons, too, which are for future chapters. This chapter is describing a complex that developed in Lehi: Heaven forbid any contact with the Bachniks.

On the other side, IZL members suffered from a strong inferiority complex in that they felt they had missed the beginning of our war. Their gross error lay in not freeing themselves from these feelings of guilt with a simple, straightforward confession. Just the opposite has occurred. They avoid and ignore the heavy guilt of abandoning the war effort, of unconditionally surrendering in the summer of 5700 (1940), as if this guilt did not exist. To these feelings of inferiority is added another: Coincidentally or not, the keener intellectual powers, those able to penetrate more deeply and express more clearly, were on Yair's side. After all, no powers at all were needed to justify and explain enlistment in the British army, the absence of war against the British. Whoever stopped rowing his own boat, whoever put aside his oars, could then lie supine in the boat; the natural current carried him. Only he who rowed against the current had to fight a war for bread and for life, had to dip more deeply with the oars of his body and the oars of his spirit. And coincidentally, or perhaps not, Yair and those who followed him had such deep spiritual oars. This, too, increased the feelings of inferiority of those who flowed with the current, right into the sandbank.

In this laundered language of mine, which refers to the "IZL," the phrase is: "into the sandbank." In stronger language, which refers to "Bach," the phrase would be: "got stuck in the mud."

Just as 5702 was a year of organizational crisis for Lehi, so it was a year of political and moral crises for the IZL. An IZL historian may one day deal with the affair from an internal point of view; I will touch only on those points I witnessed.

The first news of unrest in their camp reached me through Eliahu Lankin. A group of Betarim that had arrived in Eretz Israel via China regarded itself as neutral vis-à-vis the split. I addressed them at their invitation, and not long afterward Lankin told me of the serious crisis facing the IZL. He and a few others must decide: Should they join Lehi or try to save the larger body, to return it to the one battlefront—the war against the British regime, the battle for the freedom of Israel, which is simultaneously a battle to save the Jews of the Diaspora, while a war against an enemy in the Diaspora is not simultaneously a war for independence, liberation. This was the basic proposition that had been set forth by Yair. I spoke of it to the "Chinese." This is the message Lankin wished to bring to the IZL. Lankin assured me that the key positions in the IZL organization would fall into trustworthy hands. He wished to maintain continuous contact with me, so as to eventually bring about the reunification of our forces. This would be his holy mission.

I have never cast any doubt on Eliahu Lankin's honesty and even today I am convinced that he put his whole heart into the task. I will not claim that his efforts came to naught. Though he did not succeed, he did increase the rumblings. But at that time the spirit of Bach was still dominant, the wagon would not rise from the mud.

A side comment: I never knew Raziel, I do not know the propriety of the term "spirit of Bach." Some say other spirits, rather than his own, encouraged him, the Commander of the Irgun Zvai Leumi, to embrace British Intelligence and offer to carry out a mission for them. If this be true, only the character of his act changes; and in the court of history, perhaps a clause in the charge against him will be changed.

My following meeting with Eliahu Lankin was not private, and not "conspiratorial." (I hope Eliahu will forgive me for referring to our first night meeting on my porch as a "conspiracy"; indeed it was, though unfortunately it never bore fruit. Neither of us had the authorization.) The second meeting was at the invitation of "Am Lochem," a movement that was an attempt to merge the IZL with the Lehi and the activists in the Hagana. Michael and I represented Lehi; Lankin and Eliahu Matzadi, the others.

We could not respond positively to the proposed three-party contract. That the two spoke honestly and out of genuine pain was all we could rely on. We asked for assurances that the root causes of the schisms had been overcome. We asked to come out against enlistment. These statements were not made, could not be made, by the other two. They, too, soon learned that goodwill was not enough. Perhaps they were too weak, perhaps the IZL had not yet sunk to the point at which it would either self-destruct or undergo a basic transformation; in any case, Am Lochem was stillborn. The large scale plan prepared for an act of actual war against the High Commissioner's residence, Armon Hanetziv, was not implemented, as far as I know, because of the opposition of the old IZL commanders. Eliahu Lankin's revolution failed. Our first attempt at a union with the Hagana had also failed. But I wanted to meet one of these "strange creatures" from the Hagana, so Eliahu introduced me to "Joseph."

In our two-hour conversation, as we strolled along JNF Boulevard, I heard echoes of the "law of pressure." He asked me about the differences between the IZL and Lehi and admitted that the activist IZL approach was closer to his own: "Our actions will force them to give us more immigration certificates." Such an attitude was a War of Liberation still in its infantile stage.

For the time being, at least, even the IZL activists were beaten down. The explosives that the IZL commanders had refused to allocate to the Am Lochem operation were allocated instead to a different operation. A pigsty was blown up in Petach Tikva, and several boys went for long prison terms for this "liberating" action.

And one more typical event: Someone blew up the Steel Brothers garage. I was surprised, because by this time I was a member of the Central Command and a partner to all decisions. This operation had never been discussed. Our operations were individual actions against soldiers and police. What was this? The IZL? Maybe, finally, they have begun?

The following day we learned: the Ben Yosef story repeating itself. Shlomo Ben Yosef had broken through the restraint and complacency of Betar. He acted without orders on his own authority. This time it was Job Avtalyon, a wonderful young man with a pure and gentle soul. (I was to make his acquaintance in the Jerusalem Central Prison.) Not some show-off commanding type, but quiet and soft Job. He was the one to break the IZL's restraint. He and two friends decided to blow up the Steel Brothers garage. He was arrested and tortured and sat in the IZL prisoners' cell in the Jerusalem Prison, where his nobility and serenity shined despite the surroundings. All of us loved him not only as a comrade-in-arms, but as a brother-in-spirit. He eventually gave his life in an Underground operation "confiscating" arms in Pardess Hanna.

His deed served notice on the IZL that it could not carry the name of a National Military Organization for long without acting. He was sending a warning.

But by that time Menachem Begin was already in Eretz Israel.

3. Menachem

I am not yet talking to the Commander of the IZL, I am still talking to Menachem. The Menachem to whom I bade farewell. The Menachem with whom I was linked by the "squeaky door." His arrival was cause for joy; we had had little hope of seeing him again. Our first words to each other:

"Nu, we will continue, Israel. We stopped in the middle, you remember?"

"I remember, Menachem. We will continue."

But we did not continue together.

My memory has preserved two conversations. The first, in Menachem's room in Tel Aviv, where he wore the uniform of a Polish soldier.

"Menachem, when are you going to take off that uniform?"

He told me of the efforts being made to win him a discharge.

I offered my doubts as to the seriousness of efforts being made by Revisionists and Betarim committed to a "restrained" IZL. Why would they seek the discharge of the famous activist, Menachem Begin? "And if they don't free you soon, Menachem? Why not do what hundreds who came with the Polish army have done? Why don't you just leave that army?"

Now I was very surprised:

"And so…to desert?"

"Yes, Menachem, so what?"

And the greatest surprise of all:

"The concept of honor no longer exists for you?"

Not for nothing did this verbal interplay etch itself in my mind, not to be forgotten so quickly. Probably lacking in historical value, the conversation's educational value is immense. I attempted to put the situation into sharper terms:

"The choice before you is to be a deserter from the Polish army or a deserter from our Hebrew war."

To which he replied:

"Israel, you always liked brilliant, cutting phrases, but the brilliant phrase is not always the correct one."

No, the formulation was more than aesthetic. I do not deny that I love a sharp expression, nor do I shy from exaggeration if it will win oratorical points. But this time, I was insulted by the use of "honor" as an excuse.

I have already described the "concert" performed during Menachem's arrest. That was *Hadar*, pride, in all its beauty, *Hadar* in its place. Standing with honor, dignity.

Hadar and the concomitant honor must be an individual's *second* soul. His *crown*, not his head. A crown is meaningful on a head, not in and of itself. A crown in the wrong place is meaningless.

Even the hundreds and thousands who deserted from the Polish army not in order to serve the Hebrew nation but just "because," merely to discard uniforms their hearts were not in, merely to be Jewish citizens in Eretz Israel among other Jews, even they were not deserters. Anyone who asked me for advice—to desert or not to desert—I unhesitatingly answered: Desert. And I helped many to do so. What have we to do with these Polish uniforms? Throw them away along with the whole Diaspora and the whole Diaspora mentality. Had the Polish army been "democratic," a Jew arriving in Eretz Israel would still have been permitted to leave that army. How much more so in the case of General Anders' army, most of whose soldiers and officers would certainly have been participating in the slaughter of Jews had they but remained in Poland.

But this instance is far more serious. You, Menachem, had no intention of escaping to civilian life. You were being called to the war of the Hebrew nation. What is this game you played with "honor" and "valor?"

I saw *Hadar* perverted. And I saw the danger of detaching moral values from concrete reality. The morality of Israel is the morality of this world: the world of cause and effect. Any postulation of Good and Evil in the abstract is a metaphysics that has no place in the morality of Israel. Not the ideas of Plato, not the anti-history of Jesus, not the categorical imperative of Kant—but rather the Bible's: "And you shall live by them," and "to prolong your days on this earth."

"The concept of honor no longer exists for you?" Menachem asked.

Truthfully, no. A conception of honor, detached from my national interests, does not exist for me.

Once before and once afterward, I saw Menachem caught in the thicket of this "honor" to which he is so sensitive.

When we were still in Vilna, Menachem received a letter from Eretz Israel taking him to task for leaving Warsaw and for trying to reach Israel so quickly. The letter of complaint closed with a bombshell: "A captain is the last to abandon a sinking ship."

Menachem was quite moved when he read this and called a meeting of the Commission at which he announced his decision: to return to Nazi-occupied Warsaw.

If the seriousness of Menachem's decision were ever in doubt, the *Altalena* affair came eight years later and proved that Menachem really is some kind of knightly captain, to the point that he literally had to be dragged off the burning, sinking ammunition-laden *Altalena* ship. But *Altalena* belongs to a later chapter of history.[42]

Menachem received his discharge many months after our conversation, during which time a large portion of the Polish army was transferred out of the country. And he, too, was under orders to be transferred. Only miraculously, as he himself told me, did he succeed in remaining here.

And if they had transferred you, Menachem? If they had transferred you? The

War of Liberation would certainly have developed according to the same necessity that it did, albeit with differences in nuance caused by your absence. But where would you be with your concept of "honor"?

Jabotinsky presented Hebrew youth with a fabulous concept: *Hadar*. But he spoke and did not explain. Students do not always give the proper explanation. In Hebrew we speak of "heavens," "seven skies," "a ladder of values," and *Hadar* is undoubtedly one of the skies, but not the highest of them.

The topic of the second conversation that I remember was: framework. The location of the conversation: the street near the Metsudat Zev building. At the time of this stroll with Menachem, the busy building named for Jabotinsky stood in the shadow of the large sign above the entrance: Enlistment Center.

Why did the Revisionists have to open their own centers? What is the difference between a Jew enlisting in the British army through the old Zionist organization or the New Zionist Organization? If there is a difference, it can only reflect poorly on Metsudat Zev. The Jewish Agency and Mapai did not sell themselves in their enlistment drives. They were always sold and loyal to the foreigners. But the political offices of the New Zionists (Revisionists) and the Betar Commission in Tel Aviv and the IZL Command had what to sell, for the Zionist-Revisionists and the Betar and the IZL were independent, fighting bodies; and they were sold. Though individual enlistment may have been permissible for some reasons, and perhaps in some cases individuals should have been sent to the British army for concrete purposes (training, contact with Diaspora Jews, smuggling weapons, etc.), no one under any circumstances should have put the "Metsuda" (Fortress), which should have been the symbol of the Hebrew rebellion against foreigners, in the service of this enlistment.

Therefore, I would pass the Jewish Agency's enlistment centers with no special feeling. They were all right; they did not represent a Hebrew liberation movement. But this—which, in competition with the others, loudly proclaimed the number of thousands it sent to the British army—this aroused disgust and hate. This is how my comrades viewed the Metsuda in those days.

And this is how I described the situation to Menachem:

There are two sides. A body without spirit, a large organization bereft of meaning and reason. And on the other side, a faithful spirit that has been robbed of body, left with no organization. Menachem, I said, we were not here during the split. Perhaps we could have prevented it, for in Vilna we reached very similar conclusions, but since we weren't here we are free of the deep hatred and therefore we have the ability to straighten that which is crooked. I suggest to you today to establish on these ruins *one fighting movement*.

That this conversation was held outside the Metsuda was no coincidence. Menachem was about to enter. And I refused.

He wants to go inside and from inside to purify the house. And I am critical of the whole house.

This argument about the framework—its holiness, its dismemberment—this is an old, even ancient argument and the world has never witnessed a revolutionary movement that did not reach a crisis over the point.

How do these matters appear in light of the results? We in Lehi recovered from our organizational crisis. The spirit created the material, though the number of people open to our potential influence shrank once the IZL, and later the activist "Ahdut Haavoda,"[43] entered the fray themselves. Menachem succeeded in pulling the IZL out of the mud and returning it to the one battlefield of a movement of liberation, but . . . for all practical purposes, he destroyed the frameworks of the Revisionist Party and Betar, the good that was in them along with the bad. We cannot presume to know how events would have progressed had a united fighting movement arisen at that time, but without a doubt the two movements were ripe then for the restoration of unity. This was one of those moments. The other was years later, at the moment the State of Israel was established. These two moments were lost.

4. "Our Anger and Rage Will Bring Forth . . . a Forest"

This title is not taken from one of Ben Baladan's satirical songs in the Lehi paper *Hama'as*. This title is authentic. Leaf through the late-November 1943 editions of the *Haaretz* daily newspaper.[44] In one, you will find the complete headline: "Our anger and rage will bring forth the forest of Ramat Hakovesh."

These were the days of the Yishuv's anger and rage over the British search at Ramat Hakovesh and the murder of Samuel Welinitz.[45] Shortly after the search and murder the board of the Jewish National Fund convened and in total anger and total rage Harzfeld proclaimed the Yishuv's response to the search and murder: A forest would be planted at Ramat Hakovesh and the fundraising slogan would be: "Our anger and rage will bring forth the forest of Ramat Hakovesh."

Perhaps I would not remember this slogan, had I not been forced to stand before sixteen and seventeen year olds in my school, youth whose anger and rage were real, and explain how anger and rage over pogroms, murder, robbery and degradation can be transformed into some strange water that will bring forth a forest, together with pennies donated to the JNF.

The search at Ramat Hakovesh was preceded by other searches and by the trials of those found with weapons. Important lawyers stood at these trials and asked the judges to take into consideration that the accused were quiet working men who restrained themselves after the murders at Hulda, and perhaps the sentences should be light.

They were. Only imprisonment of twelve, ten or seven years, that was all, and perhaps a pardon-to-come on one of the birthdays of His Royal Highness King George. Of course, for every Jew pardoned, ten Arab killers were also pardoned. And therefore all the Hebrew schools in the country celebrated the birthday of the British king, each year, by order of the Vaad Leumi of the people of Israel.

There were many arms-searches, and they were degrading; and there were many arms-trials, and they were degrading. Lord Moyne and High Commissioner MacMichael had been appointed, after all, not only to implement the British White Paper policy, but also to help the Arabs finish Hitler's work concerning the Jews.

For the danger of a German invasion here passes. Apparently a few Jews may be left in the world, and they may make some noise. Under the guise of philanthropy, America may seek influence and oil in the Middle East as well as Jewish votes in the elections back home. A slaughter must be prepared here. The pogroms against Jews, called "disturbances," must become more serious. The Hagana must be disarmed. The Hagana! The British know very well that these weapons are not meant to be used offensively. Not against Arabs and not against the government. Therefore the defense lawyers and Jewish Agency officials and newspapers are so pathetically ridiculous when they sob bitterly: The weapons are defensive, only defensive! Of course they are defensive. No British soldier doubts that. But the British are not interested in Jews having defensive weapons on the day of slaughter. Lord Moyne delivers an address in which he scientifically "proves" that the Jews are not even a nation, merely a mishmash of races. And removing the Jews from Eretz Israel, transplanting them to Madagascar or some corner of Africa, would be worthwhile. He, Moyne, will accept the task of establishing the Arab League. The League is intended mainly as a block to the United States and France, but this is from the perspective of high diplomacy. The Arab masses must be given something: the treasures and corpses of the Jews, for instance. This is the goal, and the Guiteins, Eliashes, Shertoks, Ben Gurions, Meyersons and Abba Hushis are explaining to MacMichael and Moyne: But the arms are only defensive . . . the arms are pure, pure, pure.

By now the Palmach, too, is also unnecessary, having been established to serve as a sabotage and mopping-up corps for a retreating British army in the event of a Nazi invasion. Scenario: Naturally the Jews will be slaughtered, except for the leaders who will gladly fly out at the last minute. But tens of thousands of British soldiers will be saved, thanks to the honorable defense put up by the Palmach in the Tel Aviv and Haifa ghettoes. Now the danger of an invasion has passed, the Jewish "niggers" did what they were told; now they must be disarmed.

And they are. The arms are "pure," certainly clean and well oiled. But they are not holy, for if they were holy they would be defended. If these people really understood the value of the arms, they would fight for them. But they act as sheep—there is not one shot, not one battle. They have a wonderful excuse (the production of their excuses is the work of a creative genius): The regime is pushing us; it wants us to provoke them. We will respond with the forest of Ramat Hakovesh, with . . . increased enlistment in their army, and with our principal secret weapons: strikes and hunger fasts.

I stand before students fuming to the point of exploding. Fuming over the sinking of the *Struma*. Fuming over the deportation of refugees to Mauritius, fuming over the murder of Welinitz and fuming over the extermination of the European ghettoes. Their souls are searching for relief. An order—and they will take to the streets. An order—and they will mount the barricades, thousands upon thousands of good, healthy young men and women. They will come from kibbutz, village and city. They will climb the barricades. They will burn the castle with the High Commissioner in it. They will open the ports to boatloads of refugees, boatloads. Physically, with their bodies, they will open them; they are ready. Their anger and rage are capable of this. In moments of anger and rage, even the masses are capable of this. Even the war-profiteers, leftists as well as rightists, momentarily forget the good business they are doing and they, too, are ready for anything. Revolution is in the air.

But the Yishuv is in the hands of a fifth column, which does the work of the British regime. The Jewish leadership blocks the anger and the rage.

Strikes. Once, a full day. Once, half a day. Once, only two hours during the afternoon siesta (when the workers and employers disagreed over at whose expense the strike would be, they decided the strike would be at the expense of . . . the afternoon. It is the afternoon siesta; the stores are all closed anyway . . .). When this begins to grow boring, the fifth column adds a fast. Posters with black borders are hung, assemblies assemble, a fast is called. I laugh at them, I mock them, and I fast. The huge black-bordered posters have the intended suggestive effect on me, too, and I fast. And I visit the home of an ardent supporter of the Vaad Leumi and Jewish Agency, and I find him sitting at a table full of food stuffing himself.

"What's going on? What's going on?"

"What does it matter if I eat? All that is only for appearances, to demonstrate. Will my fasting save a Jew?"

And I, the dolt, fast. Outside I scoffed, at home I fasted. And he, the Mapai party man, he put on serious, even tragic, airs at school; and he spoke of a soul shaken to its core, and the unity of our hearts, and the solemnity of fasting. And inside his own home, he stuffs himself, and drinks, and laughs. And he has an excuse: "The main thing is the outward appearance. The world should know."

But not everyone makes do with symbolic demonstrations. Some struggles are serious, not symbolic. Some strikes are real. The diamond workers, for instance, strike. Sometimes they strike by the thousands. Diamonds are good business during wartime. The diamond manufacturers are profiting and the workers demand higher wages. And higher. Why not? Netanya is raging and Petach Tikva is raging and Tel Aviv is raging. Socialists and nonsocialists, binationalists and ultranationalists (among them even some who secretly contribute to our paper *Hehazit* and who are excited by its articles. They themselves will not join the Underground, of course; they are "sympathizers" who say, "You understand . . . I do not have the time . . .").

He does not have time. He earns "only" eighty lira a month. He fights—for an increase. Or when the market slows, against a reduction to seventy.

And if the diamond workers strike, why not the teachers who earn half that amount? Are they not polishing the diamonds that are the youth? So they strike: against private employers. Even I strike against some fictitious parents committee. I earn about thirty lira a month. Is this fair? Can one live like this? Honestly, no. True, in Lvov at this moment they are slaughtering my mother and my brother, but I only have to think of this on Fast Days and during official strikes. And what can we do? "We must make a living." I strike. I am not even sure against whom. Certainly against the students. And when I suggest a compromise with the administration, I am proclaimed traitor to the interests of my associates.

Where is the great director who will bring this whole grotesque drama to the stage, all of it at once? The screams of the women and children in the gas chambers, naked and suffocating, suffocating; the screams of those who drowned when the *Struma* sank; the dozens of dead from disease in Mauritius; pairs of children from the "revolutionary" Hashomer Hatzair movement wandering the streets holding boxes and seeking contributions to the Jewish National Fund; and the good Harzfeld caresses their heads and their boxes and whispers and whispers: Our anger and rage, etc., etc., etc., the old refrain; the British policeman Cafferata cleans his gun after the murder of Welinitz and reloads: Which kibbutz is next? He prepares a country-wide massacre of Jews reminiscent of the Arab massacres of Hebron's Jews in 5689 (1929); Shertok shouts into the microphone of the British radio station in Jerusalem: Enlist! Enlist! Enlist!; a Betar-Hapoel soccer game—the entire Nationalist Movement heads to the stadium! Result: 2-2. After a good and well-fought battle, they are even; thousands of workers strike for higher wages and stand silent in memory of "our millions of murdered brothers."

The country is experiencing unprecedented plenty and affluence. The kibbutzim work for the war effort and accumulate money, money, money. Profiteers in cities and villages, kibbutzim and the private sector. Blood and gold. Blood and gold. And rhetoric covers the blood and the gold. Everything is a lie, a lie. Prostitution flourishes on the Tel Aviv promenade. Prostitution taints everything. This one sells her body for a lira. The kibbutz sells its goods to the British army for thousands of lira. Shertok does the work of redirecting the anger and rage into enlistment. Three thousand younger fighters of the IZL and Lehi are destined to topple the British regime in the years 5706-5707 (1946-1947), *after* the World War, when the British are able to station some one hundred thousand soldiers in the country. Shertok and Altman, Golomb and Raziel help send thirty thousand Jewish men out of the country, thirty thousand cedars who could have undermined the British regime in one instant after the fall of Rommel, and we would have gained four precious years.

The anger and the rage were there, but a fifth column prevented their exploitation. What forced David Ben Gurion to declare in the summer of 5703 (1943) at a Zionist Actions Committee session that "The differences between us and England over the White Paper are not necessary differences. We believe that the renewal of true cooperation between us and the British Empire is a historical necessity . . . "?

Needless to say, we see this as the wrong approach—we as a liberation movement thinking in terms of "freedom" and a "foreign regime." But even in purely "Zionist" terms, has any prognosis ever proven more erroneous? Is there another statement equal to this in its lack of understanding of British policy and interests? We wrote the exact opposite in *Hehazit*: "The differences are a necessity. British imperialism is justified, in terms of its own self-interests, in its opposition to the Zionist enterprise."

And they, the proletarians, the progressives, the socialists, they found "common interests" with the Empire. Actually, there were common interests, and these were the secret of their counterrevolution, the secret of why they were, intentionally or not, a fifth column.

Between the liberation of the Hebrew people and British imperialism there were no common interests. Only conflict, which was brought to a partial conclusion against the will of Ben Gurion and his associates. The common interests and cooperation between the British imperialist regime and the regime of Mapai and the kibbutz sector and the Funds would have continued indefinitely but for the war of the Underground. The fifth column would have continued cooperating even if it had been reduced to a truncated ghetto of a state as proposed in the Morrison Plan[46] or a ghetto in the Emek-valley. The arms which were hidden were indeed for defense; and the accused and their VIP witnesses (Golda Meyerson, later known as Golda Meir) and their lawyers spoke truthfully: for defense against Arabs only. If not for the Underground, these weapons would never have been used, not even in the minimal amount they eventually were used, against "administrative British installations."

The anger and rage would have continued bringing forth forests. But no lions would have emerged from these forests. The great lions, like Dov Gruner and Dov the Blond—they didn't come from JNF forests. Some came from the forest of Liberated Thinking, purified of even Zionist dross, and some came from the forests of confusion and disappointment felt by the Revisionists, Betar and IZL over the conscience-that-was-supposed-to-awaken, that of the good British Wedgwoods,[47] et al., and the logic-that-was-supposed-to-function, and the Hebrew-army-that-was-to-rise-to-fight-alongside-the allies (Jabotinsky's last lost cause). This idea of a Hebrew army was logical—but grounded in unreal premises. The Legion and the Brigade were, in hindsight, a Revisionist version of Laborite illusions, in military garb.[48] No political facts—and no war for freedom—were born of the enlistment in the British army or the Brigade. The expulsion of the British and the establishment of the state would have come about even without the Brigade—though both the Underground and the Hagana made use, here and there, of the Brigade's existence. Dov Gruner came from the Brigade, but he would have come without it, too. Without the Underground, the efforts of the Brigade would have amounted to naught, as did the Jewish Legion during World War I. Both were dispersed leaving nothing but memories and photographs; neither had the potential of becoming a rebel force able to seize power.

The above paragraphs had to be written, in light of attempts to justify the enlistment and the Brigade on the basis of benefits occasionally derived from veterans. Without questioning the personal heroism of the enlistees, it must nonetheless be said that such national-political conclusions are misleading. In political terms, the enlistment was without any value and was, as was the channeling of rage and anger into forests, the work of a fifth column.

I have described the issue of the Brigade from today's perspective. When I wrote the proclamations against enlistment in 5702-5703, some slight doubt still existed, a gnawing in some hidden corner. Today I know with mathematical certainty: The gnawing then was an inner weakness, an anti-statehood weakness, and personal worry and personal hatred. The opposition to the enlistment was the result of the correct calculations, the state and national calculations that overcame fleeting sentiments.

The War of Freedom would have taken place without the Brigade. The Brigade would have contributed nothing without the War of Freedom.

The diversions of the fifth column failed. They failed because of those who tunneled underground in *Hehazit* toward the ideology of a Free Israel, and those who at the same time tunneled out of Latrun toward the achievement of a free Israel.

Light from Darkness

1. *Hehazit*—The Front

The decision to distribute an ideological Underground publication was one of the first taken by the Lehi Central Command organized by Michael Yizernitsky (Yitzhak Shamir).

I did not delude myself into believing that revolution is a matter of the intellect. Revolution is a matter of character. The strength to destroy and create is a strength based deep inside. The lust for the great and the willingness to sacrifice for the great are not rooted in thought but in a person's dynamics. These earthly strengths and dynamics, however, remain void and formless as long as darkness hovers over the face of the deep. The reverse is equally true: Spirit can grasp nothing, can only hover, when there is no hard surface of earthly strengths underneath. Most probably the world of the intellect and the world of the spirit only appear to us, flesh and blood that we are, as separate. But a belief in an essential unity confirms the words of Uri Zvi Greenberg, "The intellect grasps what the imagination conceives." Somewhere in infinitude parallels do meet, somewhere in the infinite the spirit is part of a higher intellect, somewhere in the infinite the intellect is actually a dynamic spirit. Perhaps only advanced mathematicians understand, when they approach metaphysics, how parallels meet. Perhaps only the poet-prophets, for whom synthesis precedes analysis—unlike most poets who begin with analysis and fall short of prophecy—reach the world of unity, which is not for nothing called "the hidden world," as what we see is multitude, while the secret is in the unity.

No, *Hehazit*, the paper of the Lehi Underground, will not deal with these metaphysical issues. The task of *Hehazit* is to provide an ideological foundation for the already existing emotional motivation and resultant deeds of the fighters. The Idea is not new. The Idea was the cynosure of the spirit of Israel in all generations past and its expression is the messiah. Even in modern Hebrew thought, and in secular Zionism and that Herzlian Zionism rooted in the negativistic approach of escaping from the Diaspora, the Idea, though weakened, has not vanished. And in the poetry of Uri Zvi Greenberg, this Idea is all.

The Idea is the messianic idea, the idea of the rise of a Hebrew Kingdom, great in relative terms but identical in an absolute sense to the kingdoms of Israel at the time of the Prophets and the time of the Hasmoneans, and identical specifically in terms of its geographical location—which is, not coincidentally, at a continental intersection—and rising, historically, at this period of crisis for all that is called Western culture, which includes Greek, Roman, Christian, Renaissance and Democratic culture, and Communism, which may be the finale of all these cultures or may be the expression of a new culture. The idea is that out of the ruins of this world we must climb again to the spiritual heights of Mt. Sinai and the physical peaks of David and the Hasmoneans.

Perhaps the messianic idea—born of religious faith, currently out of favor with the masses—has managed to creep into secular hearts only by speaking their language. The Prophets of Israel, in contrast, had the mighty courage to dare to call those who laid waste the land and nation: "The rod of My anger." We, who are not on the spiritual level of our Prophets, but whose bodies and blood are so close to the laying-waste and slaughter of our nation, we do not yet dare pronounce that judgment.

We had, however, sufficient strength to say—and this was explained and justified and repeated in *Hehazit*: We are not here to solve the "Jewish problem." The formulation of Zionism as an attempt to solve the Jewish Problem misled many good people: Herzl and Jabotinsky, for example. Only the messianic idea prevented a secular Jew of the nineteenth century who subscribed to liberalism, individual freedom and national emancipation from finding contentment in these ideologies. Perhaps the Emancipation's failure was not divinely ordained. Nonetheless, the messianic idea exploited this failure to push Jews toward their own mission. But the Zionists wished to delude themselves into thinking they had come to save endangered lives, while their mission was actually far greater —but the greatness was shunted aside, either to the high heavens or the subconscious, and on the conscious, rational, secular surface remained what they called "Zionism."

The argument with this "Zionism" was the ideological raison d'être of *Hehazit*. Ironically, to shoot a British soldier on the street we had to attack the foundations of Zionist thought.

True, most of those who shot British did the good deed without philosophizing about the Hebrew revolutionary movement. Yet the leadership of the revolution was obligated to reach the conceptual purpose, the purpose of the shots. That which seems simple to the citizens of all other nations—not to tolerate foreign soldiers, foreign rulers on the soil of one's homeland—this was not simple to the Jews in Eretz Israel. Establishment Zionism did not see itself coming to liberate a homeland, but to rescue a people. Even pure, political Zionism did not see itself coming in order to establish the Kingdom of Israel, the necessary purpose of our generation's revolution, but rather to establish a state which would solve a problem.

Our first fundamental difference with "Zionism" was, then: *Hehazit* did not bother arguing with or trying to convince non-Jews. Not the evil ones (the English), whom the Jewish Agency and socialist Zionists engaged in endless debate, and not the good, enlightened, moral ones with whom Jabotinsky dealt, with all his heart and soul. From the pages of *Hehazit* we said "no" to the entire approach of "a problem and its solution." The concept of a "problem" and "solution" lowers one from the heights of ideology to the arena of politics and means. Rescuing a people is not an ideology; perhaps a specific function of an ideology, but not an ideology. Therefore we do not travel to London or Bermuda for conferences, we do not pin our hopes on an "understanding" with the British Labor Party, we do not write thick reports and we do not deliver logical speeches and warnings to international commissions set up to solve the problems of miserable refugees. Yes, even as we stood on the threshold of the establishment of a state, Jewish establishment leaders were still in London negotiating over the issuance of 4,000 immigration certificates. A state, versus 4,000 certificates!

Years later, even the movements of the Lehi and IZL were naturally exposed to a crisis. Because they lacked the positive-ideological-messianic foundation, many fine members of the IZL and Lehi grasped the fighting of the war over territory as a change in the means of Zionist realization. With the establishment of Israel, then, the only question left is how much land, where to draw the borders. Or they said: Now that the Jewish problem has been solved, we can move on to the problem of a preferable system of government. Or, at best, those who call themselves "nationalists," still following the Herzl-Jabotinsky line, conceptually secular, claimed: The Jewish problem has not yet been solved.

I believe the nationalist underground movements failed to endure organizationally because they had not adopted the revolutionary doctrines formulated in the articles titled "Avnei Yesod" (Foundation Stones) in *Hehazit*, even though they adopted and were acting on all the practical conclusions of the political articles of the Underground publications *Hehazit*, *Hama'as* and *Herut*. They who carried out the correct conclusions without relying on the underlying assumptions eventually found themselves on a road leading nowhere.

In *Hehazit*, we are laying the foundation stones of the Liberation Movement. Ideological articles complemented political articles and formed a whole. If the aim is the establishment of the Hebrew Kingdom in our homeland, then the first conclusion drawn is: not to recognize the British Mandate over this land. The

British government is a foreign government. "We are not fighting this White Paper or any other, but the existence of a regime that gives itself the right to issue White Papers." We are not fighting the laws, but those who issue the laws; not an evil High Commissioner, but the existence of a foreign Commission, even if it be "good."

That the Commission and the White Paper were evil made our incitement and propagandizing easier, as the Jew was not yet sensitive to the concept "foreign domination." On the contrary, he had grown accustomed to it over the course of millennia.

The first issue of *Hehazit* appeared in Tamuz 5703 (summer, 1943), the first platform for the Hebrew Underground. The "first platform" because up to this point only slogans were used, slogans painted on proclamations and on walls, usually in response to some criminal action by the government, or calling for a halt to enlistment in the foreigner's army. But the slogans lacked the ideological and emotional premises to communicate the concept of a "foreign army" and they were therefore not understood by the public. If the regime is recognized in principle, then its army is not foreign. I wrote the proclamations against enlistment; to us, the concepts were clear and understood. Not, however, to the youth educated in a Zionism-come-to-rescue-Jews. After all, they say, the war is against Hitler, why not join the British? *Hehazit* appeared in stencil, the pages were gray, the print sometimes unclear, but this was the first time pamphlets about the Underground communicated with people. Till now we were seen as a gang of zealots acting emotionally, or out of blind hatred or despair. Despair was the charitable term used by those who wished to understand, if not forgive, us. The pages of *Hehazit* revealed to these people something they had not known: We have deep, ideological thought; we have cold political logic—very cold; the supposed "hotheads" analyze international political reality with open eyes and dry realism. The murder of a policeman stems neither from a desire to kill nor from madness, but rather is a link in a chain that begins in a world-view and ends in practical action. This was a great surprise—if not to the general public, which we reached only later with the paper *Hama'as*—at least to intellectual circles.

Echoes of this surprise reached us, and we sinned in listening to them. We listened too much, we overrated their value. Every compliment uttered by an adversary or even the enemy warmed us, planted the seeds of illusions. One day we will pay dearly the price of these illusions. At the time, we enjoyed them. We longed to be rid of the title "Gang." The insult pained us. Our sin in *Hehazit* was that more than attempting to educate ourselves, we attempted to convince our opponents, who could not be convinced in the least by *Hehazit*, as their opposition to us did not stem from logical considerations.

In the beginning we printed 500 copies, and eventually reached 6,000, though the material was neither easy nor appropriate for the masses, as *Hama'as* later was.

Emanuel Katz helped me with the first issue. Natan Friedman's participation began with the second; he smuggled his articles to us from the Mizra Detention Camp where he was incarcerated. His writing was mostly political analysis, from an international perspective and from the perspective of the War for Freedom. My writing was ideological and literary.

I was not involved with the printing and distribution. I did not even know the location of the press. I edited the material and handed it to my contact. A week later it was returned in print.

The paper reached me in another way, too. Three times a week, I taught Bible and literature to four private students. Once, they very emotionally handed me an issue of *Hehazit* and recommended I read it, as they occasionally heard in my lessons views similar to those in the paper. Later, I learned they had even gone a step further and recommended me to their Lehi cell, suggesting that someone make contact with me.

In one of the early issues, we headlined: "The time has come to open the battle of the Hebrew nation, the battle for the liberation of its land from the occupier" (*Hehazit*, Av 5703).

The time had come, but had the forces? Who were the few people, and what was their power to declare war? To formulate thoughts—yes. But to fight?

2. A Light at the End of the Tunnel

Our "Old Man" is a strange fellow—serious, weak, his thin beard making his narrow face appear even narrower. Ever since his photograph appeared on the first of the British wanted posters he has felt the weight of responsibility on his shoulders—for a while he even thought himself responsible for the entire movement, except that Joshua Cohen and then Michael quickly brushed him aside. Now he wanders, a loner, an amateur chemist, dreaming of a laboratory for experiments, studying chess theory. And hungry.

I have not seen him for some time, until this Sunday morning, November 1, 1943. Anxiety over the planned mass escape from Latrun kept me awake the previous night. We have lived with this escape for more than half a year, all this time remaining inactive in order to safeguard its success. This Sunday morning, on my way to the Ben Yehuda Gymnasium, I suddenly see him coming toward me at the corner of Gordon Street and I know: Here is the news, for better or worse.

"So?" I ask.

"What?"

"Is everything okay?"

He speaks slowly, as usual, his face narrowing with every word, his blue eyes growing more serious, his fingers forever curling his beard.

"There . . . should . . . have . . . been . . . something?"

I see I have erred, asked the wrong question. I try to think of a way out and, good man that he is, he comes to my aid:

"Maybe . . . a . . . robbery?"

Maybe the hunger was gnawing at him, maybe he was waiting (he was always waiting) for Michael to finally deliver on his promise to provide some lira for the chemical laboratory, and therefore he was hoping for an operation involving money.

"Yes, something like that. You've heard nothing?"

"No."

"Excuse me, I must hurry to school. Good-bye."

Thank Heaven I had not phrased my question so as to reveal the secret. I am not cautious enough; I admit and confess that more than once during the Underground years, I spoke unnecessarily. I do not recall causing any disasters, but this does not atone for my sin. This is my weakness and I wage continuous war with it.

I continue, my nerves even more tense. Had we not said I was to receive word in the morning?

Hisia Shapiro is waiting for me at the corner of Mapu, all ebullience and excitement. Obviously she cannot shout on the street but she herself is one loud shout: Success!!

Afterward, I learned that immediately following our conversation, the good "Old Man" went directly to his apartment—for whatever reason (he had not slept there that night)—and was startled to discover Natan Friedman ("Gera") there.

I will not recount here the heroic episode of the digging of the tunnel and the escape, which one of its heroes, Matti Shmuelevitz, has described in his own memoirs. I will relate only one detail, heretofore unknown, but important and edifying.

Michael disagreed with the men inside Latrun over the number of detainees to be freed. The detainees requested, from inside, the maximum. Michael argued that because of the difficulties in absorbing the escapees into the Underground, and because the quality of the escapees was more important than the quantity, the number should be limited to ten. The Central Command had to reach a decision. I barely knew the imprisoned men and so could not consider the personal aspect. I leaned toward the maximum for two reasons. First, the propaganda value—the impact of the escape. Ten men are not yet a "mass escape." Second, the emotional point—I tried to imagine the detainees standing at the edge of freedom and I argued for consideration of their feelings. I knew the difficulty that would face those responsible inside Latrun, those who would be forced to pass sentence, who will stay and who may go.

We finally agreed on twenty. Twenty-one escaped.

I soon realized that Michael had been right—not because of the burden of absorption, but because of the relation between this burden and the men's efficiency. Some of those inside were worth hundreds or thousands of others, while some were the sort who could easily be found outside, without the problems of hiding an illegal escapee. In any case, we agreed on twenty (the twenty-first, Emanuel Hanegbi, preceded the others and escaped not via the tunnel but from a Jerusalem hospital where he was feigning illness). The single justification for twenty escapees was indeed the propaganda value. The number had its effect on the Yishuv and undoubtedly gained us sympathy and support. So everything was for the best.

The escape's significance to Lehi cannot be exaggerated. Beyond the addition of the individual soldiers to our forces, our spirits were lifted; this was our first success after years of failures, so many failures that only by miracle were we not crushed by despair. This was our first compensation. For the first time, the prestige of the government is impaired; and this is itself a weapon of war. Michael's earlier escape from Mizra was the result of a moment's agility. The escape of Yaacov Levstein (Eliav) and Moshe Bar Giora[49] from the Jerusalem Central Prison was the result of a humorous trick. But the escape from Latrun was the result of a nine-month struggle with the camp administration. Chance played almost no part, thus the blow to the enemy's prestige. Henceforth the undermining of its prestige was continual. From the Latrun tunnel to the mining of roads and the driving of the enemy into "ghettoes" from which they feared to venture, and finally the blowing up of the British administration's head offices in the King David Hotel and the IZL's flogging of British officers—all these were blows to British prestige, and such blows are lethal weapons.

The day after the escape we had more hands and more legs, and above all, more hearts—burning hearts, which are motors for the hands and legs.

And another head was added to the leadership, in which the existing head and body may have been in danger of achieving a balance and canceling each other out. Between the ideologue laying the heavy foundation stones, burning with fire (me), and the body that organizes, executes, fights every day and every night the war of the Underground, on the defensive, as it expands, through the operations (Michael), between these two was now lodged a third: "Gera." Lacking the depth of a world-view, lacking philosophical bases, but logical and to be taken into account. Professionally, Natan Friedman, Gera, is not a teacher but a surveyor, one who measures every step and word. The form reflects the content, measured and considered. Emotionally, instead of Menachem Begin's dry pathos, he possesses a sense of esthetics and a tendency toward sentimentality. Judah Leb Schneerson[50] will one day describe the difference between Gera and me as that between a *Mitnaged* and a Hasid.

These three personalities provided Lehi, from this point on, a fine mesh of characteristics and responsibilities. The combination was right, the triumvirate ideal, as long as all were serving the same one cause. The day following that night of November 1, 1943, the night of the Latrun escape, this triumvirate took the initiative of Hebrew history in Eretz Israel into its hands.

A day or two later, we sat, all the members of the Central Command, the first time the Command convened in its entirety; and we rejoiced, rejoiced greatly. Natan Friedman began by teaching me a bit about the consumption of wine and cognac, an area in which he is an expert and I am an ignorant fool. He never despaired of trying to impart this wisdom to me. In his last letter from Acco Prison, during his trial after the 1948 assassination of Count Bernadotte, he still promised that after his release, with the help of Michael, he will yet teach me to drink properly.

And perhaps he would have succeeded, if the two of them had not also tried to teach me a new kind of politics, which went with the Lehi tradition like a bad combination of drinks.

3. A Time for Hits

The Underground creates its own language, not necessarily for security; perhaps to reduce verbosity, perhaps to heighten immediacy. The tendency, in any case, was away from literal, traditional, "dictionary" definitions. We spoke of "hits," "presses," "vegetarian," or "meaty" operations. I was revolted by this language, but I was usually disgusted by what this language signified, too. Yet, though I refrained from using these "technical" terms in my writing, I found them natural in conversation. I cannot imagine myself telling the commander of an operation: "Today we are going to shoot someone," or "Tomorrow there is a mining operation." Instead we spoke naturally of hits, presses.

The time for mines or "presses," however, was still far away. At this point we began the "hits" or shootings, and during this first stage we were dealing with small arms, since the only machine guns we saw were in our dreams.

Writing in hindsight, one could describe the various stages and progressions of the war as if they were planned from the start, their order part of a nice and logical construction. I am not writing historically, I am relating chapters of history as I subjectively lived them, the way they actually occurred.

In the winter of 5704 (February 1944), Menachem Begin, the Commander in Chief of the Irgun Zvai Leumi, published the Declaration of War with its detailed plans, which had a great impact on the populace. The posters were very large, the plans very wide and very promising.

To us, the entire declaration seemed strange. A battle, even a regular military war, can and should be planned. An Underground's war for freedom cannot be considered at the start. Neither the behavior of the enemy nor the behavior of the general populace can be accurately prophesied. The development of our war in the years leading to that which was achieved (I prefer this terminology to the word "victory") proved that the paths were other than those set forth in that beautiful and pathetic plan—some paths more difficult, some easier.

The well-known scenario: attacks, civil unrest (strikes, tax boycotts, demonstrations, etc.) and the assumption of power—this scenario was lifted from other wars of liberation and did not work for us. There was no civil unrest, students did not strike, government offices were not boycotted, taxes were paid. There was no rebellion and no grabbing of power as written in revolutionary theory. Reality differed from the plan—and was much greater and much more shocking, if less theatrical.

Lehi's operations during this stage were mainly hits on the street, which did not follow any strategic plan. Most were the result of encounters with the British or in response to British attacks. The escape from Latrun increased the tension between the regime that realized the danger posed by a handful of extremists prepared to do anything and that handful, which lived to fight that regime. The first clash came a few days after the escape when the British encountered, by chance, a group of escapees. Gunfire is exchanged. A first battle, in miniature. This is not Rehov Yael, not Rehov Dizengoff, not Mizrachi Bet. This is an armed confrontation. Our men have been instructed not to walk the streets without guns and not to be arrested without resistance. Begin, during one of our meetings, expressed his opposition to this policy. We continued with it for almost a year, until we realized that some of the arrests and deaths could have been avoided had our men not been armed and therefore afraid of being searched. In the long run, though, even these casualties and the tension they caused were of value. Similarly, out of the "lion's jaw" of the arrests of Matti Shmuelevitz and Anshel Spielman came the "honey" of their great trials through which they, by using the trials as a platform from which to accuse the British, were of greater help to the cause than they would have been in battle. Some "failures" turn out to be successes, and you cannot plan failures.

The escapee Yitzhak Siman-Tov fell in the first clash. Elisha was the second casualty, on a Tel Aviv street. Then something in Haifa that led to one in Yavne'el.[51] The heroism of the wounded young man in Yavne'el, hurling grenades at the enemy to save his comrade-in-arms, the besieged shooting to the last bullet— this was something new. The enemy learned that the days of Dizengoff and Mizrachi Bet were over. From now on they pay with their blood. The war grew even more violent with our reaction to Elisha's death. A decision was taken to slaughter them on the streets, whenever possible; officers and police were shot and killed.

They are no longer safe on our streets. They no longer strut like landlords. Of course they engage in brutality but this brutality only increases the tension. The Hebrew papers rage against us, sparing not a single insult found in the Hebrew dictionary. They exploit any casualties among the innocent public in order to incite against us. Until now, normalcy meant that new or illegal immigrants were murdered, drowned, or deported, the Yishuv expressed anger, and concealed behind this "anger" lay a silent agreement based on the common interests of the British and the Yishuv. The Yishuv benefited materially from the British army, which signed contracts and spent nights in the country, mostly with and in the Jewish sector, which knew how to provide more goods and entertainment than the Arab sector. When material benefits are offered, all classes participate. And banners of justification are easily hung on the benefits: "The war against Hitler."

Now somebody comes along and disrupts this idyll. People are suddenly shooting at British soldiers, police and citizens, who, of course, respond in kind with gunfire, as always occurs in a war of liberation. And innocent civilians are killed. People suffer.

But this suffering is the moral minimum owed the drowned and deported. Not-suffering is the crime of the Yishuv and no number of fasts and strikes and speeches and decisions can atone for this crime of a complacent and satiated Yishuv. The hits by Lehi members on the streets of Tel Aviv widened the rift between the Yishuv and every British soldier and policeman. And this was for the good, as London would never have thought of leaving Eretz Israel without these attacks.

In 5705, the *Haaretz* newspaper analyzed our "terrorist" war: "By their demonstrative actions, the members of the IZL intended to threaten the government into not implementing the White Paper policy. The Sternists have in their insanity gone further and their leaflets declare that their purpose is to 'expel the British occupier from the country.' Their intentions are not only demonstrative but also include acts of murder."

No argument seemed more ridiculous to us than: How is an anonymous policeman, clerk or soldier guilty?

First: He is guilty, just as every German soldier in France, Norway or any other occupied country was guilty. He represents the regime; obeisance to orders does not absolve him. If it did, the buck could be passed indefinitely, even the High Commissioner is only carrying out his orders; even the government is only executing the dictates of Parliament.

Second: All those who used the argument of the "innocent soldier" against us argued with no less fury and hate when we executed British Minister of State for the Middle East Lord Moyne and attacked High Commissioner MacMichael. And these two were certainly not innocent.

For the arguments used against "terror" were not important, but rather the atmosphere that led to them and that would have led those people to oppose any means we might have chosen. This was the atmosphere of plenty and tranquility, or the wish to continue the historical-political process, even if it was no longer historical, no longer political.

Third, and most decisive: The random hits of British soldiers and police is that which transformed the Mandatory regime into an occupation-regime, by ripping the mask of comfort and legality from the face of this imperialist regime in the colony of Palestine. If not for the heightened tensions and mutual hate we would not be sitting today in a State of Israel. And murder, "cold blooded" and by ambush, this murder is that which moved us closer to what we have achieved.

The establishment Zionists of the Jewish Agency were not alone in opposing this form of warfare. In 5703-5704 (1943-1944) arguments were also heard from the IZL.

Following the grand declaration of the "Revolt," as they liked to call the Underground war, were their first operations. They began by blowing up government offices, after providing enough warning to avoid loss of life. This would have been understandable had the purpose been to save Jewish lives. But —they attacked the Jerusalem detectives' headquarters. Their man Benziman fell and a British officer was also killed, Smith was his name, I believe (or something similar to Smith. I could check his name with the newspapers, but I will not do so—it makes no difference. According to our method, the name was of no importance). To our surprise we read in an IZL proclamation of their sorrow over this British casualty for "to us, a man's blood is holy."

The gap between Lehi and the IZL, which finally appeared to be narrowing, widened again. We are still in two different worlds. They are apparently still living in the illusion that this is not a live-or-die war, but some sort of gentleman's game. They still believe they can clear up the misunderstanding between Britain and the Jews. Not by the means being used by Weizmann and Ben Gurion, but by means of applied pressure. The erroneous premise of this theory, on which Jabotinsky also relied for some time, was: England has met with Arab opposition, therefore she leans toward the Arabs. If we show England that this is not worth her while, if we also cause trouble—she will shift her policy to our benefit. Dr. Wolfgang von Wiesel developed this theory and phrased it in global terms: If we show England that we are a force on which she can rely for the defense of Suez, she will become our ally. Von Wiesel drew a concrete image: On our Bastille Day, on the day of the Hebrew uprising, we will carry both the Hebrew and British flags, we will sing both anthems. The British will not have the heart to shoot at masses rebelling with the British flag in hand.

I have already admitted our hits were not part of a strategic plan. They were the only form of war we were then capable of waging. We had no heavier weapons. And, too, the desire to avenge Elisha's blood and the as-yet unavenged blood of Shevat 5702, this desire also motivated us.

But we had no emotional or intellectual compunctions about shooting at the soldiers of the forces we called the enemy.

We found the IZL opposition to shooting from ambush strange, a direct continuation of the same misplaced nobility which felt sorrow over a British officer's death, behind which lay the faulty and doomed theory of pressure. The

IZL is still fighting the White Paper policy, simply by different means than the Yishuv. *Rak Kach* (Only Thus), the IZL motto referring to a gun liberating all of Mandatory Palestine, still refers to a means of convincing. For nowhere else in the world, never in the past or present, has an underground movement fought on an open battlefield instead of from ambush. The ambush is the single advantage held by an underground facing greater police and military forces. Even in full-fledged regular wars I doubt that any of the "gentlemanly" concepts of the knightly wars of the Middle Ages remain. Even a submarine attack is nothing more than an ambush.

Which is not to say that we considered street hits the only means of waging war. When the IZL began blowing up enemy targets (and with great efficiency), not only did we willingly consent to the concept, but we learned the technique from them. As we lacked experts in this area, we sent men on IZL missions to learn. This technical cooperation was not yet, however, a bridge between our two organizations, which were still walking on different sides of a deep canyon. After marching in place or retreating, they had begun to progress, but still the premises differed. They were still incapable of saying, "to wage war against the enemy," for one does not warn an enemy in advance of attacks and does not express sorrow over the death of one of its officers. Is the spirit of Bach still dominant? The spirit of his death on a mission for the British in Iraq as "Captain" Raziel? Was I mistaken when I saw myself and Menachem on one side and Jabotinsky on the other? Or, and I grew more confirmed in this suspicion with each passing day, did Menachem see himself as executor of Jabotinsky's theory of rebellion, all of its faults included? In my last meeting with him on the roof of the Savoy Hotel in Tel Aviv, his Underground quarters, Menachem said.

"When I give an order, I feel Rosh Betar standing behind me commanding me to give the order."

I expressed doubt as to whether Rosh Betar Jabotinsky would have taken action at this time. Jabotinsky's final book, *The Jewish War Front*, did not lead me to believe so. But of this I am certain: If this were true, if Rosh Betar's spirit stood behind Menachem and commanded him to order operations, then this spirit was also the source of the command to express sorrow over the death of that officer. Menachem Begin was then acting not as the Menachem Begin of the last Betar conference, but in the spirit of Rosh Betar's speech at that conference—which he, Begin, had opposed, while I came to stand by his side in opposition. The war's progression quickly proved the futility of all this chivalry and humanitarianism in dealing with the enemy. From there to the blowing up of the British offices in the King David Hotel and the hanging of two British sergeants in retaliation for the hanging of three IZL men—the distance is not only far, but a leap is necessary, the crossing of a new Rubicon. And blessed is Begin who overcame his remaining weaknesses, and I have great doubts that Rosh Betar commanded him to hang the sergeants. And in all honesty: At the time, I feared that the knight would overcome the rebel, the *Hadar* overcome the necessary cruelty. Thankfully, my fears were proven baseless.

*

The IZL's entrance into the war engendered complications based on lack of operational coordination, and each unit accused the other of disrupting its activities. Coordination was necessary even though, at this time, the IZL was limiting itself to demolitions while we continued the "meaty" operations.

If our operations can be faulted, the weak spot was the one point that seemed to many their only justification: that the operations were a reaction to Elisha's murder. Some of our moderate opposition occasionally stated that both our killing and the British should be condemned. The Revisionist Dr. Herzl Rosenblum in *Haboker* and some of the *Hamashkif* writers, who wanted to help, added warnings to the regime, which they cited as the cause of the bloodshed.

The moment of revenge should not be belittled. The heart is glad, yes, glad, when the blood of our murderers is spilled. Murderers? I am confined by literary terms. Even the term "storm trooper," which we used in our propaganda against the British, even that is still too laundered. Amongst ourselves we said: We "knocked off" or we "hit" some "goyim." The term "goyim" was used so exclusively for the British that afterward, during the fighting with the Arabs, we were unable to refer to them as such. The infinite hatred with which we hated the British was concentrated in the word goyim (accent on the first syllable) even more than in "storm troopers" or "murderers." The secrets of language! Words are drawn from ancient depths, from the prayer "Pour out Your wrath upon the goyim!" and the Psalm's "Goyim have come unto Your heritage." The hate was pure and the revenge good for the heart. And I am neither ashamed nor sorry over them today.

Where acts of revenge appear powerful, though, lies their weakness. They leave the impression that they come only as a response, that they are part of a bloody circle of attack and revenge. We had to break out of this circle but had not yet succeeded in doing so. The operations of the IZL were acts of initiative but were limited in effectiveness by the constraints placed on them. Our operations were without constraints, striking at the soul of the enemy, but the enemy's attacks made ours look like revenge—while the enemy, his civilian and military representatives, deserved to be attacked even without a specific provocation.

The war did indeed develop, though meanwhile I had a slight mishap, a mishap natural in an underground war, though for me it was more than a mishap.

I Am a War Criminal

Gera, Natan Friedman, coined the phrase: "Liquidate the prisons." Meaning: Use any means necessary to avoid arrest. The rationale was that either we would liquidate the prisons or the prisons would liquidate us. Too many people "broke" in prison during the years 5701-5703, unable to withstand the torturous inactivity; they adopted a "neutral" stance, even arranged for their own separate barracks in order to distance themselves from members of Lehi, in the hope that this would put them in a better position to obtain their *fraj*, that atrocious term for freedom used in Latrun, Mizra, and other such places. Too many abandoned the struggle and too few stood firm, and therefore every arrest left a vacuum that was difficult to fill. We printed a special booklet for internal distribution with rules of behavior obligating every member of the Underground, in an effort to avoid arrest.

Every member? Apparently not. Apparently they obligated every member except the members of the Central Command, for we three violated, to a criminal extent, the law obligating maximum caution to avoid arrest. There are inevitably some who want to mock the "cowardice" of the "big shots" who send others into the flames while they hide in the safest of holes, but readers of this book have already been able to see that our war left no room for heroic displays, for knightly boldness. Of course we had to guard against being enticed by the devil, who loves to trap man between morality and efficiency, where borders are unclear and fragile. Too many chose all sorts of means to stay out of jail in order, as it were, to continue the struggle, only to be broken by their chosen means, to be rendered useless. We therefore set limits to the permissible and forbidden in the effort to avoid arrest: That which permits me to continue my role in the war—is permissible. If my cautionary measures prevent me from continuing with the war—then they serve no purpose and danger is preferable. Nonetheless, any act that is not necessary to the war and that might lead to arrest is a criminal act. And we, we who were responsible for the Lehi movement and its war, we committed crimes of this sort. That we were once or twice spared despite our foolish actions is irrelevant. And in this competition, I took first place among the members of the Command.

One morning just before the Purim holiday of 5704 (1944), at 7 a.m., Hisia Shapiro arrived with an urgent note from Michael: Word has reached us that they are going to arrest you, leave your house immediately.

And in the house, a one-year-old baby girl who has just learned to stand on her legs and look at me with warm, joy-filled eyes. And only yesterday she came down with an ear infection.

And in the house, a wife who works, is far from politics and almost unaware of my ties to the Underground. My heart breaks for them. So what, it breaks. This time I have no choice, a few words must suffice to explain the situation to my wife. When she can argue, dispute, bitterly oppose—she does. But when faced with an established fact she becomes a different person. She straightens, turns practical:

I should take sick leave from work. I can use any of several private apartments as a refuge until we clarify whether they are actually searching for me. (I will not name the first of the apartments, lest the association with me hurt the career of the family's daughter in Israel today. I will not name the second apartment lest the association with me hurt the career of the couple, who protected me until just before my arrest, and who live, at the time of this writing, in one of the People's Democratic Republics.)

One final look at the sick child, one final review of the preparations for future contact with my wife, so that I will know whether they have come to search for me, and I leave my apartment in the month of Adar 5704 (1944), to return only in Adar 5708 (1948). In that instant, as I left, I lost my civilian and my family life. The pain was deep inside, and as such, not in the way. Most people who cannot draw personal conclusions from revolutionary opinions are bothered by just this fear of losing the warm corner called home, security, calm. My conscience is clear concerning my wife. I warned her, before our marriage, in my letters. I wrote her that I need a house as a boat needs a port, but a house is not everything to me. It must belong entirely to me but I cannot belong entirely to it. This may be cruel or unjust but this is me. Perhaps my wife did not take seriously these sharp phrases of this "interesting" fellow who loved Nietzsche and poetry. Perhaps, had she known then this was more than hyperbole on my part, she would have changed her mind. Now she knows: It was not just rhetoric, it was not my point of view. It was my real character.

No. At almost no time did my conscience bother me about her suffering. That she is not a partner to my war increases her suffering, and hurts me, but does not stop me. I will not become a sinner, not for a piece of bread or a wife or a home. How will I, nonetheless, sin toward the War for Freedom? I will commit the crime because of my pedagogic work. Not because of the salary, but because of my responsibility toward the students who face their graduation examinations, for whom I am class advisor and teacher of the main courses: Bible and literature. Love is strange. Not even psychoanalysis has been able to explain the riddle of the child sacrifices made in ancient times to Molech. Sometimes we sacrifice that which we love most. I, however, certainly loved my home more than my students, yet I left my home without hesitating, and I made my mistake at school.

The day I received the warning I went to the principal and explained that I had to return home to my sick daughter. Then I went to Dr. Moshe Cohen, a fine person, doctor and friend to the Underground. After I explained the situation, he examined me and asked if I had a headache and dizziness. Of course I had, what kind of a question was that? Still, the honest doctor could not bring himself to attribute to me a serious illness, and instead made do with a diagnosis of general weakness, for which he recommended a month's convalescence.

If I did not feel dizzy, the principal Dr. Levinson certainly did. And with good reason. The eighth grade teacher of the main courses goes on vacation two months before school's end. What choice did he have? In three years of employment I had not taken even one sick day. This must be serious. My calculations were simple: After my month's absence, the two-week Passover vacation begins. If six weeks pass and they have not come searching, I will assume the rumor was groundless.

And the rumor's source? Interesting in itself. Dr. Shimshon Yunichman[52] heard the news from Joseph who heard from Chief Detective Giles that he, Giles, knows who Dr. Scheib is and what he does.

Why did Giles suddenly tell Joseph? And why did Joseph tell Yunichman? For many reasons, perhaps, but not to keep it secret.

This misled me. Six weeks passed from the day I received the message, and they had not yet come. I began to doubt the veracity of the news, and decided to return to school after Passover, knowing that I would conclude on May 1, when the eighth grade finishes and the seventh grade leaves for agricultural training. All in all, two weeks. True, the eighth grade numbers no more than . . . three students, but still I must make the final effort and in two weeks bombard them with Bible, one written test after another, more and more chapters. Of course I will not go home, only to school, only for a few hours. If they do remember and do come, they will probably come at night to the house. I spread all these logical thoughts before Michael. He relies on my logic, but not the logic of the British. He is against my returning to school even for a few days. Had I been one of the regular soldiers he would undoubtedly have acted simply: issued an order, period. But with me, a member of the Central Command and a respected intellectual, he cannot act so. He merely says: "It's not worth it." He repeats this in a note. He adds the information that these last few days, they have begun arresting people at work. They also went to the Kupat Holim health clinic offices (National-Revisionist, of course, and not Histadrut-Labor) and arrested several people.

None of his arguments move me. For it is only two weeks. Only!

And I run toward my fate.

To our rabbi and solace, Rabbi Arye Levin, with love:

Part Three

THE BODY CAST

Cell 18

1. The Lost Watch

How did the British detectives come to open a file on me? I would not ask, had the police here been worthy of the name Scotland Yard or Intelligence Service. Nothing I did or wrote abroad had been secret. We had not been thinking in long-range terms then. My 1940 *Hamedina* article on "Hostile Neutrality" could easily have been filed where necessary. The all-knowing Dr. Shimshon Yunichman had told me upon my arrival in Eretz Israel that the British police had a file on me which included the article. I thought he was exaggerating.

I do not know the skill of the British secret police in other places, but here they proved their total worthlessness. If not for our inexperience and naivety and the chattering-disease that afflicted all of us, and, last but certainly not least, if not for the collaboration the police received here, far surpassing that afforded any other secret police at war with a national underground anywhere else in the world—if not for these, the British would never have succeeded in arresting even one man, unless by chance.

How did they come to me?

Perhaps a few people surprised at the style and level of *Hehazit* tried guessing aloud, in "discreet" places like Café Sderot or the health clinic, the editor's identity. They did not, Heaven forbid, mention any names, but they did specify characteristics: a teacher at the Gymnasium, a Betari, a writer for *Hamashkif*, a recent immigrant . . . even if they added in a whisper: Israel Sch . . . surely they would never have revealed the secret.

A second possible explanation: One of the students whom I taught at night told me that Dr. Saul Levin, director of the night courses, had warned him and some others to be wary of me as I was recruiting students for Lehi. This was a lie. I did not recruit students for Lehi, and as usual in such cases I confronted him and asked for his evidence: "On what basis do you utter this nonsense?" Answer: "Dr. Benjamin Lubotzky speaks of it openly."

A third possible explanation: A few months before my arrest, Israel Epstein excitedly told me that the following brief notice had appeared in a secret IZL bulletin: "Dr. Saul Levin is spreading rumors that Dr. Scheib belongs to the faction, but he denies it."

I happen to know who passed the information to the IZL Intelligence Service, but he certainly never imagined they would publish it. He himself was only fulfilling the "obligation" to gossip. To this day, though, the reason for publishing the item remains unclear to me. I complained at one meeting, and Menachem mumbled that it really is an internal bulletin, which "only" several dozen people read. (I, of course, have added the quotation marks around "only.") True, the item did state that I denied the rumor, but perhaps the police did not place too much faith in my denial.

I do not know which of the explanations is correct. Perhaps the fourth, the one I have not considered because I have not thought of it, is the correct one. I am certain, however, that I was not on the list Chilevitz turned in, since he turned in only "his" people, of the IZL; but Chilevitz was a *schlemiel* and others operated more delicately and successfully where he did not.[53] In any case, why have I offered the readers all these possibilities? So they should read and know and learn and be prepared. What did our mothers in the Diaspora say when they bought medicine? "Oif nisht tsum badarfen" (So that we won't need it). I am not warning of informers, that would be superfluous, but rather of the idiocy of chattering, even if one's intention is only to chatter.

Three days prior to what I said would be my final day of work, I was punished for my war crime, during a seventh-grade class on the book of Job. (Teachers, speak up on my behalf! How could I not finish teaching the book of Job? Could I stop at Elihu and omit the mighty conclusion with God's speech from the whirlwind? Be character witnesses for me!)

I was writing on the blackboard. The principal opened the door and called me. He was very pale and said: "They have come . . . from . . . from the police and are asking about you."

"Yes? One minute, Dr. Levinson."

He did not understand what I was doing. But I understood. I crossed to the eighth-grade classroom opposite us, entered in the middle of the lesson, approached the window and scanned the street for guards. Seeing none, I decided at that moment to escape. I returned to my class, where Dr. Levinson was still standing at the door. I asked one of the students to carry my briefcase to my home (incidentally, this was a second war crime. In the briefcase were manuscripts of articles and translations submitted for publication in *Hehazit*). To Dr. Levinson I said: Tell my wife.

And I went downstairs.

So began a comedy of little errors within the big error of coming to work. While descending, I glanced into the administration offices. The door was open, and this led me astray. Four gentlemen sat inside. That these fools would pay no attention to someone descending the stairs never occurred to me. But the truth is they paid no attention, they continued sitting and waiting for the principal to come in, arm in arm with me, as if I were to receive three month's salary. But I did not know this. I was sure they had seen me and were on my tail, so I ran to the street. Another error: Student vandals used to make holes in the barbed wire fence between our yard and the yards of the neighboring homes. More than once I thought to myself, a time will come when I will use these holes to get out of here. Now, the only holes were in my head. I forgot.

I crossed from Rehov Mapu through an empty lot to Rehov Hayarkon. I fell once. I ran into a building at the corner of Frishman and Hayarkon Streets, climbed to the top floor and rang the bell of an apartment in which one of my private students lived. The gross error was in running. The "New High School" was located nearby and the youths were outside. When my principal reached his office and the detectives realized I had fled, they ran after me. At the corner they would undoubtedly have despaired of finding me, but they were helped by the youths—they claimed they were chasing a thief and the young students pointed straight at the building into which I had run.

In the apartment I spoke frankly: The police are searching for me. Let me hide. My student panicked but let me in. There was not much time for conversation. A loud ring told us they were right behind me. Cold logic ceased functioning; only stubborn will remained. Get out, get out, get out. By now the question was one of prestige:

I had been warned. I have sinned against the Underground. I am a criminal, a simpleton. Get out! I entered the bathroom, scrambled to the window, grabbed the outside pipe and began my descent.

An important biographical note: During my student days I had cut, chronically, my physical education classes. The physical education teacher in Lvov would not have recognized me. Though he never used pipes for exercising, he might have nonetheless made my hands a bit more agile, had I not avoided him.

And a second note, of some ironic consolation: Later, while I was in Latrun, our school's physical education instructor Zvi Even-Zahav was arrested and interned there. I laughed at him: I, a teacher of literature, am arrested climbing down a pipe. You, a teacher of exercise, are arrested prosaically in bed.

Back to the pipe. The papers reported that I jumped. Had I, I would most certainly have been killed and my glasses would certainly have been broken. Instead, I climbed down the pipe and for some reason still unbeknownst to me, and at some time still unbeknownst to me, I was separated from the pipe and fell. And because I had not jumped, I descended in a standing position and landed as if sitting down, thereby injuring the base of my spine . . . and my glasses remained on the bridge of my nose as if the whole matter were no concern of theirs.

And I have already related that I saw my Momma and Poppa in that instant, when I was between heaven and earth.

I awoke in a small bathroom, as I was being undressed by a doctor or nurse. I asked: "Where am I?"

"Everything is all right, everything is all right."

"I didn't ask if it's all right. I asked where am I, among Jews?"

"Yes, in Hadassah Hospital."

"The police are here?"

"Yes, they are. Don't worry, everything is all right."

For him it is "all right." He has a serious problem, though.

"Listen, you see," he says, pointing to my hand, "you are missing your watch."

"What watch?"

"Your watch."

"What do I care about my watch now?"

"But I must list it. You understand."

"Fine. List whatever you want."

But something strange had happened to the watch, which had been in a leather case. The case remained, the watch was gone. I did not know how, but I knew why, to teach me: Man, from now on, you are beyond Time.

My right side was swollen below, and hurt.

I was taken to the ward and given the next-to-last bed. A policeman immediately entered and stood in the passage in the center of the room. From then until they moved me from Hadassah, I was assigned not one, but a full complement of police: two inside and three in the corridor. At first, though, there was just this one, an interesting Jewish chap. Afterward, they were all goyim.

He approached, leaned over and whispered in Hebrew: "Listen, you want to send any messages?"

"No need. The school will tell my wife."

"No . . . I mean to the comrades . . . ."

Ha! They must think I left my brain with the seventh grade or somewhere on the pipe.

"No. Go in peace."

He stayed another ten minutes, for appearance's sake. Then he disappeared, never to be seen again. Too bad I have such a poor memory for faces; otherwise, I would look for him today. Who knows how high a rank he now holds.

My wife burst in, breaking all rules and against all prohibitions. She wanted to see if I were at least alive. She was crying: "Why did you do it? Why did you run? You panicked, right? For you had no reason to run."

She is very practical, Batya. She is preparing an alibi.

They did not allow us to talk. She managed only to hint that there was one nurse on whom I could rely. I told this nurse to take from my pocket the keys to the apartment in which I had been sleeping, and I asked her to give them to my wife. I was afraid the keys would lead to the apartment and its residents, my friends.

"Do you want to read a paper?" asked a neighbor.

"Yes, but I don't have my glasses."

"Your glasses are on the table."

After the surprise of being alive, and the surprise of being in Hadassah, this was definitely the most pleasant surprise possible. I am alive and reading a paper? Soon I will burst out laughing in front of the guards! Except that meanwhile I groaned, partly because I really hurt and partly because . . . I was advised to do so.

The riddle of Hadassah was quickly solved:

About an hour later, Police Commandant Ford and his entourage arrived, observed me and left. The nurse repeatedly fixed my bed and found an opportunity to whisper that which really interested me: Ford wants to have me moved immediately. But Professor Marcus is adamantly refusing them permission to touch me until after the examination and treatment.

Now matters were clear: When they found me in the yard they thought I was dead, or at least dying. Recalling several previous incidents in which they had been accused of murdering wounded prisoners in their hospital (Avraham Amper, for one), they decided to let me die in the Jewish hospital, Hadassah. As soon as I opened my eyes they regretted their decision. Justifiably, too, for my comrades had already made plans—one based on deception, one on force—to spirit me out of the hospital, though, in the end, time allowed for neither plan.

The next day my back was put in a cast three centimeters thick and I was taken to the operating room. Marcus refused to allow the guards to enter and they waited outside. The doctors were still whispering to me: People are fighting hard to keep you here.

That afternoon Ford came again and promised Marcus that I was being transferred to the Government Hospital in Jaffa, where he could visit me.

They put me in an ambulance and took me straight to the . . . Jerusalem Central Prison.

I was put on a stretcher and carried, carried, down once and down again, then turned around. I saw a row of cages, something like a zoo. A fat officer, his cap slipping off the back of his head, perspiring heavily, marched alongside my stretcher. Suddenly he said to someone in a cage: "Mr. Shmuelevitz, here is your friend."

Aha!

They tried putting me in one of the tiny solitary-confinement cages but could not fit a bed inside. By then I realized that this was one of Prison Warden Clough's games. He knew I would not be put in solitary confinement, and a bed had already been prepared in the room called the infirmary; but this was all part of his show.

Again I was lifted, turned around, up and then down again.

Mazal tov. I am in an infirmary bed in the Jerusalem Central Prison. And to be completely sure that I would not run away the warden ordered my leg chained to the bed . . . .

The room seemed nice, bright and clean.

An hour later, I discovered that cleanliness was the responsibility of the Arabs in the cell next to mine. They were called "the syphilitics" after the various skin diseases they had.

I was in a shell within a shell . . . and one more "cast" story as long as I am on the subject, one that sheds light on the preceding as well as the following events, though the story's place in the order of events is unimportant.

One day I felt a tickle on my back, under the cast, which I attributed to sweat. I made a laughable but vain attempt to reach the spot and scratch or wipe it, but it was under the thickest and tightest part of the cast. A week passed and the tickle had become an acute pain made worse by every movement on my part.

To ask for the Arab in the white apron, who appeared occasionally and who was said to be a doctor, would have been pointless; he would only have given me castor oil. By this time, I was lucky enough to have a private doctor, though I had to wait for his scheduled visits. He came accompanied by the entire retinue: the warden, his officers, the prison doctor, and the Jewish medic (Avraham, who was murdered by Arabs inside the prison a few years later). This council surrounded my bed. Dr. Troy ordered me to lie on my stomach and began searching for the itch. How? With his nose.

He put the tip of his nose to the cast and strolled around and around, up and down, all the while breathing deeply to the laughter of the spectators; and suddenly, the nose's journey ended and Troy began drilling. Half an hour later the drill reached my body. Troy widened the hole to one centimeter; and on that exact spot was a wound, already oozing pus, the result of the cast having rubbed against the flesh. A little while longer and it would have become infected . . . .

Dr. Troy hummed from underneath his expert nose. A little ointment, some cotton . . . just like any external wound.

Infection was avoided.

I am not fond of allegory. And that is the reason I am not fond of the book of Ezekiel, with its many allegories. The world is rich enough in proverbial truth, there is no need to invent artificial proverbs. One only has to know how to read this world, there is no need to invent a new alphabet. This is the same reason I do not care for Bialik's "Scroll of Fire." He said more about the Diaspora in his "My Father" than in all the allegorical constructions of "Scroll of Fire."

But sometimes pus accumulates even within the closed-cast framework of a movement. And blessed is the movement that has a faithful doctor sniffing out the trouble spot. I was fortunate enough to have a chisel; I could have drilled and cured, but I failed to smell the decay in the movement. Years later Uri Zvi pointed this out to me; he sensed it with his nose, but by then it was too late and surgery was the only option. As I said, this helped me understand many of the events of that period, in hindsight.

2. By Strength of Spirit

The months of my incarceration in the Jerusalem prison were most important and fateful for my body. The chaos inside was so complete that not even x-rays were able to make sense of things. My lower body, from the waist down, was black and blue that first month. The cast made for me at Hadassah in Tel Aviv was thick, concave and very restricting; that restrictive binding is most likely what saved me.

I received permission to hire a private doctor, partly as a result of Dr. Seligman's intercession; but more, I think, as a result of the Tel Aviv Doctors Association's angry protest over my having been removed from a hospital against the recommendation of the examining doctor and having been moved, to compound matters, not to the promised hospital but to a prison. As the supporters of Britain amongst us used to say: The English are "nevertheless." Yes, they were nevertheless . . . better than the Nazis. Some compliment! They were especially sensitive about religion and about medicine. Notwithstanding a few cases in which they allowed detained or arrested individuals to slowly die, there were also cases in which they did not allow people to die. I have already noted the futility of searching for a consistency governing their actions. Give them your bodies for their cannon, and your country's resources for their industry, and they will agree to cure you of the corns on your feet and will allow you to worship your God to your heart's content. Yes, the English are "nevertheless." And so Dr. Troy, a specialist in cases like mine, was allowed to visit and treat me. "Troy" translates to "faithful," and indeed he was. Thank you, Doctor!

The doctor diagnosed: a break in one of the spinal vertebrae, twenty-four breaks and cracks in the right hip. Final diagnosis: a miracle from Heaven.

That is what the doctor said about my body.

As for my spirit, those first months in the Jerusalem Central Prison:

A concentration of all my spiritual energies in the will to war and its joy. A soaring of emotion and imagination and logic and memory and twenty-four internal forces to counter the twenty-four physical breaks. Final diagnosis: strength from Heaven. Perhaps the same strength Jacob possessed as he dreamed of the ladder. He, the dreamer, a wretched pauper, sleeping on a stone, hunted and persecuted. Dreaming of a ladder set in the ground, its top in heaven, angels climbing and descending, and the Promise, the fabulous promise of the land that will be, that already is, his.

I lay on a parcel of land no wider than his, though he enjoyed freedom of movement while I was chained. But I, too, had my good angels with me. The boys of Cell 18, the "Sternist Room" to which I was only later transferred, came and went by means of various reasons and ruses. And what were Jacob's angels compared to these?

The boys of Israel, already "sitting" twenty, thirty, forty months in prison, their clothes brown and turbid, black caps—the sign of life sentences—on their heads. Sitting among the scum of Arab society. And guarded by the literal vomit of London, criminals pardoned on condition they would serve in the colonies. Strong boys, eating hummus (ground chickpeas) three times a day and disgusting lentil soup, boys brimming with unreleased energy, while the whistling of other boys walking in the street outside wafts in from beyond the barred windows. And voices of women (did the Jewish sage who decreed "A woman's voice is her nakedness" sit in jail?), light and merry. And Joshua, Joshua Zetler, the most macho of them all, suffers most when he hears the sounds of young children, little kids crying, laughing, talking.[54] And Eliahu Amikam sits, too. He speaks ten European languages but prefers Bengali. He is being yelled at by a British officer who does not understand when he, Eliahu, in a playful mood, speaks English with a Scottish or Welsh accent. And now Eliahu intends to study Sanskrit. He is also unequaled in his use of obscenities. Eliahu's obscenities could stand in the Holy Sanctuary itself. Some men speak simple words which sound obscene; Eliahu speaks in obscenities which sound like melodic, soft, silky music. I detest obscenity, but his never sounds discordant, not once. And Joshua Becker sits—only generations of breeding and modesty could bring forth one so tender and gentle. And Moshe Svorai, who stole the birthright from me, to be the first teacher of Israel and rebel and prisoner. And worse than the suffering imposed by the chains and walls is the guilt he imposes on himself, a guilt no one else lays on him, only he, because Yair was murdered while hiding in Svorai's apartment.

So they sit, men of great spirit, in this suffocating cell; and so they will sit for years. And they are the most powerful room in the prison, and perhaps there is not a room more powerful in the entire land, including the room of the High Commissioner, who commands armies here, and including the room of the Jewish Agency chairman, who commands budgets.

And there is one more who, if I were given the blues and colors of Marc Chagall, I would paint as he enters—not through the gate, but straight in: The walls part, step aside, move to his left and his right as he enters between them, wrapped in blue as if he comes straight from heaven, and he is a body, flesh and blood graced by beard and earlocks. And he is short, with human legs and no wings, but when he shakes my hand I sail off on the waves of precious warmth imparted by his caress, as a boat caressed by a calm sea. This must be the way people enter Paradise.

And when I see them, our boys, and him, our Rebbe, Rabbi Arye Levin, I laugh at the sight of the bars, the walls, the Arab murderers and rapists, the British "bulldogs" with rods in their hands and infinite idiocy in their eyes. Who are they? Who are they? Who are they and who are we?

Once there were among the Jews *Matmidim*, perseverant ones, who studied Torah eighteen hours every day. Who are the perseverant and what is their strength alongside the strength of the boys in Cell 18? These boys were the first to follow Yair Stern—they were the first brought in here. Not for six years, but for life imprisonment. Not for eighteen hours a day, but for twenty-four hours a day, and not to sit among Torah scrolls and sages and worshipers but rather among the filth of Arabia and the filth of London. Often without any contact with the outside, without news. This is the worst suffering of all. The feeling that they have been forgotten. Only one joy, one consolation, is known: There is a continuation; there is a reason for their sitting here years upon years. A reason.

In all my life I was never as free and strong as during those first months of prison. My bones were shattered, my body in a cast, my entire self in a prison basement under heavy guard. And just one week after my arrival I am already able to dictate to Anshel Spielman or Becker or someone else the articles for *Hehazit*. The first article to emerge from my shell within a shell is "Expressionism and Impressionism in Hebrew Policy," one of the best pieces I have ever written. All my life I will be proud of my activities during these months. I drew strength from the strength of those prisoners in Cell 18, those who laid the foundation of the movement to free Israel, and from the fingers and eyes of Reb Arye Levin. Perhaps I was also strengthened by the miracle which passed over my body, by the triumph of life over death, and perhaps also by the feeling that as of then I was entirely within the ranks of the fighters, no longer was my body divided between day and night, between a private and a fighter's life.

With these great strengths given me by Heaven and earth, I prepared for the Lehi trials.

Four of our men were awaiting trials for possession of weapons: Zvi Tavori, David Hameiri, Anshel Spielman, Matityahu Shmuelevitz. Until then, the Underground approached British trials by denying everything and trying with the help of good lawyers to avoid harsh sentences, or at least to get those sentences reduced. Members of the IZL and the Hagana followed the same approach, though the latter added a touch of their own, or a touch of Shalom Aleichem: First of all, "The accused had no weapons." Secondly, "The weapons were not intended to be used against anyone, their purpose is to defend settlements from Arab marauders, the weapons are 'pure' [well oiled?]" Thirdly, "Please have consideration for these quiet and loyal men of labor and reduce their punishment."

We decided to turn the tables. True, one gets no points for confessing to a British court, for there is more to heroism than sitting in prison. We needed fighters outside. But when a defendant had no possibility of acquittal (meaning in most cases), we chose a course of open warfare:

1. Appear without defense attorneys (we used them only at the beginning to determine legal points and provide an extra contact with the outside world).
2. Admit possessing the weapons.
3. Refuse to recognize the legal authority of the British court.
4. Exploit the platform of a courtroom to publicize Lehi's purpose and military path.

For this last was one of our weak points. Our message was not reaching the people. Our first stenciled proclamations were limited in number and difficult to read, the broadcasts weak and receivable only in a small area. The content of *Hehazit* was too heavy and the paper reached too few. The name "Sternists" was famous and feared, but the masses did not know what exactly we were.

Now we were being given an opportunity to struggle politically with the British and score propaganda points in our own community. And, of course, the educational value. The youth was accustomed to rallies against the government but had not yet realized that it is possible not to recognize this government, which is a "foreign government." The term may have appeared here and there, but our behavior at these trials was the first political act of a refusal to recognize the regime in the history of the modern Jewish community in the Land of Israel. Even the organized Jewish "illegal" immigration was only a breaking of one unjust law, but not yet a refusal to recognize the regime's very existence. This we did for the first time at the trials and, together with the manner in which we did it, this is why the trials had such an impact.

The veteran Lehi fighters were too happy to be jealous of these defendants, going where they had not. The IZL convicts were too jealous to be happy. And only the *Herut* newspaper outside actually managed to disassociate itself from our course.

My body is chained and my spirit is at the height of its ability. I do not think my spirit ever rejoiced, or will again rejoice, with the intensity it knew during that work with the boys on the speeches and declarations they were to deliver in court. They were all intelligent and knowledgeable fighters, but the platform obligated preparation and specific terminology, for on this platform words were to become spiritual, educational and informational weapons.

The "editorial board" worked like a chain. The "editors," the boys of Cell 18, took turns falling ill and being brought to the infirmary to lie in the bed adjacent to mine. I was as yet unable to sit or write, but with our spirit, our souls and minds and bodies became one. One fighter whatever his name is will not be assuming the poise of a proud, free, Hebrew fighter before the judges—all of us will be there. All of us—Cell 18, the defendants, myself—saw ourselves as one body in an a-personal act. This was a military operation of the highest order and I paid attention to each and every apostrophe. Had I been able to guess the judges' questions in advance, I would have prepared the defendants' answers, too—not because they were children unable to answer for themselves but because every military operation must be planned in advance to the last detail. Indeed, the accused proved at their trials that they were able to stand on their own two feet whenever they were momentarily surprised. Hisia Shapiro, whose prepared speech did not reach her in time, proved her ability to deliver a speech lacking perhaps rhetorical flashes, but with the same clarity and forcefulness as those speeches prepared by the "editors" of Cell 18.

In the summer of 5704 (1944), at more or less weekly intervals, the four trials were held that were a revolution in the stance of Jews facing British courts. The four speeches progressed logically, in accordance with the order of the trials and the seriousness of the charges. Zvi Tavori opened with a short but sensational announcement: He did not want a lawyer; he did not recognize the right of the court to judge him. The weapons he possessed were not illegal. He received the license to hold them from the only authority he recognized, the Lehi Command.

The judges, prosecution and Hebrew public were all surprised, but the event was not necessarily more than a curiosity. The method and principle were as yet indiscernible, the charge against Zvi was relatively light—a gun had been found in his apartment and he could have avoided the conviction, but then his landlord would have faced the charge—and Zvi was sentenced to "only" five years.

The second trial, against David Hameiri-Begin, the cousin of IZL Commander Menachem Begin, began one week later. He had been following a landlord, a member of Mapai, who had informed the British we were using his Rothschild Boulevard apartment. The previous night we had held a meeting of the Central Command there and noticed that the door to the adjacent apartment was so thin, our voices were surely audible in there. Or perhaps the landlord heard the typing, or wandered inside and found very revealing papers; in any case, he alerted the British, who waited outside and jumped Hisia Shapiro and Anshel Spielman as they entered, before either could draw a gun. We knew the landlord, a member of Mapai, was to blame, but did not know whether he had acted on his own—influenced, undoubtedly, by the incitement against us in the *Davar* newspaper[55]—or under instructions. The following day he was approached by David Hameiri and one other, who were invited to return for a conversation, and again he called the police. The boys got away, but David was stopped later on another street. He disposed of his gun while running but was caught.

David's declaration was lengthier, more reasoned. The press awoke, the method was clear. The sentence: seven years.

The suspense heightened at Anshel Spielman's trial, with the by-now expected opening: refusal to accept a lawyer, refusal to recognize the court's authority. But Spielman made more than an announcement; he delivered a speech, one that stemmed from the depths and heart of history. The motif was the tension between us, sons of the Hebrew race, sons of our father Abraham, owners of this land, and them, the strangers and foreigners here. The emphasis was on the antiquity of the Chosen People and our culture. The speech had its emotional moments, too, which we were told moved many to tears as they read it in synagogue or on newsstands. Hearts were moved, people shocked. This, of course, was our intention, not to influence the British judges. We left that task to the lawyers of the Jewish Agency and Hagana.

The sentence rose with the tension: ten years. And five years for Hisia Shapiro. The British had appended to her charge sheet a document describing, in French, the political principles of the Lehi movement fighting the British regime in the Middle East.

These events were nonetheless mere steps on the road to the summit, the appearance in court of Matityahu Shmuelevitz—the first opportunity afforded the Military Court to employ the Emergency Laws and their maximum sentence, death. This possibility, together with the dramatic circumstances of Matti's arrest—after a shootout on a public street—and also the suspense created by the preceding trials—ensured that this trial would be a focus of public and political interest. Naturally, attempts were made to dissuade Matti from following the lead of his predecessors, especially in light of the possible death sentence. He—or more correctly, we, since from the first trial until after Matti's sentence was eventually reduced, no one did anything without consultations and joint planning—rejected these attempts.

This fourth speech was purely political. In laying the groundwork, we had called to the stand "big" witnesses (the High Commissioner, for instance) who would almost certainly not appear. For the first time, we had taken the initiative from the British, and we permitted ourselves the luxury of playing with them. Shmuelevitz thus played games with his identity, making a laughing stock of the British police with their officers and experts, and he played with the distinguished judges in calling witnesses. He, Shmuelevitz, was master in the courtroom and not the British.

And more importantly, he and his words won the hearts of the people. We were behind thick walls, but even we felt the waves of support from outside. The Jewish prison guards now stood up to their British superiors and, despite the danger, freely expressed warmth toward us. Not even the Hagana prisoners could contain their feelings, though they had been ordered to do so by an internal Hagana letter distributed to lessen the effects of the trials, as well as by Dr. Zakai's column in *Davar*, in which he explained *Davar*'s refusal to publish the full texts of the speeches. But this was the first time the Hagana prisoners felt inferior to us. The IZL fighters later followed our lead, sharing in the reawakened fighting spirit and heritage. The Hagana kept till the end its ridiculous policy of haggling with the hostile and imperialist regime over charges and legal paragraphs and evidence. They never lifted themselves up, and they would have remained forever consumed by an inferiority complex had we not freed them ourselves, but this will be mourned in the pages ahead. Matityahu Shmuelevitz, at this point, took from the Hagana cell no more than one suit, to better his external appearance. And even this he returned two days later, for he had by then received from the British a finer suit: the red uniform of those condemned to die.

We are to this day bereft of great Hebrew music. Hebrew composers are still romancing the Kinneret and the Emek (the Sea of Galilee and the Jezreel Valley). Hebrew music today lacks mountains. Even the songs and music about Jerusalem are no more than soft sentimentality, in stark contrast to the character of the city. Where is the Hebrew composer who will write the tremendous symphony, our *Eroica*, to be titled "Cell on Death Row"? Opening with the death row cell of Ben Yosef in Acco, then Shmuelevitz in Jerusalem, the two Eliahus—Hakim and Bet-Zuri—in Cairo, again to Acco: Dov Gruner, and then the awesome wonder in Jerusalem: Feinstein and Barazani.[56] And from cell to cell, from condemned to condemned: The sky-blue image of Reb Arye Levin whose one eye weeps and pleads: Sign the request for mercy, sign! and whose second eye glistens with proud fire over the sheer power of this willing martyrdom. And from cell to cell and man to man and heart to heart, through all the arteries of spilled blood and unspilled blood, the *Hatikva* anthem is sung, cleaving cells, walls, pealing as a mighty bell, and blasting the enemy no less than bombs, no less.

Will this composer step forth in our generation? Or perhaps this great song will not surge because no free souls stir among us?

Shmuelevitz's bearing in his death cell recalled his bearing before the judges. He accepted the news that his sentence was to be commuted in as dignified a manner as he had accepted his death sentence.

Thus, our military operation had afforded a complete success and no loss of life. The name Lehi had been emblazoned across the country's skies and youth, just as three-quarters of a year later it would receive world-wide attention during the Moyne trial in Cairo. For any normal people, a series of trials like these would have been enough to bring the youth to the barricades for freedom. I have given much thought to the question: Why were the waves of admiration and enthusiasm which resulted from the trials not exploited organizationally? Was there a lack of ability to exploit the support of the masses? Or is the problem deeper? Perhaps Jabotinsky's description of the distinction made by the Jewish people between *stimmung* and *abstimmung*, their mood and their vote, is still valid. And even greater is the gap between "mood" and "revolutionary activity."

If the history of the War for Hebrew Liberation is written honestly, then the trials of the summer of 5704 will be valued highly not only because of the broad awakening they brought, but also because of the political act they were: The first declaration on an official, public platform that the British regime was a foreign and illegal regime, that British arms in this country were illegal arms, while the Hebrews are the sole legal owners of the land and independent Hebrew arms the only legal arms in the country. And because they are the foreigners and their arms are those of invaders and we are the owners and our arms are legal, therefore our weapons need not be purely defensive. On the contrary: Their task and legality lie in their being arms that attack, fight and subdue the foreigner's arms.

This was the logical, legal, military and educational message of the trials, and this will be the basis for assessing their place in the annals of our War of Liberation.

3. *Tikun Lel Shavuoth*: The Eve of the Feast of Weeks

In honor of Shavuoth (the Feast of Weeks) I was for the first time moved, for the holiday meal, from the infirmary to the other end of the prison. I was moved to a room that during the week held criminals but that was converted to a synagogue on Sabbaths and holidays.

I was carried on a stretcher and laid at the head of the table, here where everybody "sits" in prison and I "sit" and lie flat.

The holiday dinner was for members of the IZL and Lehi. The Hagana men celebrated in their own room, not because they doubted that our food was kosher, no, but they felt comfortable only when they were in the majority. Anyway, our tables bore no resemblance to theirs. The prison's one Jewish kitchen was, of course, the same; but the compotes sent by Histadrut industries outside went no further than their cells. They would never have considered sharing their treats at our joint, "cooperative" table. Prison is unpleasant under the best of circumstances. But when most of the Hagana men received pardons in honor of King George's birthday, not one left prison with rheumatism or ulcers, as the IZL and Lehi men later would. Rheumatism from sleeping on floors, ulcers from hummus and lentils. I no longer recall when, but I once wrote: How does one enter prison? A Lehi member enters his cell and looks immediately at the walls, for a spot to begin digging a hole for a tunnel. So, too, does a Hagana member look immediately at the walls. He, too, searches for a spot to dig a hole. A hole for pegs. Pegs to support shelves and boxes. Boxes to store the food he receives every day in plenty, shelves for the books published by the "Workers' Library" and the "Working Nation" and other Histadrut presses.

To tell the truth, they did read a lot, the Hagana inmates. Much more than our IZL and Lehi men. But they had publishing houses and the Nationalist Movement did not. Classical nationalists were not lacking: Herzl, Nordau, Jabotinsky, Uri Zvi Greenberg. But in prison, reading the classics was not enough. We needed and read different material. We devoured translations of books about the revolutions and wars for freedom of other nations. These books were a substitute for the war the prisoners wanted so much to be fighting. There was also the Underground literature which managed to find a pipeline into the prison. The mind of an Underground man was able to focus only with great difficulty on a side issue or an inconsequential matter, unlike the mind of a Hagana man lying comfortably on a bed, in peace and on a full stomach. Outside, the farms and establishment institutions cared for him. His brothers were not going out night after night on attacks; they were not hunted. Only occasionally was there a search for arms, an arrest, a trial, and again a six-month or one-year idyll. The mind of a Hagana member was more open to a wider range of literature. He began to feel a bit nervous only once a year, as that great day approached, the birthday of King George . . . and obviously he did not bother himself with plans to escape. Never! Today the Labor papers *Davar* and *Al Hamishmar* heap praise on the Hagana heroes portrayed in the movies. But a historian will search the history of the British prisons in vain for even one escape by Hagana members. On the contrary: All our prison escapees can attest to the open tunnels and open gates that Hagana members refused to use; they would not enter without a "certificate" from his highness the High Commissioner.

No. The minds of Hagana members were not occupied with the fever of the war outside or with the burning desire to escape from inside, and therefore they really were more intellectual than we. They read much while we lay on the ground in our dark cells ("preferred treatment," the right to sleep on a bed, was granted automatically to all Hagana members), while we were either digging a tunnel or planning one and checking the details a thousand times. Our men were not released by the grace of any king, our men trembled in their impatience to break out and join those who were blowing up British installations, those who were sanctifying blood.

The "arguments" in the prison courtyard highlighted the contrast between our relating to an idea and their relating to books. Most of our men reacted appropriately to every political, economic and military occurrence outside, while even the best of the Hagana stammered. When were they firm? After they had received the internal Hagana propaganda. A telltale sign in jail was a Hagana member who approached someone with sure steps and a bright face and who began to speak with confidence; this meant that the Hagana's propaganda had reached his cell half an hour earlier, with explanatory material about this or that event. There were some among them whose insides had not completely rotted away, whose core was still good, and these occasionally reacted instinctively, healthily, logically, patriotically. Their stammering came the following day, after they read *Davar* and understood that "things are not so simple."

The synagogue, like the courtyard and corridor, was also cooperative. The gentlemen of the Hagana came to pray, too, out of respect for Reb Arye Levin. Reichlin enjoys leading the congregation, he trills well. Lehi members originally held a monopoly on the position of beadle: Moshe Svorai and Michael Ben Yosef were the *gabayim*, or beadles. Reb Arye Levin, as is well known, treated all suffering Jews with love. He loved the Hagana members and the criminals. Yet his special love for the most zealous, those who suffered most, was no secret. We did not use him too often to contact the Underground, so as not to endanger him. We had other channels, but if the matter were urgent, or if the channel were closed, then Reb Arye was our contact. And if Reb Arye told us time and again that he envied us because we were suffering for the sanctification of God's name, then he was believed. But know this: He did not tell us the entire truth. The truth is that he envied not only the suffering but the fighters, and if one looked deeply into the rabbi's eyes he saw their great sorrow after the failure of the attack on the High Commissioner, and the sparkle of their great happiness whenever the hand of Israel overpowered the Amalekite enemy. He did not always say these things but he could not conceal them; they burst from within his body, through his good, burning eyes or his warm handshake.

On Shavuoth we knew: He will again be with us, and again and again he will move us, for the twentieth and fiftieth and one hundredth time, when he speaks: "And I will avenge the blood that has not been avenged," and we will repeat the prayer after him, in warmth and joy and love, for our boys outside are meanwhile avenging our blood.

Shavuoth was the first time I was together with all our men, the men of the IZL and Lehi, at one table. Had I ever in my life been so fortunate? Had I ever been so honored, to lie at the head of a table around which were sitting the lions of Israel, the mighty in strength and in love? Here was good Shimon Amrani of the IZL, who had been captured inside the detectives' headquarters (the Criminal Investigations Department of the British Police, or CID) when it was going to be blown up; and he had been tortured and had remained silent. His bones were broken while he sang *Hatikva*. Here he was, singing at the table. He sang: "What can you do / what can you do / that I am so beautiful / and like me there are none / from the sea to the River Jordan." The next day, on the holiday, all the girls from Kerem Hatemanim came to visit him, and he smiled at them all and remained silent out of modesty, his modesty in love, in war, and through torture. All this with such holy simplicity. When I later heard that he fell in the Acco Prison breakout, I began singing, without even thinking, and of course without his Yemenite grace: "Nu, what can you do, what can you do, that I am so beautiful. . . ."

That you are so beautiful, that you were all so beautiful down in that basement, in the deepest cell of the Jerusalem Central Prison.

In Jerusalem.

And I had the happiness, the honor, the privilege to lie at the head of that table of heroes. We had wine and we sang, the blood in our veins sang.

And another surprise was in store for me. The old-timers had kept a silver spoon. When they gave me the soup they gave me the spoon, too, and told me: This is Uri Zvi Greenberg's spoon, which had been sent him when he was a prisoner here.

Uri Zvi Greenberg was an occasional subject of discussion. No one cast aspersions on his poetry, of course. Had we weapons as strong, the war would have been won long before. The argument revolved around the person. Even amongst the admirers of his writing, some drew a line between Uri Zvi the poet, the prophet, and Uri Zvi the man. Especially in prison or in the detention camp, a complaint was voiced: Where has he gone? Why does he not say now, and loudly, that which needs to be said—even if this means arrest and jail? His place is in prison.

I was of a different opinion. In *Hehazit*, I went so far as to say that Uri Zvi's current views are of no interest. Once the Torah was revealed to us on Mt. Sinai, we no longer have need of Heaven's speech. We feed on Uri Zvi's poetry, which remains valid even if he thinks otherwise.

I wrote that, though I knew that he did not think otherwise, and he very much wanted his poetry to have its effect. I stopped visiting him when *Hehazit* began appearing, afterward meeting only Dr. Y. H. Yevin in the editorial offices of *Haboker*; but I had by then gleaned enough from Uri Zvi to understand him. I nonetheless wrote as I did in order to protect him from arrest, for I knew his physical sensitivity to hunger and suffering and I saw no purpose in having him wasting away in prison. And in terms of suffering, his brief encounter with prison must be regarded in the same light as all his experiences. For this was his strength—the intensity of every feeling. If another mortal needed great amounts of time to grasp something, he needed but one moment, after which it was embedded in his sensitive soul. If I needed to read a long article or book in its entirety, he needed to read but one line, and already he knew all there was to know, understood that which I understood only from the whole. He was the same with people. He learned from a detail, a movement of the hand, a variation of the voice, that which others learned from many experiences.

Those who measured Uri Zvi by their own proportions may have had difficulty understanding him. I learned to measure differently.

He was there outside, in a meager room on Rehov Yehuda Halevi, he was running about encaged and alone, more encaged than we, more alone than we, and I only wished that I could have sent him some of the joy that was in my soul at that holiday party with those boys in prison.

The Heights of the Ayalon Valley

1. From the Pit of Prison to the Expanse of Latrun

I was learning.

Learning to walk. From bed to door. Six or seven meters. Three times, then five, six. I was not doing so badly.

I was as yet unable to walk outside for visits; they carried me on a stretcher. From the other side of thick bars my one-and-a-half-year-old daughter pushed her fingers toward me; she was full of wonder. Batya spoke of her many efforts to free me; she had even spoken to the Zionist leader Judah Leb Magnes. She claimed, everywhere she went, that I had been unjustly accused. She was not pleased to see me out of bed, thinking my chances for release were better the sicker I appeared. She was able to say all these things to me because during our conversation we were watched by a Jewish sergeant who was . . . my cousin. To avoid causing her grief, I did not tell her that her promises were baseless, that I had entered a lion's den, Cell 18, the Lehi Room, and the naive entered not therein. She deluded herself. And yet . . . she was not deluded. She had decided to resume her work, social work, and our daughter was taking her first steps into life, to the doctor and to the nursery.

I was unable to pretend to be simple or ignorant or even sicker than I was. I rejoiced over every new movement I was able to make. My joy of life was stronger than my desire to deceive the English. I felt good in all respects. I was learning to walk.

And I was learning more. Learning to know people. Nothing is quite like a prison for getting to know people. Men cannot don disguises there. You are with people twenty-four hours a day, bodies and spirits crowded together. A man relieves himself in front of you. You see him in his ups and downs. Now he is a saint, an "overman," a hero, and now a pig, brutish and petty. And you learn to know yourself, too. You never completely know yourself, what positive or negative traits you will display in special circumstances. Loving your neighbors is easy when you have the choice outside of being with or away from them. But try maintaining this love when you are chained to them, your cellmates, when you cannot be by yourself for even one minute. Chattering about equal suffering is easy, while one is swallowing the good, special food sent every day by one's family, the chicken soup and pancakes and meat, while a friend two feet away is for the third time that day, and for the ten-thousandth time in all, chewing his disgusting lentil soup. I was learning a lot in prison.

I was also learning to get to know our "neighbors." This was my first close contact with Arabs. I met the aristocratic Sheikh Abu Chaled, sentenced in connection with the marauding Arab gangs, graced with a fine blackish beard, dressed to perfection, who considers himself a friend of Judah Leb Schneerson and . . . Haj Amin el Husseini. Every morning he brewed me some Turkish coffee, sat eastern style on the bed next to mine, and talked "bolitics." Every morning the same tune: We Arabs and you Jews of *Jama'a Stern* (the Stern Gang) must unite to expel the Englizi and afterward we will work things out between us, in peace or in war—but today we have the same enemy.

And in contrast, there was one Arab whose name I have forgotten, half intelligent, supposed to have been a medic, in charge of the infirmary, polished, chubby, and his greatest pleasure was in torturing the old, sick Arabs. And "torturing" means real torture. He dragged them from their beds and forced them to dance naked to the glee of the other Arabs.

The rest—criminals or political, in either case, rapists and murderers. And endless informing on each other, for every smuggled cigarette, for hashish, so as to merit the approval of the Englishman with the stick in his hand.

I learned to admire the tolerance and suffering of the boys who had lived four and five years with such Arab filth.

By this time life was easier. Reinforcements were arriving, but years had passed in a vacuum, in darkness. Nothing. Nothing. To have sat in that moldy pit and not to have known: Is something left outside? Is there reason for this suffering? By this time life was better, there were many "holidays." One night the entire prison building shook, we heard windows breaking in the city. The guys woke up and calls of "happy holiday!" rang from cell to cell. We did not yet know what had happened. We did not yet know who had done it. Each of the two undergrounds assumed the operation was theirs. The following day we knew: The offices of the secret police on Rehov Mamillah were blown up. An IZL operation. For the Irgunists, a double holiday. But our boys were happy, too. Jealous and joyous. Heads were held high, faces beamed straight into the faces of British officers who appeared to be dazed or sleepwalking. "Happy holiday, happy holiday" echoed through the prison halls.

Soon after, an operation of ours. We knew that Michael had been in the city for several months already, planning the operation against MacMichael, greatest of our foes, deserving of death eight times over. Then the news: failure. The attack did not succeed. The rabbi came that Sabbath and the pain was audible as he said: "The 'object' came through in peace." This had been our last chance. He left the country, the bastard. All that blood on his hands, and he was only scratched, only scratched.

Several days later we understood: The failure was only apparent, the attack itself was of great political value. Hitting the target is a matter of luck, but an operation is a link in the chain of war.

We considered, assessed: Was putting months of labor into one such operation, dependent on luck, worthwhile? Soon we received an answer from outside: Grasp the one and do not let go of the other. We adopted the methods of the IZL but we did not forget individual criminals.

On the great day of the Wilkins' hit I was already in Latrun. I have been told that the shots were heard clearly inside the prison and within ten minutes they knew who had been hit. Within ten minutes, Moshe Svorai was dancing in his cell over the elimination of the villain who had shot him while his hands had been raised, the man he, Svorai, had seen murder Amper and Jack while their hands had been raised. Anshel Spielman, working in the prison's carpentry shop, put together Wilkins' coffin. Eliahu Amikam prepared the tombstone; Eliezer Ben Ami engraved the name. All worked in high spirits. Thus should more fall!

The news reached me, as I said, in Latrun. I saw heavy Shmuelka running like a madman from the camp office, exclaiming: They hit Wilkins!!

After I had learned to walk, I became egotistical. Sitting in a basement in the Jerusalem Central Prison grated on me. I had not been convicted or sentenced. I pressed for transfer to the Latrun Camp, a place of detention for men not being tried.

I left Cell 18, that room forever and unceasingly planning escapes, which had already begun digging a tunnel in one corner, and I immediately decided: When the tunnel is ready I will do whatever I can to return and we will leave together. And of course, I took the solemn and holy oath that everyone takes and no one fulfills: To maintain constant contact, to write, write, write. They were so isolated, so surrounded. Every letter was like a gush of wind reviving their spirits.

I was transferred on September 1, 1944. I remember the date, because that morning's papers reported that the night before, an attack had been attempted on the Latrun Camp. When I arrived I discovered no such thing had occurred. Several weeks later we were to learn why the British had fabricated this imaginary news.

The shock of going from the Jerusalem Central Prison to the Latrun Detention Camp was far greater than going later from Latrun to freedom. Those of us who took this step went from darkness to great light, from suffocation to air. The journey was similar to leaving a besieged and degraded Jerusalem for noisy, light-headed Tel Aviv sunning itself at the seashore.

Two years earlier, Latrun had not been in the good shape I found it. Different conditions, different men; men who broke, outside or in. Petitioners for freedom, disaffected Lehi members; "neutral," they were called. Oh, those neutrals! As if neutrality is a possibility when the choice is to battle or not. At least the Betar and IZL members who originally opposed the war rose to the changing situation and joined the struggle, but there was no rise left in those neutrals. Many were among the men who had laid the foundations of the Irgun before the split and afterward, but by now they had become "living dead," just, ironically, as the war flared with a beauty that mesmerized the whole world. My heart went out to those "neutrals."

By the time I arrived, the cynicism and boredom of the neutrals and failures no longer set the tone. The pulse of the war beat at Latrun. Every time the country was shaken by another blow to one of the British fortresses, the following day would see the camp's gates open and new currents of blood flow in. They came week after week, sometimes day after day, by the dozens, the young with mother's milk on their lips, others with fuller bellies and beards. Waves upon waves. A third camp was opened to hold the daily additions.

An empire had been set up: The central Latrun Camp was the homeland, then new "colonies" were created. There were cafés, card games, chess. There were the problems involved in absorbing such large numbers, and hospitalization, and administration, and the competition between the various groups over key positions in the kitchen and in the communications section. Struggles for more rights, mail, visits, better food, a football field, books. The camp commander, his officers and guards were not to be envied. Who lived in constant fear—they or we? What had we to fear? As one wise Litvak once quipped: When I die and the angel asks: What is your name, what are your deeds?—I won't answer, not a word. What can he do to me? Will he kill me? I'll already be dead.

We were already locked up. But the camp commander and his guards trembled, day and night. By day—because of those inside. By night—because of those outside. True, those detained in Latrun were only "suspects" and when interrogated they feigned innocence and asked: Why am I here? What is my crime? But as they left the interrogation room their faces changed, the lambs became laughing wolves. Back in the camp they jokingly retold the innocent questions and innocent answers. Every man returned to his barracks and camp and movement, and his spirits were still brimming with the marvels of yesterday's operations, or the day before's, and his spirits were brimming with the desire and the hope to be back at the front tomorrow.

Three hundred innocent individuals when separate. Three hundred tons of explosives when united. How could the camp commander avoid trembling? Security was tightened daily. Another barbed wire fence, another watchtower, and with each fence and each tower their fear increased—and so did the plans for escape. Because there was an Underground in Latrun. Superficially, the camp appeared to be similar to communal life in Tel Aviv. There were forests and woodworks and steelworks and sports, elections, gossip, speeches, arguments. But there was also an Underground. In the late evening hours, one saw couples walking like shadows, circling, circling, or sitting in some comfortable, strategic corner. We knew: Do not approach! Do not listen! They are "working" on plans. Measuring meters from fence to fence. Observing, observing, observing.

Somewhere in one of the barracks a small group of Hagana detainees also spent the night, but they were unemployed, idle.

I met Arye Ben Eliezer and was anxious to hear of the new "Torah" being taught at Peter Bergson's "seminary" in America. Bergson's group, which did so much to publicize our war for liberation, this group, which found the way to open Jewish and non-Jewish hearts after thirty years of worthless "Zionist" efforts in the United States, this group suddenly invented an ideology which viewed the Hebrew nation and the Jewish nation as two separate entities. I did not grasp the point, and I needed two hours of "circling" with Arye Ben Eliezer to realize that this was no ideology after all, but only a tactic to gain the support of some assimilating American Jews who feared the specter of dual loyalty. I was not satisfied. One does not create "ideologies" or "Torahs" for such purposes. The Bergson Group's references to Ireland and Americans of Irish descent were unconvincing. Maybe the future will see a need to distinguish between the Hebrew nation in Eretz Israel and people of Hebrew descent in the Diaspora, but such a time had not (and has not) come. Not to distinguish between "Canaanites," "Hebrews," or "Jews." And today I might add: "Israelis." A mighty movement should draw in all of these, I argued, from the highest and most distant precipice down to the tiniest of factions in the Diaspora. A national liberation movement does not limit itself and its scope; it broadens its base and expands horizons.

Convincing Ben Eliezer was not difficult; he was not immersed in that "ideology." But from distant America to local worries: In our meeting outside, before our arrests, Ben Eliezer insisted that as he represented the American group, he was neutral regarding the split. The American group deliberately ignored the split when it occurred and continued to act as if we in Eretz Israel were united. They wanted to see us that way. I think the credit went to Ben Eliezer for arranging my first semi-official meeting with Menachem Begin on the roof of the Savoy Hotel, where Menachem oversimplified the problem a bit: "Return, wayward children. Return to the bosom of your parents. Return to the organization you left." In Latrun, Ben Eliezer was no longer neutral, he was an ardent IZL member. I told him we were speaking two different languages. The example I threw at him: MacMichael left the country, a new commissioner, Viscount Gort, arrived. The IZL published a proclamation welcoming him, with a "Midrash" appended: They welcomed him as a representative (*netsig*) not as a commissioner (*netsiv*). I proved to Ben Eliezer that this approach was based on the groundless, illusory "pressure theory," the hope that with the right pressure, England will be properly influenced. Add to this the Irgun's expression of sorrow over the death of a British officer—and the picture of the IZL's war becomes a little blurry. "You are still in diapers," I said. Nonetheless, the above was only our first conversation; we prepared ourselves to continue the discussion.

We prepared . . . .

Our boys were in no need of preparation. Most were in Latrun when the twenty escaped by tunnel, they were among those "sentenced" to remain behind (the barracks with the tunnel became "holy ground," the camp synagogue). They did not need to be taught the difference between representative and commissioner; they understood the meaning of war to the end with the British. They were, however, thirsty for knowledge, anxious to delve into our revolutionary thought. I was greeted enthusiastically and the intensive ideological educational work commenced. One sensitive issue was our relations with the IZL. Most of our boys had been arrested after the split, after those who followed Raziel and the IZL had surfaced and revealed themselves—for then it was obvious who was not among them, who had followed Yair, and these were arrested en masse. They had not forgotten.

I was preparing to diffuse their accumulated hatred when the first joint IZL-Lehi proclamation reached us from outside. One page, divided in half, two separate signatures, and slight differences of style. But a first step. The members of Lehi reacted with mixed feelings, the IZL members were happy. They had, after all, suffered for years from an inferiority complex as we, who stayed in the battle, really suffered. They knew the Lehi bitterness toward them was somewhat justified. Some admitted this; others hated us all the more. The joint proclamation caused a great stir in Latrun, many of the ranks longed to be united.

On the pages of *Hehazit*, I was still engaged in debate with Menachem Begin. In articles titled "Letters to a Friend," I responded to two questions he had once put to me: "Why do you declare war on British imperialism?" and "Why do you incite hatred?" The first was a political question, the second an emotional-psychological one. Regarding the war, I posit that the problem involved is not one of a "bad" British administration. This was Jabotinsky's mistake, too. The problem is rather one of a true conflict of interests. As for the hatred, it results directly from the knowledge that the British are an enemy, that they conspire to destroy us here, that they are, as the biblical Amalek, in our way. To hate them is a *mitzva*, a commandment. A year later, I no longer needed to explain to Menachem why to hate; by then the declarations and the deeds of the IZL were full of the hate that the enemy so deserved. And two years later, Menachem changed his views on the political question, too.

The debate notwithstanding, I, too, rejoiced over the joint proclamation. I received word from the Central Command of negotiations for a permanent coordination of operations. Our men were learning the art of sabotage from the IZL. The cooperation was going well.

We prepared . . . .

Life at Latrun stirred. Openly, in arguments, in "holiday" joy, in the joy of cooperation; at night, the plans for escape stirred.

We prepared . . . .

The number of detainees passed three hundred. Stirrings, stirrings, stirrings, day and night. In people's heads and in their hearts, and soon enough in their bodies, too. Stirrings, stirrings, stirrings.

2. From the Mouths of Babes You Shall Draw Strength

Introduction

I am embarrassed to tell the story of that early morning.

I am embarrassed that I was so shocked then, and that even today I have not been able to shake the shock. I am embarrassed because intellectually, I know the absurdity of being shocked by the removal of two hundred and fifty men from one detention camp and their subsequent transfer overseas, at a time when the fields of Poland are sown with the skeletons of hundreds of thousands of our brethren, and the ashes of Auschwitz are still warm, and the shoes of Jewish children are heaped into endless piles, having been taken from tiny feet before the children were gassed, burned.

I can invent a logical argument to prove our suffering here is as valuable as any other suffering. Here every victim is a volunteer, a fighter; there everything is forced. The blood spilled here is of a wounded, ravaging lion, while over there lies an ocean of blood of slaughtered sheep.

But logic loses its force, when confronted with the experience, the sense-experience of the event I am about to describe.

He who created man such that senses and emotions quicken the heart's beat more than logic—

He who created man such that he trembles when he hears a child crying at night yet reads with equanimity of a million people dying of hunger in China or India—

He who created man such that the number six means more to him than the number six million—

He will forgive me my shock.

*

Several strange things happened beforehand.

I have already mentioned the fake reports of the supposed "attack" on Latrun. A second strange occurrence involved Lehi member Eliezer Zurabin, by whom we regularly passed mail to the outside, using the good services of his mother, with whom he had the right to speak without being separated by bars. As always, he handed her a chocolate bar (Shmuelka was the manager of a Latrun "store" and we lacked for nothing. Every detainee had an account in the camp's office and made purchases against that account. Actually, we had cash, too, in the camp—everything but a stock market). The Arab officer in charge of the day's visits (he was substituting for the Jewish Shvilli, a friend of the Underground, and a special friend of the mothers, fathers and sisters who gave him a lira or half a lira, depending on the favor being granted: a special visit, a longer visit, and so forth. There was practically a set price list) was displeased with the chocolate bar and grabbed it, at which point it came apart and papers fell and fell.

Eliezer was immediately sent to solitary confinement but no one worried about that, we were all prepared to be sent there. At worst, he faced a transfer to Acco Prison after a disciplinary hearing. Most of the material discovered comprised articles I had written for *Hehazit*, which certainly saddened me, as only with great exertion am I able to write an article a second time, and even then I usually ruin it. A far more serious problem was that we included two alternative plans for a mass escape—in code, of course, a special code using numbers according to a key known only to three or four people—but this was cause for worry. Somebody says that in London, there are great experts who break every code, a respected division of Intelligence is devoted to such work. What, we wondered, will be?

The first surprise: Eliezer was released from solitary without trial, punishment or investigation. Why? One theory held that the clever Commandant Clough was looking out for himself, as he might be disciplined for allowing such open visits. So, the theory went, Clough worried first and foremost about the stars on his shoulders, and he must have hidden his "find" from Central Intelligence, he must have burned everything to maintain the calm.

The second surprise: Menachem Schiff, who long ago escaped through the tunnel, was arrested. People of his sort were ordinarily sent to the strictest kind of imprisonment: Acco. But Schiff was brought to Latrun. We were not pleased, as our theory held that he would undoubtedly be transferred to Acco along with others, and we all wondered if we would be among those transferred to Acco—the place feared by every prisoner and detainee in the country—or whether we would be lucky enough to remain in the paradise that was Latrun.

The stirrings in the camp increased. The Irgunists grumbled about the Zurabin affair, saying it endangered the entire camp. Again, new arrivals come by the dozens. A list given the British by the traitor Chilevitz. But why were young Betarim brought as well?

Night descended as usual, the packed cafés in the camp, the cards, chess, radios, songs. Around the barracks, people, always in couples, argued, split hairs. The lamb's eyes set with the sun, the eyes that glowed in the dark were the eyes of panthers. On the benches in front of the barracks sat groups of "newspapermen," not the hawkish *Hamashkif* reporter Dr. Yunichman or me, but the fourteen- or fifteen-year-olds who posted our Underground posters on the country's walls.

At 9 p.m., the Arab *nabatchim* (guards) made their rounds, knocking on the barracks to herald closing time.

The barracks were closed; one final head count. Prolonged laughter resounded from one barracks that night. Probably a "greenhorn" being initiated. All newcomers, according to the "law" of Latrun, were required to tell either three jokes no one had yet heard or about their first love. Everyone naturally chose the first option, and quickly learned it was not so easy. Just before the first punch line, someone would shout "Stop!" and complete the joke. Failure. With this crowd, finding three jokes no one had heard was no easy task. The newcomers grew tired, began sweating: Justice knows no mercy, no matter who the newcomer is. A rope has been tied to his bed—should he fail to satisfy the barracks, one pull suffices to collapse the bed. And so that night, another victim.

Slowly, even those voices grew silent. Darkness. At the end of each barracks, only the weak light of the bathroom stayed lit.

One who was unable to sleep (Did he have a visit that day? His wife? Child? Or was he expecting a visit the next day? Why the tossing and turning?) heard the calls of the night watchmen: "Halt! Who's there?" and the rustling footsteps of a dog, Clough's dog. Clough knows no rest at night. He granted the camp total freedom by day, even overlooking some illegalities, but he was possessed by one fear: escapes. Every escape has an impact on his rank. (Clough will one day gleefully tell detainee Shalom Levin of the Hagana: "Your friend Dr. Scheib has escaped and I hope I never see him again." Clough was overjoyed that I had not escaped from *his* camp or gotten past *his* guards.)

So Clough ran, gripped by fear, night after night, around and around the barbed wire fences. The many fences—electrified fences—and towers and searchlights sweeping back and forth were not enough. He awoke repeatedly, afraid. The camp contained three hundred zealous men and a plethora of plots, as proven by the previous escapes and the increase in Underground operations outside. Clough might well have wondered: What is going on in the dark now? Where is a tunnel being dug? From which corner are they crawling toward the fence? Might I not be blown up any moment in my own barracks, in an attack from outside?

Such were the fears (not all of them groundless) of the commandant, but their night had not arrived yet. Not yet. That night, too, would come. We always knew how to surprise them, how to find the fissures in their fortresses.

This night, however, is quiet. We did not even have a plan yet. The plans we had, had fallen into the enemy's hands.

This night is quiet, snorers snored, dreamers dreamed. Very quiet . . . .

Three hundred Benjamite wolves, Judean lion cubs who had not yet sunk their claws into the British body, Underground bears encaged for four years and those who had only yesterday commanded the attack and conquest of the Ramallah radio station, and the attack on the High Commissioner—now they were all asleep.

Silence in Latrun . . . .

And suddenly the silence was broken by knocking, banging.

"What is it? What is it?" A few awoke.

The shutters of every barracks were being closed from the outside and bolted.

What is it, what is it?

And those awake heard another sound:

Tum, tum, tum, tum.

Tum, tum, tum, tum.

The sound of a military march.

From the few cracks we saw an army marching row by row along the path, from the offices to the camp. By the light of their flashlights, we saw the shadows of their guns.

What is it, what is it?

The first theory, naturally, was: a search. Ever since the Zurabin affair, we had been waiting for one. The police conducted searches after all such occurrences and, in truth, we wondered why nothing had been done till now. And we had nothing to fear from a search we were expecting. The Bible commands: "Your camp shall be pure." Only the absolutely necessary—heavy cutting tools, a few pistols, and so forth—were hidden in special places. All the light material—Underground newspapers, mail and the like—was simply destroyed. So, a search? Let them search . . . .

But the army marched and marched. Why so large an army?

The second theory: Acco.

In the past, twenty or thirty men had occasionally been transferred to Acco. Not only for security or punishment, but also to deter. What detainee did not fear the name Acco? Even the inmates of the Jerusalem Central Prison were punished by being sent to Acco. During interrogations they were blackmailed: "If you don't talk you'll be sent to Acco . . . ."

Tum, tum, tum, tum.

Tum, tum, tum, tum.

The army marched endlessly, endlessly.

What time is it? Four . . . four thirty. All were awake, of course, and watching. Fates were sealed.

Every footstep—a fate.

Tum . . . tum . . . .

Someone in my barracks "joked": "Boys! They'll just line us up against the walls and shoot . . . ."

Laughter . . . and goose pimples.

The night paled, and by the pale light we saw:

The entire camp was surrounded by thousands of soldiers, tanks and armored vehicles. The soldiers were armed with Bren guns.

We were able to see the main road, filled with heads and vehicles.

The beating of three hundred hearts was almost audible. Everyone is taking his own stock: house . . . mother . . . father . . . wife . . . children . . . .

Suddenly the door of our barracks was broken open. Police and army officers entered, one after the other, higher and higher ranks. Colonels, brigadiers . . . .

Leading the pack: Clough.

My bed happened to be nearest the door. Clough kicked its side and ordered, curtly, in Hebrew: "Get up and get dressed."

(To this day I become agitated when I hear, "Get up and get dressed.")

Again, quiet. The officers spread across the barracks.

Twenty detainees dressed in silence. Soldiers with Brens stood at the door, and outside every window.

Clough held a list from which he called names. He looked at the list once more, approached my bed and said: "Sit."

My name had not been called.

Soldiers chained those who had been called, two by two. Nine chained couples left in silence. Only the chains rattled. Not a word. I looked at the faces I loved. One by one, one by one, my own flesh was being torn from me.

They left.

The doors were bolted after them.

If it were dark in the barracks, if it were at least dark . . . .

But the electric light had been turned on at the start, and daylight (it was now 5:00 or 5:30 a.m.) filtered in through the cracks.

And in that light, the picture was even more terrifying. Two men were left in the barracks: Plotkin and I.

Talking was impossible, our throats were choked, suffocating . . . and how embarrassing that I had been left behind. I felt not a bit of relief. Had they taken four or five from the twenty, I would probably have experienced a natural egotistical feeling: I remained. But there was no feeling of this sort now: What an embarrassing pain . . . they were all taken . . . taken . . . I do not know where . . . .That joke about "up against the wall" kept popping to the surface . . . .Why did they leave me behind, why did they leave me . . . ?

Two men in the barracks. A barracks that was so alive. The silence . . . the beds were still warm, the clothing scattered . . . they had not been allowed to take anything, to carry anything. Empty and silent beds. Even the beds were growing cold.

We ran from window to window searching for wider cracks, to see what was happening to these good people we loved so.

Some generous cracks, half a centimeter wide, afforded us a view:

They are walking, four in each row, chained in pairs. Only one, at the head of the line, is chained by himself. Who is it? Ah! Shmuelka Kaplan, the most senior, the old-timer, the first member of Lehi detained under the Emergency Laws. Father to three children. Good health, good spirits, good ideas. He is led out first.

For some reason, they feared he would give an order to resist. He was removed quickly, alone, in chains. Then came the pairs, the young and the veterans, according to the order of the barracks, but everyone, everyone. Even the "neutrals" who had done all sorts of things to convince the British that they had "finished," but to no avail. They, too. There was Yaacov Orenstein, one of the very first, in whom only the cynicism—toward everything, even himself—remained. And his opposite, Yaacov Poliakov ("Falach"), with a clear heart and a clear head, who refused to admit that he was finished, though he had given himself up when his wanted photo was published because, he said, of his mother, a widow . . . . He had tried to justify himself to me. A few days before, on the eve of Rosh Hashana, he got drunk and retained, of all his Lehi-ness, only his hatred for the mainline Revisionists. He ran from barracks to barracks, jumping on tables and shouting in the face of every Revisionist, Betari and Irgunist, with provocative scorn: Tel Hai, Tel Hai.

So they marched, one after the other, no distinctions being made, all those who once had some connection with the Nationalist Movement. There was not a single one of them who had not at some time been a student of Jabotinsky, even if between that time and this, he may have begun detesting the slogan "Tel Hai," or he may have not too long ago published the wanted poster of Yair in his newspaper. They went, their shirts clinging to their bodies, shaking in the morning chill, most wearing khaki shorts. They had not had time to comb their hair, they had gone straight from bed, straight outside into chains, and they walked and walked . . . .

An awful silence held everything, disturbed only by the rattle of the chains and the clatter of the many, many vehicles.

And suddenly the silence was shattered:

Suddenly song bursts forth.

Who is singing?

Those little newsmen, from Petach Tikva, Ramat Gan, Tel Aviv. Those fourteen- and fifteen-year-old children. They are wearing only undergarments. They are the Betar Youth, here only a few days. They are shattering the terrible silence of this march. A thunderous song:

> In blood and fire Judea fell
> In blood and fire Judea will rise.

They have saved the honor of this march, those precious ones. Only now does my throat clear, do tears stream from my eyes. Tears of pain and tears of joy. My heart grows wide, I want to march with them, these children who have put their elders, the commanders and leaders, to shame. Yes, sure it is easier for them, their bodies are more agile, less cumbersome; they do not carry on their shoulders the weight of wives and children. They know only Tomorrow, the battle. I no longer hear the chains or the vehicles. I hear only the blood pulsing in the veins of the singers.

> In blood and fire Judea fell
> In blood and fire Judea will rise.

And now I am sure, I feel the certainty in the suddenly warm blood of my veins:

She will rise, Judea, she will indeed rise.

So . . . why am I weeping?

3. Mud

The barracks' doors were opened about an hour after the prisoners were taken from the camp.

From the three camps, which were only yesterday bustling with life, the vestiges appeared. One or two from each barracks. Sometimes a barracks was opened and no one came out, not a single person. Those of us who did step out let our eyes take in the desolation. Then an order was given to gather the remaining detainees into one camp.

About fifty of us were left, rent flesh. Only one group remained in its entirety: the five Hagana detainees. (The two wreaths of glory which grace every liberation movement in the world had never been and were never to be bestowed upon the Hagana: Exile and Gallows.) The Hagana men, in any case, were the ones who carried my belongings to my new barracks. Only one man close to my heart was among the remnant: Emanuel Katz. At first I believed he would be better off if he did not get too close to me—the case against him was not solid, as evidenced by his having been left in Latrun. His job was already threatened by the Journalists Association, what would he gain by unnecessary contact with a man like me? He, however, decided to thumb his nose at one and all. The fool! He chose this day, when everyone was more conspicuous than ever, to form a "cooperative" with me. Until then, of course, I had been in the Lehi "cooperative"—but not a single other member remained. Now the two of us established this new partnership, putting an almost official seal on his reputation. None of this, ultimately, caused him any harm and he was released several months later.

But the man I sought as soon as I emerged from my barracks-wasteland was not a member of the Lehi, IZL or Hagana, not a member of anything, not even politically inclined. I asked and searched for Dr. Levinson and, as I did not immediately find him, I assumed that he, too, had been taken, which saddened me.

Dr. Levinson was the principal of my high school, familiar to readers of this book from the story of my arrest. He was neither a terrorist nor sympathetic to terrorists. Nationalist, yes, he knew his roots; but he was of German descent, and not too many German Jews joined our fighting family. Dr. Levinson was totally immersed in professional pedagogy and his hobbies, history and art. He had been arrested ten days after me on the trumped-up charge of having helped me escape. I was very bothered by this, both for him personally and for the school. And I assumed that when I reached Latrun I would find in him an enemy, as I was the reason he, an innocent man aged fifty with a family and a troubled high school dependent on him, had been thrown for the first time in his life into a detention camp. His reputation was ruined, his position lost. Yet I was pleasantly surprised when I found him in good spirits, bearing no grudges. He was to spend another six months in the camp and then several more months with me in the infirmary barracks. I began to appreciate him anew. I had known him only as the principal, who had been in more than one argument with his teachers. Here he was a different man. He even confided to me that being in the camp afforded him the opportunity to meet a few men he would never have otherwise encountered; and instead of hating this world which caused his personal troubles, he liked and respected it. He learned to live the "good life" of a detainee, was full of humor, organized evenings of musical studies. I cannot say the same of some of the national leaders who had been big shots outside, constantly speaking of heroism, who upon their arrests began heaping tears and flattery and requests on the secret police, even as they avoided any contact with those who were "very suspect."

I searched hard, then, for Dr. Levinson and was glad to eventually find him among those of us who were left.

We dragged our belongings, beds, mattresses, clothes, books, dragged them from compound to compound. The remnant.

At ten o'clock we were informed that the others had been flown overseas, their belongings would be sent after them.

The women with their children began appearing on the road, walking to the camp for their visits . . . . Thank Heaven the main entrance was so distant we were unable to hear the weeping or see those who fainted. Emanuel Katz had a visitor that day; I sent word through him that I had remained. At least, we thought, those who were exiled were spared the always painful—if beautiful—family visits.

The desolation engulfed us.

Before long, however, the fifty would become, again, hundreds. Once again men would be brought by the dozens. In the months to come, sixty or seventy men were actually brought straight from the "Shertokian" units of Jews who had willingly enlisted in the British army. But . . . things would not, could not, be the same.

Gone was the genuinely political atmosphere of a genuine political detention camp, perhaps because the best had been exiled overseas, perhaps because the fear of future deportations exerted a negative influence, perhaps because the traitor's list had run out of names, and the Underground armies had become, meanwhile, more experienced; thus, many truly innocent people were being brought in, arrested randomly on the streets. In any case, not only our feet trudged through Latrun's mud in the Ayalon Valley, but also our spirits which found no solid ground to rest on. The number of those who every day stood idly by the gates grew; the card players outnumbered the newspaper readers, and the number of provocateurs brought to the camp increased sharply.

The desolation—that human desolation within which I was unable to find any crystallized group for myself, and the desolation brought by the rains, falling forever on the tin roofs, and the cold, entering and tormenting my broken bones—led me to relocate to the camp hospital. I was still in a cast, so this posed no problem. Wanting to be with "the guys," I had rejected the offer of a place there when I first arrived in Latrun. Nothing remained for me now in the camp, and the hospital rooms were smaller and warmer and the food better and most importantly: I would have a corner to myself; my feet—and spirit—would be lifted out of the mud: Not, I reasoned, to see any more of that confused and coincidental crowd. Not to see anymore of that professional intelligentsia—one poet, one journalist, one doctor, one teacher, and all of them storming the gate as one, smiling and toadying to every British guard. Not to see any more of that doctor, a graduate of Hebrew University, a former member of the nationalist student groups, now a high school teacher, who gloated to me of his brilliance: Officer Hamilton of the secret police had asked his opinion of the various political groups in Israel during the Hasmonean period. "But I fixed him," gloated the doctor, "I justified the assimilationists." And he is only one of many like him.

Mud.

*

From a series of letters home:

November 27, 1944

Today is seven months since my arrest.

I was very afraid because of your illness and at night all I heard was the girl calling: "Momma!" Only Thursday's package with the address in your handwriting calmed me somewhat. Of course, a real calm came only today with your visit. While your countenance and white hands could not make me too happy—still, after days and nights of fear, your face and white hands were like a moon suddenly appearing from behind heavy clouds on a dark night.

"What do I say about the girl?" . . . How can I give an opinion about her? To offer an opinion one needs to look quietly, objectively, and in this case my look could be neither quiet nor objective. Nor would I want it to be. I saw only her serious look and I heard her say only "Father" and I heard another word, a very strong word, as if really a shout. When a man told her "Forbidden!" this one-and-a-half-year-old upstart answered "No!" and again "No!" I heard this, and I'll remember it. When she grows up, I'll tell her the story. How many impressions can a man absorb in twenty minutes?

*

February 8, 1945

Yesterday we had a surprise. They unexpectedly brought forty-nine new men, from among those under arrest in the Montefiore neighborhood, and as usual it was "interesting." It's really a bit funny to see how they bring tens of confused men, one in dirty work clothes and one spiffy, elegant (some cabaret artist), one yeshiva student who removes his hat fearfully when an Arab guard approaches, and one old man, a poor street-peddler, who has been wandering around for twenty-four hours and who still does not understand what happened. And a group of jokers manages to fool around; they tease others. Wiseacres, but still funny. Sure, one must be a little stupid or very confused to believe things like: If you want to keep your moustache you must write a request to the commandant (and there are poor fellows who sit and write!) or: Tomorrow at 6 a.m. there is a trip to the Trappist monastery [across the road from the camp], and one must register with the British sergeant (and there are those who jump at this chance, too!). Of course, there are others. Some do not waste their time. Here come four new ones through the gate and from the other side of the fence there are already shouts: "Hey! You! Do you play poker?" And half an hour later they are already "at work" in the café. Today was also "interesting." Today the High Commissioner came to visit; he went to all the barracks. A delegation wanted to speak to him but was denied permission. The entire visit was well organized. Only the Polish detainees caused trouble, two slashed their necks and stomachs with knives and four had epileptic fits. The reading situation has worsened lately. More than four hundred books were sent to the Sudan and nothing remains. This week a group of young Christians sent scientific books in English. Extraordinary! The attitude of the Hebrew establishment is awful. We received a negative reply from the Tel Aviv municipality, too.

*

February 22, 1945

Here in the hospital, life is quieter. One can learn and think more. That which a man cannot finish thinking about by day, he dreams at night. I dreamed the same dream, night after night, for one week: I strolled the streets of Polish cities, searching—for whom, is obvious—I saw horrible images of charred people. And then, suddenly, I am strolling with my laughing, radiant daughter, with lots of sunlight all around. But there are, also, humorous dreams. I dreamt once that the King and Queen of England visited, together with Churchill. They visit the hospital and I discuss the military situation with Churchill. We walk together and as we near the gate I think: Maybe I'll succeed in leaving with him . . . . But to no avail, I woke up.

Wish you a happy holiday? There's no point. Which holiday? Purim or Passover? Who knows when this letter will reach you. And even so: Of what value are my wishes?

They asked me after the visit: What does your wife have to say? Is she calm? Does she cry? And I answered: She told me, "When I think, I honestly cannot cry, but when I cry I cannot think."

*

February 25, 1945

Perhaps you've read of the death of the poetess Elsa Lasker-Schuler? If I had a volume of her poems here I might try translating it. If by chance you see one of her books somewhere, send it to me by mail.

*

But this "respite" from politics existed only inside the detention camp. Outside, things of great importance were occurring. There was mud outside, too, but the blood and the fire overcame it.

4. The Light from Cairo

I lifted my legs from the mud that filled Latrun, dividing barracks from barracks and man from man, and that dirtied the ground and those who walked upon it, who dragged themselves through it. I went up to the hospital barracks on the hill, with its small rooms offering good solitude and its closed-in porches offering good pacing (I have never been able to think except when walking) and good views, of that which lay faraway, over the barracks' roofs, over the camp's offices, across the highway, including the wide Ayalon Valley and including the ever-silent Trappist monastery opposite us.

Autumn rains are good rains, but only if the land has been prepared. There were days in Latrun when the detainees were organized, almost like permanent tenants, and they cared for their gardens and pathways which, as a result, did not disappear in the rains. But after these sturdy roots were pulled from the camp and exiled to Africa, the human material left behind was happenstance, confused, careless. Everyone wrapped himself in his own blanket, daydreamed of *fraj* and tried sending letters and pleas to the British police. In dry weather, the camp was overrun by scorpions and centipedes; and, in autumn, by mud. Therefore I left it; in political terms, I withdrew to the hilltop barracks and saw that which I had not seen below, and thought that which I had not thought below because of the many interferences and the noise of the rain pelting the tin roof and the mud, mud, mud.

News of the successful assassination of Lord Moyne, coming two weeks after that terrible morning of the deportations, reached me in the Latrun hospital, my body sealed in a cast and my spirit downcast over the departure of the camp and the descent of the human-mud.

Though actually unrelated, the attack was like a powerful rejoinder to the enemy's blow. Michael had discussed the operation with us several months before my arrest; he had prepared the attack before the British even considered exiling detained individuals from Eretz Israel. Moyne, nonetheless, was the man who gave the final orders for the deportations and who chose the place of exile, and undoubtedly had harsher edicts in store for the Yishuv, befitting the anti-Zionist and anti-Semitic views he expressed so frankly and cynically in London and Cairo. "Weizmann's demands are unjustified," he said while still colonial minister in 1942. "The White Paper is just," and "Aliya must cease." Two years later, on arrival in Cairo and even more sharply (Hitler had in the meantime eroded our numbers and our honor): "Palestine is the land of the Arabs. The Jews, racially, are a mixed breed. The Jews of Palestine must leave the country and it will be possible to find a place for them in Africa."

Meanwhile Moyne found a land of exile for 251 Jews suspected—and most of them not without reason—of having ties to the Underground. But his fate was already sealed, well before that morning he signed the deportation order. Eliahu Hakim had already trained his sights on him, after a lengthy period of tracking. Eliahu Bet-Zuri had already prepared to leave for Cairo, to participate in the actual operation. If the operation had by chance been carried out before the deportation, the establishment would certainly have justified the deportation as punishment. For this was the impressionist way of thinking: This is not a conflict of interest between two nations, between the British and the Jews, between the Empire and a national liberation movement, rather there are chance misunderstandings. There are edicts which must be revoked; there are "actions" which must bear immediate fruit. All this is called a "struggle"[57] and was close to the IZL's way of thinking, too, in its early stages.

We—and I consider this our greatest honor—ceased seeing our encounter with the British as an internal struggle within the Empire, a war against the White Paper for a better administration. We saw the war in its entirety. This was a war over the basis, not over an incidental characteristic attached to the basis. The problem is no longer a "good" or "bad" High Commissioner but rather Hebrew rule or foreign rule. And the problem is no longer a search for friends in London; the problem is a complete break with London, not only in Jerusalem, but in Cairo and London as well. In one article critical of Jabotinsky's path, I wrote that the Revisionist Party's greatest mistake was moving its political offices from Paris to London. This blocked its development from an opposition movement to the movement of Hebrew liberation. This prolonged the illusions and delays, and this placed unnecessary burdens on the shoulders of the IZL.

This clarification, as it relates to the assassination of Lord Moyne, is basic to an understanding of the ensuing trouble that erupted between the IZL and us.

I see no point in reviewing the verbal onslaught to which we were subjected by the Jewish Agency and Histadrut leaders following Moyne's assassination. From where I stand today I cannot comprehend how we were even for one moment misled into believing in the possibility of a lasting, united front with the Hagana. The seemingly inconsequential story I related above of how, after all my fellow Lehi members were flown out, the Hagana detainees took me under their wing and carried my belongings to their barracks—this was not just a humane gesture toward a man in a body cast, or even a gesture of respect toward a man of culture. This was also a reflection of the "flirtation" which took place between our two sides, which was made possible partly by both sides' hatred for the IZL and partly by the way both sides clung to marginal ideas and ignored basic ones.

Hysteria gripped the leaders of the Organized Yishuv after Moyne's assassination. The most often used expression was, "a crime despicable seven times over." Weizmann said the assassination shocked him more than the death of his son in the British Air Force. In a letter to Churchill he promised the final liquidation of the terrorists. *Davar* editorialized, of course, that this was not a blow to the British government alone, but also a dangerous blow to Jewish statesmanship, this terror being at such a level as to make us odious even to our friends. *Davar*'s conclusion: The despicable criminals left us to our fate so we must destroy them. Moshe Shertok declared this terror to be Zionism's greatest danger. The establishment institutions decided: Spew out, turn in. Israel Galili took upon himself the task of inviting the youth to join in.[58] In a special rally in Tel Aviv's Moghrabi Theater he called for enlistment in the drive against terror.

Most jarring to me in this chorus of condemnation were, naturally, the comments of the Revisionist *Hamashkif* on the partnership between the Hebrew nation and Britain, a partnership that they said must continue. Failure to understand this truth, *Hamashkif* wrote, was the root of the error of Lord Moyne's assassins.

All these comments—*Hamashkif*'s, too—contained no surprises, or in any case, they should not have surprised us. I have already remarked that the complaint that we struck against "innocent" policemen was no more than hypocrisy, hypocrisy which was occasionally revealed whenever we struck or tried to strike at criminals like MacMichael, whom no one considered "innocent," not even Ben Gurion who called him a "killer." But for some reason Ben Gurion and his associates were not willing to "turn in" or "spew out" this "killer" who killed the *Struma* refugees, while they were willing to, and actually did, turn in our boys who had attacked him.

The problem of "individual" terror was also made the focus of a "theoretical" debate. The heroes of this debate were naturally the leftists in the Histadrut union who, steeped as they were in revolutionary theory, did not find it easy to argue against political bloodshed. They referred to the ineffectiveness of the S.R. (the Socialist Revolutionary Party) actions in Russia (without referring to the fact that not even once did the socialists who opposed the S.R. turn their "terrorist" opponents over to the Czar's police. But apparently this is only a "national" characteristic of the of the Yishuv's socialism).

There was not much point in arguing with them, not even with the more recent example of the Czechs' assassination of the Nazi Heydrich, an attack which led to the Nazi massacre of the village of Lidice; not even this example could sway them. Because first and foremost they wanted to continue in their tranquility, continue playing the same disgusting game of political "struggle" in which they continue to preserve their status quo, especially since that status quo was fat and comfortable during the war years, thanks to military business. Because first and foremost was the fact that they were not a national liberation movement at all. Even if we had risen and held a revolution in the best tradition, even then their sophistry would have provided them reasons to be against us. And I regret nothing so much as the huge amounts of energy and ink I poured into these arguments with them; they, whose "revolutionary" spirits plunged the day after the assassination when Churchill said that this deed will turn even friends like him away from Zionism. And I sat and split hairs with them on the pages of *Hehazit*!

For us at this stage of the war, this was in any case the grandest and most penetrating action to date, from a political perspective. *Davar*'s comments about the blow to the British government could not but please us. This is just what we aimed for. Even the comments of Moyne's deputy on the day after his assassination, that Moyne "was the greatest defender of the interests of the British Empire in the Middle East," even this phrase only justified our action, for our phrasing was clear: There is a total conflict of interests between the British Empire and us. Most certainly, in the posters and articles we published, we exploited personal and temporal facts, as all good propaganda combines the principle with the concrete. Certainly we used Moyne's anti-Semitic speeches and deeds to reach the appalled and frightened public. But we did not make do with just this. We did not want the action to seem to be revenge upon one evil man. After the *Struma* tragedy, Wedgwood declared in the House of Lords: "I will yet see the man responsible for this crime hanged from a high tree as Haman was hanged." Wedgwood was surely a good Gentile, but it is good to sit with righteous Gentiles and make merry on Sabbath evenings and during Passover seders, not on the normal weekdays of politics—for the share of the righteous in the world to come is greater than their influence in this world. Sometimes they do damage to the cause, by deluding the ear that is listening with a pleasant, sleep-inducing melody. It was helpful that Moyne, who was responsible for the establishment of the Arab League and who prepared the massacre of the Yishuv (and who, needless to say, did not prepare the British evacuation from Eretz Israel) was not as slippery as Churchill and was not a personal friend of Weizmann, and did not attempt covering his hate-filled intentions with wrappings of "support." The "Zionists," Moyne said once, "try to stir pity with sentimental stories of their situation in Europe." It was very helpful that he was so honest and crude, so like another hateful and hated British minister, Bevin.[59] Of course this did not reduce in the least the incitement against us, just as we would not have been spared even if at the time of the Yishuv's greatest hatred we had gotten rid of Bevin himself. But if Lord Moyne had been more "Churchillian" and less honest in his hate, then our action would have awakened not only the public's fear but also hatred toward us. As it was, the establishment Jews tried to stir up hatred against us, without success. But the public was overwhelmed by fear, fear of a British version of Lidice. History has shown that there are things worse than Lidice, but apparently we were not yet a nation, for everyone, almost everyone, took his own personal stock in the face of a possible Lidice, especially at a time of such prosperity, with life not so bad at all . . . .

So Moyne's hatred for Israel was a help to us, but the main reason for the action was his being the Empire's minister for the Middle East. The theory we set forth in *Hehazit* was that total conflict existed between the Empire and us, and that this was no mere contest with a local administration; this theory took on form in the Cairo operation. And I have no doubt—though as of yet I have no evidence, either—that this was the first time the Soviets saw the Hebrew war of liberation as an ally against British imperialism. Another friend won by this action was the French people, against whom Moyne had set up the Arab League, no less than against us (France was still under the influence of De Gaulle and had not yet given up her positions in the Middle East). And a third logical but nonetheless surprising result of the action was a break in the Arab-Egyptian front. The two Lehi boys who assassinated Lord Moyne could most probably have saved themselves had they shot at their Egyptian pursuers. But the explicit order they were given before they left Eretz Israel was not to harm any Egyptians. In our hearts we harbored doubts over whether such an order endangering their own lives was justified for a political purpose, but this order proves the complete political consideration given the action, and therefore it was appropriate, even if the sacrifice did not bear the political fruit sought. We viewed Egypt in its struggle to liberate itself from the British yoke as a possible ally. The anti-British hatred in Egypt could be channeled to our benefit, while there was no necessary conflict of interest between Egypt and Eretz Israel. This was our logic. We were surprised to see the swift expression of the application of this logic, since in politics one rarely sees objective logic applied with any speed; and this despite the Arab incitement against Zionism, which was quite influential in Egypt. But lo and behold—the world was to witness the greatest lawyers in Egypt coming to the defense of Eliahu Hakim and Eliahu Bet-Zuri. And behold, the world heard of the furious demonstrations by Egyptian students after the death sentence was issued, and the police feared there might even be an attempt to free the two boys by force. The boys' appearance in court and their emphasis on the politics of the matter stirred patriotic Egyptian hearts, hearts that still bore resentment over the invasion of Farouk's palace by British tanks. No, we did not delude ourselves into thinking that these Egyptians would refrain, in the event of a victory by Rommel, from slaughtering Jews as Ukrainians, Poles and Lithuanians had done before them; but this action did prove that in a certain political scenario, under wise and free political direction, the Egyptian struggle for independence can be an ally of ours.

From a limited organizational perspective the operation was of tremendous value. Subconsciously, our members were happy over our "big" action after the IZL's recent activities, behind which we lagged.

Ironically, we were most surprised by the response of the IZL. A response born not of jealousy over our success, but rather of far more serious considerations.

I have already written of the joy that greeted the joint proclamation issued by the two organizations as a first step toward joint action. On our side the joy came hesitantly, on the IZL's side—it was total, for reasons obvious after all that has been said up to this point about our mutual relations, the feelings of hate on one side and inferiority on the other. The details of the agreement were unknown even to me. I learned of them only after the IZL announced to its ranks that the operation in Cairo was a breach of the agreement. Then the information reached me that though it was indeed agreed that each side would inform the other of any actions twenty-four hours in advance, in this case it was impossible to do so, since even the Central Command in Eretz Israel did not know when the action would be carried out in Cairo. Our Command also argued that this part of the agreement with the IZL referred only to actions in Eretz Israel, its purpose being to avoid surprises and disasters involving simultaneous operations, and to give the other organization a chance to prepare for the inevitable results of each action (searches, curfews, etc.). Our Command did not see this logic as applicable to actions outside the country. Interestingly enough, the IZL claimed that it unintentionally aided in the Cairo operation by helping to transfer one of our men to Egypt, without knowing why.

This argument over the meaning of a point in the agreement was only the superficial argument. Such things can happen with every agreement. During the "Resistance" that temporarily united all three groups, the Hagana, IZL and Lehi, the Hagana occasionally complained that a particular operation executed by the IZL or Lehi was not according to the agreement of the "rebel movement," the United Resistance, whose authority we had all accepted. Nonetheless the Hagana did not cancel the agreement over such operations. Nor would the IZL have canceled this agreement, reached after so many years of hate and anger, had this been a different kind of operation—say, had we blown up some government building without warning them in advance. They would have said, "This is not nice, this is ungentlemanly," and they would have demanded we not repeat such behavior.

In this case, however, the IZL canceled the agreement not because of our formal breach of one point, but because of the content of our operation.

In addition to the sea of incitement and blasphemy poured upon us from the expected sources, we faced a wave of IZL reservations. The IZL issued a special proclamation to express its reservations over the *tragedy in Cairo*.

And this was the sign that the Irgun was still far from the political assumptions and military conclusions that Yair had reached, that we had reached, and that we thought—or at least that I thought, for I so wanted to see these ideas fully developed and realized—the IZL had reached, too.

The Irgun's reservations about the assassination of Lord Moyne sprang from its clinging to the Revisionist policy of fighting the "bad administration" in Eretz Israel, from its belief in a "different England" which is not helping us solely because of the errors of Weizmann and Shertok. The policy of pressure was based on relying on instances of friendship, like Wedgwood's. Even the operation that the IZL once prepared against MacMichael was an action against MacMichael himself, not against the position of High Commissioner. And even then it was planned not as an attempt on his life but a kidnapping or, in military terms, "taking a prisoner."

(In the chapter that will deal with the differences in the form of our operations, we will also deal with the effects, the drama of this action, but in this chapter we are considering the political side of things.)

The IZL was still trying not to get the British "too angry." Not all the IZL's ties to the days of Altman and David Raziel had been cut. The ties held with Begin, through Begin or against Begin, but they held. And when a year later during a meeting on unification of our forces Begin opposed the formula: "War against British imperialism" and supported instead: "War against the British rule in this country," he was persisting in the same vein as the reservations about the assassination of Lord Moyne. More than the Cairo operation contradicted a point in the agreement, it contradicted the political basis of their war. I am not of the opinion that they were right regarding the formal aspect of the agreement, but even if I were to grant their argument on that point, I would still accuse them of exploiting this foolishness when the true reason was their opposition to the breadth and direction of the war as formalized and actualized by this operation of ours.

And we must be very sorry indeed, for if not for this delay (and it was a delay, for in the coming years they were forced to expand the breadth of their war because of the *objective* conflict we had identified long before, and by then even they agreed to our description of the enemy) the two groups would have come much closer together and many events might have been different. Their recoiling from the definitiveness of the Cairo operation forced them to use our apparent formal breach of the agreement to tear down the first bridge that had been built between us.

And again the waves of mutual incitement rolled verbally and in print, and again the gap widened, a gap which would become an abyss for both parties.

But if the IZL's fault in this was that it was still in its political infancy, the Lehi's fault was in a tactical-organizational error which I must relate just as it is reflected in the mirror of my knowledge and feelings.

For some months after the assassination a very strange situation persisted. First of all, the fears of a British pogrom against the Yishuv proved groundless. We in the detention camp were in a better position than the rest of the country to assess the mood of the British soldiers and police. There were no expressions of hate or rage. The repercussions from every blow delivered to regular soldiers or police in this country were immediately felt on our own flesh. The guards' looks and behavior turned crude and murderous. Supervision was tightened, clashes increased over unimportant things. Electricity filled the air. More than once we heard their complaint: "What do you want from us? We have nothing to do with politics, we're just carrying out orders; we would gladly carry out the order to free you. Why don't you 'hit' those responsible?"

The complaint had some albeit misleading justification. Some in the camp were moved upon hearing it. In any case, Lehi members were not overly moved. We defined "war" and we made war, which is to say we directed everything according to the highest justice: their leaving the country. And in this respect the operations against the soldiers and police were more effective than the acts of sabotage, or the "individual terror," because more than anything else, the British are sensitive to loss of life. "Know your enemy." And we knew the British enemy. They are not accustomed to and they do not enjoy losses on their side. Every Englishman who fell was another step toward the decision to leave our country. A political blow like the assassination of Lord Moyne did not affect the soldiers emotionally at all; therefore there was not even one minute of a pogrom-atmosphere on their side, as there would be two years later in the decisive year of 5707 (1947) when they suffered the daily losses of "innocent" victims. Of course a pogrom does not come only from the bottom. No pogrom anywhere in the world, including in Eretz Israel on the part of the British, has taken place without an order from above. But neither can one occur without stirred-up passions below.

Such emotions were not awakened in the least in British hearts. They certainly were bothered less than were the local Jews. Almost total apathy. "It's politics," they said, and what do they care. Nor was there a desire in London to commit a "Lidice" here. All in all, the English are much more political than the Jews. Though every Jew considers himself a "politician," ultimately we see that even the most primitive among the Arabs have a more finely developed political sense than the Jew. This has been proven by the behavior of the Jewish people in the Diaspora and it has been proven by their behavior in Eretz Israel. The British decided to make as much political use of the assassination as possible. This was not the first assassination in the history of the Empire, but I believe it was the first England managed to exploit so well in order to suppress a rebellious nation.

And not, Heaven forbid, a physical suppression. Worse! A moral-political suppression. The British regime exploited to the utmost the anxiety that gripped the Yishuv, the fear and trembling that struck the Yishuv leaders. A "pogrom" did indeed result, but not by the British; rather, by the Organized Yishuv. At first the Jewish leaders really were frightened and shaken. But after they recovered from the first fright they simply decided to use it to eliminate once and for all the "dissidents," as they referred to us. In the first few days, the incitement stemmed from real shock (and that they should be shocked is understandable, loyal as they were with all their souls to British rule in principle, with only a few demands to make); but afterward, the incitement was already cold and considered. Even after they realized there would be no British pogrom, they pretended that they were obligated to save the Yishuv, and the only way to save . . . was to inform on and turn the dissidents over to the British. This was, of course, accompanied by demagoguery and the lie that now, just now, we had been on the verge of achievements in London, of breaking the White Paper policy, and only the crime in Cairo prevented us from doing so. And they knew this to be a lie, but they decided to use this argument to turn the Yishuv against the Underground.

During the dark days of Shevat 5702 there were still ordinary Jewish citizens who had felt that their duty was to cleanse the plague. Flashlights had suddenly shone in the dark streets, lighting faces: "Perhaps it's Yair whose photograph has been printed?" But after *Struma*, after Ramat Hakovesh, there was a change on the street. The ordinary Jew, even if he did not yet actually assist the Underground, was no longer willing to fight it, to inform. But meanwhile, there was a "development" inside the Hagana, too: They were no longer interested in ordinary tattling by the public. Individuals who inform come into direct contact with the British regime. The Hagana was not interested in such direct contact, where people meet the government. Otherwise, today a citizen supports the administration; tomorrow he may fight against it or fight to take it over and where would the Hagana be? And where would the "National Institutions" be, whose very existence is brokerage? Brokerage between the capital, the Jewish contributions, and the Yishuv enjoying the capital (and this is why, from then to today, they are opposed to direct contact between the capital and Israel) and brokerage between the government and the Yishuv. The very term Yishuv (settlement) came into being this way. A communal, diasporic, anti-sovereign term. And therefore their lack of interest in private informing. This "industry," too, must be under "national" (read: Histadrut; definition: Hagana) monopoly and supervision.

Thus the monster named "Collaboration" was born in the winter of 5705 (1944-1945), with an office in the Jewish Agency building in Jerusalem where one man (later one of Israel's top VIPs) sat collecting all the data, all the material, all the lists and passing them straight to the chief of the CID, Arthur Giles. And in order that this should not be mere office work, in order for there to be some "activism" to satisfy the desire of the Hagana rank and file for activity—they engaged in kidnapping, torture, trailing and turning Jews in, with door-to-door service. From the door of the Hagana commander to the door of the British detectives' commander.

And the British detectives reaped the fruit, without effort or risk. The expected British pogrom did not come. It was not necessary. Jews did it.

And something else we had expected did not come. Common sense indicated that the response would be against those who had acted in Cairo, against Lehi. But what actually happened in those hard, strange months of the winter of 5705 was that all the hostile activities, the kidnapping, tortures and turnings-in, were all directed against the IZL. And this happened despite the IZL's open disavowal of the "tragic" assassination. Day after day IZL members were brought into the camp, after they had been kidnapped and tortured by the Hagana, while new Lehi detainees were few in number, comprising some who had been arrested in independent British actions (yes, there were a few of those, too) and some who had been mistaken for IZL members.

And from the outside, in letters from the Central Command, I am told of strange goings on: Lehi members are kidnapped by the Hagana and freed after twenty-four hours, with an apology for the error.

The IZL men themselves easily explain it to me: They are afraid of you. Lehi threatened "drastic reactions" while IZL Commander Begin issued an order for restraint. Begin's order contained much patriotic spirit (designed to avoid a civil war among Jews) but was, however, the road that would eventually lead Begin to the *Altalena* ship, as we shall see.

Many IZL fighters were grinding their teeth. They envied us our success in frightening the Hagana. The conflict in their souls: On the one hand they are proud of their commander's inner strength, suffering losses and in so doing preventing a civil war. On the other hand they are depressed, and their opposition to the operation in Cairo grows deeper. We acted, they are punished, and we got off scot-free.

Until one day an IZL leader with whom I was close told me bitterly that this is more than a matter of the Hagana fearing the Lehi. Rather, an agreement exists.

I denied it. I knew only that meetings are being held with Hagana Chief Eliahu Golomb. Natan occasionally relayed to me from these meetings Hagana praise for us, for our intellectual level: The Hagana leaders are especially influenced by the letters they receive from the prisons and detention camps, which tell of the high quality of individual Lehi members, as opposed to the soldierliness of the Irgunists. "They are really fascists," we are told. The flattery about our "intellectual level" was naturally music to my ears, since to a large extent I was responsible for the level of *Hehazit*. The theoretical and literary articles were having an effect.

In one letter, Natan even informed me of a Hagana proposal to merge with us. The terms: Lehi will be an ideologically autonomous unit within the Hagana, with *Hehazit* as its platform. Natan's explanation for participating in these rather strange negotiations over unification was: We must gain time.

Coincidentally or not, the internal Lehi propaganda did not reach me in the camp. Only now, as I review the material in the Lehi Archives, do I see an internal pamphlet printed that winter, somewhat surprising for its style. The style is Natan Friedman's, but the spirit is not Lehi's:

"We must take care to emerge from the crisis whole, stronger. We wanted to believe the explicit promise made by one of the Hagana's responsible leaders that informing would cease. The promise was broken. Faced with such criminal action, we posit moral means. What is required of us? Wisdom and a firm stance. Our opponents would be satisfied if we were to act rashly. We must avoid provocations. We will not give up our right to explain. The movement's Central Command is watching developments and weighing the situation and deciding which steps will be taken and which not. Our organizational activity will not cease. It will be executed with even more energy. We will enlist new men. We will educate, train. And to the two in Cairo we say: We will try to be worthy of your bearing."

Yes. In the Yishuv's turmoil, the two are almost forgotten. The eyes of the world are upon them.

I do know that efforts are being made to liberate them, but operating in Egypt is made almost impossible by British pressure and Intelligence activity. Dozens upon dozens of Jewish soldiers are brought directly from Egypt to Latrun. Among them, only a few of ours. Mostly Irgunists or people suspected of sympathy. But our groups in Egypt and in the army are wiped out.

I do not know the organizational situation. I do not know what is technically feasible in Egypt or in this country. I know only the political and the moral aspects. And both obligate acts of war, not merely organizational and explanatory activity. But because there are no such acts, I know they are impossible. "The head is bigger than the body," this has been Lehi's problem from the start. Inactivity is annoying, of course, but what can we do? And I believe those in charge when they say it is impossible to act, given the current tension.

But I repudiate completely what was done. And only what was done explains all the aforementioned oddities of those strange months. What was done: *A commitment was given the Hagana that we would not act.*

I was not informed of this, not while I sat in Latrun and not after I got out. And perhaps they knew what they were doing in concealing this cease-fire agreement from me.

I was informed of it only much later, by chance, at a time when the commitment was no longer relevant. The first I heard of it was during a conversation between Menachem Begin and Haim Landau,[60] representing the IZL, and Natan Friedman and me representing Lehi. In the course of our discussion Menachem Begin challenged Natan over the commitment. He condemned it for favoring "tactics" over principle.

The second time was when Israel Galili mentioned the commitment during one of our joint meetings.

For a third time, it was proved by the internal literature I found and cited above.

And finally, Menachem Begin told me it was the truth.

And therefore I see, in this chapter of my book, a moral need to disavow this step, even if it were done only to gain time. There is of course no dialectical possibility of showing what the results would have been without this commitment. But there can be no doubt that news of the commitment traveled beyond the Yishuv's own boundaries. There is no doubt that the news reached the enemy, too.

The strength we were able to accumulate thanks to this cease-fire, whether through new enlistments or in avoiding imprisonments, certainly aided us in fighting the war when we resumed it. But it was without doubt a tactical move that meant we were widening the gap between Lehi and the IZL, just as the IZL's repudiation of the Cairo operation was a political move that had the same effect. And it may even be that during this idyllic period between the Hagana and Lehi, the movement leftward began inside Lehi which would later result in an ideological and organizational crisis in Lehi, in the State of Israel.

And I am afraid to even consider the possibility of a connection between the commitment and the fate of the two boys.

All was quiet when they mounted the high gallows in Cairo. It was so quiet we were able to hear their heartbeats, and their singing *Hatikva*. Since the time Moses sang by the Sea, Egypt had not been graced with such singing.

5. The Silent Monastery

One opposite the other they stand, the two institutions that "care" so much for this land. In this corner, at the intersection of the Jerusalem-Tel Aviv and Ramallah-Gaza roads, they stand one opposite the other: the Trappist monastery and the Latrun police building. The crucified and the crucifiers. They reign over the Ayalon Valley and the road to Jerusalem. They have found a pleasant location.

One churns from the movement of tanks circling it at night and casts searchlights, which stab as knives the flesh of the dangerous camp that sows plots day and night.

And the other, to the right, quiet, still. The monks busy tending vineyards are silent, for they have taken vows to be so all their lives. Their wine is very good, some of the best in the country, and those in the police building opposite enjoy it. You take care of me and I will take care of you. The men of Pilate and the faithful of Peter and Paul cooperate. We will drink your wine and allow you to be silent and you will let us rule here, and may your pure prayers to the Holy Father and Mother and Son be atonement for all our sins. And make the sign of the Cross.

What did you say Arnon? The English do not cross themselves? Perhaps. I have forgotten. Actually, I never delved into the differences between Christian sects. To us they appear as one bloc. I knew one Gentile heretic: He did not believe in the Father or the Mother or the Holy Ghost, but he believed in one thing, that we crucified Jesus.

Arnon laughed out loud on the porch of the hospital with its view of the monastery and the police building, laughed into the dark of the night and said: Maybe they are only using this matter of Jesus. Hitler said it best, and not for nothing were there idolatrous tendencies within Nazism. Jesus was too Jewish for him. Maybe they hate us so much not because we killed Jesus, but because we gave birth to him.

You see, Arnon, these two buildings? (Now the searchlight sliced the darkness and passed us.) They symbolize exactly what happened to us in Europe. The slaughterers held their knives and the silent held their tongues. All the "good" goyim, the English, French, Poles, Russians, even when they were being beaten by the Nazis, they felt this consolation in their hearts: They are doing our work for us. What we wanted, Hitler is doing. He is freeing us from them, the Jews. One killed, the other was still, like this monastery opposite us. And the Pope, the keeper of mercy and kindness in the world, remained silent and the Catholics his faithful children participated in the slaughter in every country of Europe. Finally their generations-old desire was satisfied. The one compensation for their subjugation to the Nazis. For hundreds of years they had prepared for this revelry over our blood. Until he came who dared.

Maybe he really was the Antichrist—Arnon continued the chain of thought—and they are all Antichrists and we remain the last religious nation on earth. And even those among us who are not religious—their very Jewishness is a religion.

When the day comes, Arnon, I do not know whether it will be incumbent upon us to treat this silent monastery any differently from this police building. Both are enemies.

It will be interesting, Arnon says, if I succeed in cutting my way out and crossing over and have no way to go but up that hill. I will knock on the monastery door and say: I am a member of Lehi; I've just escaped from the detention camp; the British want to kill me. Shelter me till morning.

By the time you reach them, Arnon, the dogs will have torn you to pieces. They may be quiet now, but there are dogs there, and they are not bound by vows of silence.

Arnon: I am not afraid of dogs. And I think that their being French will be to my benefit. Maybe.

But Arnon never experimented. He was only in the camp for seven days. He was brought in during Hanukkah. Rabbi Ostrovsky of the Vaad Leumi came on the same day. The rabbi gave a lecture in the synagogue barracks that annoyed everyone. He libeled the "dissidents." I missed the lecture as I was walking with Arnon at the time, learning the details of his arrest. He had driven with an IZL officer to Haifa, to prepare a joint operation of great proportions. This was after the Lod Railway operation. At Lod, Arnon had been in a position of responsibility for the first time, and he had proven his worth in any position, organizational, instructive or operational. Michael wrote me that he had high hopes for Arnon. But now in Haifa they were stopped on the street and arrested. The police were after the IZL man, who was being followed; Arnon was arrested as a contact, he was told. Except that when he arrived at Latrun, the camp commandant leaped with joy over his new-found treasure. He identified Arnon based on the photos of the twenty tunnel-escapees. Arnon's photo was on the wall. "You are Saul Haglili?" Arnon could not deny it. He had been the supervisor, the camp representative, when the tunnel was being dug. Arnon was taken to Jerusalem for interrogation and returned. There was no doubt; he would not be a permanent guest. People like him were first on the planes for deportation.

One of the Jews who works in the office, who frequently comes to the hospital on administrative matters, suddenly approaches me. He says he is worried about Saul, wants to help him, and will bring pliers to cut the fences. This clerk had always been friendly to me. Irgunists warned me that he was a member of the secret police, or at least of Hagana Intelligence. The members of Hagana Intelligence in our camp complained to me that he was too frightened to be of any use to them. I say: Respect him but suspect him. His anxiety and suggestion about Arnon surprise me. Apparently he knows they are going to fly Arnon out, and apparently he likes him, which is not easy. Arnon is a mix of burning Balkan freedom fighter and intelligent Jew, wrapped in a quiet exterior. No arrogance, no revolutionary posturing. Just natural, all normalcy. An exemplary Lehi fighter. Hagana members in the camp used to say: His appearance is his identity card.

Arnon stood with me on the hospital porch, those few nights he was in the camp, reviewing over and over the chances of success. The plan was for four to six Lehi and IZL members to escape by crawling and cutting the fences and crawling again. Unless the night is stormy, the chances of slipping between the towers are not great.

And along with this scheme we are preparing a plan of resistance to any British attempt to fly prisoners out. We know there will be a flight. The air is tense. High IZL commanders have been brought in. The camp is nervous. The struggle outside has its affects on the Hagana members, too. They are also threatened with deportation. We have no need to request permission from "outside" to oppose deportation. It is not a political problem, rather one dealing with the morality of the war for liberation. We must not make the storm troopers' work easy. We have differences of opinion on the form of resistance, and we reach an agreement. A permanent watch is set up in the last (IZL) barracks. If the army and police are spotted descending on the camp, a signal will be given. The barracks will be fortified. The storm troopers will be kept out. Next, one of the empty barracks will be set afire. The purpose of these actions is to delay till daylight the deportation. The burning barracks will be seen as far as Hulda, the entire Yishuv will answer the alarm. But the main value of the action is the resistance itself. Never again like sheep.

In the middle of one night we are awakened by shouts. It has begun, though not quite according to plan.

The one keeping watch despaired after several eventless nights. We were taken by surprise. Two barracks nevertheless managed to lock themselves in, at the last minute. In the Hagana barracks they barricaded the door by dismantling two wooden beds. They yelled to the British that they were Hagana, and the officer in charge retorted: Next time we'll take you, too. The other barracks were taken without resistance. Here and there men refused to identify themselves, which complicated the removal of those marked for deportation. But soon enough the men whose names were on the list were found, so . . . why all the shouting?

It is coming from the barracks at the other end of the camp. Where Arnon is in charge. He gave the orders as agreed. Two policemen entered and were jumped, held, pushed together and shoved out by the well-built Gershon Ekdachi. The door was barred.

The British were met by blows when they attempted to enter through the windows. The men armed themselves with pieces of beds, and boards taken from the ceiling. The shouts we heard were those of the stunned police. The coordinators of the British operation gathered around that barracks; the men of the other barracks expressed their support in a chorus of their own shouts: Nazis! Nazis! Nazis!

And we sat in the hospital and worried: One more minute and they will open fire on the defenders. We did not know, of course, that only one barracks was rebelling.

The "battle" lasted three-quarters of an hour. Slowly Arnon realized the failure. No barracks had been set afire. His barracks was alone in its resistance. The pressure on the doors and windows grew and dawn was distant. He surrendered.

Fifty-four men were taken that night. One was taken from my room despite his illness. I was passed over this time, too. Dr. Troy made sure the seriousness of my condition was not reduced, even though my cast had in the meantime been replaced with a leather belt. But the shouts of our brothers, which tore at our flesh, were worse for those who remained than for those who were flown abroad. Were it not for my work, which I continued in my writing, I would have preferred to go into exile with the others. Our worries over Arnon doubled. He was obviously the leader of the revolt; those in charge of other barracks stood without a word, dressed and left.

The deportees were led past the hospital, some of them wounded, some in pajamas. The camp was still shouting, cursing. The English were shocked. They had not expected resistance, until now their missions were executed without a hitch. This time they won.

Rivers of light flooded the camp from the police building.

And the silent monastery held fast. Dark and still. The holy monks slept off their day's labor in the winepress and the exertion of remaining silent.

They keep silent the next day, too, when the road comes to life. Mothers, wives, fathers; the rain beats upon the fields and the open road and they walk the three kilometers from the main road to the camp. Soaked from rain and tears. Will they find their children, their husbands, in the camp? Will they find them?

In the camp we cannot hear but we know: Up there wives are whimpering at the gate. There is one, she is going back, a child on each side and stuffed packages under her arms. The packages, too, return home, they were meant for someone no longer in the camp. The camp is desolate and painful. Teeth are grit over those who betrayed. In the camp they wrap themselves in their blankets and only above, in the hospital, is there a covered porch on which we can stand even in the rain, and watch the road and the wives and the children and the wind swirling about them, and the police building laughing, laughing in the ugliness of its walls, and the cloistered, sanctimonious, silent monastery.

If not for our sake, if not for the sake of Arnon who was murdered after being deported to Eritrea in Africa, then for the sake of the wives in the rain on this road and for the sake of the crying children, for their sake: We will put an end to your laughter, bastards, we will. And to your blessed silence in these vineyards, too.

The Miracle Child: The United Resistance

1. "Dan Ram"

"Dan Ram" is somebody's real name, but I put it in quotation marks because for me he is only a detail that throws light on the whole.[61] I have chosen him from among all the Hagana members I met during my imprisonment, even though I knew him less well than others. We spent only a few days in conversation, after his arrival in the Jerusalem Prison from Latrun. But for me, he became a stereotype, a symbol of something very important in the development of Lehi and the entire Underground.

I have chosen him because he was the best of all I met, the most politically developed, the most morally honest. Today he also holds the highest rank in the Israeli army. And if I drew my conclusion based on the best among them, what point would there be in describing the others in whose company I spent days and nights and many months in discussions and arguments? If I tell of him, whose ears were truly open to arguments, who wanted to learn, to understand, and who did learn and understand and who did not draw the conclusions, then there is no need to tell of all those who listened and heard every word I spoke, not in order to learn or understand but only to pass detailed reports to Hagana Intelligence.

I certainly have no obligation to tell of one Hagana detainee, who despite intimate friendships with many, refrained from arguing with me, or even talking to me, and who was the bitterest opponent of the Underground. I came to understand him after I learned the secret of his hatred. The Hagana men came from many backgrounds: One was a wealthy merchant and a Hagana regular; one the son of farmers and a member of Faction B;[62] a third, a seaman and kibbutznik. Only he, who would not condescend even to look at one of us, not to mention to smile at or talk to us, his background was in . . . Betar. And as is always the case with apostates, so it was with him. His hatred was turned against his past and our present. By the 1950s he was a VIP, very close to the prime minister.

No, about such people there is nothing to wonder about. They do not pose a "problem." On the other hand, the good man, the truly good man, the "Dan Ram," is a problem and a danger.

Ram was from Hanita, where he was "village chief." This, too, is typical, for

Hanita is no mere settlement, but a border stronghold established in a dangerous place at a dangerous time. You can draw a direct line from Hanita to Tel Hai, from Eastern Galilee to Western Galilee, a line spanning twenty years from the days of Joseph Trumpeldor. The same line: the line of defense, "Hagana." Though a real Hagana and a real defense would not be the Hagana of the Organized Yishuv, which is not worthy of standing with Trumpeldor. Trumpeldor would never have put himself at the service of the British secret police; he was spiritually solid and proud. Nonetheless he was a man of Hagana and defense, and this illuminates an error made even by Betar. I called attention to this error at the Vilna Betar Conference and I called attention to it in an Underground pamphlet, *How Did Betar Fall*? Trumpeldor was a hero of defense in the truest and purest sense of the word. When we said of him that his weapons were "pure" or that "no purer blood was shed" than his, we spoke the truth. Pure weapons firing in defense, pure blood shed for his land.

But pure weapons do not yet imply weapons of conquest and battle. Though Trumpeldor had all the wonderful characteristics of a military man, an honorable man, still we cannot deduce that his political path was the necessary one for the Hebrew nation, the path ultimately chosen by the Underground, most of whose members came from Betar. The Betar greeting "Tel Hai!" is not the same as the IZL gun-emblazoned motto, "Only thus!"

There is no way anyone can call the Hagana's guns which killed Irgunist Yedidya Segal "pure," or the Hagana guns which fired on the Irgun ship *Altalena*. And the blood spilled trying to save Bet Hadar—the center of British murder in Tel Aviv—was not "pure."[63]

The hands of Hagana collaborators which carry flags to Trumpeldor's grave in Tel Hai are soiled hands. They are not worthy of presenting those flags.

A direct line leads from Tel Hai in Eastern Galilee to Hanita in Western Galilee, a direct ideological line: armed defense. Not surrender and not calling for British help. Defense with Hebrew weapons in hand.

Dan Ram was the "chief" of Hanita, and I assume he was also the best man there.

He carried out an operation in Syria, was wounded there and arrested for smuggling arms. He met Lehi members for the first time in the detention camp. A new world opened for him. A new analysis of political reality and interesting conclusions. "His heart was captured," as the saying goes, by the ideas of Lehi. He formed personal friendships and moved closer ideologically.

When I meet him in the summer of 5704 (1944), he is already prepared. I do not need to teach him the alphabet. He sees the British as foreign rulers, imperialists. He suffers from no complexes about keeping weapons "pure" when it comes to a war of liberation. At a time when the friendship and support of other Hagana members are expressed in esteem for the personal heroism of Lehi members, esteem which is always followed by reservations: "But from a political perspective . . . " or, "But from a social perspective . . . ," "Dan Ram" does not speak of personal empathy at all. He is himself courageous, experienced and ready for anything. Therefore he does not suffer, as others do, from an inferiority complex when faced with the personal heroism of our boys. This is good. It makes room for the political arena, which he enters. He identifies with everything.

While we talk in almost complete agreement in the Jerusalem Central Prison's infirmary, the Mapai Party and Faction B are struggling outside. Dan states his position almost as an ultimatum: "I'm giving Faction B one more chance; if it too proves disillusioning, then I'll draw the necessary conclusion and come over to you."

That was the last time I saw him, until years later when a Palmach unit stopped me from entering Jerusalem. (More on that later.) During the Underground war, friends of mine would occasionally run into him and apparently he remained the same "good" person he had been before. Because he was so "good," the Hagana kept him busy with all sorts of activist jobs, so he would not have too much free time, so he would find some satisfaction and not complain about wanting to be more active.

Now I realize that the benefits he and those like him brought to the war of liberation were costly. All these "almost" men, these people standing at the threshold of Lehi, all these members of the activist "opposition" within the Hagana—were ultimately used, without their knowledge, as a counterrevolutionary force. For several reasons:

Their existence in the Hagana prevented many fine youth from joining the ranks which were not "almost" but really freedom fighting. The extremist activist group in the Hagana led by "Dan Ram" and his friends led many astray and led themselves astray. This group "energetically" opposed collaboration—not only the passing of names to the British, but even the "independent" war the Hagana itself fought against the dissidents. Yes, there were many instances of these activists refusing to obey orders to act against the dissidents, even against the IZL which was further from their hearts than Lehi. I am sure that "Dan Ram" did not participate in informing, kidnapping, tearing down our posters or even in ambushes to interfere with our anti-British operations. The Hagana managed just fine without "Dan Ram." For every "Dan Ram," for every "good" boy, for every "sympathetic Palmachnik," there were dozens and hundreds of others who did what they were told out of obedience or genuine hatred or a desire to do something, anything. And "Dan Ram" could keep going with a clear conscience. To paraphrase the Bible, "His hands did not spill this blood." And to give him some real satisfaction, in addition to the negative satisfaction of "my hands did not shed this blood," the Hagana Command sent him and those like him on active operations, especially involving illegal immigration, which everyone agreed was a real battle against the regime. If not for this borderline layer of "Sternists" in the Hagana, many of those whose minds reached the Underground would have drawn the organizational conclusions, too. But "Dan Ram" never drew the final conclusion. Not in the shameful days of collaboration in the winter of 5705 when the entire Hagana was entirely at British disposal; certainly not in the Hagana's springtime, during the United Resistance. But after the "Resistance" ended, the time had again come for "Dan Ram" to reach the conclusion. And Faction B proved disillusioning, too. A retreat after the first blows it received at Yagur.[64] Dan Ram himself explained to me the secret of Yagur, two years before the search there. He told me how spiritually difficult it was for him, a kibbutznik, to join an underground war—the great efforts invested in building the kibbutz, the little that had been created in great toil, these tie a man down, provide all sorts of arguments against a war.

This is the first type of harm done by "Dan Ram"'s raising of the Hagana's prestige through his activism, thereby avoiding the healthy and clear polarization between freedom fighters and collaborators. "Dan Ram" blurred, and every blurring is bad.

The second type of harm was in the delusions he created in Lehi. A new world was suddenly opened to us. We saw that a person could be a kibbutznik and a freedom fighter. (Years later some members of Lehi would want to reciprocate and prove that freedom fighters could be good kibbutzniks. Both attempts failed.) Suddenly we saw that a person could be a loyal member of the Histadrut and a dedicated socialist and a freedom fighter all at once.

Now we confused concepts. We believed that our tragedy was in being detached from the people, a small group with no support among the people. The unique social structure of the Yishuv created the illusion that the "Organized Yishuv" and the "people" were identical. But who was this Organized Yishuv? It refers to the Labor movement and in particular the settlement movement within Labor.

Therefore we flipped over "Dan Ram"'s sympathy for us. Ah, we thought, we have made a break in the wall.

I, too, got caught in the web of this illusion. It was bewitching to see our workers' movement as a revolutionary movement, fighting for freedom, fighting the foreign rulers, with all possible means according to the laws of every war. Only a misunderstanding had apparently separated the national liberation movement and the workers. Now "Dan Ram" comes; now the heralds of change come.

During one of my enthusiastic moments over this change, Elchanan Halperin warned me: "Listen, you are new to the country, you don't know them. You'll see that they won't continue. I know them."

But I waved in his face the most recent issue of *Oz* (Strength) calling for total war. Elchanan Halperin is one of the last "Birionim" and I believe he is afflicted with Abba Ahimeirism, a virulent hatred of the Left. He is therefore not objective, is a prejudiced witness, unfit to testify. Despite what he says, the wall has been broken. We cannot repeat past mistakes. The revolutionary forces in the Hagana and on the left must be encouraged. After all, they are a force. If we had the same tools they had, they same weapons . . . the same support in the kibbutzim . . . .What momentum we could give to our actions! The Hagana really is on the verge of taking action. Nor would it be wise to extract the activists from its ranks. On the contrary, they should remain there. "Dan Ram" is very satisfied. He senses his purpose. He is proud that we respect him. For "Dan Ram" is an honest man and he feels inferior to us. But we pat him on the shoulder and tell him: Actually, there are no differences of opinion between us. To please us, "Dan Ram" curses Mapai and the defeatists. To please "Dan Ram" we criticize the IZL for being "rightist" and for conducting a war that is not really anti-imperialist.

That magical word, "anti-imperialism!" A magical bridge. True, our boys are spilling real blood in this war while "Dan Ram" is ordered even during what the Hagana called its "Struggle" not to take a British life. True, the IZL is giving British imperialism trouble even without anti-imperialist statements while the leftist Hashomer Hatzair is the pet dog of the secret police even as its mouth is full of anti-imperialist declarations. But the weight of our past relations with the IZL and our longing to see the idealistic kibbutzniks who love the land, to see them with us in the war and above all the good "Dan Ram," these are the factors that open my heart and our hearts to the illusion: There will be a united fighting force.

2. No Pardon

If I did not find uttering obscenities, or writing them, distasteful, I would use a crude expression to explain rather graphically that when a man lets his desires get the best of him, his brain is not in its normal place. And just as a person whose instincts are in control, and who has become somewhat like an animal, is embarrassed in hindsight, so must a man be embarrassed over those moments of weakness in Latrun or the Jerusalem Central Prison when illusions deceived him, when seductive snakes crawled over his flesh and his emotions whispering: Still, there will be a change. . . . Still, it is for the best, *fraj* will come, release . . . you will be at home . . . wife and daughter . . . and a good bed . . . and food . . . and strolls . . . and theater, and freedom . . . freedom.

This happens even though your mind stands aloof, laughing wholeheartedly; even though your hand writes logically and pointedly for *Hehazit* or *Hama'as*, proving that no change for the better can be expected from the two main events of the summer of 5705 (1945): the end of the World War and the Labor victory in the English elections.

The foolish emotion that swept the whole of Latrun when the war ended could not be controlled. The men were gripped by madness. They were actually packing their bags. And though everyone was sagaciously able to make jokes at the expense of this idiotic belief, somewhere in each person's heart the snake-like creature crept and whispered: Still, still . . . .

The optimists, the Hagana members, see in the end of the war itself a change in the political scenario, one beneficial to the Nation of Israel. For their political wisdom has always been: "Under these conditions the English are forced to appease the Arabs." At one point "these conditions" were the war in Ethiopia, later the pro-Nazi attitude of the Arabs. When the "danger" passes, they say, the friendship of the British will "return." With the war over, they say, the refugee problem will worsen. America will wake up and get involved. In short: Now that the last bullet has been fired, every last letter of the White Paper has lost its force. This "logic" is to be found in every Hebrew newspaper of the time.

Latrun is comprised, however, mostly of pessimists when it comes to the world's conscience and when it comes to a seasonal-scenario explanation of British opposition to us. Yet even the pessimistic majority finds a "still." The White Paper will not be canceled, they say; but still, some mercy will certainly be shown to mark the occasion.

In either case, emotion surges in the camp. A celebration, a victory celebration, is even held. Captain Clough runs from camp to camp giving speeches. We did not hear what he said in the camp of the pro-Nazi German detainees, but he gave us an enthusiastic "Zionist" speech. We concluded with the singing of *Hatikva* and went our ways, again joking and again, in the depths of his soul, every man packed his bags in expectation of release.

All of which was of course very foolish. The celebration, the shared "victory" of detainees and camp commandant, this joyous occasion lacked all logic. The victory brought us nothing. It certainly brought nothing to my brother Dov and my brother Natan and their wives and my mother, who were taken to Janovsky Square in Lvov and murdered and buried where they fell.

Real and fine emotion came only during the week we in our camp declared a "winter covering" project for the Jews of the concentration camps. A few mocked this philanthropic activity, but they were few and just liked to get others angry. The camp was very excited. Every man gathered the best of what he had and brought it to the collectors. Clothing, shirts, socks, shoes. Great warmth ran over me when I thought that soon the shirt I am donating will reach and warm the skin and bones of one who has practically risen from the grave. And maybe (at that time I did not know my family's fate), one of these things being piled here in this barracks in Latrun will actually reach my brother. The blood and the heart and the brain pound at this thought. We take great pride in pinning the notes on each sock so that those who receive the packages will know from whom the heartfelt gifts were sent: from the prisoners of the war of liberation in Eretz Israel. So that they will know that our blood is one. We did not consider the possibility of these notes disappearing into the pockets of one of the distributors, or the possibility that those who had risen from the grave and from the ovens were hardened to everything after the sights their eyes had seen.

But this was already during that naive summer of so many illusions, after the bags packed in the expectations of a pardon were forgotten.

In the meantime a second illusion, less painful than the first, but, still . . . had also dissipated.

The British parliamentary elections found me in prison. To mark the change in uniform, from plaster cast to leather bandages, I had to "vacation" several weeks in Jerusalem. There, I witnessed this second mass delusion.

The optimism was naturally less strong in Lehi's Cell 18 than in the IZL's Cell 19, and certainly less than in the Hagana's cell with its holiday atmosphere and flags raised to mark the victory of their "comrades" in the British Labor Party. One can say of the prison: He who sits longest sees farthest. Cynicism and mistrust of the British is therefore strongest in Joshua Zetler, one of the first political prisoners to be sent here. Our political analysis has no room for illusions. At issue is not a good or bad British government, a conservative-reactionary one or socialist-labor one. At issue is a true divisive conflict of interests between the Hebrew people seeking power in the Middle East and the British Empire. "Jerusalem stands and Caesaria is destroyed—believe it. Caesaria stands and Jerusalem is destroyed—believe it. Both stand—do not believe it." This political analysis from our past has been and always will be true.

Even when the war had ended we had not fallen prey to illusions, though then desire had encouraged the faith, somewhere deep in the heart, that a generous pardon would come for all detainees and political prisoners. This time, faced with a new British government, we have no such illusions. At least not in Lehi. But we do have fear. The night of the Labor victory, with songs of cheer booming from the Hagana cell and much drinking there, I predict disaster and I explain my own idea of "Still . . . ." This time: Still, the Labor Party will have to do something after all its public promises and decisions. They will throw a bone, they will immediately award 50,000 immigration certificates in the name of the urgent humanitarian needs of the survivors and, with this, they will silence Mapai. The Yishuv will be satisfied.

At the Zionist meeting in London, confusion. Weizmann has been building on the Conservatives headed by Churchill. Not that there is any danger of Weizmann turning anti-British if the Conservatives lose, Heaven forbid. No Englishman would do that. Still, Churchill is Weizmann's ally. Shertok, on the other hand, declares at the same meeting: "The victory of the Labor Party is a fatal blow to the White Paper." The newspaper *Davar* writes in its flowery language: "The victory of the Labor Party is a clear victory for the needs of Zionism. New prospects are visible, and a *new dawn*."

New dawn!

And in the skies of Britain and the skies of Eretz Israel rose like the morning star . . . Bevin.

The twentieth century, all of whose attributes are expressionist, centralized, clearly defined, whose science gave birth to the atom and hydrogen bombs, whose art borders on madness, this century gave the Hebrew nation Hitler and Bevin, as borders marking the line between the abyss of nonexistence and complete Redemption.

Small things do not happen in this century. Small things get lost among the huge boulders of history which roll rapidly on. And our fate depends on whether we too will become a boulder, crushing and not being crushed.

Neither my fears of "50,000 certificates of mercy" nor the hopes the Hagana prisoners had pinned on a Labor/Social-Democratic gesture were realized.

No pardons. No matter how an individual recipient interprets a pardon, for a community and for fighters a pardon by the enemy is a disaster. If upon taking office Bevin had granted Zionism a pardon, then Zionism would certainly have suffered the same fate as the Lehi member who later left an Israeli jail on a pardon and disappeared into Israel's Knesset. A pardon means—elimination. Bevin made a tactical mistake; true, it did not of itself destroy the British Empire. But Ben Gurion, who freed the Lehi member, was undoubtedly a better tactician.

At first glance, we thought Bevin's hostility had its benefits: It led to the Hagana's "Struggle," it did not allow for any lowering of the tension pressing on the leftist youth since the day the White Paper had first been issued. But that is the way we saw things in the heat of the 5705 summer when we, too, were enthusiastic about the cooperation between the Hagana, IZL and Lehi in a "united fighting force," seeing it as a harbinger of redemption. Only today do we begin to see things in their proper perspective. Bevin helped dissolve some illusions about the British, but also any we had about other Jewish forces. If not for us, Bevin and Ben Gurion would have colluded and engendered, with much emotion and joy, the "Morrison Plan" for some sort of autonomous province under British control, a sort of mini-pardon.

The Lehi and IZL prevented the disaster of such a pardon.

The prisons and the detention camps grew more crowded every day, crowded with men and with riffraff.

I returned from Jerusalem without a cast, wrapped in leather, and wrapped in joy over the unification of forces. A year later I put aside my leather wrapping when I left Latrun, without a pardon. A year later the Hagana people in the "United Resistance" put aside their swords. They surrendered to Bevin without a pardon.

3. The Fundamentals of Dr. Moshe Sneh

I witnessed the birth of the United Resistance movement from a distance. Because I was far from the day-to-day problems, the discussions and arguments over the practical matters, I was able to delve more into the theoretical aspects of what happened, how this miracle, this cooperation between the Underground and the Hagana, came to be. Indeed, this cooperation was the miraculous aspect, and not why they *stopped* the struggle three-quarters of a year later. The distance also helped me to understand the basis, or lack of basis, of the United Resistance movement. In November 1945, Latrun welcomed newly imprisoned Hagana members with open arms. (Why deny it? Widely open arms. We really were very happy to welcome them, these same people who only yesterday had been sending us here.) My understanding was not reached on evidence gleaned from the weak among them; I had no contact with Hashomer Hatzair, first of all because they were few in number, secondly because none of their leaders were ever brought in, and thirdly because we had no common language. I did however become friendly with logical, cultured men like Osrovitz of Givat Brenner and others from the activist Ahdut Haavoda, and by them I judge the Hagana. In so doing, I think I am giving the Hagana the benefit of the doubt.

Of course we rejoiced over the brotherhood of arms, but even we who had become somewhat close to the Hagana did not believe in the permanence of this partnership. We, who conceived of British imperialism as the darkest enemy of the Hebrew liberation movement, we could not believe in the staying power of a struggle the most extreme leaders of which never stopped proclaiming loyalty to Britain and an "understanding" of her interests.

I referred Hagana members in Latrun to the activist articles of the most active of activists, Dr. Moshe Sneh.[65]

Several months before the beginning of the "Struggle," Sneh wrote: "Our entire policy is based on the tested assumption that within the British Empire there is steadfast support for Zionism arising out of recognition of identical British and Zionist interests. Our struggle cannot be fought against British policy itself, but rather within British policy. The plan for a Jewish state is not meant to do away with British rule in this part of the world. On the contrary: The Jewish state will need Britain's protection, therefore no action is possible on our part that reveals any enmity toward England or that causes any damage to her vital interests" (*Haaretz*, 25 Tamuz).

And this man is supposed to lead the struggle! In case you think that, well, this was written before the elections in England, before the disillusionment following Labor's victory, before Bevin's speech, before the Resistance, then take a look what the same man wrote in the midst of the struggle: "We see no conflict between mass aliya in a Jewish state and large, strong British bases in this country. On the contrary, we view them favorably" ("The Nature of the Crisis," *Haaretz*, 19 Mar Heshvan).

If this was the nature of the crisis in the eyes of the man who symbolized the nature of the struggle, then we at least knew his earlier articles had not misled us.

Still we accepted the extended hand or we extended ours. I do not know, and it is not especially important, who initiated the cooperation between the three organizations. The accord had three positive aspects: a) the very existence of the agreement reduced the present and future incitement against the "dissidents"; b) the enemy's hopes for a Jewish civil war were dashed; and c) the need was met for coordination at a time when all the organizations were already operating.

But the benefits accruing to the other side, the Hagana, were no less important: a) "Dan Ram" was quieted and, with him, all those who were one millimeter away from leaving the Hagana to join us or the IZL. But experience after the Resistance ended proved that the Hagana had had nothing to fear, that "Dan Ram" would never have crossed and never did cross that last millimeter (I am referring of course to the collective "Dan Ram," a large number, not to individuals); b) the opponents of the Resistance within the Organized Yishuv were shown that the edge of the terror was blunted, dulled—if the dissidents cannot be strangled they can be slowed.

This argument was correct. Indeed, for the sake of wider action we had to sacrifice its ferocity. Nonetheless, we did not accept the restriction they tried to impose on us: not to take lives. We had no desire to fight a ridiculous war against inanimate property. This "not taking lives" policy quickly turned from being ridiculous to being criminal. Hagana members lost their lives only because, following orders, they refrained from shooting at the British who were guarding the objects which were to be blown up according to plan. A "war" like this—the world has never seen. This is one of the reasons I have quoted the articles of the leader of the "Struggle," for the basic political assumptions determined the minutest of tactical details. The Hagana never freed itself from these basic assumptions concerning Britain, and today it can also be said: not even in its new garb as the Labor movement in the State of Israel.

4. Holes We Made in the Agreement

Out of the agreement's bounds were actions involving the acquisition of weapons or money, and escapes from prison. Even these concessions were not easily wrested from the Hagana. At one point we even put forth a counterproposal: On the contrary, give us weapons and give us money and we will not operate in these two areas. Needless to say, this proposal was rejected, thereby leaving unresolved points of which we took advantage.

The parking lot operation was one of those that brought on another fit of hysteria. Ten soldiers fell. We had no difficulty in citing the clause in the agreement allowing procurement of arms. True, we did not turn much of a profit of that sort from this operation, but the side benefits were nothing to regret—losses to the enemy, which had dared to establish a military camp in the heart of Tel Aviv. The operation also allowed us to glimpse some warm hearts. In the course of the retreat through Kerem Hatemanim (the Yemenite neighborhood), doors and arms and hearts opened to us, directing us through the alleys, and a shower of blessings descended upon the retreating fighters. Not without reason does the Organized Yishuv consider the Jews of Yemen "primitive." If the "passive" Weizmann and the "activist" Sneh are to be considered progressive, then there is no more honorable title for the Yemenite Jews who hugged and kissed the Fighters for the Freedom of Israel than the title "primitive." With one million primitive Jews like them in Eretz Israel we could quickly establish a most progressive Kingdom of Israel.

One other exceptional occurrence took place at the start of the Resistance. It was definitely a violation of the agreement.

On the night of the November 1, 1945 (I usually cite Hebrew dates, but this night, with its first act of sabotage by the "United Resistance," is justifiably referred to by the Christian date, following the example of the November Balfour Declaration and the November U.N. decision on Israeli statehood. And we have already seen that as the Hagana saw it, the struggle was considered pressure *for* cooperation with British interests, so let us stick to their dates), an attempt was made to blow up the oil refinery. This was done without the permission of the Resistance Command. Just the opposite—we sent out feelers and were forbidden to act, on the grounds that this was for a later stage of the war. In reality, they hoped never to reach this later stage. Here, too, the issue involved political fundamentals. Rail tracks and bridges were not yet vital positions in terms of the Empire, at least not in peacetime. But the refineries were central to British imperialism in the Middle East. Therefore it was no coincidence that for years, we had had our eyes on this operation. In preparation, we took care to have a number of our men employed there. All the preparations were complete. The operation was so important in our eyes that the Central Command decided to execute it without the approval of the Resistance, on the assumption that if we succeed—whatever happens, happens. It would have been a blow to the heart of British imperialism here, as was the operation in Cairo. Its success would probably have hastened the British decision to withdraw from Eretz Israel, since it would have removed (or, more precisely, blown up) one of their reasons for staying.

The operation failed. The accidental detonation of one of the suitcases, which had been planted, with great difficulty, in the lion's jaw, foiled the plan and Moshe Bar Giora ("Israel"), who had once escaped from the Jerusalem Central Prison, was killed.

The "Resistance" leaders loyal to the Empire sighed in relief that the "disaster" was avoided and we, our pain and mourning proved greater than our joy that night of November 1, which many perceived as a historic turning point. Today we know, it was neither a turning point nor historic. *The United Resistance itself, in fact, was merely an episode in the war of liberation.*

The one positive result of the operation was the hint of what could be done by a fighting Hebrew youth. But the military implications of the moment were lost when it became clear that from a political perspective, there was no danger to be expected from any fighting youth. The remarks of Moshe Sneh, already cited, were enough to calm the regime; and they are the remarks of the most extreme activist, while Weizmann and his paper *Haaretz* and his main buttress Hashomer Hatzair complained against even a limited form of struggle. And then, the potency of the hint of what could be done by a fighting youth was lost, in part because of the confused expressions on the faces of those who should have been hinting. (Explaining this would require me to jump to the end of this unimportant episode called the "United Resistance" movement. If some color is still visible in the story of the "Struggle," it comes only as reflected light from the fire of the Underground war that *followed* the "Struggle.")

Therefore the question is not why the united struggle ended, but why it even began.

Many things were defined in the agreement between the organizations, many things were debated and haggled over and only one thing was not defined: the *purpose* of the "Struggle." A very strange phenomenon, perhaps unique. Even in the strange agreement between Russia and the Western powers, the purpose was defined: to defeat the Axis. But the United Resistance was for all practical purposes a movement without a definite purpose. No one will dare claim that it was a war for . . . a Hebrew state. If 100,000 immigration certificates had been granted, even over two years, the "Struggle" would have ended. So, that was not the purpose. So can we say . . . the purpose was aliya, the rescue of Jews? Let us leap forward three-quarters of a year into the future and see if this was achieved. So—why did the "Struggle" end? No, to pretend this was the purpose is to lie.

In this light, another heroic affair which has been distorted by history becomes clear: illegal immigration. Anyone who attaches the efforts for illegal immigration to the "Struggle" engages in deception. Moral and political deception.

Morally, the whole matter was shocking vis-à-vis the immigrants and disgraceful on the part of the Yishuv, its institutions and those loyal to it. The immigrants were abandoned to kinds of suffering and sacrifice that few in the Yishuv were willing to bear themselves. The immigration did not end with the sufferings of the *Exodus* from Europe but the "Struggle" did end with the trouble at Yagur. Reactions to the deportation and murder of immigrants were, to use the "sacred tongue" of the Yishuv, full of "restrained anger," very restrained indeed.

In practical terms, the immigration did not break the British blockade. In terms of numbers, no more Jews entered Eretz Israel than what was allowed by the White Paper, so all that really resulted was the bloody show. There could have been some military value in forcing the enemy to divert its troops to the shores, but this would have been of value only if the troops were needed elsewhere, if the struggle within the country had been offensive and unrelenting, which it was not. The immigration did, however, serve as a valve to release a pent-up desire for a struggle. But the Hagana blood that was thereby spared by not fighting the British within the country was paid for with the blood of these poor wretches, refugees from the hell of Europe. And so those on the left who had always scorned the "demonstrative Zionism" of Jabotinsky now engaged in the worst kind of demonstrativeness—Jabotinsky certainly never supported demonstrating with other peoples' blood.

Reverberations around the world? Yes. The reverberations were tremendous and the sympathy was great and the pity was greatest of all, and there was in this pity as in all pity something degrading and shameful. Politically all these emotions would not have moved the Hebrew ship even one mile closer to the shores of independence if not for . . . if not for the Underground which did not make do with demonstrations and the struggling of illegal immigrants. If one sees the date of the U.N. decision as the key date, and the U.N. resolution in favor of partition as the key factor in Israel's attaining independence, then he will be able to find one or two countries that voted for independence out of sympathy for the immigrants—though even this is debatable. I, however, oppose on principle overrating the November 1947 U.N. decision. Even among the Laborites in the Israeli government are some who say: The United Nations did not give us the state, our fighting youth did. (Again, Hashomer Hatzair most vocally, and in tandem with all the opponents of statehood, claims: "The United Nations gave.") Those who admit the fact that the youth won us our state, must also admit the absolute failure of the postwar illegal immigration project. No opening of the country's gates to free immigration, no heightening of the struggle in Eretz Israel, no political effect. The cruel conclusion is that the illegal immigration was for naught.

5. Bevin: An Underground Agent

So, what was the "Struggle" all about?

It had but one purpose: *to give the initiative back to the Yishuv and Histadrut leaders*. The game succeeded for three-quarters of a year. They got maximum control, with a minimum of concessions. Operations were few and far between. Whatever pressure the Underground put on the Resistance Command was met with criticism and delays. The easiest delay was the "administrative": "We are not a terrorist group, we have democratic institutions, elected leaders, and they must decide."

Admittedly, we never suspected that they lacked institutions. But we imagined that once the "Struggle" had been decided upon, its execution had been turned over to the Command, which would now make the decisions. We were wrong. This would have been a valid proposition if the goal had been known. As there was no defined goal, the institutions really did have to occasionally decide whether to do something or not. Weizmann's wild outburst at the Political Committee of the Zionist Congress in the winter of 5707 (December 1946) was not unwarranted: Bastard! Bastard! He (Moshe Sneh) blows up bridges without telling me, the president of the Zionist Organization!

We can say with total confidence that had we asked the opinion of the president of the Zionist Organization, he would have opposed the blowing up of bridges, since blowing up a bridge is undoubtedly more serious than sabotaging railroad tracks. Weizmann feared—justifiably—that the "Struggle" would destroy the bridges to London, meaning to him, too. Nonetheless, the president's fears were groundless. Not even we could have put it better than he when he railed at the Congress against what he called a "warm frost," trying to have it both ways. He said the choice was between ending the "Struggle" and adopting the path of the Sternists. He was right. So the miracle child, the United Resistance, chose to end the "Struggle."

Their desire to back out had been felt from the first moment. It was also an outgrowth of their aimlessness. Their activity came only from the need to regain the initiative, part of which had been taken by the British government and part by the Underground. True, even in the past the historic initiative had not been in the hands of the Jewish Agency. It had been, alternately, in the hands of the British regime or the Arabs, but in the past there was at least some aliya around which Agency philanthropic funds and businesses could gather. Also, in the past no other Jewish factor had been in competition for the initiative (for this was the original mistake of the Revisionist Party, that it did not know how to take the practical-revolutionary initiative into its own hands, thereby permitting the Agency to continue operating as if the Revisionists did not exist).

If not for the Underground, *Haaretz* and Hashomer Hatzair would have hailed the Morrison Plan for Jewish and Arab provinces but no Jewish state as "a great Zionist achievement under the present conditions," instead of the "minimum" they were willing to accept. And the Zionist "enterprise" would blossom for a few more years under the terms of the Morrison Plan. The Underground upset this idyll. Therefore the question of how to regain influence became the fundamental basis of Agency policy, all else was mere decoration. When the papers wrote that there was collaboration between the Underground and the British government, they were absolutely correct. But there was one tiny difference between our collaboration and the Agency's. They—Mapai and Mapam and the Hagana—operated under the instructions of the High Commissioner and the police chiefs, while our "collaboration" worked in reverse: Bevin and his representatives operated as if they had received instructions from the Underground. Nothing benefited the Underground more than Bevin's revealing his cards, than his anti-Zionist speeches, than the shooting of immigrants, than their deportations. If disaster had befallen Israel, and Churchill had been re-elected and had agreed to give 50,000 certificates a year, then the "miracle child" called "Struggle" would never have been born, and in its place collaboration would have been renewed with the police in order to deliver the final knockout to the Underground, in the name of the thousands of brothers whose rescue was, it would be said, being impeded by Underground actions.

During the Zionist Congress of December 1946, *Haaretz* wrote: "By increasing the monthly quota of immigration allowances from 1,500 to 4,000, England could in the fall of 1946 have found a way to avoid most of this year's mishaps."

The word "provocateur" was one of the most popular in the thesaurus of libels hurled at us. *I am sorry* to report that our actions—and how much more so, the IZL's actions—were not provocations. We acted out of real pain, out of the need to strike at the enemy without restraint. *I am sorry*, for to be honest, we were under an obligation to commit acts of provocation, too. *Luckily for us, Bevin acted as if he were our agent.* He alienated the Hebrew people without any provocations on our part. But what would have happened if the prime minister had been a "good" Englishman, one of those who keeps promises, who understands the suffering of the dispossessed? Then, if we had been experienced and cruel revolutionaries, as would have been proper, we would have been obligated to take action against these "good" Englishmen.

When some time later we in Lehi discussed an action against Bevin himself, and men even went to London and plans were laid and all that was necessary was the nod of the Central Command, Natan Friedman sent me to get Uri Zvi's advice. And Uri Zvi said: "No. The Hebrew nation should erect a statue in his honor."

Yes, this was the collaboration between us and the British government. The course events might have taken if Bevin had not been an "agent" of the Underground is difficult to surmise. The amount of success the Hagana would have had in its incitement of the people against us is difficult to guess. In theory, the progression should have been from United Resistance to civil war. The results of such a war at that time are hard to imagine.

But Bevin saved (whom?) from such developments.

The Hagana was brought into the thicket of the "Struggle" with no clear purpose. This kind of activity, as usual, led to much excitement and then confusion: "What next?"

6. What Did the "Struggle" Achieve?

Illegal immigration had played the role of a substitute, an alternative by means of which people were able to vent their anger, expend their energy. It had its satisfying moments, and even their supposed anger when people were killed was a form of satisfaction. A theory was concocted about "mass action." True, in revolutionary history mass action means mobs attacking the centers of government, the breaching of walls and palaces. But our so-called revolutionaries adhere to passive mass activity. They call thousands to rally at a certain place, and abandon them there to the brutality of the enemy army. Dozens of Jews fall and not even one of the enemy. The masochistic instinct willingly combines with the policy of finding substitutes for war. They stammer at the spilled blood, they stammer their anger and rage and mourning and suffering.

No one knows where this is leading. No one? Not exactly. The fog lies only in the middle. The extremes are not covered by fog. We understand the pointlessness of all this and all these victims, as do the opponents of the "Struggle," like Weizmann. But two purposes remain for continuing with the united "Struggle":

First, providing the men with satisfaction. They are doing "something." An operation they named their "Wingate Night" provides much satisfaction. Till now the IZL had held a monopoly on occupying houses, erecting roadblocks, and so forth. Now the Hagana displays an even greater operational ability. Palmach units "conquer" the city in order to permit immigrants to disembark. Lots of activity; few results. The boat of refugees is captured and towed into exile. But a young woman, Bracha Fuld, is killed by the British.[66] Thank Heaven it was not an Englishman! That would only bring trouble. But Bracha Fuld? Teeth are made to be grit! It is all right. There is a treasury of rhetoric from which to draw, stretching as far back as Tel Hai. To kill the enemy, a metamorphosis of character and style is necessary; to be killed—not so. And so the memorial meetings and proclamations of mourning have an intimate feeling about them. In contrast, we have but one answer for every member of the Underground who falls: Revenge. Revenge comes, sooner or later, regardless of whether the accounting is mathematically balanced. But there was no Hagana or establishment response to the murder of Bracha Fuld, and no response to the murder of unarmed men in the fields of Emek Hefer. Satisfaction apparently comes from the execution of the mission itself, which provides material for endless boasting around campfires and self-satisfied newspaper columns.

The second purpose: taking the initiative from the Underground and subjecting the Underground to their authority. This increases their internal prestige, allowing them to say, "You see? Apparently we are not 'so' traitorous, 'such' collaborators, if the dissidents themselves are willing to accept our authority."

Till now we had been plastering the walls with accusations of "Quislings, Petains" and suddenly—look, the Underground has accepted the authority of the Quislings and Petains. The public will think: "It must have been mere polemics, they must not really be Quislings and Petains. And if their authority is valid for the 'Struggle' and activism, so too must they be obeyed when they order a cease-fire, for 'after all' they do know how to fight when necessary." In truth, we took the increase in their internal prestige into account, but we calculated that they would not be able to retreat. We erred.

But they thought they could prove their ability to discipline the Underground, which would enhance their standing in the eyes of the British regime, which had failed to discipline us. Golda Meyerson would eventually ask the High Commissioner for permission to take independent action against the Underground, against her partners in the "Struggle." The High Commissioner will actually oppose such action, in line with that strange "collaboration" already cited between the Underground and the British enemy, a collaboration operating under its own inexorable logic.

7. One Hundred Thousand Obstacles

Warm frost is truly an impossibility. Either freeze or boil. The Hagana is confused. As a saving angel, the Anglo-American Committee appears. From time immemorial, a tested British tactic. The British may have feared that this time, the Jews would no longer cooperate with a British committee, or maybe they wanted to reduce the pressure from America. American public opinion had been roused thanks to the activities of the Bergson Group and the news from the Displaced Persons Camps.

The mantra "Committee of Inquiry," with the new "American" partner attached, appeared as a savior in the midst of the confusion reigning in the United Resistance. Now they need not reject our pressure to act for "technical" reasons, now they have a political excuse.

Tactically, the Underground was in a tight spot. Especially the IZL, because of its softer position on America, a result of close IZL ties to the Bergson Group, and also a faith in America that had replaced a lost faith in a Wedgwoodian England. Lehi's position is clearer and based more on principle, but an agreement is an agreement. As long as the United Resistance has some basis, we cannot back out. Also, public opinion in Eretz Israel sees American participation in the committee as an innovation.

Our tactical position worsened upon publication of the committee's recommendations. A proposal to allow the immigration of 100,000 refugees was for us one of the worst possible. Temptation straight from Satan. A gold mine for the Hagana. True, all the recommendations would be fatal to Zionism, but the magical words are "100,000." For rescuing our brethren takes precedence over all, no? Who will dare to display cruelty toward 100,000 brothers rotting in hunger and disease?

Internally, momentary tactics are struggling with the principle of the war. The struggle is not within our leadership. I agree to the views of the Lehi Command outside. The struggle is within the hearts of each and every one of us, and then the struggle is between the Central Command and the men in the ranks. The acquiescence of the Lehi Central Command to a cease-fire in the event 100,000 displaced persons are admitted to Eretz Israel surprised the rank and file.

In Latrun, and for a long time afterward, I was subjected to attacks in print and in conversation: How could we deviate from the principles of the war?

Actually, these attacks encouraged us.

Such are our fighters. At first glance one would expect them to be happy over a cease-fire, which offers them a break from fighting. The agreement with the Hagana relieved some of the internal tensions, but it also imposed a burden: We are no longer alone in battle; the other groups surpass us in numbers and we cannot ignore them. The agreement with them had also stolen from us our main method of combat: inflicting loss of life on the enemy. If the name "Sternists" had inspired fear among the enemy, it was thanks to this uncompromising kind of war. The IZL continued to warn the enemy by telephone that such and such a building is about to be blown up. (Even if, as time passes, the IZL stops sending warnings, still its intention is not to take lives.) Not so the "Sternists." Most of the damage they had inflicted was in lives. "How many goyim fell?" was the first question the commanders asked those who carried out the missions. It was the first question we asked each other when news of an operation reached Latrun. "Vegetarian" operations bring sneers. Now this main method of operation, the one hitting hardest at the nerves of the enemy, which is so sensitive to every Briton's life, this method to which we hold the "patent," has been taken from us. So, during the Resistance we execute acts of sabotage against trains and airports. Fine operations. Our boys quickly learn the arts of sabotage from IZL officers. Dov joins them for an operation in the south. Arnon, in Lod. The blowing up of airplanes at the Kfar Sirkin airport is the first major sabotage operation we execute ourselves. The extended periods of quiet are used for training and enlisting new members. And now, at the height of the momentum, cease-fire. Based on what? On this concession, permission for 100,000 immigrants? This is a total contradiction of everything that we have taught our fighters. We have inculcated them with the knowledge that we are not fighting for immigration certificates, but over the foreigner's right to issue certificates. Now the first test . . . and the Central Command fails. Maybe, ultimately, we also intend to be nothing more than a form of pressuring the British.

In writing and debate, inside and outside Latrun, these are the arguments used by the members of Lehi.

More than once a member of the Command finds himself in an uncomfortable position because of the collective responsibility imposed by secrecy. More than once I am forced to explain and justify deeds with which I am not fully at peace. But such is not the case with our acceptance of a cease-fire if 100,000 Jews will be let in. There is no comparison between this cease-fire and the earlier cease-fire after the assassination of Lord Moyne. The earlier one was a surrender to an ultimatum issued by the Hagana. The current one is a wise and correct tactic. In our organizational literature, someone writes that in any case, the British will not allow 100,000 Jews to immigrate. This is a weak argument. The Empire's official representatives could, after all, allow themselves to accept the committee's recommendations (which were less than the Morrison proposals would later be). And we should not rely on the theory that they will not do so. Usually, it is wrong to rely on an enemy's foolishness. The main argument for accepting the cease-fire is internal Jewish relations. The month of Shevat 5702 (February 1942) taught us not to operate in a vacuum. If the Hagana had stood waving in its hands 100,000 certificates for the European refugees, and then pointed to us as an obstacle, it would have been more successful in inciting hatred against us than it was even in the fearful days after the elimination of Lord Moyne. Only a minority can grasp principles, and in fighting for them that minority must lean on what is concrete. Thus we used the *Struma* disaster to expose the British face. Even though to us Britain was the enemy even without *Struma*, to us Britain was first of all *foreign* rule and only secondly—cruel, nonetheless, public opinion was more interested in the cruelty.

Had the British been smart and accepted the proposals of the Anglo-American Committee, they would have delivered a tactical blow to us far greater than gallows and detentions. Tactical, of course, not permanent. With the force of the idea of freedom already refined, and the will to freedom already steeled in the blood of Shevat 5702, we would have found a way around this, too, but we would have stood more alone and weaker than we did stand in the year 5707 (1947), the year the Underground reigned.

Explaining to members of Lehi how to transform themselves from freedom fighters to activist "Zionists" was not easy. But the Command did have the complete trust of the ranks, and perhaps of more importance: The course of events was on our side.

The British rejection of the committee's proposals nonetheless came as a surprise, considering that Bevin had promised to accept whatever was unanimously agreed upon. The committee's decision was unanimous, and Bevin rejected it. The rejection itself was foolish and the way in which it was done, more so. Clement Attlee insisted in a special address that as a condition, all the private organizations had to be dissolved. Yes, only an "agent" of the Underground could make such a demand. At that time, he had the ability to start a civil war, had he but distinguished between the armed groups and demanded the dissolution of the Underground while allowing the Hagana to retain its "unstained" purely defensive weapons. But Heaven "hardened Pharaoh's heart."

A great psychological, political and historical truth is expressed in that biblical verse.

The British demand offended all the organizations. We breathed a sigh of relief. The danger of a civil war passed, a war which would have found us in an uncomfortable position. The Hagana would have held 100,000 certificates and we would have held . . . a just principle. We had a second reason for being relieved: the end of the cease-fire. Another illusion had been shattered. There was no going back. We put pressure on the plodding administration of the Resistance (which delighted in its plodding). Natan Friedman wrote the joint communiqué that was approved:

1. Hebrew arms will not be laid down.
2. The war is not for 100,000 certificates, but for freedom.
3. Attlee's demand is an expression of hypocrisy.
4. The security necessary to save our brothers will not be compromised.

The above announcement was distorted as it was read on the Voice of Israel radio. I do not recall the changes, but I do recall that we in Latrun listened, and that I was greatly depressed. Several days later I learned that the wording was corrected, following a bitter protest by our Command.

Now, however, that the political objections to our ideas for operations were removed, the "technical" rejections resumed. The counterrevolutionary elements exploited the cease-fire, used the time to weaken the tension in the ranks, lower the desire to fight. Hashomer Hatzair's main worry was that the Hagana's agreement with us and the joint communiqué were tantamount to official recognition of the dissidents. Heaven forfend! But in the Ahdut Haavoda labor movement, party concerns also began devouring military concerns.

Precious months are passing (Iyar, Sivan). They discuss, examine, reject ideas for operations. We are steaming. The rejection of the "100,000" proposal should have been the signal for heightening the "Struggle," not relinquishing it. Unless behind the scenes, someone is still trying to save himself by selling us out . . . .

No doubt, the "sellers" were ready, all of them, minimalists and maximalists, Weizmann and Sneh, Meir Yaari and Israel Galili, and they would have silenced any "Dan Ram." But? They had no buyers, for Bevin was acting as if he were the top agent of the Underground.

During this long interlude, we engaged in several operations not subject to the official authority, such as confiscating weapons from the enemy. And since spirit and pen are also weapons, the Command decided on another "expropriation": an operation to free . . . me.

Torah

1. Rabbis

A. Rabbis of Different Sorts

Only one city's rabbinate is allowed to visit the camp.

The English are far from being lovers of principles. The Englishman is not willing to shed his blood for faith, but neither is he a heretic. Perhaps in all the world, only the Jews are willing to endanger their lives for the sanctification of God and to prevent the desecration of God. The Englishman is very careful. Little remains of the monarchy in England, except the crown and royal celebrations. No more than this remains of the Englishman's religion, but he still says: "God save the King!" even if he is not a hundred percent sure there is a God, even if he himself grants his king no rights at all. Therefore the English maintain more than any other people the balance between the Bible, which they call the "Old Testament," and the Gospel which they call the New.

This affinity for the Bible, which misled so many naive Jews or Jews who chose to be naive, does not spring from any philosophical acknowledgement of the justice of the biblical world-view, or any deep emotional faith, as it does, for instance, in some Slavic sects. For the English, this is simply a matter of being . . . careful. Who knows? What if? Can it hurt? And if in this approach they weaken their dependence on the Christian Church, well, this is a good by-product. To say that the Englishman believes in God is difficult. But his nature is such that he cannot decide and state: "There is no God." Or even more cautiously: "I don't believe in Him." Why not? Better not to take the risk. Why risk losing the world to come, even if its existence is doubtful? The English national drink: tea with milk.

The religious tolerance of the English, for which they are well known, derives from this nature. Their tolerance does not emerge from a world-view, but rather from unbelief that does not dare to be heretical. And if this spiritual condition can be crowned with the title of tolerance, so much the better.

And if we can benefit from this hypocrisy and assumed piety, and win contact with the world outside through regular visits by rabbis, so much the better.

But wait. Are we really benefiting?

Were the matter of rabbinical visits to the prisons and detention camps in the hands of the civilian administration, perhaps we would have made real gains, spiritual and organizational. But the entire matter was subject to the supervision of several additional factors:

1. The British secret police
2. The Hagana's secret police
3. The Chief Rabbinate.

Each group had its interests and its own policies. The interest of the British secret police was first of all—negative. To reduce the visiting rabbi's work to truly religious needs. As God must be neutral in this war between them and the "terrorists," they reasoned, so His representative, the rabbi, must be neutral.

In Jerusalem, the secret police failed on this point for one simple reason: When Rabbi Arye Levin began serving the Jerusalem Central Prison and visiting every Sabbath, there were not yet any Jewish political prisoners and the secret police paid no attention. When political prisoners were imprisoned there, beginning with the "Birionim" and concluding with members of Lehi, it was too late for the police to do anything; Reb Arye already had "tenure." But the British were able to deal as they pleased with new prisons and detention camps. Therefore Reb Arye's struggle to be awarded visitation rights to all camps and prisons, including the Women's Prison in Bethlehem, was in vain. The Chief Rabbinate would seem to have been under an obligation to intervene; the appointment of a rabbi for the prisons should have been in its hands. In any case, it had the option of making a recommendation. But Reb Arye was unable to hide two facts:

One, he was a disciple of the late Chief Rabbi Abraham Isaac Kook. And Rabbi Kook's stand against the entire Organized Yishuv on the Stavsky case was remembered well, like a dagger in the Yishuv's heart. When the Revisionist Stavsky was falsely accused of murdering Labor's Arlosoroff, Rabbi Kook was one of the very few people to defend Stavsky and other accused Revisionists against the libel. And no one familiar with Rabbi Kook's life and thought could have any doubt about the position he would have taken on the war for freedom, had he lived to see it.

Two, even beyond Reb Arye's loyalty to his rabbi, Rabbi Kook, Reb Arye was himself spiritually and emotionally close to those who were sanctifying God's name and people, and this was no secret.

These facts were enough to discourage the Hagana and the rabbinate from intervening to have Reb Arye appointed chaplain to the prisoners and detainees of Zion. Reb Arye himself was so modest, so quick to flee from honors and so hesitant to seek any position . . . yet this was one position he sought with all his might, so he would be able to visit his "children" all the time. Despite his age and shaky health (shaken in part because of his constant worrying over the suffering of the imprisoned) he even wanted to travel to visit the deported who were languishing in Kenyan and Sudanese exile. But the Hagana and the rabbinate did everything to prevent that from happening. There came a time when Reb Arye's strong will finally wore down British resistance, when Prisoner Supervisor Col. Scott was ready to sign Reb Arye's appointment, but someone intervened and the appointment was canceled. Which organization intervened, or if both had a hand in it, is unimportant. The love with which even the Hagana prisoners loved Reb Arye was no match for the "higher interests" of the National Institutions that control everything including the Chief Rabbinate, which—what luck!—contains no men of God like Rabbi Kook, who knew he represented the Spirit of Israel and the spirit of the Torah, which are greater than the institutions of the Organized Yishuv. One can argue that perhaps Rabbi Kook would not have so vigorously defended the Underground's actions. No one, however, can imagine that he would have cursed the Underground heroes as the Yishuv's Chief Rabbi Herzog did, calling the operations "despicable crimes" and, in so doing, tightening the noose around the necks of the accused Hakim and Bet-Zuri and Dov Gruner.

Rabbis of Israel!

Yet, Latrun was not lacking in rabbis.

B. Kosher and Honest

The regular one, he was kosher. He was all right in almost all respects. We had no reason to complain to the prison administration or the Chief Rabbinate. He was a kosher, honest rabbi: Rabbi Eliezrov.

A good Jew, impoverished, whose income derived mainly from the pittance he received for his visits to Latrun. His already pale face appeared even whiter surrounded by his black beard and garb. Soft, innocent eyes, in which we could see the ever-present struggle between his desire to help and his fear. He was so apprehensive. Once they searched him on his way out and he almost gave up the ghost, though he had not even a single smuggled message on him.

He used to arrive on Friday afternoons, always carrying a package of food. He did not eat the camp's food since not everything was completely kosher. He ate only the cold food he brought with him, from Friday afternoon till he returned to Jerusalem Sunday morning. He slept in the Hebrew officer's barracks near the camp office. He walked down to the camp for services Friday night, Saturday morning and Saturday night. The regular worshipers gathered in the synagogue. The rest of the camp remained unaffected, almost unaware. Men occasionally continued milling in bathing trunks outside the synagogue, smoking cigarettes. Sometimes the rabbi gave a Saturday afternoon lecture on chapters of the Mishna or the *Ethics of the Fathers*. Probably the same lecture he would have given in a study hall outside. That he wanted to give us more was obvious, but he was so weak, so weak. We made no demands on him, no. We did not trouble him with Underground missions. At most, some family request. Once, the Jewish sergeant told us the rabbi was going to be fired and was very upset. We submitted a request on behalf of the detainees to retain him and raise his salary.

His heart definitely ached for us and ours for him, but his heart was not with us, nor ours with him.[67]

He brought us his fine soul every Sabbath, but infused no new spirit in us.

The Sabbath was the property of the neutral Chief Rabbinate, supplying only "religious needs."

The holidays, on the other hand, were the monopoly of the second organization, the Hagana.

C. The Hagana Intelligence Rabbi

A different rabbi came each holiday, one who volunteered to leave his own home and spend time with the detainees. Because the Hagana had its hands in every sector of the country's life, the Hagana also had "rabbis" of its own. Sometimes members of the Hapoel Hamizrachi (Religious-Labor), sometimes "kosher" members of Mapai. We in the camp never checked the ordination certificates of the rabbis, and I have no desire to stain their reputations; I will not contest their claims. They responded to our trust with mutual trust and, unlike the other rabbis, they ate in our kitchen. They usually knew what to do in the synagogue, though there were cases (one, whose name was Canaani) of "rabbis" who did not know the order of the blessings or prayers, or who forgot to wash their hands before eating and were therefore not obligated to recite the Grace after Meals either. The common denominator was that they were most friendly and happy with the Hagana detainees, though they visited other barracks as well. Some of the camp's residents claimed all these rabbis were working for Hagana Intelligence. I doubt it. First of all, all members of the Hagana, especially the educated, served the Intelligence anyway. So nothing special was happening here. Secondly, what need was there to send Intelligence operatives when news from the camp, including detailed notes on each and every man, was already being compiled and sent from the camp by the Hagana detainees themselves?

My friend Dr. Kurtz twice took advantage of the possibility to volunteer. He was given the opportunity as an ordained rabbi, as an active member of Hapoel Hamizrachi, and as a Hagana member. He even left his family on Yom Kippur to come to the camp. I think I can be sure that in this case, aside from his wish to see me, he had no "suspicious" motives.

One holiday, I think it was Shavuoth in the year 5705 (1945), the top IZL man in the camp appeared before me in the hospital barracks and said: The rabbi sent for the holiday, Rabbi Halperin, has been identified by IZL members as the leader of the kidnappers and informers in Jerusalem. His name has been mentioned in internal IZL literature and he has been recognized by men in the camp. The camp is steaming. The extremists want to rough him up. The moderates will make do with preventing his entry into the camp.

I expressed my opposition to both responses. If he is so well known, I do not see why the working-over must wait till he comes here. I have nothing against his receiving his due outside. Here in the camp we cannot provide this pleasure to the goyim guarding us. They will not say that a Jew was attacked here; they will say a rabbi was attacked, and this will do no honor to the camp, our religion or our holiday. I was asked if honor is done to a synagogue, if an informer-rabbi worships inside. This was a strong argument, but I held to my view and suggested a compromise. In a break with tradition, he will not be received by camp representatives. He will not be invited to any barracks. He will be in the synagogue under the beadle's authority and will enter the Hagana barracks as their guest.

But someone had to inform the rabbi of this, and I accepted the mission. First, I told the Hagana members. They welcomed the rabbi and after services, he took a walk with me and heard what I had to say. He was tall, with a blond beard. His voice and mode of speech were typical of Hapoel Hamizrachi. He denied the accusation. Moreover, he said he had been opposed to the kidnapping and the turning over of men to the British and any form of collaboration. He was prepared to submit to an investigation, yes, let the men submit evidence.

He was quite emotional; which of course proves nothing. It might be a sign of righteousness but also of guilt. After all, being on the Underground's blacklist is no pleasure. Though a Hagana man on the Underground's blacklist is better off than an Underground member on the Hagana's blacklist . . . . And Rabbi Halperin, who is alive and well today, not buried and rotting like Yedidya Segal who was killed by the Hagana, is proof enough of this.

To this day, I do not know if I did the right thing.

D. The Dog in "Had Gadia"

Rabbi Dr. Jacob Goldman, who had been appointed chief prison chaplain, came for the last Passover holiday before my "liberation." Previously, he had been a military chaplain in the Jewish Brigade of the British army.

With all the respect and sympathy I feel toward him today, now that I know of his deeds and intentions, the truth is that when he first appeared before us I did not trust him much.

First, because of the official nature of his position, especially since we wanted to see our rabbi, Reb Arye, in his place. Secondly, as I myself was the product of a rabbinical seminary, as I was cooked in the same kitchen, I did not like this combination of titles, "Rabbi Dr."

Thirdly, and certainly this is a subjective weakness: It was he who unintentionally deprived me of that which was mine. I had led the Passover seder in 5705. I had "reigned" over two hundred and fifty detainees; and it was a deeply emotional experience for me, and from what I sensed and what I was told, for all the participants. I had clearly and joyously raised the wine cups, toasting all that was dear to us: The first cup to our families at home, who are sitting these very moments with tearful eyes, the eyes of mothers, fathers, wives and children. The second cup to all the prisoners of Zion and the detainees, and especially to the three hundred exiles in Africa. The third cup to the fighters outside. The fourth cup to the liberation of our homeland and the establishment of the Kingdom of Israel, *Malkhut Israel*. In this company, at the tables, after the fine wine, after the melodic and forceful reading of the Passover Haggada, the words I spoke were like redemption coming to suffocating souls, an expression of all our longings. I was able to tarry and prolong that prayer which in my father's mouth was the most sublime, which he sang with supreme pathos: "Nishmat Kol Hai" (The Soul of Every Living Being). I said a few words about the greatness of the prayer and then I sang it as Poppa sang it, with fervor, strong and proud, every word an entire world. "From Egypt You redeemed us!"

"Who is like Thee—Who is equal to Thee!"

Every holiday I would wait, trembling inside, for "Nishmat." And that seder in 5705, my first outside my home, with a wife weeping and a child at home who does not know how to ask, seven days after Hakim and Bet-Zuri went to the gallows in Cairo, and here before me, to my right and to my left, two hundred and fifty shining faces, precious faces, all of them with a corner of sadness in their hearts and all with their blood joyfully singing of the battle for freedom, all of them potential Hakims and Bet-Zuris, and I—how good it is that I am privileged to lead a seder for the likes of them.

Now—there will not be another seder like that on Passover eve, 5706 (1946). I do not know this rabbi's abilities, but I know my own. It is not possible that we will rise to the same heights. Circumstances would seem to be more favorable now. We are in the thick of the United Resistance movement; the number of Hagana men has increased. We are partners in the war. Blood has already been spilled in this joint war. Everything demands a greater stirring and greater fusion.

All my fears about the rabbi were not directed at him personally, for I did not know him. He had just taken a job. This was another reason for my lack of confidence in him.

Later, I learned that he won the hearts of the detained men and, even more, those of the detained women. He was warm and honorable, honest and dedicated. But that seder night he just did not do anything special, the seder would have ended in great disappointment if not for my intervention.

I sat on his left. On his right sat . . . Camp Commandant Clough. This goy who frequented Jewish homes in Tel Aviv, who spoke Hebrew well and who, when the World War ended, delivered a speech on the realization of the Balfour Declaration, had no evil intentions. The wine was good, the rabbi was an army officer, Clough always aimed to please—that is why he came here, after all. Perhaps the Hagana men appreciated Clough's presence, too—the "good Englishman." We did not appreciate the "honor" at all.

Rabbi Goldman led the seder according to tradition, *too precisely* according to tradition. He should have known *where* he was. *Who* were the people sitting before him? What was their spiritual background, what were their desires, for what were they suffering? The rabbi ignored all this. He led an abstract seder. He read the Haggada, spiced it with inconsequential jokes, without a word on the location or the historical epoch. He seemed beyond place and time. No wonder people were anxious for the *food*. No wonder that during the food an argument broke out with the Hagana members. The Betarim began singing a Betar song, the Hagana members rose and announced that this was not in the program and they would leave in protest. The rabbi was without a doubt bewildered. After the food, people began drifting out, dispirited.

Then I decided to move. I asked the rabbi's permission to raise the third cup and without waiting raised it in honor of the war for freedom. I do not know whether the goyish commandant recited the blessing over this cup, but I know he drank it.

And I raised the fourth cup, too, though the rabbi did not agree too enthusiastically to my doing so.

The honorable rabbi no longer exists. I see his confusion, but I also see the stirring among the participants. The demonstrative exit of the Hagana members also clarified the situation. As of now we are again among family, and the Passover seder has always been made holy by families. Only one remains here who does not belong, a foreign body: the commandant. I have no reason to be bitter toward him personally. On the contrary, he treats me kindly. Some say this is because of his two illegitimate sons by an Irish-Christian woman, who were students at the school where I taught. But I think he treats me well for a different reason: He is a clever goy. The war with the Yishuv does not interest him. He is interested only in the rank insignia on his shoulders. For their sake, he guards against escapes from the camp. And there is a head sitting on those shoulders which he cares about no less than the insignia. He wants a good "file" with the Underground, as far as possible. He does not find the fate of his friend Wilkins very encouraging. He knows that my recommendations carry some weight. So he does little favors for me.

Once he was on his way to the camp and saw my wife walking; he gave her a lift. He allows her to visit more than the official once a month. Once he allowed us to meet in his office. He arranges a visit for me with my private doctor in Jerusalem whenever I want (I eventually took advantage of this favor to be rid of him once and for all). All these "favors" are deliberate and just so that I will speak well of him, when the day comes that we find ourselves speaking of him. And all those who sang the praises of this "good goy" and did not see the calculating side of him, remember: When the warden of Acco Prison refused to hang Dov Gruner and his friends, Captain Clough was brought in and he neither refused nor hesitated. From where did his "courage" come, so suddenly? Simple: By that time he was already safely out of bounds. He was then the warden of the Shchem Prison, with no Jewish inmates.

This seder night I am not settling any "personal" accounts with him. The moment I took the throne from Rabbi Goldman, I ceased to be a private individual and became instead a representative of the kingdom; and if I am part of the kingdom, then this British captain at the head of the table is an enemy of the kingdom. Maybe it is not good manners to attack him; he is our guest, but, I confess, I do not know how to act tactfully toward someone I hate, even if he is my guest. Manners have their limits, too. If a man is my opponent, and our differences of opinion are truly a matter of different opinions and nothing more, then I know how to listen and I try to understand, too. When the difference is not one of opinion but of interests, and the conflict is an end in itself, with an either/or aspect, and especially when the matter concerns two warring parties, and especially when the first party imprisons the second, then I do not indulge in politeness. Captain Clough sits at the head of the table, the representative of the regime imprisoning us, the regime we are fighting; I think that honesty is better manners than hypocrisy and toadying. The days of chivalry in war have passed, no matter how many tears Don Quixote sheds.

I am angered by this goy who mocks us, knowingly or not, and who sits with us celebrating as if we were all equals, in *his* detention camp on *our* holiday of freedom. And even if he is here reading the Haggada, I will not suffer him gladly.

Before the seder's end, I decided to wreck the idyllic atmosphere. When we reached the "Had Gadia" song I again rose to say a few words. The Anglo-American Committee of Inquiry was at the time in the country "inquiring" of both sides, Arab and Jewish.

There is a serious problem, I began, in "Had Gadia" (this is a joke told by the poet Saul Tschernichovsky in one of his idylls). The cat that eats the goat (in the song) is plainly a murderer. If so, the dog that bites the cat is a fair, just judge, following law and tradition. If so, why did the stick beat the dog? The stick would then be evil. If the stick is evil, then the fire was right to burn the stick, the water wrong to quench the fire, the ox right for drinking the water, the slaughterer wrong for killing the ox and the Angel of Death right for slaying the slaughterer. The result appears to be that God commits an act of injustice when he slays the Angel of Death. Can this be?

The audience had fun with the problem and so did the goy.

The solution, I continued, is: True, the cat is a murderer. But you, the dog, who made you the judge?

I concluded: I am occasionally reminded of this story when the English come to create peace between Arab and Jew, when they undertake inquiries and aim to pass judgment. Whatever will be between the Arabs and us will be, either they will ravage us or we will ravage them. But you English, you dogs, who asked you to be the judges here?

What happened next cannot be fully described. Thunderous laughter and applause shook the wooden barracks. Even among those diners who usually took such care not to allow any slips in their behavior or speech, who pretended to be innocent victims, even they were swept up in the collective roar. A real political demonstration.

I did not see the goy's face, for the rabbi was between us. The rabbi was in a tight spot. I understand him. He is the official "king" here, an official person at any rate, a representative of the official Yishuv and, here in his presence and under his supervision, words like mine were spoken.

And who saved him from this bewilderment? The goy.

Even though he had long ago finished the four cups of wine and to be totally "kosher" he apparently drank to the four sons and the ten plagues as well, still his mind worked quickly. He jumped from his seat and asked the rabbi for permission to speak.

Nothing could have restored the room to silence as this did. Everyone strained to listen. He opened in Hebrew and apologized for his crude language, switching to English. And this is what he said: Although a dog does not usually answer, I will do something unusual and answer Dr. Scheib.

This sharp opening was successful, and the impression was given that a sharp debate was about to begin. Instead came . . . a Zionist speech.

First of all, the actions of the British government are not approved by all members of the government. Sometimes those carrying out the decisions do so of necessity and not out of malice. Secondly, this is not the will of the British nation, which sympathizes with the Hebrew nation. I am not free of course to say all that I feel. We are here carrying out instructions and they are not always to our liking. And finally I can say only this: I wish you what we have just read in the Haggada: Next year in Jerusalem.

He was most certainly applauded. Whether we believe that he was a "good Englishman" or, as I believe, that he was a very smart one, in either case this was a brave and wise move on his part. Any other response, of anger or of humiliation, would have brought laughter. If the Hagana members had been there, they would probably have swooned with joy, seeing this as evidence supporting their theory. For this is just what they hope for, the appearance of the "good Englishman" who will unseat Bevin and write some new MacDonald letter and give the Jewish Agency "in consideration of the suffering of the displaced Jews and without jeopardizing the political status of the country and the natural rights of the Arabs" . . . 5,000 certificates a month. Obviously they, the Hagana members imprisoned because of the "Struggle," would be immediately released, and woe to the dissidents who would dare spoil the renewed "traditional friendship." This was the question I used to ask the detained

Hagana members, day and night: In return for how many certificates per month are you willing to renew the hunting "season," hunting the Underground in collaboration with the British?

The Hagana members, however, had earlier left the room in protest over the singing of "In blood and fire Judea will rise." Now they were being punished for having done so. They were deprived of the pleasure in which they would have basked had they heard the reply of the clever Captain Clough.

But Rabbi Goldman was happiest of all. He was "a righteous man saved from trouble." We never met again. Perhaps he felt some resentment toward me; perhaps, inside, he felt a little suppressed joy, too.

E. The Chief Rabbis

As one might expect, the visits of the Chief Rabbis had an effect on the camp. The basic attitude of most of the detainees to religion was one of respect, even if they were not devoutly observant. Religion was, for them, a national value. And men "resided" in Latrun only because of national values. As far as we knew, no members of Hapoel Hamizrachi or Agudat Israel were arrested in a zealous war for religious values, or socialist members of Hashomer Hatzair for fomenting revolution (though some Communists did spend time in Mizra and Acco).

I have no doubt what would have happened in a detention camp had one existed in Rabbi Kook's time and had he come for a visit. A political detention camp can serve as a barometer of any country's political atmosphere and sensitivity. If the country's Chief Rabbis visit such a camp and hearts do not pound, this is a very bad sign, very revealing about the nature of the Chief Rabbis.

In all honesty, some distinction must be made between the two Chief Rabbis. Sephardic Rabbi Benzion Chai Ouziel made a fine impression in his outward appearance, the festive dress he donned in honor of the occasion, his sword-bearing bodyguard walking before him. In our Ashkenazic eyes, this was all unusual, like the kissing of his hand by the Sephardic detainees. Unusual, but fine. Anyone who entered a synagogue for the first time to hear the rabbi's greeting was also impressed. He spoke of the detainees' suffering and consoled them. And his consolation made a pleasant impression on me, too. To be precise: cold and pleasant. The rabbi spoke of Joseph who also sat in prison, but that was God's will and he left prison as deputy to the king. "And you, dear children, do not know whether in your imprisonment here there is not some hidden intention of Divine providence, too."

What the hidden intention of Divine providence was—I do not know. In any case, it was our clear intention to come out of here real kings, meaning free men of a free nation in a free homeland. If this is what the rabbi meant, then his consolation was pleasant. So why did I perceive a chill in his blessing? Maybe because of his fine appearance and because afterward, I heard this blessing four or five times, that is to say, every time that Chief Rabbi Ouziel visited. Yet, we certainly had no reason to find any fault with his visits, as we had after the one and only visit, during my stay, of Chief Rabbi Herzog.

I cannot say we did not have preconceived notions about him. We knew him well from his occasional declarations against our "despicable deeds." We never heard him use such language when speaking of the English. When Jews were murdered or doomed, Rabbi Herzog always managed to find polite, stylish words of protest filtered through seven layers of diplomacy. But if the blood spilled was not Jewish, but English, then the rabbi suddenly forgot the commandment to keep to clean language and vented his spleen. The Chief Rabbi, who we should have seen as a representative of the generations-deep spirit of Israel, was no more than the director of the religious department of the Organized Yishuv, and closer to people like Meir Yaari, to the unbelievers, to those who mocked God for mockery's sake, than to us.

Had the camp been as homogenous as it was when I first arrived, it would certainly have had the courage to tell the Chief Rabbi that he was unwelcome. Simply unwelcome. But the camp was not such a clearly defined political entity. The men here were only "suspects." The only instances of solidarity involved the kitchen. The fear of being sent to exile in Africa hung above us all. Also, the possibility of obtaining a *fraj* by means of bribing police officers Hamilton and Curtis, then partners with some Jewish lawyers, discouraged many from political activity. Under these circumstances, Rabbi Herzog's visit assumed the air of a Theatre of the Absurd. He came as if he were a Jewish middleman, his secretary sat at his side running a fill-out-your-request office. One by one the detainees approached the Chief Rabbi, each declaiming his troubles, and the rabbi ordered his secretary to make notes. Needless to say, nothing came of any of these requests. The Chief Rabbi could not recommend the release of someone of whom he was not 100 percent certain that he was not a terrorist. Therefore, the final opinion was always in the hands of Hagana Intelligence, which could check a person's case history.

The rabbi reached the heights of derision, however, upon the conclusion of this comedy of supposed "individual treatment." The speech or lesson he delivered was so absurdly inappropriate for this time and place, that because I know the rabbi is not stupid, I am forced to conclude that he was just naive.

On what will the Chief Rabbi of Israel in Zion in the year 5706 (1946) lecture, before two hundred nationalist detainees? On the fate of the nation? The fate of the land? The suffering of the detainees, of the families? The hopes for the future?

No. In this time and place, he found a need to deliver a convincing address on the oneness of God. He took the verse "Hear O Israel, the Lord is God the Lord is one" and homiletically examined it to prove that God is indeed one.

The few listeners whose patience and manners enabled them to stay till the sermon's end were, I believe, totally convinced that our God is one, in heaven and earth, and also in the detention camp.

Therefore, we waited with twice as much longing and love for the visit of he who was certainly, certainly one of the world's thirty-six righteous men, the visit of Reb Arye Levin.

F. The Rebbe

He was forced to endure seven humiliations and seventy-seven insults before he was granted permission to visit the camp. True, he was rabbi to the prisoners in Jerusalem. But his spirit was not satisfied. A real "imperialist." The territory he craved to conquer was the suffering of the youth of Israel, all suffering, especially suffering in prison, and above all: suffering for the freedom of Israel.

He who has not seen how the camp welcomed Reb Arye, does not know the power of love and faith. He does not know this, either: No person in Israel ever disbelieves completely. Every Jew really does have a portion in the world to come, because in every Jew there is always one corner hidden deep in the soul in which can be found the Divine Presence, in which can be found faith, even if it is encased in many, many shells. And when is it revealed? When a *tsaddik*, a righteous, saintly person, comes and lifts it up.

The same fellow who would arrogantly or apathetically stroll outside the synagogue during Sabbath services, smoking a cigarette, this same fellow would suddenly run from barracks to barracks in search of a yarmulke to cover his head, and he would push to reach the rebbe and say hello and gaze into his beautiful face and beautiful eyes. And if this fellow were an "enlightened" heretic, he would be slightly embarrassed and would justify his excitement by saying: I am not honoring the man of religion but the man. Of course the heart paid no attention to the mouth's idle chatter. Of what relevance was this distinction when talking of Reb Arye? And another matter the mouth could not explain: If so, why was a "man" of this sort never found among the nonreligious? Is it coincidence that this man who everyone thinks is a higher man and holy, is also a man of religion and total faith?

The camp's best days were the days Reb Arye visited. Even a blind man could see the Divine Presence accompanying Reb Arye. He brought no bodyguard and no secretary. He brought only his heart. And the heart took notes and the heart felt. He rejoiced with us as would a child who has found his mother. He arrived laden with love and left laden with more, for we all gave him our love. He arrived laden with regards and information and left with more regards and information. Some information was of the kind none of us would share even with those closest to us, but with Reb Arye, we share. Addresses, names, dates. Reb Arye makes a mental note and he will remember. He remembers . . . now he begins calling names. "Mr. So-and-so." Where is he? Why is he not here yet? And people run across the camp looking for him. For sometimes Reb Arye comes unexpectedly, and the inmates are dispersed. And Reb Arye must see everyone, everyone.

One stormy day when he, Reb Arye, is himself dressed only in a thin frock coat, he rubs my arms and says worriedly: "Why have you come out like this, without a coat?" And I felt like Momma and Poppa were standing above my cradle covering me with warm blankets and caresses.

Now look: Seemingly these are the same men who yesterday crowded around Rabbi Herzog's table, where he *forced* them to deceive him, to lie, to swear that they were innocent, that they had nothing to do with the crimes and that they oppose the crimes; seemingly these are the same men, yet suddenly everything has changed. No one can lie to Reb Arye, no one needs to. True, Reb Arye is powerless, he does not have the ability to free anyone, and no one in the secret police would pay any attention to his recommendations (perhaps this is the greatest compliment one can utter about Reb Arye!); but apparently people need something other than *fraj*, and there is not a raw material in the world that cannot be ennobled by spirit. Only the pipeline matters, and there is no pipeline like love and therefore there is no human material in Latrun so raw—and oh, there is plenty of rawness here—that the pipeline of love flowing from Reb Arye's soul does not affect him, make him more gentle, soften him, better him. No shell can withstand him.

Reb Arye recites the afternoon service, Minha. What in Israel is simpler and yet often shown more disrespect than the weekday afternoon service? Reb Arye says the "Shemona Esreh" (Eighteen Blessings) out loud. What's this? Why do tears suddenly form in our eyes? Why do our hearts rise to our throats? Reb Arye says the Eighteen Blessings.

"Restore our judges as at first," says Reb Arye. And you, it is as if you suddenly heard the prayer for the first time, as if the meaning of the words has for the first time become clear to you. Here, here in a British detention camp in Eretz Israel, the meaning of the good and simple words spoken by Reb Arye suddenly becomes clear: "Restore our judges as at first."

And so it is with blessing after blessing. Every word in its simplicity. They come from the heart and your heart joins them. The hearts in the synagogue barracks are like waves, waves rising and descending, rising and descending.

After the prayers, Reb Arye lectures. Lectures? No, Reb Arye does not lecture. He does not know how. Other rabbis speak better than he. "Better," if "good" means oratorical artistry or rules of rhetoric, if good means outward structure. Yes, these qualities are lacking in Reb Arye's speech. And even his accent, which is half Ashkenazic, is not understood by many, yet people stand and listen, or perhaps they do not listen, they drink, drink the good words. For Reb Arye speaks from his heart, and it is as if he is speaking from our hearts. And Reb Arye knows how, in every speech, to hint at the matters of most concern to us. At an edict issued, at a battle fought, of victims who fell, of the hanged. Reb Arye lives with all these matters. He is one of us.

I do not know why I merited his occasionally sharing additional bits of Torah with me, after the lessons he gave the whole camp. I am not always worthy of this. I face many people, fully cognizant of my own worth; but whenever I face him, I feel like an empty glass and all I can do is absorb.

When the time comes to leave, he finds it difficult to part. I envy you—he promises and repeats—I envy you. For you have the great privilege of actually suffering for Israel, while I . . . what am I? I can only share in your suffering. Your privilege is greater than mine.

Another time, in speaking of the slaughter of our people in the Diaspora: Here I am returning to my home, my family, I will sit at my table, the world goes on, but you, you are the only ones who are really tormented, not like the Fast Days proclaimed outside which are held just to fulfill the obligation.

And we all believe him, believe that he does indeed envy us. Deep in my heart I know that he envies us and not only the suffering, but also the action we take outside, for which we are suffering here. And if he were young . . . .

Reb Arye leaves the camp. Again and again he looks back. Again and again he shakes—no, envelopes—your hand, and again and again he whispers as he always does: God's salvation is as swift as the blinking of an eye, the blinking of an eye.

And long after, long after his departure the warmth remains in the camp, in the eyes, in the hands he shook, and the prayer has spread in our hearts. Our emotions stir and spin, spin, and all, all of them meet on this one point: It is good to be a Jew if there are Jews like this. Even if there are many others, oh, so many others, it is enough that there are a few like him. By these, a race is judged.

2. Joshua Bin Nun's Order of the Day

On one of those heart-rending nights, the morning after which a man felt both joy and shame that he had remained in the camp, a dear friend, whom I loved more than any other outside of my own Lehi men, was torn from me.

To say "I loved him more" is not easy. Is defining and classifying all the loves with which I loved the imprisoned Jews of Latrun easy? Many and varied were the characters and the relations. Not to speak of the personal closeness of the Lehi members, the men of the smallest of all movements, born in actual blood—each of whom was worth entire units of other organizations considering what was demanded of us, in being able to grasp concepts and in readiness to take individual action. Perhaps I lost sight of personal deficiencies. My love for them resembled the red twilight I saw nowhere else in Eretz Israel, only here as it poured into the Ayalon Valley on autumn and spring evenings, filling the entire valley until even the police building opposite glowed prettily, until even the stupid face of the Arab *nabatchi* beamed. Or how should I differentiate between the love with which I loved Kritzman, for instance, and my love for "Von Foxy." The former, a lawyer who left almost no clause unviolated, from British legal clauses to those of respectable social manners. One minute he talked to you, with a heavy heart, of our most serious problems and the next minute he was running wild in the barracks. One minute he talked to the camp commandant as a master to his slave, the next he was leading services in the synagogue, reciting the Blessing of the New Moon as a repentant son before his father. There is nothing you can say to Kritzman for which he will not have a biblical verse or rabbinical maxim ready to support his own view (though sometimes the reference was clear and sometimes he had to extrapolate). And the latter? I do not know the origin of the name "Von Foxy." I do not recall his real name.

Only this: He was a driver from Petach Tikva and his face did not appear especially intellectual. But from his mouth came pearls. One song was his favorite: "Oy, der Rebbe, der Rebbe" (Poppa is whispering that I should quote the song now but Momma forbids), and the guys would gather round him calling, "Foxy! 'Oy der Rebbe,'" and he sang and the whole audience, all of it, sang the refrain—one could not help but join in—and Foxy was happy. Once, during a Purim party I think, he was asked to climb a table and sing for everyone and no one was happier than he. When news of his release reached him, he sang the song as a parting hymn. A table was placed between the gates, the entire camp gathered and he sang till he was hoarse. He had been arrested on suspicion of participating in an IZL operation with his car. When questioned, his alibi was that he had spent that particular night in the fields with a woman. When pressed to reveal her name, he replied, "Nu, I'll tell you the truth, she was a prostitute . . . nu . . . for what respectable woman would go out with me?" But his face became suddenly beautiful and holy whenever he read of a respectable blow delivered to the goyim outside. All alibis disappeared from his eyes, which then glowed with joy, and his hands, which he then rubbed together, also betrayed him and the envy he felt for the men outside. His face grew beautiful when he went—I once saw him like this because we went together—to visit his mother. You see that he is willing to give his soul for her just as he is willing to give it for the war. It does not detract from his love that after the visit his mother stands another half hour on the road five hundred meters away waving to him with a handkerchief, waving again and again, and she, the old woman, the weak one, does not tire and he, the healthy one, tires and jumps on a chair and shouts with all his strength: *Oy, Momma, gey shoyn a heim* (go home already) and ends in a Russian triple curse. When she is out of sight, his eyes shed tears.

And I love the both of them, the scholarly lawyer, the proud representative of the camp who knows how to be so simply childish, and also the one whose holiness shines through his coarse language. How does one describe levels of love?

Nonetheless, I love Dr. Haim Hanani, who was torn from me one night, with love of another kind.

Maybe because he filled an empty page of my life's calendar. Between the time I was a son in my parent's home and my university years lies a year and a half as wide as the ocean, the years in which I finished the Polish-Hebrew Gymnasium in Lodz. What is left me from that year and a half except a diploma? It was there that my teacher and educator Dr. Jeremiah Frankl began prophesying a future for me as an author. It was there that he himself pushed me in a different direction. In the classes dealing with Ahad Haam, about whom he was very enthused, he of necessity lectured about Ahad Haam's opponent, Berdichevsky. Then I gravitated to Berdichevsky and through Berdichevsky I found Nietzsche. What else is left from those days? I lived in one room with three friends, and all three were members of "Gordonia" and our nighttime arguments were furious. Once they invited me to go with them to the home of Pinchas Lubianiker (Lavon) for lunch on Yom Kippur.[68] I refused, even though by nature I am rebellious. But I never felt the need to rebel against He who rules from heaven. I recalled this "revolutionary" spirit of Lodz's Gordonia members in 1928, when years later I sat in the spiritual home of Pinchas Lubianiker, Hulda, reading his *Fundamentals*. I talked with the Hulda farmers and saw how submissive they were, how nonrebellious toward the earthly regime that was by all counts crueler than that of Heaven.

The Class of 1928 was dispersed across the world. One day the British bring Dr. Haim Hanani, a member of that class, to Latrun. I had no contact with him in Lodz, perhaps because he sat on the first bench and I on the last, perhaps because he was the top student in mathematics and physics and I was the worst. And now he is entering the camp of those detained on suspicion of terror. I am both surprised and happy. He obviously has not been brought in for failing to solve some logarithmic equation (I picked "logarithmic equation" at random, only because I remember the trouble I had with logarithms, whose rules I could never absorb). First, because the British Emergency Laws do not apply to such problems; secondly, because he, Haim, could not possibly fail to solve them. If my teachers discovered some literary ability in me, they found a mathematical genius in him. The fact that for years to come he will be an administrative clerk at a university says more about that university than about him; eventually he will be recognized and given a professorship at the Technion in Haifa.

When I see that Dr. Hanani is part of our fine Latrun family, my feelings toward mathematics suddenly warm.

How did Hanani get here? Apparently, even in Lodz he had been a member of Betar. When he arrived in this country he worked and starved in the Plugot Betar units. His heart is certainly with the Underground, though as far as I know he is not now active, except for being a relative of the IZL's Jerusalem commander, and except for being on friendly terms with Menachem Begin. I had seen the two of them walking together in Jerusalem when Begin was still wearing a Polish army uniform. But the British CID decided that he was a member of the IZL's "Brain Trust" and arrested him. All the character references he brought from his university's presidium were useless. All the efforts of an important Australian scientific institute, which asked the university to "loan" Dr. Hanani for a year or two, were useless. His file with the secret police was in inverse proportion to his thin face and body, and in direct proportion to the suffering of his family (a wife and two little children with no means at all).

My intention is not merely to tell of a personal friendship, or of one arrest out of many hundreds. The story of Hanani's Latrun spell is worth recounting. He walks here in a special world. In terms of the camp's organization, he is not just one of the crowd, he is almost a model for the crowd.

Many of those in the camp, including me, try to avoid the "dirty" work given us as barracks or camp members. Who, for instance, enjoys kitchen duty? Or whose heart is excited by the idea of sorting rice? Dr. Hanani is different. I plead with him to win exemption from this work on the basis of his spiritual service to the camp, but he does not want to be excused. His small philosophical beard does not interfere with his washing the barracks' floor, and his philosophical contemplation does not interfere with his stirring a pot of lentils in the kitchen. As nature would have it, who are the most depressed in the camp? Those who were falsely arrested. They move about gloomy and mournful, telling everyone their troubles and showering the police and anyone who has any connection to the police with letters and more letters. Not Hanani: He is a man of thought, an "idealist" in his world-view. *Physically* he has done no wrong, at least not recently. But *spiritually*? Whoa! What a "criminal" he is. For he is a religious believer and also a student of Jabotinsky. Anyway, national pathos and political realism combine in him. And the man of science in him commands him to scientifically find a way to put these characteristics at the service of the Hebrew people, avenging and fighting for greatness. Though the Emergency Laws do not penetrate his mind very deeply, he cannot ignore them and therefore does not consider himself "innocent." Perhaps for this reason, or perhaps because of some of the other characteristics in the catalogue of nobility, he is one of the quietest prisoners.

But he does not waste a single hour. He studies and teaches. Mostly teaches. Many in the camp are preparing for the high school graduation examinations and more than any other subject, mathematics needs to be taught. Hanani teaches groups and individuals, all who ask his help, as many hours a day as are necessary. From beginning math to advanced. Almost from his first day here to his last, to his exile in Africa. From a political-organizational perspective, he is not involved in any of the existing structures in the camp. To me he seems closest to the IZL. The IZL members do not know him at all and consider him a member of Lehi because of his friendship with me. In reality his spirit belongs not only to these two fighting undergrounds but, more deeply, he belongs to the Underground of the ancient Spirit of Israel, conquering the world and all that is in it without leaving the ground.

Even if this ground means a detention camp in the Ayalon Valley.

Although I long ago despaired of any knowledge of math beyond the multiplication table, I have developed an interest in those areas of math that border on philosophy. From the perspective of pure science, it is absurd for me to ask Hanani to make clear to me something of the mysteries of Einstein's thought.

We take long, long walks. When we halt and Hanani points to something in the sky, the guards in the watchtowers most likely assume that we are planning an attack on the camp involving parachutists, but actually this is only a lesson in the cosmos according to the newest theories of physics.

My father used to joke: This Jew does not know how to swim, but he *understands* the idea of swimming. I was like that when Hanani tried to explain the meaning of a world both infinite and limited. Much clearer to me was the concept of curved space. I was happiest, almost happy as a child, with the bringing together of the concepts of time and space, as Einstein had done. "The horror of a vacuum," the abhorrence and fear of a material or spiritual vacuum, is that which made me uncomfortable about the two tunnels (time and space) in which the world's activity flows, whether they are tunnels existing transcendentally, beyond our senses, or the tunnels of our consciousness, as Kant taught. In any case, the two are separate. And I could not escape the question that is at once childish and philosophical: What came before? The Kantian solution only transferred the problem from the external world to the world of thought. Perhaps I am far from understanding matters correctly, but I was engulfed in a feeling of happiness when listening to Hanani's explanations or attempts at explanations. Not an empty tunnel anymore, not even space any more, but a moving, contracting, expanding, living creature, which blends with time, being born and giving birth, as "they become one flesh." The entire world suddenly became more intimate, as it moved further from being comprehended by the small intellect, as Uri Zvi says. Perhaps Hanani will be astonished to read of the effect his explanations had on me, certainly men of pure physics will mock me.

I never again felt cold in the infinite world. I no longer minded the numbers that Hanani referred to, the trillions. I am not afraid of them. I am not made inconsequential by them.

The fine grain called Planet Earth speeds through space, worlds larger than it burn up; they are pulverized minute by minute. On this grain, two "molecules" move about, Hanani and I, each of us to a real molecule as the sun is to a pinhead, and I am not afraid, and I am not made inconsequential. I begin to understand the Torah's prohibition against worshiping the stars and constellations. Do not bow down to them. Do not bow. Do not become inconsequential in the face of millions of light years, the infinite distances, the tremendous bodies of fire of which our whole planet is only one spark. Do not bow and do not consider yourself inconsequential. In the beginning God created the heavens and the earth. "The" and "the," two times the word is used. The first verse of the Bible could have been: " . . . the heavens and earth." What is the purpose of the second "the"? To demonstrate equality. Around this point I later built the central part of my ideological courses, regarding the verse: "I will see Your skies, the work of Your hands, the moon and stars which You have established. What is man that You should remember him, the son of man that You should recall him?" And the answer: "And You made him little less than God, crowned him with honor and glory, You have given him dominion over the works of Your hands, You have placed every thing beneath his feet."

The long walks circled the barracks; near, so near, the barbed wire. Hanani explains the characteristics of the stars, their sizes, distances, cycles. Hanani takes me on a tour of the cosmic nebula and from there we leap into the world of an atom before, during and after its explosion; into the secrets of power in the smallest particle, into the secrets of time in the largest particle.

As is my wont, I translate everything into my own language. "The sun is the face of Moses, the moon the face of Joshua," the rabbis taught (as a child I really did look for Joshua's face in the moon) and here I am in the Ayalon Valley, and here in this valley thousands of years ago the sun and the moon and the hosts of heaven were ordered to stand still, to come to "attention" before the hosts of man, the army of Joshua, before the spirit of victorious man.

This, I know, is no allegory, but one world on a different plain. And here we are walking around this atom of a British camp and I am not sure whether we fall into the category of "protons" or "electrons," and I am not yet sure by what technical, chemical or physical means this atom will be exploded, but I do know that it will explode because we will it and because Heaven has given us the consciousness of will, and perhaps by this consciousness He divided us from all else and caused us to rule over all else.

Spirit hovers over Hanani in these distant and awesome worlds, while darkness engulfs us. The darkness is broken only by the beams of searchlights sweeping by from time to time, and the flaming eyes which flash from time to time from faces unrecognizable in the dark, on these walks around the barracks, so near the electrified barbed wire fences. Everything is electrified here. The fence is electrified. Our spirits are electrified. And the power plant of our spirits' electricity is beyond the enemy's reach, this power plant is under the command of Joshua in the Ayalon Valley.

Therefore we calmly and quietly rise with Hanani to a world both infinite and finite, and to space curved by time, and we reach the limit that is no limit, for which man has no word other than God, and our heads do not grow dizzy and our souls do not crumble and our spirit is not stunted, for our feet are planted firmly in the valley, this valley.

And when one night was torn—I was living in the camp again, my bed facing Hanani's, my heart facing his, my spirit facing his spirit—and in the midst of the tearing we heard his name listed among those doomed to be sent from the camp to African exile, he just looked at me with smiling, sad eyes. Smiling because his spirit is so strong and sad because his two playful children due tomorrow or the day after for their once-a-month, just once-a-month, visit are so weak. When he dressed and began singing some loutish Latrun song, I felt such power that I could not look at him. I could not even say, "Shalom."

3. Torah, Weddings and Good Deeds

> Rabbi Shimon of Shilo taught: When the evil Nebuchadnezzar threw Hananiah, Mishael and Azariah into the furnace, Yorkenai the Prince of Hail stood before God and said to Him: Master of the Universe, I will descend and cool the furnace and save these righteous men from the fiery furnace. Gabriel said to him: This would not show the greatness of God, for you are the Prince of Hail and everyone knows water extinguishes fire. Rather, I, the Prince of Fire, will descend and chill from within while burning outside and I will perform a double miracle. Then the Holy One said to him: Descend!
>
> Talmud *Psachim* 118a

At winter's end, I rose and descended to the camp again. First, because the rains had ceased and with them the mud. Secondly, because the hearts were once again warm. The population inside Latrun grew and with it the spirit rose. And in the third place, when the spirit rose so did the thirst for "Torah," for the teaching of the law.

I had been engaged all this time in the written Torah, the written law. The hospital barracks lent itself to writing. It was quieter than the camp, there were fewer evil eyes. I usually do not fear the "evil eye," but some "evil eyes" are connected to evil tongues. While writing itself was permitted in Latrun, everyone knew that I was not writing a dime novel or standard reportage. Before the deportations to Africa, I had been ensconced in the Lehi barracks, with heavenly angels watching over me, some to the right and some to the left; I was able to leave my briefcase and notebooks without worrying. But since that night when I was left bereft, no such fortress as the Lehi barracks exists, and the barracks are mixed and all sorts of men mill around and one cannot be certain that someone else will not leaf through one's writings.

The "written law" with which I busied myself was of course material for *Hehazit* and, with the closing of *Hehazit* upon the capture of its stencil machine, for *Hama'as*, which began as a monthly and later, when the battlefield grew hot and I was freed, became a weekly. Also, most of the ideological and political booklets of the Underground were created in this same hospital barracks, as well as the broadcasts for our radio programs, especially after we found a permanent solution to the problem of smuggling out the material that I had written. Were I to describe the various inventions used in organizing this ongoing postal service, I might satisfy the curiosity of some readers, but I would be revealing one of those Underground secrets which may one day be needed again.

While the "written law" kept me busy, my teacher's soul craved some "oral law." So when people from the camp began asking me to teach and lecture I answered: More than the calf wants to suckle, the cow wants to nurse.

This nursing, however, involved not the secrets of milk but those of fire. That this fire burned mostly among the Underground's detainees is no coincidence. With only one exception, my students never included Hagana detainees. Apparently because of the plenitude of dairy products they received from the Tenuva dairy cooperative outside, they had been weaned on milk; and their fear of mixing dairy and meat kept them away from the classes. They were neither students nor teachers. There may have been an additional reason. They saw themselves as temporary residents of the camp, while the Underground members expected to be permanent residents.

Of course, the members of the Underground did not openly declare themselves, but their faces gave them away. For example, one man sat in the same barracks as I did for fifteen months. Moreover, he did not miss a single one of my classes. On the day of his release he came to me, said "shalom" and confessed he was a member of Lehi.

There was another man, who introduced himself to no one upon his arrival, who became friendly with no one during his stay. He found a corner of his own, books of his own, and he sat in his corner and studied. No one knew who or what he was. Seemingly he arrived only in order to study. Even when the camp went through emotional "imports" or "exports" of large numbers of prisoners, even during the peak excitement of the "exports" when long lists of names were read at the gate, this man sat in his corner and studied. And when one day his name was read almost no one knew who he was, they searched for him barracks by barracks until he was found. He was very quiet, he gathered his few belongings and his many books, and he was gone. A real *Lamed-vavnik*, one of the hidden righteous.

And there were youths who were fifteen when they arrived. One in my barracks, for instance. Outside he was a laborer during the day and a "journalist" at night, pasting up our wall-newspapers and posters. Now he thirstily plunges into the books. He had always wanted to learn and never had the opportunity. Now he learns. For two years, three years.

The fire burns not only in secret. There are group lessons, too. We tried organizing a complete school, covering all subjects, with a schedule of classes, but there was not enough continuity for it to last. We do have permanent subjects, though: Hebrew grammar and the Bible. Moshe Gold does most of the lecturing in grammar and I cover the Bible.

I have always enjoyed teaching Bible. I was arrested during a Bible class. But in my entire pedagogic career, I never before tasted this taste, the taste of teaching Bible in a detention camp in the Ayalon Valley.

I never enjoyed Biblical Criticism, even when I was outside. Since the time I had studied Biblical Criticism in the Rabbinical Seminary of Vienna, I have been weaned a complete and healthy weaning from the foolishness of that barren analysis, that dissection of chapters and sentences and words and letters, in order to arbitrarily reassemble them according to the imagination of the biblical critic and his desire to be original. For too many trees you do not see the forest, and for too many letters you do not see the sentence, and for too many sentences you are left without prophecy, without poetry, without prose; nothing, nothing, only errors. What is a chapter of the Bible according to Biblical Criticism? More or less what any healthy person is after psychoanalytical criticism: a chain of errors, neuroses and complexes. Nothing is left of the simple, conscious, precious, good person, nothing at all.

Therefore, I pushed aside all the commentators when I taught Bible. In this valley we are alone with the Bible, in an isolation of devotion that needs no intermediaries. Only one exception was permitted: During the Passover holiday we study the Song of Songs according to Rashi's commentary, that the love expressed in it between man and woman is an allegory for the love between the Jewish people and God. But even then we know we are alone with the body and soul of the text. The longing of the body and the spirit, the longing of the individual and the nation, come together in this valley behind the barbed wire fences. Perhaps in no place else in the world have the yearnings for the love of woman and the love of God, the love of land and the love of beauty, come as close as they have here. For this love of the Assembly of Israel and the freedom of Israel, boys filled with desires and filled with fire in their blood are sitting here. Where else in the world can we so understand the verse: "Go forth and gaze, maidens of Zion." Here everything is transformed into one reality: Jerusalem and the maidens and King Solomon. Our ancestors trilled the verses of the Song of Songs and closed their eyes in order to avoid seeing the plain meaning. Just like the learned professors who opened their eyes but closed their hearts in order to avoid seeing the allegorical meaning. And only we in the detention camp understand the Song of Songs according to its plain meaning, its allegory, its hints and its secrets, which are all one, one song that is all songs, just as the blood spilled yesterday in an attack on British airfields or on the streets of Jerusalem in an assault on British government buildings is one with and the same blood which sings its longing melody for a maiden in Jerusalem, or a girl in Petach Tikva, or a prisoner in the Women's Prison of Bethlehem.

"For your caresses are better than wine," and "how beautiful are your steps in sandals," sings his blood and sings her blood, sings the ground of this Ayalon Valley under our feet, sing our feet treading on this ground, on the same ground upon which marched the soldiers of Joshua the son of Nun, and the soldiers of Judah Maccabee.

Our ceilings are tin roofs? Our furniture, wooden beds? So what? "The voice of my beloved here it comes, leaping across mountains, bounding over the hills."

We hear them, the voices leaping and bounding from between the rocks, from between the bushes.

And in Bethlehem the maidens sit, the Shulamites, the palm trees, and they watch. Here the men come as cedars, here they will burst from the depths and free them and free Jerusalem.

The British watchtower stands twenty meters from the synagogue barracks in which the classes are held. Near the barracks is the spiky barbed wire fence. And the picture of the screaming skull: Caution! Mines and electricity and death! And we, twenty or thirty men of Israel, sit here burning with the fire of this song or the fire of a prophecy or the fire of the love of the Psalms or the fire of the very chapter which tells of this same valley in which the sun stood still and the hosts of heaven entered the fray by order of the commander of the hosts of Israel, and these events occurred and were recorded three thousand years ago. And fire comes from within the fire. The fire of Scripture in the fire of longing, in the fire of love and joy!

It is good to be a Fighter for the Freedom of Israel; it is good to be a member of the Underground Army of Israel on this land of Israel; it is good to adhere with blood to these clumps of earth, these songs, these precious words. And when you lift your head and look out the window at that wretched soul standing on the watchtower and at that barbed wire, you can do nothing but laugh a mighty, healthy laugh which rolls from here, across and beyond the barbed wire, and which reaches the ears of your commanding officer and your comrades in the Central Command, who are sitting somewhere right now and marking on maps where the enemy will be attacked. And the song which bursts forth from your mouth reaches the walls of the Bethlehem Prison and breaches them and causes the hearts of the maidens there to tremble, the maidens of Jerusalem who are in Bethlehem. And the forces accumulating within you are like those within the man who ordered the sun to stand still. These forces are within us.

This is how we studied Torah in Latrun. This is how we quenched the thirst for Torah. Fire within fire, miracle within miracle.

Only the thirst for "good deeds" could not be quenched. On the contrary. The fire of Torah made this thirst burn all the more.

Thus we burned in Latrun, in this triple-headed fire.

We walk around the barracks, round and round, like our father Abraham in the furnace. (Has it yet been noted that Jewish legend adorned the nation's father with the crown of a rebel thrown into a furnace?) The heat of the sun burns from above. There are no trees and no shade. We cannot sit in the barracks for long, for they roast us alive with the heat of the burning tin roofs. The ground opens up and hundreds of scorpions crawl forth. One summer game involves lighting a fire around a scorpion and watching this Japanese noble of a creature commit suicide by doubling over and sticking the point of his tail into his head. Some distance above us we can see the Latrun police station . . . . We will surround and burn it, we will burn it.

During the day there are no secrets in Latrun; the studious learn, the workers work. Once a month someone comes, a mother, sister, child, wife. Once a month a gift is given. Something woven, etched, sculpted. Once a month parched lips cling to soft lips, the very soft lips of a wife, to a wrinkled forehead, the very wrinkled forehead of a mother, to the very gentle cheek of a child. Once a month a gift is given. "Is it nice?" "Yes, pretty!" "Thank you." "Next month . . . ."

One's heart aches for those who have no such "month." No mother, no brother, no sister, no children. No family, and no one visits them. He is imprisoned here a year, two years, three years and he has never been privileged with the joy of a visit. Never! He stands here for months, months, and sees the others going with gifts in their hands and returning with packages in their hands. Packages, food, cake, fruit, chocolate.

The days are not his. The months are not his. What is his? The nights are his. They are his. They are his.

At night all the other torches are extinguished. At night no one studies. At night no one watches the faraway road, no one searches for a fragile girl wearing a light dress blowing in the wind. No fire of Torah and no fire of the wedding canopy. At night, the fire of good deeds breathes here.

Men press, press into the coffeehouse to hear the news on the radio. Tense faces: Was there an operation? Then they light up.

The first question: Where? The second: How many goyim fell? The third: Were there any casualties? Fourth: Whose operation was it? And only the very, very miserable become gloomy: Apparently the *fraj* will be further delayed . . . .

Not always is there this kind of news that gives meaning to our life here. But always after the news everyone disperses, in couples, to walk around and around. The voices are almost inaudible. Searchlights follow the walkers, follow and tremble, tremble.

Here is one who was brought in only a week ago, only yesterday. The face of an innocent lamb. And at night, a panther. At night he feels he must tell his companion everything. The operation in all its details. Who commanded and who participated. Everything, he tells everything. For in the telling and hearing of the story, the fire burning for "good deeds" is somewhat quenched. Just as the day after every operation the description in the newspaper is read once, twice, three times, with lust, and then the different newspapers are compared. So that no detail, not even the smallest, will be overlooked.

But when you see two members of Lehi walking here, you know and everyone in the camp knows: Here, no one brags about operations, perhaps because in Lehi there are few braggarts and perhaps because most of Lehi's operations do not lend themselves to exaggeration anyway. They are narrower and deeper. Therefore everyone knows: A pair of Lehi members walking around and around means a plan to escape. A tunnel or a hole or a charge or some new plot. Lehi members are few and each is therefore comparable to many, each feels more responsibility; his absence outside is more noticeable. And then there is the well-known heritage, the heritage of escape in Lehi that the other Underground lacks. Almost every member of Lehi has at one point either escaped or attempted to escape from a prison or camp.

During the day the ground of the valley burns beneath our feet. At night the blood that is imprisoned here burns.

Good deeds burn their way toward me. To be again with those who will take action tomorrow, who will stand under fire and who will shower with fire.

Circle after circle, walk after walk, round and round and round and round. Soon the barracks will be closed, soon the lights will be extinguished, and only the searchlights will sweep the paths between the fences, back and forth, back and forth, and the wooden beds will creak beneath the bodies. Someone laughs, someone argues. The good, healthy, diligent, zealous boy from Haifa takes another look at . . . the nude pictures he has hung above his bed.

And silence.

And only a very attentive heart hears the pounding of the hot blood in the veins. The pounding: Get out. Get out. Death to the enemy. Freedom for the homeland, for this valley, and for Jerusalem, and for the maidens of Jerusalem.

The pounding of the blood at night is very great.

4. Unbound Holidays

I was not overly meticulous about descending from the hospital to the synagogue to worship on the Sabbath. But holidays were different, especially that Shavuoth holiday in 5706 (1946), which was to be my last day in captivity. In high spirits all that day, I asked to be allowed to read the "Akdamoth" prayer for the congregation, for there is so much fire and joy in that song and my entire soul seemed to be singing. And when we recited "Hallel" the implications were clear.

"Out of distress I called upon the Lord." (Tuvia the milkman used to read this as: "Out of prison I called upon the Lord.") "He answered me by setting me free." (The meaning of this freedom I understood only the following day, twenty-four hours after this prayer, when we sped through the open expanses in a car going from Jerusalem to the coastal plain.) "This is the day which the Lord has made, let us be glad and rejoice on it." (Wait, wait, I say in my heart. Don't count your chickens before they hatch. True, the operation is like all Lehi operations, planned to the last detail, and we have every chance of success, but who knows? The devil may trip us up . . . .) "The Lord is God who has given us light, form the dance with boughs." (No; I mean, this time, God willing, the dance will be done without boughs or chains.)

Only two of our men in the camp know of my planned escape. Our "foreign minister," Dan Zamir, called foreign minister because of the diplomatic work he enjoys so much. If not in Baghdad and if not in Prague—two places to which he has been on missions—then at least in Latrun. I leave him responsible for our men in the compound and for my personal belongings. Without anyone noticing, shortly after my departure from the camp he will go to my barracks, pack my things and take them with him.

For several weeks we have lived with the tension of this escape. The plan is not new. For over a year I have been pushing for it. About once every two months I am taken to my private doctor, Dr. Troy, to have my cast or belt changed. After one year, the cast was changed to a belt and the advantage is like the advantage of a detention camp over a prison. I am allowed and able to remove the belt at night, and my body is then as free as my imagination. The laces of the belt no longer bind the body and the barbed wire is no longer seen. Darkness and silence have wings.

Usually, I am not accompanied by a heavy guard. Two or three policemen or, more often, detectives. Two or three times only one detective entered the doctor's office with me, staying with me for about an hour. Then I curse myself and am ashamed. If my body had the strength of my spirit, then I would free myself with one blow. Oh, if only Eldad "the ideologue" were not here, but rather one of our other boys, of agile body and muscles, if only someone like Uzi the Redhead were here, or Dov or . . . listing the names is pointless; I think anyone else in my place would easily take advantage of the opportunity. The detective is sitting reading a newspaper. The doctor is out of the room, and right by my side are the various instruments of an orthopedic office, some of them quite heavy: hammers, pliers. Just pick one up and give him a single blow to the head and walk out to the bustling streets of Jerusalem. Just one blow! But I cannot rely on the speed of my movements or the strength of my blow, having no experience in this area. If I take too long? If I miss? If I do not crack his skull and he . . . quickly draws his gun and shoots? I do not want to die, at least not this way. Not when it is not necessary, for they are preparing a foolproof plan for me. Once, I was angry that they had not sent a stakeout. One detective took me from Rehov Haniviim to the Russian Compound, on foot and unchained. Passers-by had no way of knowing that here were walking a prisoner and his guard. Just one man, if he were walking behind us, could have hit him from behind . . . or if I were a little athletic I could have knocked him down with one move.

What I am writing depresses me, and I am ashamed of myself. If only the detectives would have taken "Meir" (Joshua Zetler) the way they took me! Or anyone else from Cell 18 at the Jerusalem Central Prison, where from time to time I spend a few days, when my treatment is extended or when Dr. Troy, at my request, extends it.

The visits to the Jerusalem Prison also delay my own escape, as we have a plan for a great prison breakout there. A tunnel is ready in Cell 18. At first only Lehi members are involved. Later, the IZL boys in the adjacent cell are let in on the secret and a hole is made in the wall between the two cells. But they are dependent on help from the outside. The plan is for a big escape, and I must arrange my visit to Jerusalem for the same time. This is not easy. The date of the breakout has already been postponed once so that I could join them. It cannot be postponed again, for the operation is tied to attacks all across the country and in Jerusalem itself.

The operation failed. The prison was not breached. We suspect the enemy knew of our planned assault. The attacking units were surprised by guards in places the guards had never been before. Only miraculously did our men and the IZL avoid many losses. How did word filter out? Maybe that provocateur in the IZL, who would later reveal the operation planned for the Jerusalem train station, and who would escape the IZL's revenge by crossing the seas, maybe he was already at work? Or perhaps there was too much talk? In either case the hopes of many were dashed and the darkness certainly grew thicker in that basement cell with the old-timer convicts, Svorai and Zetler. My conscience bothered me: Because of me the operation had been delayed seven days. A special request had been sent the IZL, they understood the reasoning, accepted it. Who knows, perhaps on that earlier date our luck would have been better.

We have no choice, we must return to the plan I have been recommending for a year, to free me during my visit to the doctor. The operation will be easy, in my opinion, considering my earlier visits. Nonetheless, Michael does not rely on the normal; he takes into consideration the possibility of a much heavier guard than usual. He sends the choicest boys on this operation, the best commanders, and in charge—Dov. Dan Zamir guesses in advance the make up of the group that will take part. They are so few, our boys, but their worth is inestimable.

I set the date for about two months after my last visit. So as not to be late, the boys begin their wait early. The location is in midtown, with much traffic, it is not far from the seat of government. Detectives run about like dogs there and are a danger, but there is no alternative. Most of the boys are not from Jerusalem. Every day two cars come from Tel Aviv. As I write today, I cannot recall which bank or insurance company footed the bill for all the expenses involved in this operation . . . .

I am privileged to enjoy one last family visit. Those precious moments when my eyes cannot see enough of my daughter and when I have so many things to tell them. We barely speak. Batya takes a letter for Natan. She has a contact. By now, the Underground is already able to help support families (again, thanks to that same bank!). A fair sum has also gone to treat my daughter who has been ill. In the letter I send an urgent message: An IZL man of such and such a description will be taken with me to Dr. Troy. I must decide whether to let him in on the secret, in case he wants to join my escape, or in case he wants to cancel his trip. In any case, this complicates matters. The devil intervenes: The letter falls from Batya's nervous, tired hands. But no one notices. She, of course, does not know what is in the letter; perhaps if she knew she were helping me escape, she would have hesitations about delivering it. Still, she senses something and asks that I promise not to escape, it is best for me to sit a while longer, she is trying to have me freed in ordinary ways. What is an "ordinary" way? Some say a release can be arranged for 600 lira. The British detectives are on the take. Prices vary according to the seriousness of the case. There are Jewish lawyers who help in this business. I promise my wife I will not escape. And what is she afraid of? The risk, life underground, the fear that begins after the escape. When someone is under detention there is no danger he will be arrested, but when he is outside, and especially when the situation worsens and curfew is imposed, with searches day after day and night after night, then no moment is ever free from fear. She is of course right. "But deliver the letter immediately, immediately!

It's very urgent! It's about an informer who was discovered in the camp!" I do not know whether she believes me. I see her leaving, running down the road dragging our poor, tiny girl, quickly, quickly . . . .

Thursday is a big day in the camp. On this day the Atid Company delivers private packages and in them is all that is good: fruits, vegetables, cake and . . . mail. Of course, the packages are opened by the British duty officer, with the help of a Jewish officer. The Jewish officer knows more or less which packages he can leave for the goy and which he should open himself. Occasionally he throws a fit over an illegal item in one of the packages. A bottle of wine, some cigarettes, or something similar. He screams to high heaven and thus proves his loyalty. In his fury he "forgets" to check other packages, boxes, containers. And the Englishman thinks he can rely on this man. Later, the Atid car leaves with empty boxes, containers and bags.

Not completely empty.

The man responsible for this box-mail on the outside is Gideon, and all I can say is that if the postal service in the State of Israel operated as smoothly as Gideon's there would be few complaints.

On the last Thursday before my escape, as Atid reached the gate on its way out, a messenger from Captain Clough came for me: Come to his office at once.

I was stricken with fear and with trembling. I had no doubts: This time the boxes were checked and my mail was discovered, and because of my confidence in this postal system, already operating for over a year, I had not bothered to encode my message. Now everything is revealed. There will be an investigation. Otherwise, why would the commandant suddenly call for me? He has never done so before.

But our internal supervisor, I think it was Kritzman, and a third man were called along with me. This must be serious.

Clough sits opposite us and when he turns to me as the camp's senior inmate, he begins to pour out his heart: "You are witness to the fact that I always treat you as men of culture, and I rebuke all those under my command who do not behave toward you as they should. Now this is how you repay me?"

What happened?

Something horrible. During a soccer game a fight erupted between the detainees and the duty officer . . . Officer Rogan, an Irishman who served with the British police during the Irish rebellion, who was sentenced to death, fled England and is now afraid to return there, and who, when he has had nothing to drink, is in a very bad mood indeed. This time he refused to station policemen outside the camp to throw the ball back in; the energy-filled boys, having no other outlet, spent their energy on the ball and it flew out. The camp boiled. Could it be? A little longer and the revolution would begin. Rogan rang for the officer and called for help. Clough came running like a madman. The young prisoners were standing behind the fence shrieking. Still, none of this is really serious. Clough would not have bothered the communal elders over this. What else? He continues excitedly:

"One of the young men yelled to me: 'Only here are you so smart, wait, wait, we'll fix you outside!'"

This sentence he says in the original, in Hebrew, to emphasize its seriousness. Then he again reviews the way he treats the camp, and really he does not care, he will gladly give an order to allow soccer playing from morning till night. Then he again refers to the drunken officer with some fine and proper English words.

Now I understand why he called me. If something or someone is going to be "fixed" outside, then there is only the "Stern Gang" to do it. The IZL does not settle individual scores. Lehi does.

Now that the weight was lifted from my heart and my main fear allayed, I was in a good mood and decided to return his kindness and calm him: "Why do you pay any attention to the words of some young fellow? No one has ever been 'fixed' because of a soccer ball."

So, the conversation ended in idyllic endearment. I exploited the moment to complain about the delay in my being taken to my private doctor in Jerusalem. He asked that I write an official letter to the office, after which he would do his best.

Usually, a detainee was not informed when he was going to be transferred, but this "friendship" with Clough served me well and on the eve of Shavuoth he told me I would be seeing Dr. Troy the day after the holiday. At the last minute, I found someone whose mother could get word to Jerusalem.

The camp was accustomed to my good spirits, but never had they seen me as I was then. The only mishap was in the philosophy class later that day.

About three weeks before my escape some of the men had asked me to give them philosophy lessons. One of the men was Avraham Rubinstein from Kfar Hasidim, an IZL member but too intellectual to be given a high rank in that organization. As a matter of fact, I was surprised that he and Reuven Rosenkranz never attempted to escape. Both were longtime students of mine in the camp, they studied and they taught. Ever since Warsaw, I had been wary of the IZL's militarism, which derided the world of the spirit. These two understood that this was a fault, but they were loyal members and loved their organization. And they taught me not to generalize; in reality the human material in Lehi and the IZL was the same, the good or bad winds blew from above.

The second person who asked for a philosophy class—and he turned out to be the life of the class—was Shalom Levin, a Hagana member arrested before the United Resistance was born. In the days of the Jewish Brigade he had worked with Moshe Shertok. In the camp, he managed the affairs of Hagana Intelligence, but this was not his only reason for seeking my friendship.

To this strange group—two Irgunists who happened to be studious and a Hagana Intelligence man who happened to be a disciple of mine—was added Moshe Gold, the Betar commissioner who sought to ease his bitterness by playing chess and teaching grammar; one of the reasons for his bitterness was an unsatisfied desire to complete his education, a desire unsatisfied because of his work for the movement.

One or two others also joined the philosophic circle. And it was not practical or national or religious philosophy, rather the most abstract. I lectured with the help of S. H. Bergman's book on the basic concepts of philosophy. After this final class, a student told me I had not been up to my usual level. I knew this better than he, but how could I explain the reason? The next day I celebrated the holiday by distributing drinks to residents of the hospital. Then I went down to the camp and met our men in a barracks on the side, and I drank with them to the success of the upcoming operation, without saying any more than that.

One more evening in the bustling café. One more circling of the camp with Dan Zamir, one more with Shalom Levin of the Hagana and one last conversation with Moshe Gold.

In the morning the van comes from Jerusalem. Traveling with me are two other detainees. I am usually dropped off at the doctor's office accompanied by a detective or policeman, and then the van continues on to the Government Hospital with the others. This time the order is reversed. After the two are dropped off at the hospital, the heavily guarded van takes me to Dr. Troy. Entering, I sense no one. Usually my handcuffs are removed before we enter. The man in charge of the guard is an aging sergeant with a friendly face and he tries to unlock the cuffs. With great difficulty he removes one but cannot manage the other. He asks my forgiveness, he feels bad. I take advantage of the delay to look around. Normal traffic. The driver remains in the van with one policeman. Two cops are posted at the office door. The sergeant enters with me. The waiting room is crowded with women and children, more than ever before. Things get worse. Dr. Troy is out. We are taken to the doctor's room to wait. The sergeant puts his Tommy gun on the table and sits down. I am in a chair facing the door. The sergeant tries again to remove the second cuff and again he apologizes, warmly and honestly. To tell the truth, I feel sorry for him. I ask the nurse for a newspaper. As usual she offers me a cold drink. She brings me *Davar* and brings the sergeant the *Palestine Post*. He spreads the paper out and avidly reads. I peek at *Davar* and my ears are listening and my heart is pounding and my entire spirit is breaking in long, tense waves.

Suddenly an uproar in the waiting room. If the sergeant were not so goodhearted he would have been stirred by the noise. But he continues reading the paper. I hear: "What happened? What happened? Quiet! Quiet!" I do not know how long this continued. Only later did I learn that one of the boys was brought in on a stretcher, as if injured in an accident, and only when another two white-gowned boys entered did the accident victim suddenly "recover." They jumped the policemen at the door with guns drawn. Women began screaming.

By now I am certain all is lost. But "my" sergeant is still reading his paper. The door is suddenly broken open. One lad stands opposite the sergeant, the former's gun pointed at the latter's belly, and he orders: "Hands up!" The sergeant jumps in panic, with trembling hands raised. I spring forward. That is my mistake: Instead of walking around the sergeant, I pass between him and our lad. I hear a shot from behind. (Our instructions were not to hurt anyone unless necessary. The lad claimed that as I passed in front of him, the sergeant grabbed his Tommy gun and therefore he had to shoot. The goy was wounded but recovered completely; I had not wanted him to die.) The waiting room is a mess, I run toward the door, which is blocked by an obese, panic-stricken woman pushing hysterically to get out. Someone pushes her aside and clears a path for me.

I am in the yard. One lad shoves a sheathed gun into my hand: "Hold this." I do not accept it: "What will I do with it?" Since my course with Avraham Amper in Vilna I have not held a gun, and I am simply afraid that I might hold it the wrong way and cause trouble. I run. It seems to me dozens of lads are around me, because for the tens of yards I run they are on either side of me, as if forming two chains. This was afterward revealed, of course, to be an illusion, there were only seven or eight, but two guarded me from the sides and showed me the way.

A car is waiting. I jump in. The handcuff chain is dangling from my left hand. The car is jammed with our boys and with weapons confiscated from the guards: two Tommy guns and several pistols. And some more taken from some passing soldiers. Someone shouts to the driver: "Fly!" and the car flies. The same person hugs me around the neck and yells: "Now we're even, Eldad!" It is Dov. But why "even" I do not yet understand. A shot is fired at us. Dov orders not to return fire. Duck. We duck. A bullet passes through the roof. The car has already made two or three turns and entered quiet, empty alleys. It stops. Dov and I get out and enter a second, waiting car. Drora is sitting inside. Again the order: "Fly!" and in three or four minutes we are outside the city, off the road, in the fields.

Slowly, slowly the noise in my head dies down. It is ten o'clock. If everything goes well we will be in Tel Aviv in another three hours. We drive through the "Triangle" north of Jerusalem, the long way around. We will try to avoid the roads and keep to the fields. They will certainly be checking the roads, mainly the highways. We will use a small section of the road near Ramallah and then return to the fields.

We are, of course, peaceful citizens. Unarmed. I am also without identification papers. In their place I have the much less helpful chains on my left hand. There are no tools in the car. Dov makes an effort to pull the cuffs off. I urge him on, even if it means snapping the joints of my hand. If we are stopped—the chain will finish us. Dov pulls with all his might. They are off. After all that, Dov does not throw them away, saying, "Things like these are always needed. Anyway, he should keep them. A souvenir." I remember what he said and ask: "Why did you say 'even'?" He answers: "Because you freed me from Vilna, I decided I had to free you."

Well, I do not recall. I do remember him coming to Vilna, a child almost, fifteen, in 5700 (1940). He came with Kotlicki. Two young boys. For some reason Batya took an interest and helped them. Afterward, Dov reminds me, I tried to get him an immigration certificate from Youth Aliya.

In Eretz Israel I saw little of him. In Latrun, I had heard rumors that he was making us proud. A journalist once referred to him as "the tall blond," and from then on that nickname instilled fear in enemy hearts.

He was the only one of the boys I recognized. The others I did not even see. As the years go by, they come, one by one, and introduce themselves: I participated in your breakout. Not all of them come. Some—I never have the privilege to know, to see their eyes, to shake their hands, the hands of freedom fighters. Uri and Ptachia—this is their penultimate operation. Two weeks later they go on the Haifa rail works operation and do not return.

The path is desolate but pretty. Dov sits next to the driver, they are holding a map. "See how pretty," Dov says once in a while. The beauty of desolation. No houses, no people, almost no trees. Only once, a shepherd and his sheep. We fly at tremendous speed. A cow does not move quickly enough and is run over. An old Arab shouts. It is a miracle the car is not damaged.

We fly.

I did not know Dov. But I got to know him immediately. Despite the map, Dov and the driver err, they drive straight, straight. Suddenly Drora stops them; she thinks they should have turned a sharp left at the bend. They had previously checked the route. The road we are on leads straight to a police station. We back up about one hundred yards. Yes, left at the bend.

I am in a tight belt. Maybe it is not the belt, maybe it is the excitement, or maybe the speed, or maybe all these together. I am gripped by nausea and vomit.

I joke even during the vomiting—a heritage from my father, who all his life dreamed of telling a joke as he was dying.

Later I feel better; and by the time we leave the desolate areas, I can quietly and happily listen to Dov's account of the attack on the Kfar Sirkin airport, which he tells as we pass the site: We came from here. There is the airport. Eight planes. Withdrawal through the fields, many hours. No losses, not even an injury. We were very proud of this operation, our valor was proven.

We are now on the Haifa-Tel Aviv highway. Another quarter of an hour. There is no danger. The British will not think to search for me, escaping from Jerusalem, on the road from Haifa. They are stupid enough; they spend that whole day searching the length of the Jerusalem-Tel Aviv Road.

Not three hours. We made the trip in under two. At exactly twelve o'clock we enter Bnei Brak. Of course, I feel as if everyone is watching as we get out of the car. This feeling will stay with me for quite some time. I find it hard to believe that I look like everyone else, that I do not have horns or a suspicious face. How little coordination between what is going on inside me and my face! Dov does not get out. He goes on to Tel Aviv. In another fifteen minutes he will appear before Michael, the director of the operation, and inform him, without a salute or any other military trappings, "All is well." And Michael will express his joy as he usually does, with a long laugh.

I enter my first human-civilian household, that of "Yoske the carpenter." I do not want to eat or drink, no, nothing, nothing. Only this: To remove the cumbersome body belt and shower, shower under flowing cold water, to be rid of everything, the sweat, the dirt, the excitement, the fear, the two years of detention, the barbed wire, the captains, the visiting commissioners, the investigations, the Arab *nabatchim*, the nights of deportations, the arguments, everything, to wash them from me, to be cleansed by the falling water, and to cling from now on to the Underground, directly and with all my body and all my arteries and all my might.

Part Four
EROICA 5707

The Red and the Black

1. The Lehi Command

How will I get to Tel Aviv?

My guess is probably in the dark hours of the night, after double and triple checking the road, under armed guard, ready for anything . . . .

Just the opposite. Gideon and I leave on a bright morning in a nice car, as two quiet civilians. Only with great difficulty do I work up the nerve to pass Sarona.[69]

How do the members of the Command live?

When I was taken from them, they had been in the second stage. The first stage had been Yair's sleeping in bomb shelters and later the era of the orchards, the Kingdom of Joshua Cohen. In the second stage, the intermediate level, Michael lived literally between an orchard and a real town, in a small house in Ramat Yitzhak that bordered on an orchard. From there he spun the first organizational web and spread it over cities and settlements, man by man, cell by cell. In his own home there was no furniture; his wife Shulamit cooked whatever was available in the same, one pot. And did it matter?

Natan lived in some basement, half-room and half-shelter, grumbling about the darkness and dampness. Working there was impossible.

Only in the third stage did we reach actual apartments. First, because the financial situation eased and secondly, because apartments were more secure. Experience taught us that the eyes of the police were open wider to poor neighborhoods and to separate houses. This country's poor have a reputation for being close to the Underground. Michael is privileged to be the first to become an orderly, respectable citizen. With a well-furnished, family-style apartment, he and his wife do not attract their neighbors' attention. Especially since Michael, the husband, is bearded and garbed in black like a Hasidic rabbi. This is how I found him in his doorway, in a nice building on Adam Hacohen Street, and he was brimming with real joy. A little later Natan arrived, with a thick black Stalinist moustache, though his own hair is red. Great is the joy in this home.

The Lehi Central Command in its entirety. Everyone with equal rights. The three of us have been detainees, the three of us have escaped. But we are all equal in other respects, too. There is no "leader" in Lehi. Within the ranks, it is well known who is the organizational pillar, who the political mind, and who the burning spirit. Not only is there no leader, but there is no commander. I say this neither in praise nor reproach. A time comes when we will turn this fact of life into our unique treasure, we will deride "Supreme Commanders" or "leadership." We had de facto coordinators. Michael was first, later Natan, known as Gera.

None of this had been discussed in the past. Yair had not appointed a Central Command. Many of those he put in charge disappointed or deserted. From then on things were run on the basis of those "responsible." The term "commander" is almost nonexistent;[70] at the most it signifies the man responsible for a particular operation. In time, an entire theory is constructed to support this structure, as opposed to the IZL's structure. During the Underground war, this is good and makes our relations friendlier and more personal. It does not interfere with our operations, which are not battles in a military sense.

Needless to say, we do not hold regular meetings or keep minutes. We meet only when an urgent problem arises. Other matters are settled by small notes folded very, very well. Gera's notes are the handsomest. His handwriting is fine and straight, the pieces of paper are cut straight and even the tape is cut straight. Michael takes less care but he does not like "corresponding." He writes infrequently; and when he does, his notes are no more than a sentence or two. Gera's notes are enjoyable because of their style and humor, too, and because of the personal friendship and concern apparent in each. I can only speak ill of my notes: Whatever paper is at hand becomes stationery. Unlike Gera, I do not have paper, scissors to cut with or adhesive tape. My handwriting is not overly beautiful. Even I sometimes have difficulty deciphering it. We once referred to our styles as a disagreement over "pressed pants." Our meticulousness in notes and style corresponds to our meticulousness in dress and the creases of our pants. It pains me that I am not strict in these matters. I am not trying to develop a theory in praise of outward negligence; I am just incapable of applying myself to these matters. The argument over pressed pants sometimes spills over to nonsartorial matters. During meetings with the Hagana leaders I more than once arouse ire because of a strong phrase, some unpolished language, and Gera reproves me: The same thing can be said in a different, less provocative manner. I do not have this problem with Michael, because he does not come into contact with outside organizations, his meticulousness is focused on matters of life and death. Every operation he plans, he thinks out to the last detail. He relies on nobody in anything; he leaves no detail up to those "responsible." He must see everything with his own eyes, speak to almost everyone participating in an operation. As a result he is much loved by his men. But I am not sure whether this will endear him to history. History, especially in a stormy period, takes long and quick strides, and overmeticulousness holds her back. Later, when we take stock and ask ourselves why we did not grow numerically when the IZL did, then the "responsible" people, led by Gera, will offer Michael's slow pace and severity as an explanation.

Yes, the eternal answer: severity. Pressed pants are fine, severity and meticulous attention to detail, too. The only question is whether they are appropriate at all times, in all places.

This triumvirate, each man with his strengths and faults, comprised the Lehi Central Command, the nerve center of the War for Freedom, for since the year 5702 (1941-1942) we have been the vanguard of this war, by our formulating its principles most clearly and by our drawing the conclusions from the formulations; though not always in the frequency and force demanded, for our body is too small. Yes, the journalists are justified in using against us the argument: Who are these people who give themselves the right to dictate policy to the Nation of Israel? Who are these people who decide by themselves if the country will enjoy calm or suffer military rule and searches? They issue "death sentences," declare "war" and "peace"? Who elected them? Who made them? Who sent them? They sit like madmen in hiding somewhere and take over the life of the Yishuv.

This is true.

Dozens of institutions in this country represent thousands and hundreds of thousands of voters: the Histadrut, the Zionist administration, the Vaad Leumi, the municipalities, the party councils . . . . During the United Resistance, one Hagana man explains to me how difficult it is for them to carry out an operation. After the Staff has approved it, then the proposal goes to secret and not-secret circles. Opinions must be expressed by the Actions Committee of the Histadrut in the name of the workers, by the Agricultural Board in the name of the kibbutzim, and of course by the Jewish Agency leadership. Party representatives sit on these boards and committees, and the debate is in principle or in form one of party polemics, so the institutions of each party are sitting in judgment. If the kibbutzim protect their interests, then Tel Aviv Mayor Israel Rokach can also protect his (this involves less selfishness than the kibbutzim, since the city is not actually his property). In contrast, the Lehi Central Command sits off by itself somewhere, three—and soon to be only two—men, sometimes after a short discussion and sometimes without any discussion but with two minuscule notes, four centimeters by six centimeters each. Written on one note is: "There is a need to respond immediately. The plan is to hit in Tel Aviv or Jerusalem or Haifa." Or: "The big goy we talked about will be in such and such a place tomorrow. The plan is feasible. What is your opinion?" And if "Yes" is the brief reply, then the next day the Yishuv is "appalled," and the British regime is shaken, the lives of such and such a number of foreign soldiers or policemen are cut short, and cut short with them is the continued existence of their foreign rule. The Yishuv suffers a siege, searches, even shootings and deaths. Yes, all this was decreed in two brief notes. Without elections, without councils, without five- or six-hour speeches, without polemical articles thousands of lines long in the pages of *Hamishmar* or *L'ahdut Haavoda* which cite Marx and Engels and Lenin and Bukharin and Stalin and Ber Borochov and Berl Katznelson and tens of theoreticians and experts on revolutions in order to prove that we may strike at English soldiers expelling boatloads of immigrants or, alternately, that to strike at them is forbidden for one hundred and fifty different moral and political and humanistic and practical reasons.

Yes, true. With us things are quite simple. Michael usually executes the operation. The proposals are usually Gera's or mine. A short consultation, and almost always unanimity of opinion. The decision is made and the instructions are given. And if several quiet weeks pass over the homes of the British and the palaces of their commissioners and officials, this is not because of doubts on our part, of the Lehi Command, but only because of a technical lack of opportunity to operate.

And if the British Parliament and Buckingham Palace and the Foreign Office have not yet been blown sky high, this is not because we do not want to provoke or anger them, or because we are afraid of the results, but only because our boys in London have not yet submitted the practical plans to us, though they are working on them and we are waiting for their letters, and we are sending explosives from France to England.

From where do we draw our authority?

Jabotinsky wanted to be given the authority to lead the people in rebellion by the people itself. If not for the World War, he might very possibly have actually been granted this authority. But the national destruction which accompanied the war is itself the proof that he should not have waited to be given authority by some vote, petition, or congress. The destruction which for years hung over the necks of millions obligated the few who saw it, who prophesied it, to rise and act on behalf of the millions who stood on the threshold of the ovens without realizing it. The nation was like a sleepwalker on top of a cliff, at the edge of the abyss. Who will claim in the name of democracy that we must first wake him and ask him whether he wants to fall?

The sleepwalker metaphor is not complete, however. There were not only sleepwalkers in this nation and this Yishuv. There were those who deliberately raised obstacles. Our Marxists were real imperialists and wanted to encompass everything. All the above-mentioned institutions which were said to have the authority to decide, as opposed to "three madmen" who were not elected by anyone, these institutions represented narrow economic interests. The good business being done by the kibbutzim and Solel Boneh, the chief contractor of the British Mandatory government, dictated to the "ideologists" the "argumentology" against the "criminal terror." The coagulation into a class of the thousands of clerks in the Histadrut and the "National" Funds is what created the law of unsullied "pure weapons." Without these narrow class interests, Weizmann could never have stood at the head of the Zionist movement after enduring defeat after defeat.

We did indeed take upon ourselves, we three men, and later only two men, the authority to plunge the Yishuv into war, to embitter relations with the British regime, to prevent the possibility of compromise and peace. Therefore, we spilled British blood even if it caused material damage to the Yishuv, even if it resulted in the spilling of Jewish blood.

For we were not Marxists, and we did not rely on economic crises, which would foment a revolution. We acted on account of the Vision of a Free Israel, which can be forced upon the people until they declare: "We want it." In 1938, rumors spread in Poland of an antigovernment conspiracy hatched by one of the "Pulkowniks." The conspirators' program was fascist and its Jewish clause included forced evacuation: The confiscation of the property of the 100,000 richest Jews and, using this money, the transfer of millions of Jews to Eretz Israel. I should like to hear one complaint today against this program in the name of "democracy." It would have been a *mitzva*, a divinely ordained commandment and a good deed, to transfer millions of Jews without asking them. And perhaps it would have been best if this conspiracy had succeeded and the cruel program carried out.

A small group of people did indeed give itself the authority to force the Yishuv to fight the British. And if Yishuv affairs had progressed not according to this group of "crazies" but according to the majority of the authorized and elected, then the fate of everyone here would have been the same fate to which they walked in Poland, following their elected institutions and the opinions of the "sober" and the sedate, and momentary concerns and interests.

We drew our authority from the blood already spilled, and from the blood about to be spilled, though this blood was still unaware; we drew our authority from the babes and infants who are today reaching adulthood in their homeland and who would not be doing so had we not fought without asking permission of their parents. We drew our authority from the historical experiences of other nations, and from the historical failures of the Zionist movement which was established to save our nation and did not save it, which was established to attain Hebrew rule in this country and not foreign rule, and which betrayed the nation and the land. And I personally drew my authority from the poems of the man who renewed prophecy in Israel. Prophecy, too, is not chosen in democratic elections; prophecy, too, rises from the awareness of responsibility itself, a responsibility toward the Whole without asking the Whole. As the prophets of Israel were once, so Uri Zvi was for me. I questioned his songs like the Urim and Thumim, like oracles,[71] and they charted my course and I walked in complete surety.

And the strength of these three men chosen by no one, who sat and decided the fate of British rule in Eretz Israel, was finer than the strength of the democratically chosen who sat in the offices of the British police and decided that the fate of the youth of Israel, the Fighters for the Freedom of Israel and the members of the IZL, should be one of arrest, deportation, torture and death. And our strength was finer, we who took for ourselves the authority to "dictate the path of war to the Yishuv," than the strength of the "president" and the chairman of the Jewish Agency, later the president and prime minister of the State of Israel, respectively, Chaim Weizmann and David Ben Gurion, who were then prepared—in return for 5,000 immigration certificates a month—to agree to the continuation of British rule in our country, and even to the bringing, with their active help, of the Lehi and IZL Commands to the British gallows.

If our hearts were sometimes heavy, this was never out of pity for enemy lives, never out of worry for the suffering of the Yishuv. I am not afraid to say these things openly. Needless to say, we took seriously the fact that we had defined the British as our enemies, and our deeds as war; in short, the simple slogan: Death to the enemy—Freedom for the homeland. But we also saw the Yishuv's suffering as necessary from every perspective. The crime was not the suffering, but rather the complacency of the Yishuv. The Yishuv grew wealthy; the price was blood. If the Yishuv had begun a war for freedom the day the White Paper was published, then it certainly would not have enjoyed the prosperity it did during the World War; but it certainly would have forced the British regime to open the country's gates to immigration, and this would have been possible just because that regime was in the midst of a war for the survival of Britain itself. And if our war forced Britain to remove the mask of the gentleman, then our job was well done.

Nonetheless our hearts were sometimes heavy as we reached a decision, but only if the operation endangered the lives of our members; they were so few and so elite. Drafted not at the end of a whip, not with notices in hand. Every one of them was a *Lamed-vavnik*, one of the thirty-six righteous. And reserves did not exist. Every one who fell was irreplaceable. Therefore we scorned the "effect" of "face-to-face" battles. Therefore Mazal[72] and Dov and the members of our technical department strained their brains to invent ways to deceive the enemy, yes, by means of ambush, without worrying about the epithet "coward" bestowed upon us by the papers *Davar* and *Haaretz* and *Mishmar* with all their military nobility. When reaching decisions like these we were not afraid, we were terrified. Terrified for the life of every young Fighter for the Freedom of Israel, for whom there was no replacement, certainly not in the great herd that was bleating and mooing within the fences of the Yishuv, and which would still be bleating and mooing its tears and its laughter today, in the Jewish Agency sheep-pen and the Histadrut cowshed, under the close supervision of the British High Commissioner, to this very day, were it not for those precious bodies of the few, the very few who were not chosen by the people, not authorized by the people, not sent by the people, and yet nonetheless they were sent and they went and they gave their blood.

Thus the Lehi Central Command sat, comprised of four, three, or most of the time only two, and decreed the fate: peace or war, for this land, for the Yishuv.

We were not elected; there were no voters to dictate to us their desires, which were often petty, fleeting. It is good that the fighters we sent to fight and to die chose us not with votes but with their blood, their hearts, their trust, for they were like us, free a priori from any personal requests, from any binding personal possessions, with only an awareness in their hearts, and the Vision.

The authority came to us from the blood, from the song, from the wisdom, and if God is He who resides in the holiest blood, the prophetic song, and the historical wisdom, then we were doing His work though we did not play with, as some others did, mentioning His name.

2. Our Red Night

The Underground's agreement to a cease-fire if 100,000 certificates were issued was a risky card to play; we played it and won. This was one of the miracles we were lucky to have bestowed on us. Afterward began the heroic period of the Underground war which had one fault: the unheroic ending. This fault must, however, have deep roots, and perhaps some of them will appear in the telling of the story.

My first meeting with the members of the Central Command was after the decision to renew operations. Such a decision was not easy to pull from the lugubrious body known as the United Resistance movement; lugubrious organizationally and even more so ideologically and politically. But really they had no choice. The bow of their youth had been drawn too tight. Had they withdrawn at that point, perhaps many youth, especially the urban, would have joined the Underground. Maybe even "Dan Ram" would have crossed his eternal last millimeter.

The distribution of operations was to our disadvantage, in terms of the order. First came the IZL operation against the railroad and police buildings, then the bridges blown up by the Hagana, and finally our operation at the rail works in Haifa.

This operation was one of the most difficult. The site was well defended, and the preceding operations had naturally increased the tension and the security. The importance of the operation was great, because its complete success would have silenced the rails. Gera told us of Galili's excitement when Lehi had proposed the attack. The Hagana wanted this operation for itself. After all, the people of Haifa and the Bay area might lend support.

Our previous experience in Haifa should have been a warning to us. Haifa will be remembered, as far as the Underground is concerned, with sorrow and bitterness. We did have some successes there, mostly afterward: The IZL operation at the oil refinery, our demolition of the detectives' headquarters. Many British officers and policemen lost their lives in Haifa. Last but not least was Lehi's exploding eight oil tankers in the bay. Still, Haifa has a reputation for disasters. Most of our prisoners had been arrested there; and many of our dead fell there, too. Coincidence or not? Haifa's population is divided between an established working class and a tranquil bourgeoisie. The down-to-earth Jew of Tel Aviv or Ramat Gan is rare in Haifa, as is the zealous Jew of Jerusalem and the poor-though-precious neighborhoods of Hatikva and Kerem Hatemanim. In any case, safe shelter was difficult to come by in Haifa. A man sent to Haifa bade farewell as if he were going straight to jail. Enlisting new members there was also difficult.

Lehi's account with Haifa is long and bitter, beginning with the heroic death of Jonathan in the spring of 5703 (1943) which led to the tragedy at Yavne'el, through the bloody story about to be told, to the beginning of Lehi's moral and organizational tragedy with the arrest of Natan Friedman-Yellin in Haifa after the assassination of Count Bernadotte in 5708 (1948).

The rail works were chosen not only because of their own importance. We also had ambitions for our organization. The ranks of the IZL were growing, partly because of their operations. The majority of the youth is not fluent in political terminology. Our ranks may have paid much attention to the differences in the first joint proclamation, in which the IZL wrote of "oppressive rule," while we wrote of "foreign rule"; the IZL, of "traitorous English statesmen," and we, of "traitorous England." Politically, there are certainly differences in these phrases; but as for the war, even the IZL has abandoned its original hesitance. The good youth, who want to give their blood and strike at the enemy, naturally join the larger force. The Lehi Command is under pressure to execute a large-scale operation. Authors' jealousy increases wisdom; fighters' jealousy increases blows to the enemy. (Except that this time, our own blood flowed.) In the annual report which Gera wrote in Tishrei 5707 (1946), he openly and honestly records our calculations during the deliberations. He writes of a deadly, closed circle: We cannot carry out more serious operations because we lack large numbers of fighters, and the number of fighters has not grown because of the limited scope of our operations, compared to the IZL's. The next year, in an internal pamphlet, I warn against this competitive view; still, I cannot say with any certainty that had I escaped earlier and been there during the deliberations, when the decision was taken in Iyar 5706 (1946) to attack the rail works, I would have opposed it. The numbers, in any case, were an additional argument in favor of unification with the IZL.

The boys were sent. The operation was well planned, in keeping with Michael's meticulousness. The operation itself was executed almost *in toto*. The tragedy occurred, as did the later tragedy during the Acco Prison breakout, while our forces were withdrawing. The boys remained at the site longer than called for in the plan; they were searching for two boys who had seemingly disappeared. But the failure stemmed mostly from the high level of alert of all British positions following the IZL operations and the Hagana's blowing up the bridges. They knew it was Lehi's turn.

I had spent ten days moving from one place to another. Two days after I moved into my permanent apartment, a survivor from the killing fields arrived, by coincidence; he had come to visit the children of my Hungarian landlords. I heard the story from him, though he was hard to understand. He did not know how it happened. It happened with terrible speed. Ambushed during the retreat. Within seconds, thousands of bullets rained upon them. He leaped from the vehicle and crawled; only miraculously was he not wounded or discovered. Two or three got away. Eleven fell, twenty were taken prisoner. Elimelech, who later fell in the escape from Acco, described everything, every terrible thing, in the booklet *We Did Not Return to Base*.[73] He failed to describe only what happened inside those of us who were not there, and certainly what happened inside Michael and Mazal, who had planned the operation. Michael will not rest until he has planned a vengeful massacre for the goyim. He promises this, though he does not know that he will rest, he will be forced by the British to rest for almost two years. And Mazal had good reason to hesitate so much a year later before again sending dozens of people to Haifa to blow up the refineries. Again and again he drove there to check the site, and especially the escape route, and finally he decided, against the opinion of impulsive, courageous Dov, to postpone the operation. He re-established a fighting unit after the tragedy at the rail works only with the greatest difficulty, and he did not want to do it again. The truth is we never recovered from the blow, certainly not qualitatively.

The Hebrew population of Haifa was called upon to participate in its entirety in the funeral of Weitz, who died at the E-Ziv bridge. On that same day, eleven of our dead were buried with no one accompanying their coffins. The Yishuv is not called upon to mourn these, its sons, and the Voice of Israel radio of the Hagana or, more correctly, of the United Resistance movement, does not mention the operation at the rail works.

And this while the agreement is still in effect. And the operation at the rail works was under its orders.

And we are bleeding, and we are bitter. For we do not yet know that this was the swan song of the Resistance. They never stopped hating us, and all our cartwheels and all our patriotism had no effect. They hated us for making them fight, for fighting before they did, and because we would continue to fight after they surrendered. There was not a bit of sadness in their hearts over our boys who fell, just as they would later fail to mourn when Dov fell, though by then he would be in their army, under their full command. They are not like us and not like the IZL; they never, ever forget the internal front. Maybe this is the only thing worth learning from them. For the sake of a united fighting front, we gave up methods of fighting that raise the number of enemy losses and minimize our own. Was this worth it? Our wounded prisoners in Haifa were visited by representatives of the establishment institutions. The boys were happy, really and truly happy. For *we* cannot visit them. And the next day the newspapers announced that the visit had been an error. The visitors had not known that these were Lehi wounded.

No, not worth it. Even our greatest supporter of the agreement with the Hagana, Gera, even he cannot forgive the indignities heaped upon our fighters' blood by Galili. When Gera is one day on trial he will suffer further indignities at the hands of Galili. But this is not yet the Natan Friedman-Yellin who will stand in that same city of Haifa asking the court once, twice, three times to free him on bail because of the *difficult conditions in prison*. No, this is still *Gera*, proud and cruel, sending people to war and death yet feeling their pain and hurting when their honor is besmirched. During the next meeting with the Resistance representatives, he casts doubt on the entire arrangement: It lacks a moral foundation.

3. Their Black Sabbath

I was called to spend Sabbath in the city, for consultations. I slept at Gera's apartment on Rehov Sokolov. Early in the morning, we woke to the sound of the curfew siren. I still had no identification papers, and, what is worse, the two of us are together. We told ourselves countless times: The top men cannot sleep in the same place, not even on nearby streets—the further away from each other the better. But principles are one thing and behavior another. There is no one above us to take disciplinary action.

The radio announcement calms us—this time we were not the target. In truth, we were more than calmed, we were "not overly distressed," to use Natan's diplomatic language. I can speak more plainly if roughly: We were happy. Not because we rejoiced in others' misfortune, but because we were confident that now, with this, their hesitancy, which so racked our nerves, will end. This will end their method of fighting, in which every action is followed by an extended period of hoping for a single kind word from London, a half-smile, the shadow of a promise. In my ideological classes I like to teach people with Maimonides' deep explanation of one of the Divine policies which seemingly contradicts the principle of free choice. If God hardened Pharaoh's heart, why did He punish him for the acts which stemmed from this hardening? Maimonides gives the apparently theological question a wonderful, historiographical answer: If Pharaoh had agreed to free the children of Israel at once, he would have avoided punishment for all his previous crimes and for the 400 years the Jews were enslaved in Egypt. Therefore, God is obligated to harden his heart, so he should not so easily become a penitent and escape his just recompense. In other words, Maimonides is saying: Evil that does not exhaust itself is very dangerous; it is like a wound that has closed before all the pus has come out.

But the elders of the Yishuv stood after every operation alarmed by their own momentum, hoping for the moment when the "misunderstanding" in our relations with England would be cleared up.

Therefore, we were happy, honestly and out of patriotism, over the "Black Sabbath." "We have crossed the Rubicon," Galili told us in a brief note. And indeed they themselves felt festive in those first few days. It must have been a bit uncomfortable for them, purporting till then to be underground leaders and yet walking freely outside and participating in public gatherings. Now finally they are in a real underground. During our first meetings afterward, Galili and his friends ask for advice: How to disguise one's face? How to live, with one's family or alone? How to set up contacts? They were playing like children who forget they are only making believe.

The Voice of Israel radio reached the heights of rebellion. Golda Meyerson delivered a really revolutionary speech in Haifa and told a crowd of thousands: "We will not surrender. We will continue." How can you not believe her?

True, there are omens. First of all, they went quietly when arrested, without resistance. The excuse was: the British will not be able to identify them anyway. Instructions are not to identify oneself during the interrogation. But practically, this was of little importance. The Palmach has already been badly hurt. Individual identities neither added nor detracted, and before several weeks had passed the first fissures appeared, people identifying themselves during interrogations. Once more, the United Resistance distributed tiny notices in the Tel Aviv area, calling on people not to show their ID, but to no avail, for meanwhile the residents of Rafiah have broken.

The second omen: Yagur. Yagur as a symbol. Abandoning weapons! It cost the enemy nothing. He searched and destroyed with pleasure. There was no resistance. What was called "heroic resistance" was nothing more than the hysteria of some women, not a firm stand by men or women. He who so easily parts with his arms is not dangerous. Had there been armed resistance, with losses on both sides, then the searches for arms would definitely have ceased and the position of the Jewish Agency would definitely have been strengthened. A display of real strength. Their chatter about "moral strength" as resistance nauseated us.

Another omen: *Haaretz* became the rag of the "moderates" calling for withdrawal. The paper's editors would not have dared to do this unless they saw that the people in the thick of the struggle were not firmly committed. This was a blatantly quisling-like move on their part. And Weizmann and Kaplan and Shertok would not have dared risk appearing to be traitors unless they knew that no such accusation would be forthcoming from the activists, from the friends and comrades of the heroes of the E-Ziv bridge and Sarona, just as Ben Gurion would never have dared turn against the Underground as he later did unless he knew that he was in no danger from them. This quisling-like call in *Haaretz* (there are apparently different degrees of quislingity) had an immediate effect. The activist leaders were faced with a powerful coalition: some civilians, Aliya Hadasha (the New Immigration Party),[74] part of Mapai, all of Hashomer Hatzair—all these made for strong pressure, especially at times of general hardship. The alternative was to make a pact with the IZL and Lehi and go all the way. And this, Ben Gurion and Galili would never do. If we had deluded ourselves about this once, we had done so from a failure to understand their spiritual and economic make up. Uri Zvi Greenberg and Dr. Abba Ahimeir understood them better. But by this time, newcomers were leading the Underground, who had not yet felt the force of Histadrut artillery on their own bodies, who could not yet understand why these people *will never be patriots*. Today the reason is obvious: The activists in Mapai are first and foremost opportunists. Their activism is derived from their opportunism; and when other quislings threatened to rise, they transformed themselves into quislings first. The truth they express is: If someone is going to struggle—it will be us. If someone is going to surrender—it will be us. If there will be a state—it will be us. The thing is—there is only us.

After our red night came their Black Sabbath. This is not the name given the day in the British log; this is the name given by the Jewish Agency and Hagana historians.

And rightly so. They used words without realizing what they were saying. Why a "black" Sabbath? What happened? The leaders of the Agency were arrested? "And what did you think," Weizmann later asked, "that you would get candies for the 'Struggle'?" And deep in his heart Weizmann was happy, for he knew these men who wished for "warm frost," he knew (and this was obvious from his sarcastic comment about the candy) that they were not prepared for the suffering of Yagur and Latrun, he knew that this was the end of the "Struggle" he hated so much. This was his victory over Ben Gurion and Sneh.

Oh, the Voice of Israel still thundered: "There will be war." But this was not serious. The "Struggle" ended on "Black" Sabbath. The arrest of the leaders and the events at Yagur determined the course of these "revolutionaries."

And the King David Hotel only helped them abandon the business.

A Little Bit of Grammar

Perhaps one day a perceptive researcher will turn up, one who will write this generation's history in conjunction with this generation's linguistic deceptions.

Take for example the transformation of active verbs to stative. "Something is puzzling," "something is surprising." As if the possibility exists for something to be "puzzling" in a vacuum, in and of itself. As if a characteristic existed in some object that made it puzzling, rather than that a subject is puzzled. As if puzzling objects exist in the world and not puzzled subjects, who are puzzled because of the lack of coordination between their understanding and the object. The same holds for "surprising," which has suddenly become stative and an independent entity. How can something be surprising in and of itself? For everything is a link in a chain and if it appears sudden, this is only in the eyes of he who fails to see the chain. Something can surprise me, you, him, us; and after a while, you begin to see it, and there is no longer any surprise. So the object was not surprising, but rather you were surprised, a surprised subject. This linguistic error slowly clouds people's thinking.

Indeed, nothing was "surprising" in the events that shocked us after our tragedy in Haifa. So why was it surprising that the operation was not mentioned on the Voice of Israel radio? Why was it surprising that the citizens of Haifa were called upon to honor Yichiam Weitz, who fell one night before our eleven, yet were not called upon to honor the eleven who fell after the explosion of the rail works? If you drop the solecism and no longer say "it's surprising," but say instead "it surprised us," then you will understand that the blame lay with us, with those of us who were surprised, we who were surprised then, like those in the IZL who were surprised later when Ben Gurion ordered their *Altalena* ship sunk with all the Jewish arms and Jewish sailors on it. The facts themselves were "all right." We were not all right, not in our naively believing in a vast love of Israel which led us to rejoice over the united fighting spirit, not in our believing that as with us, so with them—as we loved every drop of holy Hebrew blood, so they loved every drop of holy Hebrew blood; as we were shaken over the blood of Weitz and Welinitz, so they would be shaken by the blood of other Hebrew fighters falling by British bullets; as we recoiled from spilling our brothers' blood, so they would recoil.

And because our understanding was willing, we corrupted our grammar. We told ourselves they shed their former being. Because we ceased to see these subjects—Galili, Sneh, Ben Gurion and Abba Hushi—in their stative and eternally stationary forms, we began to be puzzled by "surprising" things like their hatred for the freedom-fighting destroyers of British installations, like their hatred for IZL sailors bringing desperately needed arms to the homeland.

The edifying lesson to be learned from the grammatical crime: No, there is nothing in them to surprise someone who knows them. The blame lies with us, we who were surprised.

In the grammar lessons taught in Latrun by Moshe Gold of the IZL and by me of Lehi, neither of us delved deeply enough to differentiate between the verb that remains forever stative, like the character of a traitor, and the active verb, forever active on behalf of others and not on his own behalf, as the members of the Underground were active, and the dead of the rail works and the dead of the *Altalena*, with the Organized Yishuv scornfully silent and the Palmachniks joyfully neighing behind the coffins of our red corpses.

These Are the Things Enjoyed

1. Practicing Kindness[75]

The last note sent by Sneh, before he left the country, is the order for the Underground to carry out the operations code named "Malonchik" (Little Hotel) and the house of "Your servant, Your anointed," in Jerusalem, as agreed.

The Lehi operation, the blowing up of the "House of David" ("Your servant, Your anointed"), which housed the offices of British Intelligence and others, was not executed. We had a scheduling conflict with the IZL (neither the first nor the last; they were apparently busy trying to make up for lost time). They demanded a long period of time for their operation before we could begin ours (the buildings were nearby). Our people said that once the IZL began, execution of our operation would be impossible. Without a doubt, the value of their operation was greater than ours. Their target was the center of government. But we did not want to give up our operation. The lessons of the rail works were still smoldering within us. The tragedy there was a result of our being last in line for operations.

We wanted revenge. The IZL will, in accordance with its policy and as agreed upon with the Hagana, send a telephone warning to those in the King David Hotel to evacuate before the explosion. We—whether we promise to or not—will not send any warning, that is obvious. We are Lehi.

The debate concluded with an agreement to leave a few minutes between operations. Dov, responsible for our operations, was prepared to assume the risk, but Levi, responsible for our Jerusalem branch, was vigorously opposed; the age-old conflict between "military" and "administrative" authorities. The "military" was right but the "administrative" won. Our operation was not executed.

The King David Hotel, the Mandatory government's headquarters, exploded together with dozens of high officials and with a huge amount of British prestige and self-confidence. Perhaps quite a few documents were destroyed, too, but only someone who values documents values their destruction. We value people.

The controversy that later flared and that from time to time still surfaces over responsibility for the operation seems to me most peculiar—at least from the IZL's point of view. The formal order originated, without a doubt, with Sneh. But the truth is that without a doubt, not Sneh, not the Hagana and not the

United Resistance bore responsibility for the *results* of the operation. None of them wanted these results. The result was, as IZL Commander Begin repeatedly emphasizes, the ultimate destruction of the British civil administration in our country. This resulted just because of that which left Begin in shock, that which Sneh certainly did not intend: the loss of life, including precious Jewish life. Had warning only the Jews been possible, it would have been worthwhile. We had intended to do this when we were planning our revenge in Adar 5702 (1942), the elimination of the British administration in the Mt. Zion cemetery. British rule was not shaken by the destruction of the King David, but rather by the destruction of the administrative staff and the fear instilled in those not killed. If Begin's assumption is correct that this was a "provocation" on the part of Sir John Shaw, the Mandate's Chief Secretary who refused to evacuate the building, then this is another example of the same phenomenon involved in Bevin's "provocations." There is an objective collaboration between the revolution and its most extreme enemies, between the Hasmoneans and King Antiochus. "Will the oppressive and repressive Government building and Staff headquarters explode?" asks Begin in the Hebrew edition of his book, describing the moments before the explosion. And one might ask, in contrast: Was the *building* oppressive and repressive? The stones? The documents? Or perhaps it was the bureaucrats, those who were killed or who survived.

After the attack, Begin tried in vain to transform Sneh and the Resistance into partners in one of the operations decisive to the undermining of British rule in our country. After a furious argument between Begin and Galili during one of the following meetings, Begin suggested submitting the matter to arbitration and that I be one of the arbitrators (Lehi was considered neutral in disputes between the Hagana and the IZL), along with Dr. Magnes, I think. Today I can reveal that had Begin's proposal making me an arbitrator been accepted, I would have ruled in favor of the heroism and ability of the IZL soldiers, but against Begin's claims and accusations.

For the kindness done by Begin to Moshe Sneh in laying the "blame" on him or making him partner to it—this is a kindness Sneh does not deserve, while Begin does an injustice to the IZL, which despite the Jewish casualties whose deaths served no purpose, is deserving of having the entire operation credited to its account, without any partners.

In psychoanalytic terms, perhaps a Freudian explanation lies behind Begin's forgetfulness, when in his memoirs he does not specify whom he proposed as arbitrators.

2. Visiting the Ill

I can find no better title for the meetings between us and the Hagana leaders, following the explosion at the King David Hotel, than "visiting the ill."

In that pleasant, especially beautiful building with the steps leading upwards from King Solomon Street, where these meetings were held sometimes with and sometimes without the IZL, I began to discern our and my error in assessing our third partner in the War of Liberation. If the long respites between each and every operation till now, if the Hagana's behavior after our bloody battles in the rail works, could still be interpreted as momentary weaknesses, vestiges of the past, in these meetings I came to realize that these were not weaknesses but rather a chronic illness for which there is no cure. The three-way meetings forced me to realize that there were not three partners here, but two—the Underground and the Hagana. And this, despite the contrasts between Begin's views and my own. Thus, for example, together with Galili I disagreed with Begin's plan for a great, coordinated revolt to seize power, the main part of which was the conquest of Armon Hanetziv, the High Commissioner's Residence, in Jerusalem. Galili asked: How many days can we hold it? I asked: How many hours? Galili understands military matters better than I, while I am sharper in debate. Indeed, Begin did not pretend there was a possibility of victory. He believed holding out for four weeks was possible. We could take the heads of the British government prisoner, and hold them in the Residence to prevent its being bombed. Perseverance in the face of siege and hunger would not be easy. But Begin valued the demonstrative and even political worth of such an operation. Not just the raising of a flag, but also the establishment of a government. This would automatically change our status; if we have a government and an army, the Emergency Laws would end. The British would be forced to deal with us as rebels, to end the trials, etc. After the presumable defeat, operations could continue in the new government's name, either underground or in exile. (The Bergson Group in America, whose representational aspect was until then rather fictitious, would be given a legal status by means of this revolt.)

Aside from asking about the hours, I asked Begin if it was not obvious to him that in such an operation perhaps two thousand fighters would fall, and since the IZL wanted to take upon itself this conquest of Jerusalem, most of its men would be lost? Is the raising of a flag, a demonstrative act, worth this?

I viewed this proposal as an outgrowth of the romantic school in which Begin was educated. The many Polish rebellions we learned about in our Polish high schools, in history and literature courses, in song and dance, with all the heroic glory, with all the tragedy, with all the deep educational values inherent in them, all these influenced Begin when he prepared such plans. And, too, maybe the impact of the Jewish war with Rome, which ended at Betar, with its heroism, a wonderful page in history, was too deeply etched into Begin. This operation we were discussing would have written another wonderful page into history.

In opposing the plan, I suddenly found myself in a strange coalition with Galili; of course, not for long. I argued for continuing our partisan methods, minimizing our losses and maximizing those of the enemy. Galili readily agreed to a minimum of losses on our side but continued to demand zero losses for the enemy.

Despite these contrasts and "coalitions," the situation at these meetings was perfectly clear: Differences of opinion between Begin and us about the *method* of operations might exist, but there were no differences about the need to continue and to escalate.

So we sat: Israel Galili at the head of the table. Begin on a couch to his right, I on a chair to his left. Opposite Galili—Natan Friedman. A second representative of each the Hagana and the IZL at either side of the table. And on the table, lots of food.

The speakers' style alternates: one minute bitter, one sweet; but the food and drink are all mixed together, bitter sandwiches and sweet cakes, hard spirits and sweet wine. The two who share a manner of speaking are those at the head and "tail" of the table: Galili and Natan. Galili talks to Natan with an Ashkenazic accent, calling him "Nusan" with such intimacy that surely it was the cause of Natan's foolish idea two years later (despite my objections and pleas) to call Galili as a witness in the Bernadotte trial, at which time he will be able to hear Galili, the man who once greeted him so warmly and with such a hearty, brotherly smile as "Nusan," spit ugly, dirty phrases in his face, and libel and desecrate our hanged martyrs as well. At the table, Natan used to answer Galili with the same softness. Not in the friendly slovenliness of an Ashkenazic accent, no, Natan was too fastidious in his use of language, in his grammar as well as pronunciation, so he would purposely say "Yisrael," accenting the final syllable. Nor would Natan concede to Galili on the main points under discussion: continuation or cessation or a respite. No. In this respect he and I did not yet differ. But whatever I would hurl at Galili in bitterness and in polarizing terms, Natan would smooth over in soft terms. Not without reason will Galili one day ask Dr. Kurtz, who organizes these meetings with the Hagana in his house, to have "Nusan" come to the meetings instead of Scheib.

And Natan has another good characteristic. He does not rush his replies. Or perhaps he likes giving diplomatic answers that can be interpreted in more than one way, after which he will do as he pleases. Galili will complain: "Nusan," can it be? But you said such and such . . . ? And Natan will only laugh and say: But I also added such and such . . . . And Natan's greatest characteristic is his silence. He knows how to reply in wonderful silence. "Nusan!" Why are you silent? And "Nusan" is not silent at all. He takes something from the table after glancing in every direction, smiles or even laughs aloud, but he says nothing. In short: His mouth is sealed and his hands are free. And who can say later that he broke a promise?

Menachem is usually the main speaker at these meetings. He is always there with a prepared speech. And the speech is always strong. He always opens by analyzing the political situation, then draws the conclusions and then makes the proposals. His speeches always take a long time, but they are well put and logical.

I (and I think I must add: to my sorrow) do not know how to speak softly as Natan does, and I do not know how to be silent as he is. It is no wonder that I occasionally upset Galili and cause his eyes to bulge. His face reddens and swells and his eyes seem to want to jump right out of their sockets and pounce on me.

He speaks of changing the form of "Struggle" and I correct: "Surrender." Sometimes (in the meetings at which the IZL is not present) he speaks not as the leader of the Hagana but as a member of Ahdut Haavoda and he explains that what I say may be true, true, true—but he has to accept his movement's "authority" and I correct: "budget." The United Kibbutz movement (the backbone of Ahdut Haavoda) behind Yagur will never rebel, not because it respects authority, but because it is dependent on a budget and fears financial sanctions. Their weaker-natured members panicked as soon as they saw their work destroyed, and they are no different than any property owners.

When Galili hears the word "budget" it is as if somebody has stepped on a spiritual soft spot. Outbursts are not in his nature; only his eyes boil, and his mouth speaks: "Do not belittle budgets."

From there the illness spreads. New viruses appear at every meeting and with them, paralysis. Every meeting, the number of limbs of this big, cumbersome body that are paralyzed grows; but instead of a healthy limb girding its strength to make up for the deficiency caused by the sick limb's paralysis, the healthy limbs seem to rather enjoy this state in which they can lay the charge of paralysis on others.

As an alternative to an active struggle involving sabotage, civil disobedience is suggested: not paying taxes, not making use of the British authorities. The burden will fall mostly on urban shoulders. The kibbutzim do not pay taxes; a kibbutz has almost no contact with the authorities. It can live without police, without mail, without courts. Its very basis is nongovernmental, bordering on anarchism. Understandably, the kibbutz movement has long opposed a Jewish state. Why does it need a state? Therefore, after Yagur, the kibbutz sector pounces on this treasure called "civil disobedience." The ball is passed to the "civilian" court. The "civilians" are in any case already shouldering the burden of the war. Curfews always hurt the cities. The members of the Underground are for the most part from these "civilian" homes. So we begin tiresome negotiations on the forms of "rebellious" disobedience. What is to be done, what not. Suddenly salvation arises from a new corner, one whose sun had seemingly set forever.

Weizmann.

Ben Gurion and Sneh are in Paris. Hashomer Hatzair is engaging in sophistry about a hearty struggle, meaning one at the expense of immigrants who will be starved and killed. Shertok does not want to "sit" any longer (in detention, where he has been since Black Sabbath). The agreement reached is for civil disobedience; that is, we agree to the expansion of the "Struggle" at the expense of its force. When we express our doubts, Galili promises, adopting an insulted tone: There will be reactions to provocations. We will not remain silent when faced with expulsions of immigrants and searches for weapons; but instead of planned operations against enemy installations, activity will consist of civil disobedience, in which the entire nation can participate.

Natan Friedman reminds Galili of the folk tale about a newlywed husband who goes to court to complain about his father-in-law, who promised him food. The father-in-law lists various foods, the best a Jewish kitchen can offer, until the husband is finally able to interrupt: Yes, judge, this is all fine except . . . he gives me nothing.

We agree with the Hagana leaders that sometimes the value of widespread disobedience is not less than infrequent operations. But when? When will this disobedience begin?

Weizmann.

This is the excuse. Weizmann has requested a delay of ten days. Everything is ready. Just ten days. "Will you break the agreement over ten days? And ten days later a new date appears. Give us four weeks, Galili asks/demands (in his official position as chief of staff he demands; personally, as leader of the "activists," he asks).

Why four? What will happen four weeks from now? What is the logic of this date?

I ask him. And he admits: Really, there is no logic to it, I chose it at random. I could have said: Give us seven weeks.

Meanwhile, boats are coming. Boatloads of refugees are deported, and there is no response. Meanwhile the prisoners from the rail works stand trial. The British court is surprised by new tactics. In a Central Command meeting I propose that we stop making speeches. Speeches have already fulfilled their purpose. Now we must go further. We decide to instruct our men not to participate in the trial; on the contrary, to interfere with the proceedings. In song. These instructions are received in Acco Prison enthusiastically. Singing lessons are now conducted in Acco Fortress. At the trials, confusion. The courtroom comedy is brought to an end, the accused are removed and the trial takes place in their absence. To do so, the British regime must enact a special law; after all, the British democratic tradition must be preserved. And so, overnight a law is created whose force applies retroactively (someone in Mapai must have taken notes then on how to do this, for exactly two years later a similar law was passed by the government of Israel). The sentence is death. Death for eighteen people. Who is afraid? Least of all: the sentenced. Most of all: the heads of the British regime. They know what hanging eighteen Sternists would mean. They know what would happen the day after such a night of gallows. All restraints would be off. We, of course, do nothing to calm their fears. Our paper *Hama'as* appears week after week, a warning posted at the top: "The enemy will drown in its own blood."

Next in the line of fear, after the British, are the members of the Agency. There is no room in their hearts for the condemned men; they proved this with their behavior toward those who fell in the rail works. They proved it by their apologies the day after the members of the so-called National Institutions visited the military hospital by mistake. Still, they do not want the boys to be hanged, for they know they themselves would be forgotten were an ocean of blood to sweep the country after the hangings. And they are still knocking at London's door. Did not *Haaretz* write that with a monthly increase in certificates from 1,500 to 4,000, England could have prevented, in the fall of 1946, most of the mishaps that occurred this year? Four thousand! That is the price. It is no secret. That is the price asked by Weizmann. Perhaps Ben Gurion could not be bought at that price. But faced with 5,000 certificates, not even he would resist.

Weizmann wants a cease-fire at any price. The civilians succeed in reducing the plan for civil disobedience to one "brave" operation. The councils and municipalities allot 100,000 (that number! that number!) lira for immigration purposes without asking the government's permission. What a revolutionary move! Yes! The sum will be raised from the populace in a special appeal. (It is a means for educating the masses: Give a donation and your conscience will be calmed. Now you can quietly stand opposite ravaged boats and children's blood. You can pat yourself on the belly: "I made my contribution. We are with you, brothers.") The Voice of Israel radio is still screaming, "We will not surrender," while in Rafiah they are already lining up to identify themselves. From Latrun we hear: David Remez is still standing firm, studying and teaching. Shertok and Joseph are behaving disgracefully. Golda Meyerson, in her new position as director of the Agency's Political Department, gives a speech in which she states no more and no less than:

"If the authorities would give us a real guarantee that the Arabs will not attack Jewish settlements, then we would have no need of any arms at all."

And all this happened without them having to endure any really difficult tests. Members of the Palmach were never sentenced to death. They were not sent into exile. Only one Yagur, one Black Sabbath, and all the activists are on their knees.

Had Galili been a true "fighter," we would have seen it in him in these meetings during the disintegration of the "Struggle." But he showed no sorrow, no bitterness. On the contrary, he seemed happy that he could pass the blame for inactivity to others. He has a plethora of devices: Weizmann. The civilians. The need for a *slick* (a hiding place for arms). And when on occasion he makes use of a new argument for renewed restraint he smiles, for he knows that we know that for them the "war" is over. So why does he drag us from meeting to meeting? The answer is obvious: The leader of the Hagana has an additional job now, to prevent operations by the "dissidents." The main purpose of the whole "Struggle," from their point of view, was now being put to the test: If the dissidents' actions cannot be prevented, then the whole "Struggle" was pointless, and even worse; for by now many in the Hagana have had their appetites whetted, their fighting spirit ignited, their desires to avenge their comrades' blood heightened. The "Struggle" is dead and we live. The three-way meetings become shorter each time, more cynical. By this time, Galili sometimes issues warnings and threats.

At December's Zionist Congress, the official burial ceremony is held for the body which has been a lifeless corpse for so many months. Britain sends a splendid wreath to the Congress. In the words of *Haaretz*: "The British government's only contribution to the Congress was the release of eight detainees from Latrun, among them three members of the Agency board of directors." Obviously, no tears will be shed for the "Struggle," R.I.P.

3. And Escorting the Dead

In a meeting with Golda Meyerson, a few hours before her flight to the Congress, I was given an opportunity to escort the deceased on its final journey.

The meetings with the Hagana Command, the tasty sandwiches and bottles of cognac, are over. The Hagana Command is no longer a relevant factor. All its time is spent searching for *slick*s, hiding places (not for arms, since there is an unofficial British promise that the searches of kibbutzim will end when the "Struggle" ends, but rather for their activist ideology). The activist-oriented *Oz* paper of the opposition in the Labor movement is dying. Ahdut Haavoda is mired in party politics, after one year as a militant factor. Slowly, slowly, the ranks are being prepared for a renewed struggle . . . against the dissidents. Hagana Intelligence has been given responsibility for these preparations. The initiative has passed once again from the Hagana to the Agency leaders, or the supposedly democratic Congress. The elections to the Congress center on the debate over the "Struggle," which is to say, over a corpse, a dead issue. How can Mapai run with a list uniting activists and defeatists? Apparently the differences of opinion are overshadowed by their common interest, that the party retains power.

The manner in which Golda opens her conversation with me is therefore laughable: She wants us to help *them* (in her words, "us"), the "activists," to become a majority in the Congress.

Actually, this was not her opening. It was preceded by a declaration: She would not be sitting with me were it not for her assumption that we are patriots, though this has no bearing on her objective evaluation of our activities.

The meeting was held in Dr. Jacob Weinshal's apartment. The veteran intermediary, Dr. Shimshon Yunichman, had asked if I would agree to meet in the apartment of the late Eliahu Golomb ("There is a special atmosphere there," according to him); but I preferred Weinshal's. And if the Agency's Political Department director agreed to this, and if she opened with such a declaration, then obviously the King David Hotel is not the only building that crumbled. Much has apparently changed.

I was not moved by her compliment, for I knew with whom I was speaking; and I did not need the gift of prophecy to know that in a few months she would ask the British Chief Secretary for permission to completely eliminate the "patriots," who suddenly became "despicable criminals."

The heart of the discussion was her request that we refrain from operations for a little while, a month, maybe two, for the duration of the Congress, then for the duration of the negotiations in London.

Regarding the Congress, the rationale is clear: The Congress must decide on the continuation of the "Struggle." There are as everyone knows, many opponents of the "Struggle." But the "activists" hope to win a majority anyway. If we continue our extremist activity it will bolster the wing opposed to the "Struggle." It will frighten many who have not yet decided which way to vote.

To her credit, she explained all these things in good taste and with logic, simply and without rhetoric or sophistry (in contrast to her friends David Remez and Levi Skolnick [the future prime minister, Levi Eshkol]). And if one added to this her external appearance and puritan dress, he might just have fallen into the trap and believed in her goodwill and honesty. I did not. I had fallen into "Dan Ram"'s trap; I had been tempted to believe in the Palmachniks, those "fine lads," but this time I was constantly aware: This is the Mapai leadership, which automatically means absolutely everything is a tactic. Principle, consistency and truth are not binding. This is Mapai.

But because I was indebted to her for her "patriotic" compliment, and because in any case we had already decided to halt our activity for a short while—not for political reasons, but for technical reasons involving preparations for other, larger operations (we had also announced an end to rail sabotage, to avoid wrecking the citrus-fruit industry which was then shipping produce by train)—I was able to repay her kindness, display generosity and promise: We will consider this argument with understanding; after our consultations we will announce our answer. I think it will be favorable.

Our discussion of extending the cease-fire for the period of negotiations with London was totally different. In truth, Golda "in truthed" a lot. "In truth," she said, she was not sure that the Congress would decide to go to London. "In truth," clearly nothing would come of a conference in London, but *just for that reason* a cease-fire was necessary. Then she displayed some hackneyed acrobatics that lay somewhere between the "in truth" and the "just for," acrobatics that were typical of the Yishuv but are found in no other nation. Not many sages survive in Mapai, but what does remain from their grandparents who used to study Talmud? That digging, waving talmudic movement of the thumb that comes to strengthen arguments.

Just because there is no possibility of anything coming out of the London conference, we should not provide the English with a pretext ("terror") to reject our demands.

I have no respect for the art of formal logic. Of all the wisdom in our country, perhaps this is the cheapest: argumentology. There is no "in truth" that cannot find a "just because."

During my Vienna schooldays, Moshe Arye Kurtz and I would play a game: We argued over a particular problem, each of us piling up mountains of arguments, and the next day we said: Now we reverse the situation—you be against, and I will be for. And again, the syllogisms and inferences were piled high.

I also remember, from my studies at Vienna's Rabbinical Seminary, Professor Avigdor Optovitsur taught Talmud with extreme sophistry. He would enter the classroom and present a terribly difficult problem. Of course, he also had the solution; but if Heaven forbid one of the students came up with the same solution, then he invented another solution and also contradicted, logically and intelligently, the first solution, which he himself had also prepared, but which someone had "stolen" from him. I am not criticizing him; he was my favorite teacher, having opened the gates of legend to my understanding and love. But I mention this as another argument against the wisdom I call "argumentology."

Another memory comes to mind: After I had excelled in my university philosophical examination, when being examined by Professor Reininger, a Nazi, a hater of Israel, and especially strict in the history of philosophy in general and of Kant in particular, I had a mishap with Professor Karl Biehler, a very pleasant, kindhearted man and a liberal. He asked me to define logic and I answered according to Sigwart: It is the "laws of correct thought." He jumped as if bitten by a snake and failed me. Naturally I reviewed the definitions and when tested again months later I knew, "Logic is the law of formal premises for science."

Today I thank Prof. Karl Biehler from the bottom of my heart for teaching me this lesson. For indeed, a sentence can be in full accordance with formal logic and still be incorrect.

I remember all these school-day events whenever I encounter the spinnings of logical argumentation, which spin themselves and nothing else.

Of course, to reply to Golda's proposal, to cease operations during the negotiations in London, I did not need to confer with my colleagues (to be precise: colleague); I was able to say "no" loudly and clearly right then. There was at least some minimal sense in giving a chance to a Congress of Jews, but there was no sense in giving a chance to new negotiations in London.

Suddenly the thought occurred to me to put my "just because" on the table and simultaneously furnish additional proof of our true patriotism.

On the contrary—I told her—if you possessed a greater political wisdom, you would have to support us secretly and benefit through us. The two of us could reach an agreement: We (Lehi) will permit you to repudiate and even condemn our operations, and you will permit and also help us to continue operating. This could be a card in your hand. We already proved ourselves in the matter of the 100,000 certificates, when we went along though it contradicted our military principles and political ideas. We went along and even exploited it.

I continued in this vein for (I am slightly ashamed over my naivety) I truly and very much wanted to see them as real patriots, putting the national interest above the party interest, even though in this case I was from the start abandoning any demand for our own authority. In effect, I was asking: Use us! Our blood!

I waited for any one of several possible replies, all of which I knew already. But apparently there is no end to the number of replies hidden in Mapai's soul. The reply was short and delivered in a self-righteous and, actually, offended tone: "These are tactics and I do not know and I do not like tactics," says the leader of Mapai, and even her puritan black dress blushes. Probably she flew in this black dress to the congressional burial during which the tombstone was erected over the linked and continual "Struggles," to the open joy of Weizmann/Aliya Hadasha/Hashomer Hatzair and to the concealed joy of the activists Ben Gurion/Ahdut Haavoda. But any potential splits in the Labor movement were healed in the Fiscal Committee.

And dressed in black elegance they flew to London.

An Intimate Chapter

1. Fears

Our sages said: "A man does not incriminate himself, call himself evil." How much more so would a man not consider himself a coward. In truth, evil is worse than cowardice, but a person is not humiliated if he is called "evil" and yet he will never forgive being called a coward. I will not bear witness that I am a coward, but I will say that there are—and specifically, that I had—moments of fear during the Underground period. Intellectually, I cannot explain why I feared some things and not others. If someone were to say, for instance, "Go through fire and water," I would have to draw a line and say: Through fire, yes. Through water, no. To this day I have not learned how to swim, as I fear great amounts of water. Maybe because I almost drowned when I was five? But I do not fear fire. Bullets flew all around us as we escaped from Warsaw in September 1939. German airplanes flew right over our heads and shot at the panic-stricken people scattered among the bushes and trees, and I felt no fear. Not during the bombing of Warsaw and not during the bombing of Tel Aviv and the bombardment of Jerusalem. Maybe because I had grown accustomed to such fire in my childhood, when I was in my hometown Podvolochisk, a Galician city on the Russian border, at the beginning of the First World War. I was four years old then. And I was five during the street fighting in Tarnopol and I was seven, eight, nine, ten as grenades and gunfire continued in the streets of Lvov. They exploded around the windows of our rooms. My father played chess with me; the pieces scattered. My father set them up again, said something humorous, and we continued playing and the grenades continued exploding. Since then it has become natural for me to joke during bombardments. In any case, I do not fear fire and I do not fear death.

But I greatly feared arrest after my escape from Latrun. This fear had no logical basis, but neither my self-mockery nor intellectual arguments were able to overcome it. I was not even afraid of prison, only of the arrest itself, the very act, how they will appear, how they will identify me, how they will laugh and be happy and take me. Perhaps there exists a fear whose root is—shame? But if so, then why was I afraid only when I was alone in the house, not when someone was with me? Perhaps the arrest was only the garment worn by that other, deeper fear, the primal fear of being alone. Perhaps an analytical psychologist would reach that first childhood memory: a dark and long corridor, a locked door.

Momma and Poppa leave the house and I am three and I am shouting horribly because of the dark, because of being alone, because of the locked door and because of Momma and Poppa who are gone.

But underground, this was not just a fear. It was very defined. It wrote in very black letters on a black background: I do not want to be arrested. I do not want to be arrested. I do not want to be arrested. Big letters and small letters, written horizontally and vertically, shouting and whispering, speaking logically and speaking confusedly. I do not want to be arrested.

Well, who does want to be arrested? So what is this fear?

The first time it came upon me it enveloped me in a hot wave, on one of the first days after my escape.

I was living temporarily on Rehov Hagedud Haivri in the home of a Jewish merchant, well-to-do, well educated, and friendly, very friendly. I have one room. It has a good library, and I stick to *Orot Hakodesh* by Rabbi Kook.

Why has the contact not come yet today? I do not yet have any identity papers. Why has "Trumpeldor" not come yet? (Trumpeldor is Little Jacob's nom de guerre; Trumpeldor had lost his left arm in the Russo-Japanese War, and Jacob's left hand had been blown off in a grenade explosion.) Besides, someone innocently mentioned to me that across from this house (and he pointed) lives a deaf Jewish policeman who has received several warnings from the Underground and who is even under a death sentence. (Why in heaven did they put me—me—in a house under his nose?)

Suddenly . . . shouts. Someone has jumped from the street, over the railing, straight onto the veranda of the house. He is wearing a policeman's uniform, and after him comes a plainclothesman. Sweat covers me. It is obvious. We were followed. Or they just became suspicious, and now they will search. I hear knocks, shouts. The housekeeper is home alone, and steps outside with them. More shouts.

At first I think: Get out. I take off my shoes so my steps will not be audible, and I run through the back door to the yard. There is a shack there. I look for a way over the fence; but it is high, and it is midday, and I will be seen in the street or in the neighbor's house, and they will begin to shout. I have already been burned once in flight. I return. The shouting gradually settles down. The "civilian" disappears, the policeman remains talking to the housekeeper.

Afterward, I find out it is only a family matter. The policeman is the father of the housekeeper; he does not want her to work and he is telling her to go home.

I am embarrassed and tell no one. But the fear is there.

The next time I felt the fear was in Drora's room. By this time she is my contact, my permanent residence is in Ramat Gan; I go to Tel Aviv only for meetings.

Drora's "room" is no room; it is a basement cell. A barred window near the ceiling. Rather "unsympathetic" people live next door; we must be careful. Better for them not to know a strange man is in the room. They are curious and might knock when Drora is not there. I must not make any noise. I cannot move, not even in the cell's two open feet. But if I cannot move then I cannot think and if I cannot think a lucid, purposeful thought, then what is left? Feelings are left.

Children are playing in the yard. I have not seen my daughter since she visited Latrun. Yes, Latrun. There I was imprisoned and here I am free. Shhh . . . I turned over in bed and it squeaked. Did anyone hear? The curtain over the window must remain drawn, too, in case one of the children looks inside.

Would that it were night so that I could go out. How beautiful are the nights. On the first night—an argument with Drora. She makes her bed for me, and takes the floor for herself. I am not chivalrous, but this I cannot stand. No reason or power can convince her to trade. She has a reason: I have not yet completely healed from my broken bones, I am still "sick." Even in Bethlehem Prison the women enjoy "preferred treatment" and have beds, while here Drora is on the floor as if nothing were the matter! And I am stealing her bed. Much later I will hear from certain people, especially those who were never "underground," suggestions accompanied by winks and twisted lips about "contacts" and "rooms" and "sleeping," etc., etc. For these subjects are for them, leading their legal, boring lives, a sort of underground. And the poor souls do not know that there is a loyalty which is greater than love.

But I cannot sleep this night on this bed. The room does not seem good to me, even though it has served Drora and many others as a good shelter for some time. So narrow that there is not enough space for a second bed. Cold in the winter and hot in the summer and bars on the window and water when it rains and plaster peeling off the walls and the sky is not visible from it though the horizon shines within it. And Drora does not move out, not for a long time, not until it is "spoiled" when we find it listed on one of the Hagana's lists as a Lehi room. From then on it is used only for short meetings.

In this basement cell, after that sleepless night, the fear re-emerged. Drora is out and I am alone and suddenly there is a knock at the door. Not one of "our" set knocks, but the knock of a stranger. And again a knock, and again. After the knocks, a loud English voice: Who lives here in this room?

Can there be any doubt? No, there is no doubt. I can only wait till they break down the door. But they do not do so. They disappear.

That night Drora brings Batya to the room for our first meeting since my escape, and now Batya's burden is doubled. Until now there was only the pain of separation, of my arrest. Now fear is added, every day and every night—I might be arrested. Therefore she cannot rejoice in my liberation. What kind of liberation is this? And again the same question I was asked in Hadassah on the day I was arrested: "Why did you do it?" She knows why I did it, and still she asks, the pain asks from inside her, and the fear, too.

After she leaves I tell Drora about the knocks and the Englishman. She calms me. He probably wanted someone else who speaks English, who lives on the top floor. She must, in her heart, be amazed at my "cowardice," though she does not say so. She accompanies me to Rehov Sokolov. From there I walk alone to Natan's apartment.

I did not sleep in Drora's basement any more. But I did hold many meetings there. With Oren, who dared cross that final millimeter from the settlement movement, perhaps because he had revolutionary forefathers or perhaps because he was not really a "settled" man. And in this same basement Dr. Lubotzky threw his "divorce" papers in my face, as he distanced himself from Lehi, on the way to Mapai. And meetings with outside groups, and meetings fraught with friction and hope and disappointment. And here Amichai pressed, in the winter of 5708 (1948): Save Jerusalem. He had come from there and he sounded the alarm: Men, arms!

And I descended to that basement one final time on Drora's wedding day. She no longer lived there, but from there, from this site of her suffering in the Underground, she left for her wedding. These were half-underground days in themselves, actually, with the British still in the country, though not in Tel Aviv. I brought flowers and I brought a gift: Abel Pann drawings of the Bible. I inscribed in the album: "The tie knows no bounds." I meant the tie to the Bible, and I meant the tie of loyalty, any loyalty. And I took leave of one of the warm, living treasures of underground life.

In that basement.

2. Ramat Gan Refuge

They had intended to put our press in a small Ramat Gan house, but after my escape from Latrun, Michael decided I should live there. I noticed then, and continued to note through the nights spent underground in the State of Israel following Bernadotte's assassination, Michael's tendency to keep the spirit somewhat distant from the body. The organizational man must live in the city, but the spiritual man is best kept at a distance.

After allotting me the Ramat Gan apartment Michael sent me a note with instructions to go to Pardess Hanna, as widespread searches were expected. I went, and replied by note: "Take care of Gera, I am not worried about you." Indeed, he wanted to protect Gera and sent him, too, out of the city; but Gera returned to Tel Aviv on Monday for a meeting with Menachem Begin and remained to sleep, and before he was able to leave, the big curfew was imposed.

I was not worried about Michael, he was after all so in order, a rabbi with a beard . . . but I alone was in a safe place: Pardess Hanna, at the edge of the town, in the home of Sara and Mickey, an employee of a brick factory. A year later this house would become Lehi's regional base of operations. After I arrived, Drora arrived to bring me news of the miracles that had saved Gera and of Michael's arrest.

Even Gera's poor makeup did not give him away. And Michael's excellent disguise did not help him. He was identified and arrested. We "hit" the detective who identified him, and this gave us, and Michael, some satisfaction; but it was, of course, no compensation for the organizational loss. Much of the organizational work now fell to Gera.

The Ramat Gan dwelling had been built especially for us by a sympathizer, one of the first Birionim in the country. Krinitzi issued a permit for speedy construction and knew to whom he was issuing it. Yes, the building was built in too much haste and with too little care, so that today it is only a ruin. But in my day only one fissure was visible, along the wall in my room. And even that I attributed to the double wall, which had been built with a special entrance . . . but why should I reveal everything? I sat in that hiding place only once, when there was a huge search in Ramat Gan and the army surrounded the whole town, round and round, but failed to include the corner on which my house stood, between the slaughterhouse and the Elite factory. At 4 p.m., when the army began pouring into Elite, I began to fear the widening of the search and entered the hiding place. An hour's wait revealed that the army had only been assembling after the end of the search. I breathed deeply when I came out of the hiding place. Literally, for it was full of mold.

But the house was good. A separate house of two rooms in an abandoned orchard where houses were first beginning to be built. One could come or go in any direction without any neighbor's noticing.

My first wanderings ended there. I lived there for over a year.

The landlords: a gypsy couple. Real gypsies? No. Gypsies are not a fighting race, and these were freedom fighters. Which teaches that Jews, even if they are "gypsies," are still Jews.

Why were they considered "gypsies?" First, they were a musical couple. They played in cafés, military bases, at weddings. In any case, their body clock was different. Their days were not days and their nights, not nights. And they did not live ordinary "civilian" lives. Also, they arrived as illegal immigrants with nothing of their own. Finally: From the very first they sought and found a way to the Underground and they said: We want to help.

She, Miriam, was dark with a light face, a mother to two boys and quite childish herself. She always complained to me, asking why they do not involve her in more work; she wants to take a course, go on operations. I explained the value of her supporting a central member of the Underground, how we need "families" with whom we can live, but all this was to no avail. All those years she retained the sense of inferiority, as if she were not contributing enough.

"And the danger, Miriam? If they come here and catch me, you will suffer, too, and Dov will be arrested, maybe you will be, too . . . ."

No, to no avail. There, boys go out at night on operations. There, boys are falling and she is here, in the rear guard.

How happy she was when I told her that her two brothers were abroad working for Lehi, one in Hungary and one in France. A coincidence? Not exactly. Their whole family was in Betar. Still, their enlistment in Lehi came as a surprise and Miriam wiped tears of joy from her eyes.

They are four. And poor. The increase in our operations further reduces the amount of work available to the public on military bases. Curfews reduce the amount of work available in Jewish cafés. The children are already reduced to eating stale bread, but after every successful operation the house celebrates. I do not understand their Hungarian language, but Dov's eyes when he reads the newspapers to Miriam make us all happy.

I search and search for the Marxist basis for this happiness but I cannot find it, just as I cannot find it in the sympathy of their opposite, the prosperous and established property owner: Reb Avraham Krinitzi. Why do they and why does he bother with this thing, this War for the Freedom of Israel? Why, when all their economic interests cry in distress: No war!

I enjoy being with them, with these gypsy-fighters, though there must be husbands more orderly than Dov, housewives with more culinary talent than

Miriam.

There are, however, nights when the two of them are working and I am again afraid. Such silence and darkness. Only two children are sleeping in the next room. And suddenly: heavy clattering on the nearby road. Military or police vehicles. A searchlight from Sarona combs the trees. A rustling. What is it? Steps. Steps. Someone is approaching. No. Jackals. Jackals and not people. Thank God.

I do not fall asleep till 2 a.m., till 3 a.m., till they return.

Usually only Dov works, and then the darkness is good. We sit on the porch. I come out after sitting in a closed room all day. Miriam smokes cigarette after cigarette, and I tell her what I have written during the day. She has difficulty reading Hebrew and wants to know everything. "I'm stupid, I'm so stupid," she repeats endlessly. And she is not stupid, she is only childish, and her soul reaches farther than her hands can.

She does not ask questions she thinks she is forbidden to ask. She does not have the least bit of curiosity. She does not even ask when she sees me pacing nervously, day and night, back and forth. Perhaps she already recognizes my walk: There is going to be an operation. But she will not ask.

"The boys, they moved tonight, Miriam. My heart is heavy with worry."

Miriam does not know many of our boys. Only a few, those who come to meet me or who happen by. She knows Uzi the Redhead. He built the hiding place. And I reveal an Underground secret to Miriam. This Uzi, Miriam, he is our mining expert. There is no one like him when it comes to "pressing." And Uzi is always cheerful, he runs through the streets of Tel Aviv looking for goyim, for the British.

Only, I never get around to telling Miriam how Uzi the Redhead was arrested when a member of Hashomer Hatzair informed on him (Uzi himself had once been a member of Hashomer), and how he escaped from the detention camp, how with his bare hands he tore a hole in the barbed wire, and how he reached Jaffa—naked and bleeding—in an Arab car, and how his wounds took weeks to heal. He fell, Uzi fell in Jerusalem. I never finished telling Miriam the story of Uzi the Redhead. But she did hear the story of Shmuel, and then she cried into the rainy night. Shmuel had been in our Ramat Gan place. He was a photographer. He came to photograph me and took the opportunity to photograph Miriam's children, Naomi and Gabi. Shmuel was fatally injured in a monetary operation on Allenby Street in Tel Aviv.

How silent all around, and dark. But somewhere out there, these very moments, the blood of our boys may be dripping, dripping into the ground of an orchard similar to this or onto a paved street. Miriam's face pales, as if the blood were dripping from it.

Drora comes twice a day, morning and night. She brings newspapers; she brings mail; she takes material for the newspaper, for *Hama'as*. At first, she also escorts me to meetings. But, slowly, I fill myself with Ramat Gan-confidence.

There is nothing like Ramat Gan for confidence.

Here, you can knock on almost any door when you are in danger, without having to fear being turned over to your pursuers. Ramat Gan is not like Tel Aviv, with its corners full of eyes. Eyes, spying eyes. One need not fear to walk the streets, roads or alleys of Ramat Gan, as one fears to walk in Tel Aviv, the "first" "Hebrew" city. There are no Tel Aviv cafés here, in which an Englishman sits over a glass of whiskey or of his misty national drink, tea with milk, or in which a young man, a Palmachnik hero, sits with his "gal" over black coffee or coffee with milk (known here as "upside down coffee") always black or upside down, sits and scours the street with wide eyes, till he winks to someone, gets up and follows someone else until that person sees him and disappears, or until that person does not see him, enters a house and then the Palmachnik records the address in his notebook and returns, smiling, to "gal," proud that he has completed his mission.

In Ramat Gan you can walk alone the length and breadth of the city without encountering such eyes, such "fine" young men. Here the streets are more curved, more winding. Here there are many slopes, yet I walk these streets more confidently than I walk the straight, too straight, streets of Tel Aviv.

Most of the time I hold my meetings in Dov the Blond's house.

And where else would tall, blond Dov live except our tall, green village, Ramat Gan? His house is the tallest of all, with many steps to climb. The building is five stories high. Dov lives in a nine foot by nine foot room on the roof.

The Lehi broadcasts emanate from there.

Dov's courage emanates from there, and he himself leaves on his ravaging operations from there. He neither climbs nor descends the steps of his house; he leaps, as he leaps over the barbed wire fences of enemy bases. As he leaps into an enemy armored vehicle and takes control of a Bren gun.

And he returns to this room, with its view of the distances, and to Judith. Here he tries to write poems, too, and he gets angry that I do not print them. Here he probably dreams his single personal, egotistical dream: a son.

And to this room in the heights of Ramat Gan, into which a cool breeze blows even during the hottest of heat waves, Gera also comes to briefly reside, for he suffers greatly from the Tel Aviv heat.

From outside, this room was never "spoiled." "Outside" meaning from the perspective of security. No Hagana spies ever found it, though the through traffic was great. But the room was "spoiled" from within. Dov went abroad. Judith had no desire for it without him. The room was abandoned and neglected and cracks appeared in it.

When I stayed there for the final time, in the blustery days of winter in 5708 (1947-1948), the room trembled in its desolation. True, flames were visible from it, flames from the direction of Abu Cabir which was being attacked by our men, but the shutters were cracked and dislodged from their hinges and the nights were cold, rainy nights. Many shutters were dislodged.

I tried to fasten them again. In vain. They broke together with the shutters of the Underground. Below in Tel Aviv we felt nothing; but up here, above, we were gripped by shudders. It's cold, right, Drora, it's cold? You take all the blankets and coats upon yourself. In vain. The rain penetrates from outside and the wind shakes the withering planks and the bones and the shutters of the heart and the shutters of the mind. Drora cries. Are you cold? She does not answer, she only cries. The first time I have heard her cry. Apparently all the shutters have been dislodged. They had been sealed shut, sealed shut, and now the wind has dislodged them in Dov's abandoned room. Now she cries, the tears of the one corner of her soul that has been left alone, always alone. Now she cries the tears of Arnon, who is taken on such a winter's night. Arrested, flown out of the country and murdered far, far away, and she cannot even lay a wreath on his grave. She cannot lean her body against his. She cries the torture of those difficult days when she is ordered to return day after day to that house near the Yarkon River in which she spent one year, one full year, with Arnon. She begs: I can't, I can't go there. And there is no mercy. So she goes there and again sees everything and she bolts the shutters of her soul. Do not break. Do not break. And so she carries everything inside. In increased work, day and night, day and night, on the stencil machine, on the typewriter, as a contact, and in a few operations, very few, for no one is better than she in printing and as a contact. And she carries with her a serious illness, the fruit of eating and not eating in the Underground, during years in the orchards with a budget of five grush a day, and the pains of the body are sealed together with the pains of the soul, sealed. For Lehi, Lehi.

Now suddenly the shutters are dislodged, the rain pours into the room, deep inside, and her weeping bursts outside, over all those years.

I try again. No. There is no repair for these shutters. It will no longer be possible to live here. Not possible.

And in Dov's room the wind whittles away in abandon, and the rain.

In another year, Dov will also be gone.

A last night in this precious room. I was never afraid inside it. That night I moved about feeling the beginning of the end. And I wrote a wild song the next day, which I kept somewhere.

I looked but I could not find it. In the winter of 5709 (1948-1949), when I again bolted tightly the shutters of my room in the post-Bernadotte Underground, the song was confiscated and it has never been returned.

3. Sabbath Eve

Slowly, slowly, Batya grew accustomed to the new circumstances. Slowly, slowly she retreated from her original decision not to see me for fear of being followed. She agreed to come see me in Ramat Gan. With our daughter.

Leaving the building through the rear, going by way of the dunes, and after traveling circuitous routes, she arrives with dusk on Sabbath eve and goes home on Saturday night.

This is my first meeting with our girl in many months. She is three and one-half years old. I have in the meantime grown a little beard. She has not been told the purpose of this strange journey. Her mother pointed to me and said: "This is Uncle Joseph." And she stopped at the door, thought and thought with her wise eyes and said only these unforgettable words: "You are my father, right?"

And she jumped into my arms.

From then, she was the best conspirator in the country. To be extra careful, she erased the name "Father" from our household conversation. Even from her mother's: "You aren't allowed to speak about Father." When she came across my photo in the presence of other people, she would push it aside so they would not see it.

A current of deep seriousness, very deep seriousness, flowed down the impetuous river of her childhood.

I do not know what her intellect grasped from this mysterious atmosphere, but I have no doubt that she understood. If not for her deep understanding she would not have been able to keep her tremendous secret for two full years.

Thus they came for the Sabbaths. Sabbath candles are lit in the room. Naama recites the blessing together with Mother. And she adds her own blessing: "God, preserve Father from evil." That much she learned from Mother, but she adds her explanation so God will understand: " . . . so nothing will happen to him."

And so the two precious souls stand over the candles. Mother and daughter cover their faces and recite their prayers and I stand behind them and suddenly everything disappears and I am holding my mother's dress somewhere along the paths we wander during the First World War. Candles must be lit, there is no Sabbath candelabra. Then Poppa takes two potatoes. He bores holes in them, places them on a box, and Momma lights. I do not know where this was . . . in a forest? In a room? A carriage? I only remember those two potatoes with Momma's candles in them.

Just as they, Momma and Poppa, appear again and again, so they appear, intentionally and unintentionally, in the list of my Underground noms de guerre. My first was Sambatyon (the violent river beyond which live the ten lost tribes, according to legend). I no longer remember if someone gave me this name or I chose it. Either way, its meaning was clear: It hinted at my stormy character, heaving rocks. The name Eldad came after my arrest. I chose it because of its connection to Sambatyon. For Eldad Hadani was the man who told the story of his journey beyond the Sambatyon River. But in addition to these pseudonyms, names were needed for identity cards, which had to be changed from time to time. I was unable to pull these names from thin air or from telephone books. I chose David as a first name. I thought: because of its simplicity. This was before I received an identity card. Miriam asked me what she should call me (at first she had no idea who I was), and I merely said without thinking: David. Only later did I realize that it was not so "merely." David Arye were Poppa's first and middle names.

In contrast, I chose a family name intentionally taken from my mother's family: Laifer. And when sometime later I was forced to change the name, I again intentionally chose a name from my mother's family: Zimmer. Only with my third choice did I decide to free myself from these familial ties, when I sat down and wrote without much thought: David Gottlieb.

But this was no accident. Once someone asked me: "What is the translation of the name 'Fruma'?" I was surprised and asked: "Why do you want the name 'Fruma'?" He answered: "My mother's name was 'Fruma' and I just had a daughter and I am looking for a Hebrew name." I said: "My mother's name was also 'Fruma' and it means a woman who believes in God and observes His commandments, and in today's Hebrew we have no one word for this." But in the course of our conversation, the psychoanalyst in me leaped out and yelled:

"Is not my 'Gottlieb' really a disguised 'Fruma'?" For Gottlieb means lover of God.

Maybe I am engaging in exegesis? So? Is exegesis groundless?

"God, preserve Father from evil. So nothing bad will happen to him," my daughter whispers over the Sabbath candles when she comes to visit me underground, to brighten my Sabbaths.

The little one received much compensation for the suffering she was forced to bear. Gifts and stories that I would tell her every Sabbath. The only difficulty was finding compensation for her mother's suffering, for an adult is not as happily forgetful as a child.

Poppa would trill the words of the Psalm "A Woman of Valor" on Sabbath eve, fully concentrating on the meaning of every word; and Momma was worthy of having this song sung to her. Batya is worthy, too, but how shall I sing her this song of the home when we are in a stranger's home? The only words I fulfill are "Her husband is known at the gates . . . ." For better or worse, but known in any case. Except that Batya would gladly do without this honor, she wants a quiet corner and house, a real home without all the fear, without sneaking off through backyards, without the sadness in our girl's eyes and envy always in her heart, envy of children whose fathers are home every day, every night; to sleep and know, there is nothing to fear.

"I am trying to grab fate by the throat,"
wrote Beethoven while he was creating the
Third Symphony, *Eroica*.

In Deed

1. "May You Fight for a Good Year"

You will not be inscribed for a good year, you will not be sealed for a good year, if you do not fight.

The leaders of Israel do not believe in the benevolence of Heaven, and do believe in the benevolence of the goyim.

Poor in deed, shaken and afraid, they stand before every general and commissioner and plead for mercy. They are heading for British judgment.

They will inscribe hundreds of thousands of brothers for death and for hunger and for plague.

This they inscribe and seal in impure London. They are writing a very bad year there and Zionist leaders are inscribing and signing with them.

Therefore we call upon brothers everywhere: You will not be inscribed for life and you will not be sealed for freedom—if you will not immediately fight:

Be poor in deed when facing Heaven, but tremendous in deed when facing the devil's rule.

Be givers of strength to the holy, but breakers of the strength of the impure.

May you fight for a good year.

Hama'as, Erev Rosh Hashana 5707 (New Year's Eve, Sept. 1946)

We gave our blessing to the beginning of the united "Struggle" with the Hagana. We gave our blessing because we were very patriotic and very . . . naive. We gave our blessing because we believed it would help bring the War for Freedom. Today we know: We should not have blessed the beginning of the "Struggle," but rather its end, and especially the way it ended.

What remains of the "Struggle"? And what remains of the prototype from which this fiery word was taken? What happened at the end of our father Jacob's struggle with the angel? What remained for Jacob, the supposed victor?

A broken thigh. A new name (for the old contents): Israel. And some blessing, which is not specified and not explained.

The name "Israel" in return for a broken thigh.

Only when this "Struggle," this pseudo-war, ended could the Underground set out with full momentum on the heroic war of the year 5707 (1947).

It is still too early to speak of a Revolt. We always opposed the use of this term for the war we fought, as a Revolt is a one-time action for the military expulsion of an existent regime and for the taking of power by force. We did not yet consider ourselves (the IZL and Lehi together) ready for such a one-time operation. Events might very well have developed in this direction, had Bevin not realized the need for a tactical withdrawal in order to deliver a strategic blow. But there was no military expulsion and no taking of power by force. There was a war for freedom against a foreign ruler, who withdrew politically. Had the "Struggle" in its ridiculous form continued, the withdrawal would also have been ridiculous: It would have resulted in ridiculous borders or, simply, larger immigration quotas.

The enemy's wise withdrawal will be discussed below. At this point, the subject is "*Eroica* 5707."

The underground war developed into a partisan war. Until now the means were: centralized and planned attacks on predetermined targets. From time to time the enemy suffered "black days" or "black nights," and the newspapers were covered with large black headlines; but between these times the country lived and the regime lived their normal civilian lives—with occasional shocks, beginning with the small shocks of the first "hits" in 5702 and 5703 (1942 and 1943) and ending with the big shock of the explosion of the King David Hotel. And the enemy responded with a civil-police response: searches and arrests.

There were many reasons for this form of warfare: the small number of Lehi forces; the obstacles within the IZL when the war started (the abstinence from shedding the enemy's blood); the lack of self-confidence that we really "could" strike at the enemy; the lack of wide support among the civilian population.

Only with the passage of time were these obstacles removed. When thanks in part to Bevin the Yishuv's support grew, and when the final obstacle, the "United Resistance," was also removed, then the forces which had been gathering in our bodies and blood overflowed everywhere and washed the Land.

In the year 5707 (1946-1947), only two factors in the country continued to be relevant: the attacking Underground and the defending British regime; no "Zionist Congress" and no "Agency" and no "Histadrut" and no city hall. The

British military command on one side and the IZL Command and Lehi Central Command on the other. In terms of the outward, momentary effect, the operations of 5705 and 5706 (1944-1946) were certainly more "pleasing." They lent themselves to larger headlines. But in practical terms they were surpassed by the value of the hundreds of "small" operations executed by the Lehi and IZL in the heroic year 5707, operations during the day and at night, against property and soldiers and roads and trains and oil and banks and armories and offices.

The constancy of these actions is that which sealed the fate of direct British rule in the areas of the country inhabited by Jews.

In these areas, rule was taken from the hands of the British by the Underground in the year 5707. We became masters of these areas and that which appeared in the Underground newspapers about the British being locked in ghettoes was not rhetoric but reality. Then came the explosion at Sarona and the explosion of the Haifa detectives' headquarters by Lehi, and the IZL operations against the Schneller military base and Bet Goldschmidt soldiers' post—and the regime discovered that it was not safe even inside its caged ghettoes.

The operations just mentioned were based on surprise, cunning, and personal bravery. As Lehi was numerically small, cunning played a large part, as at Sarona. After the blows we received at the rail works, it was not easy for us to send platoons on direct attacks. The IZL, with its reserves and vast experience, was more able to initiate such attacks, though as the enemy entrenched itself their minds also began concentrating on cunning, inventive methods of penetrating enemy fortresses. Thus they tried to tunnel into Bet Hadar. We also tried getting in there to plant explosives. Our success was guaranteed, as the operation was similar in type and even identical in terms of the planners and executors to the Sarona operation. But the announcement of the intended British evacuation of our country saved the lives of the two hundred British soldiers and officers who were camped in this fortress in the heart of Tel Aviv. Actually, we gave serious consideration to carrying out the operation even after the British announcement. The blood of seventeen-year-old Lehi member Alexander Rubovitch, kidnapped in Iyar 5707 (May 1947) by a British policeman and murdered, was still warm within us; the blood of the hanged martyrs had not yet been avenged. Had the building been outside a heavily populated Hebrew area we would have blown it and all its residents without mercy, except that where the building actually stood, there was the chance of injuring passers-by (though according to the plan, we would have cleared the street at the last minute), and the decisive consideration was: public opinion would be against us because the evacuation had already been announced. So two hundred enemy soldiers were granted a pardon and our Operations Division sadly dropped its well-constructed plans.

But while operations such as these were once planned in between other operations, there is no longer any "in between." Even the time spent by the United Nations Special Committee in the country did not bring our activity to a complete halt. The United Nations called on all sides to cease hostile activities. But the British side does not obey U.N. instructions, so why should we? A proclamation is issued with the conditions under which we will agree to cease operations: an end to the expulsion of immigrant refugees, an end to the farcical trials, cancellation of all restrictions on freedom of movement.

During the United Nations Committee's stay, the cessation is partial. The continuous war ceases, but it continues under the excuse that we are "responding to provocation." And where there is a will, there is no shortage of provocations. And we had a will, a will to strike the enemy without respite, but real provocations were not lacking either. In principle, we claimed that the existence of British rule in this country was a provocation. But this was not enough for public opinion, which needed crude kicks to feel the foreign rule. The *Exodus* ship, the gallows, Rubovitch—these were heights of the enemy's cruelty, heights which caused even very cold blood to boil.

The weapons almost never leave the fighters' hands. As of Tishrei 5707 (October 1946), we publish every month a list of that month's operations. The boys are already "playing" all the "instruments," small and large, but the most popular this year is the mine. Even the IZL no longer shies from this means, combat by "ambush," but Lehi enthrones the mine as king of the roads and rails. The enemy is unable to defend itself; it cannot constantly comb all the roads. The main strength of this method lies in the small number of losses for the attacker. There are many instances in which we do not succeed. Everything depends on maximum precision. A fraction of a second determines whether the jeep or car will explode or only turn over from the blast. We have experts, of course, experts in planting the mines on the roadsides, experts in pressing at the correct second. Only once are boys caught in the mining of a train and even then they are caught because they are late in withdrawing; they had so wanted to see the results of their work.

The blowing up of such trains caused one tragedy, which, of course, drew heaps of curses and condemnations. Once, a locomotive driver was also killed, a Jew and a father. But not one of those who cursed us knew that the driver was an Underground sympathizer, and that he had been supplying us with the train schedules. He fell victim to a schedule change which occurred that day before he could tell us. Only in the Cameri Theater, when *Nights of Rage* is performed, does the audience applaud the heroism of the French underground, which in its war with the enemy gives no consideration to the fate of an individual locomotive driver, who is French and who is an underground sympathizer. In the theater, it is good. For others, it is good. But for us, it is a "despicable crime."

And no one among the revilers in prose and newspaper columns felt the pain of this loss as we felt it, except the family. Yet he who once says "war" must know in advance the meaning of the word and all its consequences. Somewhere in a hidden corner of the soul there is room to mourn the loss and to suffer. Some losses and some circumstances shock this corner more and some, less. But neither the former nor the latter have any place in decision making. Only he who was unsure when he entered the war, only he who was unclear then, only he can put this blood and this suffering on the scales and weigh and ask: Is it permissible? Is it worthwhile? One hurts over the losses and the suffering and then one goes on with the war.

Only those losses whose blood is not avenged, only those dead who fall in a war that is not completed, only they scald our souls, only they have the right to shout from the earth. The Hagana's losses at Sarona shout from the earth, the losses of Givat Haim shout, because those who sent them betrayed them. They fell in vain. But those who fell in the Underground war, even if they were chance victims, innocents, even if they were children, fell not in vain, because their blood was added to the score and was avenged seventy times over.

There is no *Eroica* without tragedy. *Eroica*'s power, and that of any *Eroica*, is to lift the voices of pain onto a higher ladder of values, not to see the pain in isolation, and not to ignore it. Is not this the meaning of God's answer to Job from the whirlwind?

And this is the meaning and the answer to any claims of suffering and losses that consciously or not stemmed from the Underground war. This is not merely an aesthetic view, as the Greeks saw tragedy, as Nietzsche was first to perceive the secret of tragedy, but rather a matter of historical meaning, as befits the children of Abraham who passed between the divided carcasses in the covenantal "Brit Ben Habetarim" (Genesis 15), as befits a people whose first king was the tragic Saul.

With all their instruments, Israel's youth played the heroic symphony of the year 5707.

All the theories of warfare which were discussed within Lehi or within the

IZL, all the arguments over individual terror or over "meaty operations" or open battles as opposed to ambushes, all these ceased, as if they had never been.

War.

The boys and girls set out almost every night to impose their will on the country's roads. To instill the goyim with fear.

Until now we had discussed almost every operation; now there is no longer any center of operations. Every person in charge in any area is permitted to send his fighters on an operation, any operation, as he sees fit. We know in advance only of major operations, such as the explosions at Sarona or the oil refineries. The Central Command discusses only financial operations or punishing informers, but to discuss operations against the British? What for? Thank God we are not obligated to bring each and every operation before the seven institutions of the United Resistance movement for discussion. Partisans know where the enemy is and they are permitted and commanded to strike at him.

Only the issue of operations against the rail line, which are holding up citrus shipments, is brought before us. The discussion is not easy. The problem is not only the producers' economic losses. The problem involves much unemployment, for tens of thousands depend on this industry, directly and indirectly. But principles are also involved: There will be no end to this, tomorrow people will complain about the paralysis of a different industry because of curfews on roads or martial law. We consider the possibility of transferring the citrus fruit by car. Technically it is not possible. The decision is to temporarily halt the sabotaging of trains and to proclaim this publicly.

There are whispers: A secret agreement between the producers and the Underground! Cynics ask: How much of a "ransom" did the producers pay? The truth is we held no discussions with any interested party. The truth is we did not even think of such an idea till after we had made the decision. Then we thought: It is only right that we turn to the producers and ask for a donation to the Underground; we did save the season's produce. And the truth is we rejected the idea so that our decision would not appear to be a "business deal."

But we were not lacking for British targets. Unceasingly, we prepared to eliminate the top military and civilian officials. In Jerusalem we carried out observations, we planned—and small details ended up preventing—the elimination of General Barker and British Chief Secretary Sir Henry Gurney.

The economic losses sustained after the renewed sabotage of the rail road in the summer and Haifa's oil refineries also added to the loss of British prestige, not to mention life. The imposition of artificial taxes to recover these damages raised no real money, only pale protests by *Davar* and *Haaretz*. The joy of the immigrants on the ship *Moledet* (*Patria*), who stole ashore while the refineries were burning, is certainly worth the curses of the powerless *Davar*. And meaning is given to the deaths of the four Hagana men in Sarona by Yankele, who blows Sarona up. Yankele will one day mount the ladder of heroism on the walls of Jerusalem and fall there.

The 5707 Freedom War is played by and on all the instruments. Lehi is most effective in inflicting loss of life, the IZL reaches new heights in lowering British prestige. When the British whip a young member of the IZL, the IZL retaliates by publicly whipping British officers—and the stunned British never whip another Jewish boy. The symphony is complete: There is song in the heart, song in the blood, the song of the Hebrew youth that was in Exile even *in* Zion and that only now stands up straight. A Hebrew plough is not enough to straighten the Hebrew stance. And Hebrew speech is not by itself a sign of freedom. Only arms, not those hidden in a *slick*, not those purified and preserved in pure olive oil, not those ready for the Hagana's defensive use, but only arms raised in battle against every foreigner's rule here, only such arms straighten a person's stance. They forged the song sung by the eighteen defendants in court; they forged the song sung by Dov Gruner on the gallows.

Such an instrument is not "musical," not gentle? Oh, but it is. It is an old, ancient instrument, and also ultra-modern. *Any instrument* can be musical, *any instrument* can play. The question is what it plays, the question is who conducts, and from what spirit the tune bursts forth.

The Hebrew War for Freedom plays its *Eroica* in the year 5707.

It is not the first symphony of our people on the road to freedom. It was preceded by the World War I "NILI" underground led by the Aaronsohn family, and then by Jabotinsky's Betar youth. This is the third symphony, which began in 5701 (1941) in the depths of Yair's warring-loneliness, and which reached its peak in the Hebrew Underground War for the Liberation of Eretz Israel from the British in the year five thousand seven hundred and seven.

2. The Broken Moon in Kfar Shmaryahu

The Yishuv has two sectors: urban and kibbutz. The British are searching for the Hagana leaders in kibbutzim such as Yagur and Na'an. They are searching for "terrorist" leaders in the urban sector (as is the case in every progressive revolution).

But there is another sector in the country, the most modest and quiet and farthest not only from "terror" but even from the establishment "Struggle," and struggle of any sort. This is the rural sector. Not the established villages of Zichron Yaacov and Binyamina, they are hornet's nests of terror. The percentage of Lehi members there is so high that the Shomron region is considered "ours." Nor do fighters of other organizations seeking shelter or in need of a base have anything to fear from these deep-rooted farmers. And of course the Aaronsohn family vineyards in Zichron Yaacov provide fine wines, and fine cover to fighters in training or about to set out on operations. Blood speaks to like blood, heroes whisper secrets to other heroes.

For these very reasons, however, Lehi's Central Command will not move to Zichron or Binyamina when times are dangerous. Where will we go?

To Kfar Shmaryahu.

Of all the *yekke* (old German-Jewish) villages in the country, none is as *yekke* as Kfar Shmaryahu. I am not insulting, merely describing, its character. In addition to the external order and the cleanliness and the German speech and the musical evenings, it has two more blatantly German signs:

1. Between 2 p.m. and 4 p.m., the still of night descends. The village sleeps; the afternoon nap is enshrined in law.

2. There are so many doctors among the farmers.

The world-views and Zionist views of the village members should be obvious. First of all, that they even have a world-view is a fact made necessary by their country of origin. In Binyamina, some healthy and normal farmers can be found without "world-views," but not in Kfar Shmaryahu.

And there are two guarantees concerning their Zionist views:

1. (I am taking care to mark everything 1 and 2, because the "order" of the place under discussion makes it necessary.) The village's name memorializes Shmaryahu Levin, the preacher and propagandist of the Keren Hayesod (Palestine Foundation Fund) and, as far as I know, the only Jew Weizmann praised in his book.

2. Weizmann himself is a regular visitor to the village.

Could we find a more ideal place for the Lehi Command?

Maizler rents a house on the western edge of the village. Not in his own name, of course, but under an assumed name, for he is being hunted in Tel Aviv, or at least he thinks he is being hunted, ever since his factory blew up while mines were being prepared inside. It is a shame about the factory and a shame about the mines, which were supposed to play the next day, but what can you do? Meanwhile Maizler (whose Underground name is, for some reason, "the

Rooster") leaves Tel Aviv, he is suspicious of his factory's landlord. So he takes his belongings—his wife and handsome twin sons, Ehud and Gideon ("Udi" and "Gidi" in modern, un-biblical Hebrew)—and he moves to Kfar Shmaryahu.

When the situation in Tel Aviv worsens, with curfew following on the heels of curfew and search following search, Gera decides to follow in Michael's footsteps and scatter our members, beginning with those whose presence in the city is not absolutely necessary. As we are in the blessed year 5707, during which the war is progressing without complexes and without internal or external obstacles, there are almost no policy decisions requiring oral consultation. My written work can be done in Kfar Shmaryahu, too, perhaps even better than in Ramat Gan, where I was ensconced off the main road opposite Elite, a short distance from Sarona (whose fate has already been sealed, etched into the notebook of Mazal, responsible for our Operations Division).

So "half the Command" is already in a completely secure area. But my solitude comes to a speedy end. On the night of March 2, Gera accidentally leaves his radio on after the final news broadcast and soon he hears the announcement: "Beginning at midnight, martial law will be imposed on the areas . . . ."

After the experience of the search in which Michael was arrested and from which Gera was miraculously saved, Gera does not tarry. He leaves his house, finds a car and, in the dark of night, before the rooster crows, he reaches the Rooster's house.

Several days later it becomes clear that this time, there had been nothing to fear. The martial law had not been intended to facilitate a "search for terrorists." The British have already given up trying to do that. Now, martial law was meant as blackmail, to force the Yishuv to liquidate the terror, after even the Hagana's attempts to do so on its own have failed.

Martial law, however, was more than just blackmail, and we were properly happy even before we knew what would happen.

Imposition of martial law was the clearest outward expression of the Underground's primary accomplishment in 5707: *the abrogation of British law*. Martial law was actually the British "Amen" to the concept of "foreign rule," which Yair had defined as the one political concept that described the reality of the British being in Eretz Israel. The concept is also found in Uri Zvi's poetry, though on a deeper level, since cultural values are also included there. The concept is found as a *rhetorical* expression in the speeches and articles of Jabotinsky, who refers to the "occupier of Judah." But this term as a basic political concept obligating he who utters it first came into use in this country with Yair.

Not an "oppressive rule." *Hebrew* rule can also be oppressive. "Foreign rule." The term was deemed strange for many years, though today Ben Gurion and Dr. Moshe Sneh and the reporters of *Davar*, *Al Hamishmar* and *Haaretz* use it as if they had been born with it.

Martial law made this concept real and was welcome, as far as we were concerned. And if the streak of operations that preceded it and the Bet Goldschmidt operation that invited it served no other purpose than to turn this potential into reality—then they served well. On all counts:

1. During the period of martial law in the spring of 5707, the two bodies that faced each other, *the populace and the foreign ruler*, did so more clearly than ever before as two totally foreign and hostile bodies, without the mask of a legal Mandate to rule the country, without the intermediaries and abettors of the crime, the Agency and Vaad Leumi. The regime's intention was to cause the population to suffer and thus to turn it against the Underground. This was a significant psychological error. The masses were then with the Underground (and the masses are not to blame if the Underground lost them one year later). The hatred was turned in the opposite direction, toward the collapsing regime.

2. Martial law placed the problem in its proper light for the whole world to see. This was a "knife in the back" of the Jewish Agency, which had again and again tried to shrink the Underground in the world's eyes, to portray us as a small gang with no support from the people.

3. Martial law was a weight added to the British economic burden.

4. Ultimately, when the Underground began to strike during the martial law, inside the protected British "ghettoes" and outside them, it led to a sharp drop in the British army's morale. And the soloist of the concert was the grenade; it was all the fashion. A sign that our nerve was increasing.

The hidden wires that so wracked the nerves of the drivers of British armored vehicles and jeeps, were linked to Kfar Shmaryahu. A button is pressed in Kfar Shmaryahu and Dov flies swift and predatory as an eagle from region to region, from Haifa to the Shomron, from the Sharon plains to Jerusalem, supervising the operations. Without respite. Chief of Operations Mazal is in Tel Aviv under martial law. The military's control fails to deprive us of freedom of movement. Dov certainly does not recognize the existence of boundaries or borders. Many enter the area and leave. Drora, who has until now served as my contact with the city, becomes the contact between the Central Command and all our divisions; not a day passes when she does not cross the barbed wire fences in both directions. Every day by different means. Contact is not broken for a single moment.

Our nerves are tense as we wait for a major operation in Jerusalem. The plan: the wholesale elimination of twenty to thirty top British detectives, including all those assigned to fighting the Underground. A prostitute close to us is organizing a "birthday party" in the Savoy Bar on Rehov Ben Yehuda. The plan is ready. One problem remains: the Jewish orchestra in the bar. We are looking for a solution.

Suddenly an obstacle: The IZL intends to attack the Schneller Compound, an actual fortress, the same night. If our operation is carried out they will be unable to move.

Dov is flying again, zooming between Jerusalem and Kfar Shmaryahu, back and forth, back and forth. Which is preferable: breaking into a military fortress or eliminating an entire dangerous department of the police? If the IZL and Lehi were cooperating, or even coordinating actions, then perhaps both operations could be arranged. But coordination does not exist. During this period, it does not exist. Only the people on the spot sometimes meet, some of them coordinating their activities and some merely informing the other organization of what will happen. (Perhaps it was at this moment, or some other, that Dov met the commander of the IZL Combat Unit and they discussed applying pressure from below, from the ranks, for a unification of our two organizations.) But as of now, the situation in Jerusalem is tense. Neither side wants to give in. Dov comes to see us again on the final day. Gera makes the final decision. After much hesitation he decides: Carry out the operation against the detectives.

But the instructions arrive too late. Members of the IZL announce that as soon as it is dark their men will begin the operation, and they are already in their positions around the Schneller complex. Any other operation in the city may mean disaster for them. The members in charge of our operation decide to cancel it.

Late that night, Schneller Fortress is blown up.

How do our deliberations look now, in hindsight? Had this been a year earlier, we would have had cause for much resentment toward the IZL, which refused to give in for the benefit of our action; one year earlier, the detectives were still active. By 1947 they were already in a state of despair. Rule was already in military hands, arrests or individual searches almost never took place. And if a complaint is nevertheless to be lodged against the IZL, it must be because our operation was tied to this one date while the operation against Schneller could have been postponed. And more than one of the detectives who were guests at that party must have had the blood of Underground fighters on his hands. I cannot rid myself of the feeling that the IZL's dominant consideration was its ambition, its desire for IZL-success.

This was one of the few cases in which inter-Underground jealousy did not lead to increased blows at the enemy, but rather saved the enemy from a blow.

In an unrelated but simultaneous incident, we received an urgent letter from Menachem proposing the immediate unification of the two organizations. In light of the circumstances, he proposed agreeing to a temporary basis and structure.

Our response was not uniform: I immediately said yes; Gera said: What's the rush? We'll meet and talk, the first chance we get.

I thought then that the different responses derived from our different characters. I am quicker and jumpier, more excitable. He is mild, mild. Balanced, balanced.

As time passed I knew: No, the different responses went deeper. Gera is diplomatic and, in accordance with the famous saying, when a diplomat says "maybe" he means no. When he said then: We'll see, he already knew most definitely: No. But he did not want to say it, either on principle, to avoid saying anything explicitly, or because he knew of my desire for unification.

Gera soon returned to Tel Aviv. The complexity of the matters he had taken upon himself was too great for him to be away too long. Many people had joined the fighting Underground, and many were the Underground's needs.

When martial law ended, I, too, went to Tel Aviv for the talks with the IZL on the proposed unification, and afterward I returned to the terror center in Kfar Shmaryahu. From there I saw the pillar of smoke rising from blown-up Sarona.

And there news reached us of the IZL break-in to and breakout from Acco Prison. Great was the mixture of emotions: Before the operation, there were prolonged negotiations with the IZL over our participation, over the number of our men to escape during the breakout. Afterward, there was the mix of blood and joy. So much heroism and so much blood.

And one day, a spruced-up lady arrived with red hair and a lot of makeup on her cheeks and eyes and lips. She was actually a dark-haired Yemenite, and she had escaped from prison where she had been under a seven-year sentence imposed while I was escaping from my captors. Now she is here in Kfar Shmaryahu, having come in this dress from Jerusalem with rouge on her face and pneumonia in her chest and a burning desire to stand at the microphone and broadcast to the nation, to the youth: This is the broadcasting station of Lohamei Herut Israel, the Fighters for the Freedom of Israel—Listen, listen.

And there, in the depths of the green silence, I counted the *omerim*, the sheaves that we raised heavenward in blood and fire, in Acco and Jerusalem, sheaves and sheaves, and two sheaves in song and in brotherly embrace with a grenade between their hearts. Meir Feinstein and Moshe Barazani—two young men, one from the IZL and one from Lehi, both on death row, to be hanged one morning—had blown themselves up in their cell hours before they were to ascend the gallows.

> When the Temple stood—
> we raised the sheaf of the wave-offering to You.
> And now that the Temple is destroyed—
> we raise the spring of our sons.
> We count the days of 5707,
> we raised four golden sheaves to the gallows.
> We raised to the sacrificial fire two boys in Jerusalem
> and now in the Zvulun Valley we brought a basket of blood
> to cleanse us of the impurities of Exile—
> to cleanse us of the filth of enslavement—
> so that all the souls of Israel will be cleansed of the filth of the fleshpot—
> We count.
> In joy we count and in sadness
> In the joy of giving and in the sadness of the blood.
> The land asks in blood.
> May the heavens answer.
>
> *Hama'as*, 4 Iyar 5707 (April 24, 1947)

One of the three-year-old twins (who can distinguish between Udi and Gidi?) opens his wide eyes to the partial moon and shouts in pain:

"Momma. The moon is broken!"

3. Talks on Unification with the IZL

"We'll set aside seven days each year for talks on unification with the IZL," Gera once said to me. And since these words were full of wise humor, I laughed long and hard; and only after I laughed, did I realize that this was more than a joke. The humor had a point, as did almost everything Gera said or wrote. Once, he returned from a meeting with Sneh or Galili with a description one of them had given of his writing style: "utilitarian lyrics." He derived much pleasure from this description and, afterward, he more than once demanded of me, as editor of *Hama'as*: "Eldad, give me a little . . . nu, you know . . . utilitarian lyrics." Except that I could not do so upon request. And if Gera wrote a lyrical piece in honor of the "Valley Festival," a blessing for the settlers of the Jezreel Valley, I am not saying it was artificial. On the contrary: I can testify that he was truly sentimental, and from his childhood, his upbringing in his grandfather's village home, he has retained a true love for the land. Yet, he would not have written such a fine piece without the secondary-not-at-all-secondary intention to show the Left: See, we are not enemies of your settlements in the Valley. I am sure that I also sinned by writing this way, with my eye on somebody, but though I was able to do so in print, I could under no circumstances direct my emotion to such utility.

Humor, like lyricism, has deep roots. Even humor can be pure, full of inherent beauty, but it can also be "utilitarian humor," and then it approaches sarcasm.

An example of such pointed humor is Gera's joke about unification with the IZL. After talks on unification in the springs of 5706 and 5707 (1946 and 1947), one could refer humorously to setting time aside each year for these talks. But Gera spoke these words purposefully and after consideration, as he spoke and wrote all that he did. His intention was to say, and say especially to me, since I returned over and over to the subject: We will not unite with them.

There could have been no reason for Begin's proposal, during the period of the 5707 martial law, other than a patriotic desire to unify the forces. There was no crisis within the IZL at that time that could have motivated the proposal. On the contrary, the IZL was standing with both its legs in a real war, without restraints or hesitations. This is true for the means with which they were fighting as well as the political perspective.

After the wounds opened following Lehi's assassination of Lord Moyne had healed, the first talks were held on unification. This was in the middle of the United Resistance, during the spring of 5706. I was in Latrun then and received by letter the details of the negotiations. The main arguments, as I learned from the letters, were over two points. The IZL insisted that Zev Jabotinsky be proclaimed Father of the Revolt. On the other hand, they vigorously opposed defining the war as a war against British imperialism.

I expressed my opinions on these two points in a detailed letter, which I sent to Menachem. I had my doubts about the first point, since it might encourage those in the nationalist movement who still believed that England might change her policy, if only she could be convinced through Underground pressure that it is in her interest to ally herself with the free Hebrew nation.

But I was mainly opposed to the IZL's position on the second point. Fuzziness in describing the enemy might lead to halting the war whenever a new illusion arose. I knew that somewhere in the heart of the Irgunists, the hope still lived that England's interests were not in total conflict with ours. Also: Clearly defining a war against British imperialism offers the possibility of winning allies who are interested in weakening the British Empire. No entity, on the other hand, will agree to help us if they know that we might tomorrow compromise and ally ourselves with this British imperialism.

The idea of unification was so dear to me that in my letter, I even dwelled on the details of the unification, should it take place. I wrote against the IZL emblem "Only Thus" (with its rifle emblazoned across a map of British Mandatory Palestine, including both sides of the Jordan River), mostly because of its map. What point is there in waving a map of the British Mandate? This is not our true country, this is not an historical truth; it is only an imperialistic truth. Educational and political damage are done by clinging to this map. It is a continuation of the "revisionist" policy of 1925, based on the demand that England *fulfill* the terms of the Mandate, "which it had betrayed." At that time such a demand was understandable, but we have meanwhile matured, we have grown in experience and in strength. We are not coming with weapons to realize the Mandate but to end it. And therefore, we should not accept the borders of the Mandate as a symbol.

I also thought about a name for the unified movement and made a suggestion. Little problems like these can sometimes be obstacles. Each organization is devoted to its external forms; this is understandable. They have been sanctified in blood. I therefore thought of a way to combine the names: I.L.H.I., the first letters of *Irgun Lohamei* or *Irgun Leumi: Herut Israel* (Fighting Organization, or National Organization: Freedom of Israel). Seemingly, I favored my side in this suggestion by leaving more initials from the name Lehi (L.H.I.); but this was not my reasoning. I wanted to include a slogan within the name. And the name I.L.H.I. can also be read as a slogan: *El Hai* (The living Lord). For a long, long time my heart has pined for this slogan, which would replace the time worn slogan, "Tel Hai!" Tel Hai is clearly a defensive slogan. From Tel Hai the road does indeed lead to the heroic defense of Yad Mordecai and Negba; but it in no way leads to the expulsion of the British, to the King David Hotel, to the assassination of Lord Moyne and to the IZL's hanging of two British sergeants. While the slogan *El Hai* is not a battle cry, it does give expression to a world-view I wanted to lay at the foundation of a national youth movement. *El Hai*, the Lord of *life*, the *Lord* of life. Just drop the "T" of "Tel" and begin with the aleph of "El," the aleph which is the beginning of the Hebrew idea in the world. The Maccabees used a similar slogan-concept. Maccabee derives from M.C.B.E., "Who is like You among the gods, O Lord."

Gera would have been the last to agree to such a slogan. It was mystical or, worse, it might alienate us from "progressives." After we left the Underground, he was to go even further and refuse to describe us as a national liberation movement, since that word might also be misinterpreted.

In a similar vein, I fought for some time to establish the Temple Sanctuary depicted on Bar Kochba's coins, minted during his revolt against Rome, as the Lehi symbol. Gera opposed this, too, as he opposed a speech I gave in Jerusalem, "The Temple Will Be Rebuilt."

But the talks with the IZL in the spring of 5706 failed not because of trivial matters like the symbols and name, and not even because of important matters like the definition of the enemy.

The negotiations failed because Natan Friedman opposed unification. He exploited the existing differences of opinion, but he would have found other reasons had he had to. And he opposed unification because he had clearly and programmatically planned his future move to the left. The proof is the renewed negotiations, in my presence, in 5707.

The two points upon which the 5706 argument focused were easily disposed of. Menachem no longer insisted that in our joint platform we proclaim Jabotinsky the Father of the Revolt; and more importantly, he agreed to our definition of the enemy: British imperialism. When I asked him: What has changed? I received a strange enough answer:

"I have been convinced by letters from our friends in the United States that we have nothing to fear from such a definition. On the contrary, there is deep emotional opposition in America to British imperialism, and even among the highest politicians British imperialism is not very popular."

This was a slightly strange argument coming from a political man like Menachem Begin, but there is nothing bad in it, as long as one learns from and develops the thought. We were not born with our ideology, and political positions wither. Our ideas were the fruits of developments, too, the only difference being that we reached them before the IZL did.

Gera whispered that I should ask Menachem if he accepts the conclusions of our booklet, *Fundamentals of Hebrew Foreign Policy*. This booklet contained all that we were so proud of in our independent political thought, the foundations of which were laid by Yair, from which we drew the realistic conclusions in the given international situation. Including our approach to Soviet Russia. Menachem's answer was: "Yes."

Now I assumed all hindrances were taken care of. More than this could not be demanded.

The IZL was at that time at the height of its military ability, at the height of its moral standing, and Menachem reached the heights of political consistency.

Then Gera decided to refer the question to an internal Lehi forum, to include people with responsibility and long-time Lehi members. And in that forum he arranged for the proposal to fall. Not with a clear "no." He had no reason for a clear no, and anyway this was never his diplomatic method. But he did it cleverly, by raising doubts and fears and question marks.

One example of such doubts: As long as we exist separately, they are forced to fight. They cannot withdraw, for then their members would join us. Who knows if behind this proposed unification is not a hidden desire to eliminate the competitor, who pulls them toward war?

In the consultations we held with the "responsible" parties, I tried to sway them toward unification. Some feared the IZL's military structure. In Lehi relations were more personal, intimate. The main fear, though, was that we, the minority, would be swallowed by the huge majority and our character assimilated without trace. This was accompanied by the question of what guarantee exists that this majority will not one day stop the war. Has the spirit of Bach really disappeared?

I tried to paint the structure of the leadership as the guarantee, since there, at least qualitatively, we would not be a minority. Also, the spiritual education of the ranks and the written political positions would be our responsibility. Even IZL members admit that our *Hama'as* paper is superior to their paper, *Herut*. What more can we ask than this agreement to our political positions and concepts? And then Hisia Shapiro asked the heavy question for which I had no answer:

We are in the Underground. We cannot be sure that tomorrow or the day after you or Gera or both of you will not be arrested. We do not have many more people of such quality that Menachem will be forced to listen to them, and what then? How will we preserve our consistency in the event of such a disaster?

I had no answer, for questions such as these are without end. What guarantees could there be? As time passed we learned that we could not be sure of our own members, not even of the leadership.

The fears increased. Without a doubt, the past abyss of hatred influenced many.

Here and there, the new winds which began to blow in the ranks must have had their effect, too.

A vote was not held, since we had no authoritative institution other than the Central Command. But Gera could justifiably conclude that most of the members were doubtful. Had he wanted to go ahead, however, we probably would have found that most of the members had overcome their doubts, for they knew Gera was against it.

Another hour of opportunity was missed.

Begin approached Natan Friedman with a proposal, for the third time, to merge the organizations, on the eve of the state's establishment. Then Gera, the man responsible for Lehi, replied: I am ready to agree to this combination if it will be joined by . . . Sneh.

One cannot write a history of "ifs." One cannot assume that during the year of heroism 5707, a merger of our forces would have increased the attacks upon the enemy. But very possibly the next year, 5708 (1948), the year of the Underground's dissolution, would have developed differently. Perhaps we would have stood differently from the way we did in the months preceding the state's establishment, the months which were internally decisive for the Underground. And it is beyond doubt that a merger would have completely changed the situation in Jerusalem. Jerusalem fell for many reasons, not least of which was the division between the two Undergrounds.

Perhaps if we had seen Jerusalem while we negotiated, we would have overcome the terminology and fears. And Jerusalem would not have been divided if the Underground had not been divided.

And in this Jerusalem, in the deepest of its basements, on one of these same nights, a merger of flesh and blood took place for which there is no parallel. Two hearts clung together, ignited each other, poured into each other, and became a single Elijah breaking through the Walls of Jerusalem and rising in a chariot of fire; and we were left below, we who were supposedly at the top, we were left below, far below, twisting in a river of blood and fire. Barazani and Feinstein left us below.

4. A Vision of Sorrow and a Vision of Joy

I was asked: "Why is no expression given to the Underground's heroic war in Uri Zvi's latest poetry?" I answered: "Uri Zvi is the epic poet of the future. He did not need to see the heroism take place. It took place in his blood before it did in reality. He sang it in his songs before our bodies played it."

Many of those fighting in battles and commanding the battles had assimilated into themselves the explosive material in Greenberg's *Sefer Hakitrug Vehaemunah*, the textbook of the War for Freedom, and the songs thundered when the men pressed the detonators. But the tie to Uri Zvi was much deeper than that of a prophet with those who actualize his preaching. Many people blew up bridges or were hanged exactly as described in "A Vision of Sorrow and a Vision of Joy," the last poem in the Book of Books of the War for Freedom, though they had never read the book and the song was not in their blood. But the book itself and the song itself came to Uri Zvi from their blood, the blood they joyously sprinkled on the earthen altar, and he smelled this blood many years earlier, and he smelled it as a grown man who suddenly whiffs the scent of his mother, an intimate scent hidden deep in one's senses and forgotten, forgotten but not gone.

A dark blood from ancient times runs in us, says Uri Zvi. The blood of Datan and Aviram and the calf worshipers and Josephus Flavius. But that does not mean the good blood has evaporated from the nation; and this good blood has burst forth in our generation.

There is a law of cyclical ascents and descents, and the cycles are sometimes astounding in their detailed similarity. We read over and over the accounts of the lives and deaths of Ben Yosef, the two Eliahus and Dov Gruner and we read the story of the Ten Martyrs killed by Rome. The same generosity of spirit, the same freedom in death. And from Sarah Aaronsohn's suicide when being tortured by the Turks to Yaacov Raz's suicide when being interrogated by the British and Barazani's and Feinstein's suicide before the British could hang them—those who came later may or may not have learned from their predecessors, but they were all of one stock.

Unlike the days of Ben Yosef, we were now able to look directly into the eyes of those singing on their way to death. When Rosh Betar Jabotinsky lifted us to heights of holiness and pride I "squeaked" in response. Why? Because then we were "restraining" ourselves over Ben Yosef's blood, because we were not worthy of having Ben Yosef's crown bestowed upon us. But in the spring and summer of 5707 (1947) we looked straight into the eyes of Gruner and Avshalom Haviv[76] and Barazani and Feinstein. The vision of sadness could be borne because it came with a vision of joy. The joy of revenge and continuation. Bracha Fuld was escorted to her grave by thousands, as ordered by the establishment institutions; the hanged martyrs were buried as Yair had predicted in his poetry, "They will bury us stealthily by night," and the blood of Rubovitch, whose tortured body was never found, played, played in us and played from us on the streets and roads, in the days and nights, and we all felt it and the murderers felt it, and the hangman felt it at the hand of more Gruners and more Rubovitches. They knew: They can kill one hundred Bracha Fulds, and it will cost them nothing; but every drop of blood of a hanged member of the Underground verily costs them dearly. When Shertok and his flock were asked in Latrun: "If we release you, will you continue the 'Struggle'?" they answered loudly and under oath: No, no, no. Despite the blood which had been spilled because of their orders. But when the Gruners and Rubovitches and Feinsteins were asked: "If we give you pardons, will you continue?" they answered, all of them, all of them, with their bodies already impaled and torn, with their necks already in nooses, they answered in song and joy: "We will continue, continue and strike at you. Death to the enemy—Freedom for the homeland!"

How pitiful Shertok and his flock seemed opposite their true liberators, and how pitiful the hangmen seemed opposite those who were hanged. What similarity was there between the forces? What could the British use against the forces of Ben Yosef, Hakim and Bet-Zuri, Mordecai Alkochi?[77] What?!

Obviously, the military strength of these boys was not decisive. Obviously, the patriotism of the Underground fighters was much greater than that of the Englishmen. The heroism of Rubovitch's murderer Farran was weaker than the heroism of the murdered Rubovitch. Behind Rubovitch stood comrades ready for anything. Behind Farran stood more people whose only reason for fighting was to obey orders, whose lives were their most precious possessions. They did not want to die; they saw no reason for dying here, nor did their mothers and fathers in England. And just because of this, there was more political sense in killing them than in their killing Rubovitch. Dov Gruner's strength was not only internal. The British were not overly impressed with his heroic spirit. They are not overly sensitive, or in any case, they are not prepared to operate, in a political sense, on the basis of moral heroism. Dov Gruner's strength was that the entire Underground was one Dov Gruner. All were prepared for the same fate. All of the same flesh, the same blood. If Ben Yosef had become as real as Dov Gruner, we would have sped up all the historical developments. Ben Yosef became a hero, whose heroism inspired us all, but he did not become real strength because his gallows was not seen as obligating his friends to do anything. He created a potential spiritual force, which remained potential. He readied the ground for the heroic stance of Hakim and Bet-Zuri, of Gruner and all those robed in purple majesty, whether they endured the final test or whether they were pardoned before the final test, which they all would have withstood, all of them, as did Gruner, as did Ben Yosef. This was Ben Yosef's personal influence. From the distant past we still read of the Ten Martyrs. From the recent past the blood of the NILI fighters Naaman Belkind and Joseph Lishansky, hanged in Damascus, and the blood of Sarah Aaronsohn in Zichron Yaacov was still warm.

The British did not have forces like these to use against us.

And the force of the excitement stirred by the Underground war all across the Jewish world, and in non-Jewish circles, too, could not be countered by the British, either. Whether the support of non-Jews stemmed from a dislike for England, from common interests or from pure idealism, it in any case gave us encouragement while England had only trouble back home, over the economic crisis, the tiredness from the Second World War, the tactical foolishness of their behavior toward Jewish immigrants.

All these provided a favorable backdrop to the War of 5707. On this backdrop we were able to write with our heroic script, with our blood, with our inventive minds—to write and to dictate.

In 5707, British law in Eretz Israel came to an end. The undermining of the law had begun the day Yair established the Underground. The force of the British courts came to an end the day the first Lehi member declared his refusal to recognize the authority of these courts. These courts turned ludicrous on the nights the IZL matched their punishments by whipping British officers and hanging British sergeants.

The problem under consideration was serious: What to do when the enemy tried to use sentenced prisoners as hostages? The enemy attempted to gain time by means of delays between the sentencing and the confirmation of the sentences, and between the confirmation and the executions. Hints came from many directions that if there were no Underground operations, pardons would be granted. This was terrible. Terrible not in terms of the regime, but in terms of public opinion. We were no longer naive and we had already taken the gallows into account as an almost necessary part of the war. In any case, history does not provide any examples of a war for freedom that managed to avoid them. But the people of Israel are merciful, and sometimes the pressure by families and their tears were added to the incitement mill: "Here!" screamed those who incited against the Underground, "They want hangings! They instigate provocations so there will be hangings!"

Clarity and consistency of thought were necessary to withstand these temptations. I had once bitterly criticized Rosh Betar's efforts to save Ben Yosef's life. There had not been a door in London on which he had not knocked those last nights to find a legal way to postpone the hanging. He was a real father, or real humanist, perhaps the single one of his nation. I had argued strongly against this approach. Perhaps it is a law that every holy deed must also be cruel. The laws of war are different than the laws of peace.

Lehi did not play the game of kidnapping hostages. During the trial of the eighteen prisoners from the rail works, the IZL recommended kidnapping British soldiers and even offered to help. We rejected the proposal. There were reasons of principle, but the main reason was the organizational burden involved. A half-year later the IZL learned that kidnapping is not at all easy, and holding the kidnap victim is even harder. For months the IZL lived with taut nerves and a taut organization because of its kidnapping operation. Holding British hostages did indeed save Michael Ashbel and Joseph Simchon from being hanged; but the second time the IZL tried to save prisoners from the gallows, it failed. For the British, it had become a matter of prestige.

With their prisoners threatened, the IZL asked us to refrain temporarily from operations. This was indeed our "obligation." During the trial of the eighteen, we had asked the same of the IZL, except that when we saw that the government was using the sentence and the delay of its confirmation to win a de facto cease-fire, we released the IZL from its commitment. Now a serious danger existed that the enemy would continuously dangle men by the rope, for many had fallen prisoner and there was no offense for which a sentence of death could not be passed.

Added to this was the Rubovitch affair. Our members were gripped by fever. We had announced our agreement to a six-week respite during the United Nations Committee's deliberations, but we had explicitly conditioned this on its being a mutual cease-fire. We announced that we would not initiate operations but we would respond to hostile activities such as the expulsion of immigrants, death sentences, etc. Now immigrants were deported under the eyes of the United Nations Committee. The British showed no signs of self-restraint. We therefore had no reason to continue ours. To act while the committee was here became a political necessity. And kidnappings became more and more difficult. IZL members waited in ambush around the clock for high officials; only the kidnapping of high officials would actually prevent the hangings of our fighters. The Hagana declared a holy war to protect the British, to prevent kidnappings, and to find kidnap victims. The logic of this Hagana crime will be discussed in the next chapter. For the Hagana's behavior, without a doubt, hastened the hangings.

Meanwhile, the British began shooting at those who were posting our proclamations. We decided to end our restraint. So one Saturday night, instructions were given to provide our "poster boys" with armed escorts. British soldiers and officers were killed in Tel Aviv and Haifa, while "walking innocently," as the newspapers that were allowed to publish under British law put it. *British* soldiers and officers just walking *innocently* on the streets of Tel Aviv and Haifa.

The blood of Rubovitch was avenged. The IZLers grumbled; but they were unable to claim that a continued cease-fire would win pardons, just as they were unable to claim that our prisoners or theirs would want to save their own lives at such a price.

When the British sergeants were hanged (in retaliation, after three IZL members were hanged), a load was lifted from my heart. I was very much afraid that the IZL would surrender to the pressures that were coming from all sides. Every once in a while I thought: Now this is the epitome of the absurdity to which the Organized Yishuv has succumbed; but in the matter of the kidnapped sergeants, I really think that this was the truth. What terror overcame them! And with what means did they not try to influence the IZL, this time as one wide front, from right to left. Chief Rabbis and revolutionary admirers of the Spanish Communist La Passionara, "civilians" and the leaders of Mapai (those future murderers of IZL members on the *Altalena*). All, all, some with blessings and some with threats, some with flattery and some with curses, all, all worried greatly over the lives of the two sergeants.

We, as I have said, did not play this game. We did not play the whole game of courts, whether British or Underground. Courts and sentences for Jews—informers or other criminals—yes; but for the British? What relevance do courts and sentences have? But because the IZL operated according to its own style, we were very worried they might yield to the pressure and offer a gentlemanly gesture. I remembered well my argument with Menachem in 5704 (1944), when he attacked me on two points: Why do you talk of British imperialism? And, why do you incite hatred against the British? I answered him with two "Letters to a Friend" in the pages of *Hehazit*. Now I was worried that perhaps he did not yet hate enough to withstand the pressure.

I was happy to see he had matured this additional step. He hated. Blessed is the hatred for one's mortal enemy. We took revenge simply. For the murder of Rubovitch, for the British car-bombing of Rehov Ben Yehuda in Jerusalem, which killed fifty-two civilians[78]—we massacred the enemy with all the means at our disposal wherever we found him.

The IZL's mode of response had this value: The Underground fought its war not only against the British, but also against the manifestations of their governmental authority, such as courts. The whipping of British officers (which provided some good war humor, too) and the hanging of the sergeants demonstrated: courts for courts.

In this light, it was absurd that the rabbis of Israel were for some reason recognizing the goyim's legal system while slandering the Jewish. Maybe the IZL judges had not been ordained by Rabbi Herzog, but had the British officers been so ordained?

Perhaps the IZL was able to act because it had undergone a deep baptism of blood in the Acco Prison breakout. There as in Jerusalem blood mixed with blood: The Irgun's Dov (Shimshon) Cohen with our Shimshon (Shemesh) Vilner; and our Elimelech, who had led the singing at the trial of the eighteen, he fell there, too. And Matti Shmuelevitz closed Amrani's ("What can you do? What can you do, that I am so beautiful, and like me there are none from the sea to the River Jordan?") eyes. Yes, there were small disagreements around the breakout. We wanted to participate in the actual operation. The number of Lehi men to escape was also a subject of negotiation. And only the blood is the same, and the hearts which beat in life and cease in death are the same hearts, and the heroism is the same as in the days of Samson and Saul who fell dead upon his own sword, and every one of us is a Gruner and a Yaacov Raz and every one a Bet-Zuri and a Barazani and there are no real borders separating us in that marvelous year, the year of the *Eroica*, the year 5707. Only this heroism, this blood on one side and the impure blood of the enemy on the other. Who will be victorious?

5. Fearsome Bartholomew's Eve

I do not know if the name Bartholomew's Eve, referring to a massacre by French Catholics of French Huguenots in the sixteenth century, was the official name given to the operation prepared by the Hagana against the Underground, or if someone else gave this name to a plan that was canceled before it was ever given a real Hebrew name.

There is something else I do not know. I do not know why Menachem Begin, in his book, passes over this episode in silence. Maybe because in his book he deals only with facts, not in the roots of those facts. Maybe for some other reason. One could argue that because the plan was not executed, it is not part of history. But I believe otherwise. In my opinion, the very existence of this plan provides a key to the understanding of many other phenomena, and in its light even the *Altalena* affair seems much simpler. Since all the evidence indicates that Begin did not recall this 5707 (1947) summer-night's plan during the *Altalena* incident, I feel that putting it into writing at least this once is worthwhile; for, who knows what tomorrow may bring, what may happen tomorrow night? And there is no joy in being surprised twice.

The fact is that when word first reached us, we of course did not believe it. But the signs kept coming, ever stronger. They showed: The Hagana is preparing a bloody night. It has prepared a list of three to four hundred commanders in the IZL and Lehi. It is gloating that it even knows the addresses of Begin and Friedman. In one night, within one-half of an hour, units of the Hagana will simultaneously burst into hundreds of apartments and "hit" all those on the list. No kidnappings, no arrests, just quick and final liquidation.

And the dissent in Israel will end.

This seemed fantastic, even with all that we knew of the Hagana. But our sources were reliable. The leaders of the Palmach prepared the plan and Ben Gurion approved it (shades of the future argument over who held the copyright on the *Altalena* murders).

And still I refused to believe, until I received a final assurance from Mr. Israel Rokach, the mayor of Tel Aviv.

I met with him several times in his home and in other homes. I do not know whether Mr. Rokach was considered an IZL sympathizer. He certainly was not considered a Lehi sympathizer. We were much too extreme for him. On the pages of *Hama'as*, I did not mince words in reproaching him for not returning the British medal which had been bestowed upon him, and I reminded readers that David Yellin had responded to British provocations by returning his. And we attacked Rokach because of the public relations work he did for British bonds. For me to find a common language with him on political questions was difficult. I saw them in the widest aspects of the international situation, the interests of the Empire, etc., while his view would encompass—and I admit: reasonably and realistically—the relations between the Histadrut and the middle class or, as it was called here, the "civilians."

I did not, however, meet Mr. Rokach to discuss general political matters or class issues. Most of the time our discussions centered on matters concerning Underground life in Tel Aviv. I cannot recall any opposition by Mr. Rokach to our operations . . . in Jerusalem or Haifa: "But why here in Tel Aviv?" Sometimes he asked for a meeting to lobby on behalf of Barclay's Bank, with which the Underground had "very close connections," of a sort, in 5707. I need not add that his efforts were not very successful, and he could have been referring to me as well as to many others when he said to me jokingly, "What is the difference between us? You speak from the walls and I speak to the walls." After one of the largest of our many confiscations from Barclay's Bank, in which we "withdrew" 200,000 lira, I was about to suggest to the Lehi secretariat, which was debating how to use the money, that we should extend a loan to the City of Tel Aviv—when Mr. Rokach preceded me by appearing before the City Council and forcefully demanding that we return the money . . . to the English.

Mr. Rokach's reputation rose in my eyes, and in the eyes of many others, with his dignified behavior while under detention in Latrun. Unfortunately, this is not the impression with which I was left, for my last meeting with him in the winter of 5708 was when he came to ask a favor not for the English, but for . . . the Arabs of Sheikh Munis, that we should not carry out our threats to drive them out.

But in our meeting in the summer of 5707, in a house at 6 Rehov Zamenhoff, we spoke of a serious matter and not of returning money to the English or preventing the flight of Arabs. We spoke of the danger of civil war. I asked him then if there were any truth to the rumors about Bartholomew's Eve and he said clearly and explicitly: "I am sorry to tell you that there is a basis to the rumors." He later added that thanks to the vigorous intervention and threats of Rabbi Abba Hillel Silver, the disaster was prevented.

Understanding the background to a decision of this sort is a matter of life and death. How and why did this matter even come to be considered? And should not anyone who hopes to take the historical and political initiative from the current government into his own hands, at whatever time or with whatever means, try to understand this? For this is the sole key to comprehending that which has happened and that which has not happened in Israel, before and after it became a state:

Protecting the internal rule of the Histadrut administration, with or without Mapam.

Marxists might point out the economic interests of the Trusts and the administrations and the bourgeois kibbutzim that are hidden behind this rule. Our analysis is not going into that area. Before us is the fact: The existing Jewish administration began the "Struggle" in order to take for itself the initiative; and after it ended this "Struggle," after suffering one or two blows, it decided to liquidate those who took into their own hands the historical and political initiative.

Their political and moral "argumentology" against "terror" has no real meaning. These are not the men of pure morality who can be found in the "Brit Shalom" peace group with philosopher Martin Buber. These are very sober parties, Mapai and Mapam. All their gushing about "innocent blood" was lies and hypocrisy; Natan Alterman's rhymes about "a child's blood" were lies and hypocrisy. It was not Alterman who really felt the pain of that Jewish locomotive driver killed when we blew up the train; we felt that pain, and we felt it twice as much because he was a member of Lehi and we used to receive train schedules from him. The Altermen and the Alterwomen applaud such heroism when it appears in the French *Nights of Rage* on the Cameri stage; but when it appears on our side, they call it "disgusting" and they run to save the British in Bet Hadar and the enemy's trains.

Why? Why? This is without precedent among nations and cultures. It is worse than Vichy. The aged Petain did what he did because he no longer believed in an Allied victory, and he wanted to save what he could, and he at least received some form of autonomy. And had, for instance, Germany won, who knows if France would have been any less independent in its alliance with Germany than it was under the Marshall Plan. But not even Petain persecuted the French underground as the Hagana persecuted us, and the Hagana got nothing in return, nothing!

Golda Meyerson stood before the Chief Secretary and begged: Recognize the Hagana as a "militia," permit it to violate some British laws in order to defend the British. For indeed, some Hagana boys had been arrested while posting their *Hachoma* broadsides *against* the Underground separatists.

And this at the same time the British were killing and deporting immigrants, a time of hate-filled speeches by Bevin, a time the "100,000 certificates" were denied, the time of the *Exodus*. At this very time, thousands of Hagana members fought a holy war against the separatists. Tens of thousands of lira were allocated to bring Palmach members to the cities to crack the heads of children hanging posters and to clear anti-British mines.

None of this is comprehensible, unless the deep meaning of the year 5707 in the history of the War for Freedom is comprehended.

In 5707, only two relevant factors existed: the foreign rule and the fighting Underground. The foreign regime was losing all possibility of civilian rule. Had things continued in 5708 without the surprising turn they took at the close of 5707, then events would have developed with an iron logic, as is the case with every liberation movement: the expulsion of the British regime and the taking of power by the Underground, which is meanwhile winning over a majority of the populace.

In that heroic year 5707, the Zionist Organization and the Agency administration and the Vaad Leumi and the city halls and the parties of the right and the left all ceased, for all intents and purposes, to exist. They became nothing more than political fictions. The British did not recognize them, the Underground did not recognize them, and thanks to the propaganda work done by the Bergson Group in America, even world Jewry ceased to recognize them, meaning: ceased giving them money and began giving to the Underground. And ceasing to give them money means in short: an end to the Mapai-Mapam rule, an end to the kibbutz, and an end to the bureaucracy of the Funds and the Histadrut. The initiative moved as with all revolutions to the city, and to the classes "that have nothing left to lose other than their chains," meaning in our case, the poor Florentine, Hatikva, Kerem Hatemanim, Bukharan, and other such neighborhoods, all of which were already walking in the light of the faces of the fighters and martyrs.

The *Haaretz* newspaper expressed this simply and clearly in "Luach" 5708:

> The situation in the country showed that the "political" initiative in the Yishuv had gone from the hands of the elected institutions of the Zionist movement to the dissident organizations.

And who anywhere in the world knew that during that year a Zionist Congress was held? And what value did that Congress have? The blowing up of Sarona and the oil refineries by us, and the King David and Bet Goldschmidt and Acco Prison and the hanging of the sergeants by the IZL, made more history than the last ten Zionist Congresses put together, with or without Revisionist participation.

Since "Black Sabbath" and the Hagana's surrender, the Agency administration was no longer relevant. During the ten months of the "Struggle" they were at least there (though we could have done without them); but after its cessation, the natural process of an unfettered War for Freedom began, leading toward a Revolt (I emphasize: *toward* a Revolt).

Of course this competition between the British regime and the Underground and this Revolt could not have taken place in a vacuum. Many factors played a part in facilitating the possibility: Britain's economic woes, her soldiers' weariness, their traditional unwillingness to fall, to be whipped and to be hanged for no idea or reason. Certainly, many entities in the world had eyes that gleamed at the prospect of weakening the British Empire; many, yes, and very different types. They were a background. Only one entity lost all relevance: the *organized* Zionist movement. "Organized" Zionism, because the Zionism that was in the hearts of the people was swept up and would have been swept even further up in the waves of the war, while people completely forgot about that flock of public hacks which was still knocking on Bevin's door, and which would have, as with all revolts and revolutions, disappeared together with the British commissioners and generals, all of them together: Golda Meyerson with Gurney, Reuven Zaslani with Giles, Weizmann with Churchill, Shertok with Creech-Jones. All together. No, not without reason did Ben Gurion shout at a Vaad Leumi meeting (the date: 11 Nisan 5707; April 1, 1947): The Yishuv must escalate its efforts against the "insane, impure wildness." These were his words one day after the oil refineries were blown up by Lehi and the immigrant ship *Moledet* (*Patria*) sent by the British into exile.

Mapai's nose naturally smelled what was happening. Mapai suddenly saw the vacuum. All that was left to it were its board of directors and . . . the Palmach. A tense Palmach. A hurt, embarrassed Palmach. Embarrassed because of its withdrawal from battle, but hating even more those who did not withdraw, who remained at the front, who fought with heroism, who blew up Sarona. The Palmach thirsted for blood.

No. Not motivated by humanism or a concern for the lives of British soldiers and not with any hope of political concessions from Bevin. These were not what motivated the Hagana to kidnap Underground fighters in 5707, to sacrifice its own men to save Bet Hadar, to spend thousands and to spill the blood of children hanging up posters of *Hama'as* and *Herut*—no, they were motivated by the feeling that their own rule was coming to an end. The Agency and everything that was a part of it died together with the Mandate. It and everything that belonged to it were unbreakably linked to the British regime. Perhaps this is what *Al Hamishmar* unconsciously meant by the name "A linked Struggle." Linked, indeed, *very linked to the British regime*. And the Hagana and the Palmach go on operations in defense of the British regime because their well-being depends on British well-being. And when all other methods fail (the kidnappings, the beatings, the informing, the guards on the roads and around British targets), when all these fail and all over the world doors are closed in their faces with the question: "Who are you, really??" then they have no choice and they decide to grasp at the final means: Bartholomew's Eve. "I cannot stand this nightmare any longer!" one of their leaders shouts every morning in the Vaad Hapoel building. And what is the nightmare? The hanging of Hebrew boys? Perhaps the spilling of English blood? No. The nightmare is: Where are we? Who is in charge here?

The day after Ben Gurion's speech to the Vaad Leumi, *Haaretz* writes in its lead article:

> After this speech, the separatists have a choice: to stop or to take upon themselves all the serious consequences hinted at in the open threats of Mr. Ben Gurion.

The ground is fertile for the idea of Bartholomew's Eve. They have nothing left to lose. All they have is their rule.

For several decades they have been accustomed to determining everything in this country, and now this power has been taken from them. They are very afraid and they are already whispering among themselves about the possibility that all Begin really wants is for the British to invite him to negotiate. I know this suspicion is groundless (Altman might have entertained such hopes when he was a Revisionist Party leader, but not Begin). During martial law, the Histadrut leaders are gripped by a new hysteria: "Civilian leaders are coming into direct contact with the government." Several months later they begin whispering, loud enough for the enemy to hear: "These civilians, Rokach and Krinitzi and Ben Ami, they are Underground sympathizers." Then it is the turn of these mayors and councilmen to be arrested, which they turn into a victory, because they behave in Latrun as the Agency leadership had failed to behave there, in other words: with dignity.

Another attempt at joint pressure is made. The Agency appears before us in its coalition form, to appear more representative, more authoritative, more general. We, the heads of the Underground, are invited to a meeting with the members of the Agency's coalition. On our side: Begin and me. On theirs: Rabbi Fishman, David Remez, Yitzhak Gruenbaum and Peretz Bernstein.

Again we go round in circles. The same hackneyed arguments. Rabbi Fishman reminisces; very interesting. I tell Peretz Bernstein that I miss the golden period of his writing, in *Haboker* in 5703-5704. Remez speaks gently: "On your part" or "even on your part." A pleasant breeze blows from Gruenbaum—he, too, is opposed to us, but he has strong reservations about his friends' arguments. He, as he puts it, looks upon us with the view that history will judge us. "You have a part . . . ." And in a more personal vein he says, "If I were younger, perhaps I would be with you."

But the coalition has no effect on us.

The road is open for Revolt.

6. Our Orientation Is Victorious

We were surprised, we ourselves were surprised, at the speed with which our political perspective was proven true. This was Lehi's perspective alone, concerning the common interests of the Hebrew war of liberation and the Soviet Union.

We were happier then, on the day of Soviet Ambassador Gromyko's speech, than we would later be on November 29, the day of the U.N. decision for partition.

This was a day of victory for Yair's foreign policy, which we had adapted to the concrete political reality of the time.

The Soviet Union did not reach its turning point because of Mapam's support and toadying. And not because of the "progressive" works of the Histadrut and the kibbutzim. These were not new; and even with all their economic collectivism, they could just as easily have been anti-Soviet.

A personal friend, the Communist in whose home I found refuge in the days immediately preceding my arrest, meanwhile won himself a respectable job in the intelligence service of one of the People's Democratic Republics. As part of his job, he maintained contact with me. Of course, since Gromyko's speech he, too, was singing a new tune, but this is not important; after all, Communists have no choice but to make after-the-fact loving declarations of Amen to Moscow. What is important is that my friend, who is not just a party member, but is an intelligent man with a deep and wide knowledge of Marxism, immediately found the Marxist explanation for this change in Moscow's attitude.

This is typical. A system which appears to be scientific and to have laws, could not—as laws require—predict the developments or the possibility, but after the fact there is an explanation for everything. There is no chain of events for which an explanation cannot be found after the fact, proving that the events necessarily developed this way and no other.

So, this is my Communist friend's Marxist explanation: Soviet Russia cannot rely on any but progressive countries. In the entire Middle East, the capitalist state of Israel will be the strongest ally. How can this be? The other countries are feudal and, therefore, lacking a conscious proletariat. Many years will pass before they develop one. In contrast, a Jewish state will be at the capitalist stage, meaning—industry; meaning—a class-conscious proletariat. Even if the left-wing parties are not a majority, they will have enough strength to neutralize any attempt by the Right to integrate the state in an alliance against Russia.

Of course, you cannot interject and ask him: If so, why did the revolution succeed in agricultural-feudal China, and not succeed in industrial Japan? Do not create difficulties; a little sophistry will always be able to explain the situation over there.

We, of course, attribute the change in Soviet policy to the appearance of a Hebrew force fighting for true independence. At the moment, the Soviet Union is honestly interested in true independence, since it considers neutrality the most it can hope for in this region currently in the grips of British imperialism.

This was our reasoning. When people asked me if we are fighting against imperialism in general, I replied, in an internal booklet:

> Short and simple: No. We are a concrete national movement and our war is therefore against concrete imperialism. And if some other imperialism enslaves us, we will fight it. We do not have a surplus of forces or a surplus of time to use fighting imperialism in general. We do not rule out being aided by another imperialism, if it is anti-British. Of course, we will fight against American imperialism if it helps the British, but we will also fight nonimperialist nations which oppose us. A nation's war can only be fought against a real, not an abstract, enemy—we will be neither Sancho Panza nor Don Quixote.
>
> Be concrete.

Therefore in our meetings with the official representatives of People's Democracies, I never hid the fact that the IZL was closer to us than Mapam, because the IZL was *fighting* British imperialism in practice and Mapam was not. Regardless of what theories lay behind the fighting and the not-fighting.

And when Mikunis[79] tried to find that which united us and that which divided us, I gave a concrete formula based on a chance autobiographical detail:

"I went through Moscow to get here. They warned me that from Moscow, trains also lead to Siberia, but still I went. The difference between us is: You go from Moscow and to Moscow and by chance you come to Jerusalem. I go from Jerusalem and to Jerusalem and if the road leads through Moscow—so be it, I'll not hesitate."

Indeed, we preached a pro-Soviet orientation without hesitation. Because we saw the *objective* commonality of interests. This was solely an aspect of foreign policy, with no connection to an ideology about government. I repeated and emphasized in all our ideological classes that the problem of government is not one of principle. It is subordinate to our national needs. Whatever best helps attain independence is also the best form of government, at this time. We will not choose the finest socialist regime unless it moves us closer to freedom. And the opposite is equally true. Freedom of the individual is not an ideal at this stage in our people's history.

Therefore, when I spoke with foreigners I never pretended that we were a socialist movement—we deserve Russian support not because of socialism, but because of common national interests. We *really* do not want to fight Russia. We *really* are not enemies of the Soviet regime. We *really* can learn much from it, though we will oppose any attempt at Soviet domination no less than we fought British rule.

The Fighters for the Freedom of Israel addressed the problem of orientation. By 5707 this was clear to every Fighter for the Freedom of Israel. Therefore, we were greatly and deeply happy to hear Gromyko's declaration of support, because we knew that our *national* war had encouraged it; our war, which was more effective than all the anti-imperialist chatter of Hashomer Hatzair, which effectively supported imperialism.

With our blood, we proved that we did not want foreign rule. With our blood, we removed the British tanks from our land. With our blood, we proved that which we wrote: "A foreign base will not rest on our backs." Not because it is directed against Russia, as Mapam and Maki (the Communist Party in Eretz Israel) argued. We do not have to worry for Russia's sake. But because it is directed against our freedom. And because it is also directed against Russia, we see Russia as an ally.

This is the healthy foundation upon which we built our political orientation, and therefore we were not surprised by the change in Russia's policy, only by the speed with which it occurred. And I had to be twice as cautious to ensure that this victory would not lead to the same self-effacement before Russia that the Balfour Declaration had encouraged in many people vis-à-vis England.

To the degree that we heighten our war, we will heighten the trust of our friends.

And when representatives of our country's Communists met Dimitrov[80] and told him about the split between the Palestine Communist Party and the Hebrew

Communist League, Dimitrov asked: Which of the two blew up the oil refineries in Haifa?

To him, this was worth more than all the arguments by the two Communist splinters.

Therefore, our hopes and our opportunities multiplied. Therefore, we said: There is a reward for consistent political thought. We will continue and will fight any oppressor, as broadly and as forcefully as possible. And allies must appear.

And we sent representatives to Czechoslovakia and to Bulgaria, too.

Part Five
COMING APART

Only yesterday I held heroism, like a stone, in my fist,
For months legions sang to you, Jerusalem—and today:
Yesterday's heroism slips as sand from my fingers;
My Vision grasps your stones, and is as red as the setting day;
And I and my stomach are hungry for bread and for Dominion.

Uri Zvi Greenberg, "Hagavrut Haola," 5688 (1928)

Dunkirk

1. The Big Sack and the Little Sack

"Do not look at the sack, but rather what is inside it." Our forefathers who were wine growers and wine pressers and who said of wine that it gladdens the heart, and of woman that she is like a fruitful vine, our forefathers said: "Do not look at the jug . . . " (*Ethics of the Fathers* 4:27). And we, who because of our many transgressions no longer know the taste of real *joie de vivre*, we who have become merchants and peddlers, we deal with sacks and not jugs. In any case, do not look at its size and thickness, look at what is inside.

Because we forgot the wisdom of our sages, we suffered much pain at the start of the year 5708, on 13 Tishrei by our calendar, September 27, 1947, by theirs.

Everything goes as planned. Better, in fact. It is an exemplary operation executed by our Tall Blond. In broad daylight, in midtown, next to Barclay's Bank, with unequaled courage and the speed of lightning, he overpowers a British armored vehicle; and, using the same vehicle's Bren gun, he covers our men as they confiscate the bank's money. Four British, who are there to legally take Jewish money from the bank in order to give the money to the Palestine government's treasury—just as the ship *Exodus* is being turned away from our shores, but, after all, the government has many expenses—these four British fall and Uzi the Redhead, who has not yet forgotten the blood of Rubovitch, is running around looking: "Where are more goyim? Give me more goyim!" (During the operation Uzi was seen by a friend of his, a member of Hashomer Hatzair. The friend informed and the next day Uzi was arrested by the British.) Meanwhile, our "porters" are running with the baggage, two sacks of money, which are taken from the bank and loaded into a car.

At this point, the devil begins darting about the wheels of the operation. A Jewish policeman wounded in the shooting approaches one of the taxis waiting for the "porters." He asks to be taken to the hospital, immediately. And the hearts which sing when felling British enemies melt at the sight of Jewish blood. The taxi takes the wounded Jew and leaves. And when those carrying the sacks look for it, it is not where it should be.

British reinforcements have meanwhile arrived, more British armor appears, and a battle begins. Not much more time can be lost. Not even Dov, who took the Bren, can hold out much longer. He runs with the Bren, covering the other boys. There is room for one sack in the car. But which sack should they take? The larger and heavier one, of course.

Larger and heavier.

The small and light sack is tossed to one of the yards, temporarily, until they can return for it. But they will not return for it; somebody sees them tossing it, the British search and find it.

Why is this important? The main thing is the operation succeeded; all the boys are all right. There are no casualties among the passers-by and . . . the large and heavy sack is in our hands.

A day later we learn: The large and heavy sack contained lira coins. Forty-five thousand individual coins. By their count and ours. In the small, light sack were fives and tens, totaling 150,000 lira. By their count.

Regret mixes with joy. Except that the regret is quickly gone while the joy remains over that which we have, except even that goes too quickly; but how we spend our money is another matter.

On that same day, during which we had our success and our mishap at Barclay's, on that selfsame day, 13 Tishre 5708, by our count, September 27, 1947, by their count, Britain published in London for the first time and with great fanfare the declaration of its decision to end the Mandate and pull its forces from our country.

We grabbed this large and heavy sack, lifted it to our shoulders, and shouted with joy: Victory!

To be precise: Our first reaction was different; it was the same as everyone else's: disbelief. We published a proclamation, and we published articles in which we brought seventy proofs, and then another seven, that this was only a tactic, only deceit.

It was indeed deceitful and tactical, but not at all in the way that we thought. We grasped at all the minor events: The families of British clerks returned here, winter residences were built for the army, and so forth, to prove: Here! The whole declaration is a baseless lie. They will not leave. But as it turned out, these were groundless suspicions. They were leaving.

No doubt, deep, deep inside, behind the constant refrain: "They will not leave," was hidden the wish: Do not leave yet.

I am not afraid to say this, and I am not afraid that those who dislike me will rejoice over this "treasure" that I am giving them: Here! Just as we said! The main thing for Lehi was the "war." Fighting for fighting's sake.

I am not afraid, because I am not writing this book for them. I am writing for us, for all the fighters, who paid with the best of their blood, lives and years for this battle and for whom this was not a "struggle," for whom this was serious. For the sake of the account of this serious war I want in this chapter and the following chapters to put some order into the thicket of feelings and thoughts in which we were tangled, beginning the day that proved decisive for the entire Underground, the day the withdrawal was announced.

Just after November 29, in an explanatory talk with our members, I said hyperbolically: "The British have fixed us! They are leaving." This hyperbole sprang from our confusion. True, the British played into our hands for some time more. Several days after the announcement of the withdrawal, we announced that we would cease our activities during the U.N. debate. We never did resume our full war against the British. We did fell many, many more of them, but occasionally, only in response to provocations.

The taste of 5707 was still fresh in our mouths. At the time, this might have seemed the only taste we enjoyed, our arms striking at the one-hundred-thousand-soldier-strong regime, which was armed to the teeth. This was what David tasted when he struck Goliath, the taste of revenge for years of torture. But *today* I know that the reluctance to believe, to see them go, which spread amongst us after they announced their withdrawal, had within it—alongside our blood, which had not yet fully expressed itself—also an *unconscious*, deep understanding that this was not a true victory. Our expressions of joy, and the IZL's, and the recurring cheer: We chased them out, we chased them out!—these were the clearest expressions that something was not right here, something which at the time we were unable to identify and only today do we know what it was, or at least those of us who have the courage know.

Only today do we know, *must* we know: We did not chase them out. For if we had chased them out, then:

1. They would not have remained in the country to the extent they did.
2. We would not have to return to this point in books and in speeches: Who expelled the British? The Underground or Ben Gurion? It would have been clear to everyone.

There was no military expulsion. So, what did happen? Did we force them to *leave*? This is a more reasonable claim, but in this case, leaving instead of being expelled, the enemy retains much more initiative regarding the conditions of its departure. If it is as experienced and as flexible as British imperialism, then it may turn its departure into a return, its tactical failure into a strategic victory.

This is exactly what Bevin succeeded in doing. Churchill had Dunkirk, Bevin had Palestine.

The year 5707 was a year of blows for the British, to their bodies, their money, their prestige. Compared to all that had taken place in our country till then these were records, and under the conditions that existed here—the limited geographic scope and the Vichy-style Jewish regime with all its resources—this was an operation of which we can be proud, with which nothing in the world can compare. But all of this was only the overture to the Revolt, which should have come and could have come if not for this "Dunkirk" engineered by Bevin.

The first gallows shocked. The first martial law frightened. Since then, though, the war was on; and it swept more and more forces into the ranks of the fighters. The Agency and the Hagana ceased to exist from a political perspective. They retained only a *military* option: Go with the war or go with the British. Either a more vigorous renewal of the resistance, or "a militia to save the British." All the other functions of the "Institutions" were no longer relevant. Even the immigration, which had substituted for the "Struggle," a form of atonement by the Hagana for its surrender within the country's borders, had reached a standstill. Tortures and no breakthroughs. Martyrology. At the most—demonstrations. World public opinion sees only the fighters. We stand—on this point I speak only of Lehi—on the threshold of real achievements in our unceasing efforts to win allies in Eastern Europe. And according to the law that nature abhors vacuums, many eyes would certainly have soon opened in the United States and France, which may be considered the IZL "spheres of influence."

The year 5707 was the year of the beginning of the storm. Had developments progressed in the same direction, the pillars of British rule in the Middle East would really have been shaken. In 5707 we passed from the underground stage to the partisan stage; in 5708 we certainly would have passed to the higher stage, the military stage. Certainly the time would have come one day for the IZL's plan to conquer Jerusalem and Haifa, not only as a dramatic demonstration and to raise a flag, but with a chance for real success, with assured support from the public, with allies abroad, and with a confused and disintegrating enemy army.

We were ascending the steps toward Revolt. If not for these steps, lined with the bodies of the hanged and the prison-breakers, Bevin would have continued to simply laugh at the United Nations and all of its committees. If not for these steps, a far greater number of Jews would have been willing to settle for the Morrison Plan. The Aliya Hadasha Party, whose representative, Pinchas Rosenblitt (today: Rosen), later became a cabinet minister in Israel, published this statement in 5707:

> The terrorists rule in our streets. They and not the Zionist administration are determining the character and the methods of our policies. Even the Morrison Plan could have served as a basis for negotiations. It can serve as a basis even today.

I wonder if the Israeli cabinet minister, Herr Rosen(blitt), remembers this statement.

But we who bled paved the way. Step by step, body after body, we paved the way. Why?

We were preparing for the Liberating Revolt.

And we won the difficult battles. The external enemy was unable to defeat us with its prisons and its gallows, and the internal enemy was unable to defeat us with its collaboration and its own sort of terror and the direct aid it extended to British fortresses.

We won all the battles.

And we lost.

The already banal saying, "The British are losing all the battles and winning the war," is not really that banal; in any case, it proved true with us. In any case we cannot conclude from Bevin's many slips in matters of details that he was, politically and strategically, a fool.

The decision by the British government, a decision approved by the "evil" Bevin, to "withdraw from the country," became a strategic victory for British imperialism in the Middle East and a defeat for the Hebrew Underground, to the extent that the Underground had intended to win more than mere "concessions" or the abrogation of the White Paper. For as far as these were concerned, Bevin lost. The White Paper was canceled, though not in its entirety, of course, since in large parts of our homeland it is still in effect even today. But the Underground had—at least I thought so—broader aims than this and we were on the verge of realizing them early in 5708, when Bevin's Dunkirk interrupted us.

Which is not to say that Bevin was planning for the State of Israel which was eventually established. He most likely continued to hope for a limited tactical victory as well. He could still hope for any one of a whole array of alternatives made possible by his withdrawal:

1. The chaos would force the Jews to agree to the Morrison Plan and to the final repression of the Underground.

2. A majority would not be found in the United Nations to support Zionist demands (Note: "Zionist" and not "Underground").

3. Arab forces would physically exterminate the Jewish "National Home" and entire Yishuv.

Given any of these possible developments, Bevin would have been able to return to the tactical battle he had already lost in direct warfare with us. But even if none of these actually occur (as they more or less do not, for the Jews "win" at the United Nations and on the battlefield with the Arabs), a tactical British surrender is still worthwhile in order to ensure a strategic victory, on the main and most important point: *the preservation of imperialist rule throughout the region*. This rule was seriously threatened by the Underground's continued and widening war. The fire would have burned from Iraq to Egypt, and first to collapse would have been that firm fortress (whose survival today is ensured only by the existence of Israel), Trans-Jordan.[81] The map of the Middle East would have changed. Some form of competition between the world's powers would probably have continued, but Britain would have been totally out of the picture.

The announcement of the withdrawal prevented this development and prevented the great Hebrew Revolution. True, thanks to international support (which came for various reasons), thanks to the forcefulness of the lead dwarf,

Ben Gurion, during the critical moments, and thanks mostly to the temperature and the preparedness of Hebrew blood, Bevin was unable to buy his victory at the cheap price he had undoubtedly hoped for. But even the price he did pay, the State of Israel as it exists, was worth it to him and to the British Empire, which survived the danger of being forced from the entire region. Britain extended its rule in the Middle East by quite a few years, once the force that endangered its rule—the Underground—dropped from the scene.

The old regime of the Zionist Movement, led by Mapai, was saved together with England. As soon as the White Paper was canceled in part of Eretz Israel, the "misunderstanding" (as the establishment Zionist lexicon referred to the years of blood and sunken-*Struma* immigrant ships) was forgotten. That Weizmann was president and Ben Gurion the prime minister of this "state," this is the clearest outward expression of what really happened. Bevin, who had been acting as if he were an "agent of the Underground," betrayed us and went over to the "other side."

The British withdrawal saved British rule in the Middle East and saved the rule of the "Institutions" in the Yishuv. And it delivered a decisive blow to the Underground, which joyously shouted "victory" too early because it had traded its goals for the goals of the "Struggle," and which rejoiced over the large and heavy sack with many, many coins, individual and single lira.

But the sack that was abandoned contained what was most important: the direct assumption of power in this country, power taken from the British and from the Jews at the same time. These were the bills of five and ten which we abandoned, which we left behind, because we gave our car to save a wounded Jewish policeman, *because we were very patriotic*.

And the British remained in the country; and only Dov, the hero of that day, is no more because he fell in Uja al Chfir, and Uzi the Redhead is no more because he fell in Jerusalem and for Jerusalem. And many, many other dear ones are no more.

2. The Night of Abandon

> And all the people took the golden earrings, which were in their ears, and brought them unto Aaron. And he took them from their hands and fashioned it in a mold and he made of it a molten calf; and they said, These are your gods, O Israel, that brought you up out of the land of Egypt . . . .And they got up to laugh.
>
> Exodus 32

And I also got up that night, to see what was so humorous.

Had I overcome the desire which drove me to go look at the crowds of Jews, celebrating what was not worth celebrating, still I would have looked, because the walls had fallen. Had I still been living in the Ramat Gan orchard-corner, or on the edge of Bnei Brak, where I was for the last three months of 5707, then I probably would have sat over a cup of coffee with a little cream on top, listening to the "dramatic" U.N. vote. I would have peacefully thought whatever thoughts I had, and lain me down to sleep, allowing the turbid cream to settle, and rising the next day to again see everything with the wise and cruel eyes of a Fighter for the Freedom of Israel. Except that to do this is impossible if one lives in a new apartment on Tel Aviv's Rehov Dizengoff, only a few feet from the Casit Café, the center of the riotous celebrations marking the U.N. vote for a Jewish "state."

On this spot, in the Hebrew city last to suffer and first to celebrate, the abandonment knows no bounds.

For the first time I abandon myself, unburdening myself of the constraints imposed by underground caution; and I descend to roam and see the nation at its worst. They can barely finish singing *Hatikva*, for all the throats have burst from shouting, all the windows have burst, all the gates of the houses have burst, all the radios have burst and their volume has been raised to the maximum and the loudspeakers are screaming from every corner. Rehov Dizengoff is no longer a street, the houses are no longer houses, and men are no longer men who can step where they please, quietly and while thinking. Everything is swept up in the ever-growing riot that is encompassing all. Women are running with babies in their arms, houses are dancing with flags waving, the honking of cars competes with the wordless, tuneless shriek:

Yaaaaayyyyyy! howls the joy.

Yaaaaayyyyyy! howls the cultured progressivity of Casit.

Yaaaaayyyyyy! The singer spins his dissonant rhymes: I don't care, what do I care, what difference does it make to me? And really I don't care, what do I care, what difference does it make? Is there a choice? There is no choice! Long live the "state."

I continue.

Yesterday, I had still been afraid to cross the corner of Frishman and Dizengoff in daylight. Café Pinati is there, where the members of Hagana Intelligence sit, just as progressively as those in Casit, though somewhat lagging in culture. Anyone who fights against the British and for the freedom of Israel must stay far away from both these cafés. Tonight there is no fear. Tonight no one at Pinati will get up to spy on you. Not because their jobs have ended tonight. They will yet have their hands full with work, and full with Jewish blood, in the course of the winter that follows the U.N. decision. But tonight, tonight they are drunk. With abandon, continuously and as if strung together, the bottles are broken on the ground. Independence! The dogs of MacMichael and Barker have been freed from their leashes. Freedom.

I pass by and continue, in loathsome anger. I had come down to see the happiness of the Jews.

And on the simple level there was happiness. The simple, apolitical happiness of Jews, the happiness of "we will have a state" of our own. Yes, many of those who are happy today were only yesterday scornfully turning up their noses at the word "state," either because they did not believe it possible or because they did not believe it necessary when they were thinking soberly. Tonight they are dancing and happy. Their understanding has passed along with their sobriety. A "Jewish state," the magical words of the past decades.

Below this level lay another, and it dominated the night. Abandonment.

You see it in the formlessness of the happiness, the lack of all self-restraint normally present in deep happiness. As if demonstrating the psycho-physiological truth that pleasure is only the release of tension.

The tension had been so great these past years, even if not of one kind. The massacre in Europe, the danger of a German invasion, the Underground war and all that it involved: assassinations, curfews, searches, gallows, demonstrations, illegal immigration, the fear of pogroms, the threat of civil war. Only a very few are ready to continue on and on with this kind of tense life, for their characters are of steel and their nerves of steel are tightly strung, from the depth of suffering all the way to the distant messiah; and on these steel paths the messiah will definitely come. But they are few. The nation is a nervous nation. It cannot wait more than forty days for Moses to return. A mixed multitude does not withstand the suffering of desert and fire. A mixed multitude wants rest; whatever happens—happens, just let there be rest. A decision, period. A large state or a small one, with Jerusalem or without, the main thing is: an end to this tension, to this "cycle of blood," as it is called by the right- and left-wing bourgeoisie, which wants stability, stability, stability. These past months, the tension has risen, naturally and also artificially, in anticipation of the U.N. decision. Naturally, as for a condemned man waiting to hear his sentence; artificially, by the Zionist leadership, which has always grasped at all sorts of dates and committees and meetings. Indeed, they are their life and the length of their days and they will meditate and hang their hopes upon them, day and night, day and night. They can use them to avoid fighting. They can use them to gore the "separatists" who are "stabbing us in the back" "just" "in these decisive days." And what will happen if Heaven forbid a positive decision fails to be taken? Then they will have no choice and they will have to "struggle" again. . . if no new savior appears on the horizon in the form of a special session of the Zionist Congress or another committee.

In the midst of this tension and the suffering, which is so natural during a war for freedom, comes the U.N. vote. Any vote whose outcome is unknown contains some hazard, some gamble, and now the masses of Israel stand in this hazard-filled tension and watch: Will they win the gamble, will they be given a state or not?

Millions of Jews are standing all around the world, thousands of Israeli youth are standing, healthy as cedars, wonderfully combat ready, prepared to sacrifice, and they are standing with their hands in their pockets and their mouths open, watching . . . how Costa Rica will vote. Costa Rica. Costa Rica. On them, on the votes of Costa Rica and Nicaragua, our fate is dependent, whether there will be a State of Israel. Our youth is standing and counting: Four, already, are for us, and one is against. What about Siam? Where is Siam? Siam? Siam is missing. Siam is wonderful! And ink gushes, pens run to the paper, counting, counting. How many now? Hurrah! Nicaragua voted for us. Nicaragua voted that the descendants of Abraham and Isaac and Jacob and David and Isaiah and Judah Maccabee should also have a state. Hurrah. Nicaragua. Where exactly is this Nicaragua? What kind of a nation is it? Who knows? Ask one, two, three, ask thousands of people from among the mobs waiting for Nicaragua's decision, ask them: What is Nicaragua? No one knows. No one knows. But that is not important. Long live Nicaragua, it is on our side. Ours. Do not confuse us with geography and history. If Nicaragua and Costa Rica will Heaven forbid be against us, then there will not be a Jewish state and millions of Jews will be very sad, and only the Arabs will have a state. State? Seven, eight states.

Suddenly, curses: Cuba, be damned! Cuba voted against. Anti-Semites. And when the big ones vote—people lose their minds. The United States—for. Long live democracy. The Soviet Union—for. Long live the great Russian Revolution. And I, too, am happy, for the triumph of our orientation. We were first.

Waves rise and fall, rise and fall. The hearts beat, beat. How many now, how many for us now? And how many against? How many are needed? Thirty?

Thirty-two? When I was a child Poppa used to play cards with me on Hanukkah, the "31" game, and my heart used to beat like this when I got to twenty-four or twenty-five. Will I get thirty-one, the magical thirty-one?

Another picture from Poppa's house appears before me. (As with any whirlpool, the depths rise.) I am twelve years old. I am walking on Poppa's right, my ten-year-old brother is on his left. We are dressed up, wearing shirts with blue and white collars, marching in a holiday parade on the streets of Lvov. All Lvov's Jews are marching, with flags everywhere. This is the second time I am walking with Poppa in such a crowd. The first time, we went to the funeral of the Torah scrolls, which burned together with the Jews who leaped into the synagogue to save them; and we were in the cemetery in November and snow covered everything. And in the snow were thousands of Jews dressed in black, and they were burying Torah scrolls together with burnt Jews; and the cemetery was full of crying and the wailing of women and men, and the snow was not melting. It was frozen and evil. But this time we are in a holiday procession. Thousands and thousands of Jews are marching: the San Remo decision! Fifty-two countries voted for us, for a "National Home." Everyone's heart rejoices, rejoices, is truly proud; I am, too, as is my brother in his handsome new suit. For we were very naive. We still believed, we believed in the value of decisions like these, we believed in the world's conscience, many believed then and many wanted so much to believe.

But also: What did we have behind us then, when our nation was in the infancy of its renewal? A lot of justice and a few settlements. With them we stood before the world. Therefore, we were glad we won "understanding" and agreement. But today? Today when we are for all practical purposes the only *nation* in the Middle East with culture and with strength, today when we have behind us a heroic war against the British Empire? Today we stand like a doltish herd and dance circles around every vote on our behalf? Today, *after* all our experience, after we have seen the worthlessness of the votes of such institutions, institutions which strut for a day and whose decisions are of momentary significance, we still grasp at them? Still, and to such an extent? With such determination? With such belief?

The association I make with the golden calf was not born that night, and I did not father it. It was brought to my attention by Uri Zvi Greenberg, who with the glance of an eagle encompassed distances, distances in time, and who lived with the past as if it had happened before his own eyes. He said to me: "Only once before has the nation experienced such a horror, such an abomination, like the dancing of that night. The dancing around the golden calf must have looked the same."

And Uri Zvi must have intended the comparison between the calf and the state, too, which had been decided upon, which could no more live than that calf. (Can anyone imagine, today, such a "state" with those borders, and that population, the state that was decided upon and over which Jews danced?) Certainly, Uri Zvi had in his thoughts the betrayal of Jerusalem, at whose expense the decision was taken; for in return for our conceding her and abandoning her, several "Catholic" or "Christian" countries voted for us, allowing the dancers to dance on the severed body of Jerusalem. But that night I concentrated mostly on two points: The phenomenon of this self-abandon, and the self-abasement. From where, I wondered in amazement, did this great people get this foolishness? They who heard the Divine "I AM," they who saw the Divine glory, they dance in circles and shriek: "These are your gods that have brought you up out of the land of Egypt"? *These*? Nicaragua and Costa Rica? Because of these? The strength to dance comes from them? The right to live? From where does this great people get such a low, slavish spirit? Were our fathers who believed in the messiah also capable of dancing like this over a decision by the goyim? In all our vast Redemptive literature, which is very realistic despite the mystical garb it wears, is there a hint of something like this happening? There is Elijah the herald, there is the war of Gog and Magog, there is the Valley of Jehosaphat, there is the messiah descended from Joseph, but there is not a trace—nor should there be, given logic and realism—of any such herald of redemption as this, the goyim deciding by a vote to establish the State of Israel, and this becoming a holiday and a celebration. In all the cultural heritage of our people there is nothing of this sort.

So what is this, from where is it coming? Is it not that the light of the movement-of-blinding-light, the Emancipation and the Enlightenment, has reached this far? The self-abasement, the looking to the goy's words, and for the goy's kindness, began then. They praise the Bible, so the Bible is good. They disdain the Talmud, so the Talmud is bad. All the rejoicing over hearing praise from an enlightened Gentile. The whole absurd fight for equal rights in the Diaspora, the happiness over a French author who opposes anti-Semitism and a Russian politician who is a liberal, this retreat from the realistic, extremely realistic, notions which our Sages held about the nations of the world. There was more light in the cave of Rabbi Shimon Bar Yochai than in the Enlightenment; there was a deeper understanding. A belief in the messiah is more realistic than a belief in the League of Nations and a United Nations. Those who are dancing in Dizengoff Square are not the grandchildren of Rabbi Shimon Bar Yochai and the Baal Shem Tov; they are the grandchildren of those who danced in Paris and Leningrad and Warsaw and Budapest to celebrate the "equal rights" they had won. Perhaps Zionism has not reached the deeper levels. She is one hundred or one hundred and fifty years old. She is not the same messianic belief our forefathers held, she is the same age as the Costa Ricas and Nicaraguas. And she abases herself before them, before all the votes of these United Nations.

I will not say that I formulated this whole analysis as I roamed through the riotous crowd. But I will say I pulled it from that night's thicket of thoughts and emotions, about this abandon and unburdening, about Jerusalem which had been placed on the altar, about dancing spies, about my being a stranger among them. There was no October victory, no conquering of the Bastille, no expulsion of the enemy; this was some vote which took place somewhere, and youth howling. This, too, is Diaspora, exile. And to say that a new generation has arisen is to lie.

Is this not the dance of the beggars in *The Dybbuk*?

That night passed, dark as it was despite the lights flooding it, and it passed and it smiled with a sneer, for it was followed by days by the light of which the dancing figures appeared even more ludicrous.

But together with that night, the night of our Underground also passed and disappeared, a night which had so much brightness, in which everything was clear, and a day began which was neither day nor night: fog.

Fog

1. My Explanation: Barely Satisfactory

When in the course of my background talks with those who held positions of responsibility in Lehi, someone accused the Central Command of not having foreseen the possibility of a partition of Eretz Israel, I could have easily disproved his complaint by quoting an article that appeared in *Hehazit* in 5705 in which the possibility was considered. But it is not enough for partition to have once been mentioned as a theoretical possibility. A liberation movement that opposes such a solution must also indicate the means to prevent it.

During the discussion days we held after November 29, Natan Friedman with one group and I with another, I could only come up with a fatalistic explanation: "Part of the land is liberated, just as part of the nation came here and just as part of the nation fought."

This excuse was evasive. *Blaming others*. Those who did not immigrate and those who did not fight.

Certainly an additional million Jews in Eretz Israel and another five thousand fighters would have been capable of preventing partition, and certainly even without them the Underground conducted a war which would have to win first prize if prizes were given to freedom fighters. But he for whom the main thing is not patting himself on the back: "See what heroes we are," he for whom the yardstick lies between the aim of the heroism and its achievement, he should not be too evasive or blame others for the not done.

As 5707 turned into 5708, we lost the initiative, not only the military but also the ideological. This was not a necessary development. We slid into the arms of the defensive-Zionist ideology, perhaps because we viewed incorrectly the fictitious British withdrawal, perhaps because of our latent longing to be on the same one front as the rest of the nation, perhaps because of the realistic assessment: *How* can *we* fight to liberate the entire land?

In the course of the background discussion in Gideon's house in Bnei Brak, I repeatedly declared to the tens of participants (the following quotations are taken from an internal booklet that included my oral explanations):

> We are closing a chapter and opening a chapter. We are discussing chapters and not Torah. Torah does not change. Our "Torah" is the liberation of the homeland for the nation. The return of the nation to the

> homeland and the establishment of the Kingdom of Israel as an instrument of and an expression of the collective Hebrew creative force.

Of course I also acknowledged the confusion and explained its causes:

> The focusing of our eyes, words and arms on this enemy (the British) is what caused some people some confusion. On the one hand we all know, and we repeatedly emphasize, that the imperialism which has vital interests here has only retreated to new trenches. But the withdrawal of the military and the government's direct rule has hidden from our sight the enemy in its most concrete form, that form to which we had grown accustomed and against which we had devised such successful means of striking. Now a new situation has come into being. The imperialism, buffeted by American imperialism at its rear, will rule not with its concrete body, but with new forms against which the means of warfare we have until now employed are not appropriate.

When I was asked by the regular freedom fighters for more clarity and consistency, I proclaimed clearly:

> We will not recognize any agreement to allow a foreign army in any part of the land.

Yes. Everything was correct. The explanation for the confusion, the feeling that the withdrawal was a big deception, and the promise not to "recognize." But when they began asking: How??? I began to stutter.

There were differences between my explanations and Natan Friedman's. He did not speak of the goal of *Malkhut Israel*, the Kingdom of Israel, as I did. He emphasized mostly what had been attained, rather than what had not. But both of us saw clearly that we would continue in two ways: within the state—as a legal party; outside the state, meaning abroad and in Jerusalem—underground.

I tried as much as was possible in those psychotic days to minimize the achievement by lifting it from the static plain to the dynamic current:

> The "state" is of course in quotation marks. It will not pass muster in terms of a freedom-fighter's ideology. It will not pass muster in terms of the realization of Zionism. Finally: It will not pass muster in terms of a

> lengthy existence. We must ensure that this stage, the "state," never ceases to be in movement. Our main task is to transform this "state" from a National "Home" to a national "Corridor" and in a corridor no one stands, no one sits, no one sleeps.

(Only a year later were we shown that even in this "corridor" you can stand like a pauper at the door, "sit" in Acco Prison, and sleep in the Knesset.)

But as clear as the analyses of the past and the future may be, reality was the *fact of the U.N. decision.* There were two ways to prevent its implementation. The first we considered and rejected, and the second we saw when it was already too late, if not objectively, then subjectively, because of the tiredness of the members of the Underground, *from top to bottom.*

The first possibility, which I had already suggested to Begin during the bright days of 5707, was stopping the Underground war. As the date of the U.N. debate approached, we saw more and more clearly that *we* were pushing toward the partition solution, which would satisfy most of the Jews, return authority to the Jewish Agency and the establishment Yishuv, and end the suffering of the refugees. I put the question in its starkest form to Begin: What will happen if we stop, in order to prevent partition?

Our conclusion: The Morrison Plan would be implemented, and in its worst form. Yet, we did not have enough inner strength to stop fighting. We were afraid to choose the path: "The worse it is, the better it is." We did not dare. We were not cruel enough, or we were not certain that it would bring the revolution. To use dialectics with complete certainty in hindsight is of course impossible: "What would have happened if . . . ?" In any case, we considered the option of stopping then and rejected it because . . . we were too patriotic.

I now argued, this time before my surprised listeners: We had once decided to halt operations if 100,000 refugees were allowed to immigrate. A partitioned state means at least 100,000 refugees will immigrate, so why should we treat it any differently than the original 100,000 proposal?

And only one person accused us of treason. In protest, or in confusion, he turned . . . to the Hagana. He was a casualty of the fog.

There was a second possible means of confounding the partition plan, a possibility which was not considered by us or by the IZL; and only the prophet saw it and considered it and mourned it, and he does not have the title "Doctor" as I do, but he understands history and geography better than I, and he conducted no journeys and no diplomatic meetings, but he understands politics better than

Natan Friedman-Yellin, and he does not have the title "one of the great military commanders" like Raziel, Meridor, Gidi, but he is the greatest strategist of our generation, *because he is a prophet.*

Uri Zvi.

And the possibility was: Jerusalem.

Had we left all the glorious and not so glorious battles in Jaffa, Yehudia, Sheikh Munis, had we left them in the hands of that "force which knows how to defend," the Hagana, and had all of us gone up, from the Central Commanders and the Supreme Commanders to the last of the soldiers with the last of the guns—to Jerusalem, in those days when she was abandoned, had we seen her not only as the center of our hearts but also of our country's map and of the defense of our country, then we would have determined the fate of the country; and we would have prevented the disaster of partition, and we would have continued to be a national liberation movement as we were destined to be, and not as we traitorously ceased to be, in those days when ideological and organizational fog descended upon us after the two strategic blows we suffered, we and the IZL both: the apparent withdrawal and the real partition.

2. On Two and a Half Fronts

To the political confusion into which we were thrust was added the organizational confusion into which we thrust ourselves.

Two mistakes by Natan Friedman added to the confusion.

After the Arab attack in Gan Hawaii, our enlarged secretariat met in Bnei Brak, and I sought to have certain divisions (primarily our Intelligence Division) transferred to the Arab front, and to prepare our Operations Division for this new front, too.

The proposal met with Natan Friedman's vigorous opposition. He said: There won't be an Arab front.

This shortsightedness was almost certainly a result of the "Neutral Middle East," the desirable theory of neutrality he had been first to formulate and justify. This theory had its roots in the principle that we were fighting British imperialism, and it rightly saw all our Arab neighbors, who were also enslaved by Britain, as potential allies. In Paris there was even an intelligent member of the Egyptian opposition who promised to form a joint Egyptian-Hebrew political movement to fight the common British enemy. It was all *so* logical.

But I alluded in our background meetings to this policy as one possibility, the farthest away in time, while other possibilities were more immediate (such as exploiting the competition between the various imperialisms, exploiting the existence of non-Arab and non-Moslem minorities, or exploiting the conflict between Egypt and Syria on the one hand and the Hashemites on the other). Friedman, however, placed his hopes on the progressive leftist movements in those same countries. That is why he wrote the Arab chapter in our booklet *Fundamentals of Hebrew Foreign Policy*.

This *desirable* situation—an alliance against British imperialism—as well as a sharper turn toward the left, caused Friedman to see the Arabs of our country, too, as potential allies. Up to this point we had had only one experience with them and it was entirely positive: Yosef Abu Ghosh, an Arab member of Lehi. A marvelous phenomenon in a muddy ocean of hypocritical Levantinism. Uri Zvi, the poet who penetrates beyond his own time, said to me: The blood of ancient Hebrew rebels must run in him, he cannot possibly be an Arab. But he is a single phenomenon and has no relevance to socialism, to progress, or to anti-imperialist countries. His is simply the character of a true rebel, who loves other rebels. Friedman is not relying on him when he says to me, and to the secretariat, and to Begin when we hold joint meetings: There won't be an Arab front.

Begin, free as he is of ideological conceptions in foreign policy, sees most clearly and is the first to proclaim the danger of an invasion. Of course, to turn the IZL into an army able to halt an Arab invasion is beyond his power. But now, at last, there is a rationale for the IZL's military structure. In Lehi, we ran up against our ideology. A neutral Middle East is not a baseless concept. It does, however, require basic conditions that do not yet exist—mainly, the independence of the Middle East, a precondition for which is: the great strength of a great Kingdom of Israel. Without this, there can be no independence, no neutrality. Without this, the concept is no more than an obstacle blocking a realistic view. It dazzled and blinded Friedman. No preparations were made in Lehi for the Arab front.

This was the first reason, but there was a second, deeper reason for the mistake Friedman made those first, foggy days: the desire for abandon; to unburden. Since then it has become visible, growing stronger, eventually culminating in his humiliating stance at his Acco trial and in the establishment of the stillborn "Fighters Party" as his entry ticket to the Establishment Yishuv. This desire for a quick unburdening is the second reason for his sudden order to dismantle the Lehi Combat Unit, except in Jerusalem. The order increases the confusion in the ranks. In the middle of the night, I am called from my home by people who have come from our branches all over the country, and with tears in their eyes they ask me what it means: "Are we finished?" And I know nothing. We had spoken of budgetary cutbacks, but the word "dismantle" had never been used.

Meanwhile, the Arab front grows. Meanwhile, the IZL takes up defensive positions, though it also engages in offensive operations. Meanwhile, the British front still exists. In the midst of the utter chaos, which reigns for four weeks, the original order to dismantle is canceled and we somewhat belatedly open our anti-Arab front.

I am not of the opinion, Heaven forbid, that this delay was of serious importance to the front itself. The front developed on a scale and in a form that were beyond us. Our small numbers, the spirit of our members, and their training were all inappropriate for defensive positions. But the delay was of critical importance to Lehi, internally—it testified to the confusion within the movement's leadership.

Nevertheless, we executed several operations important to general developments. First and foremost: the blowing up of the Saraye (the "palace" that held the Arab headquarters) in Jaffa. Just the fact that two boys were able to penetrate into the very heart of the Arab uprising was itself the cause of much confusion and panic among the Arabs in the city, in addition to the loss of life that followed. Will anyone in the State of Israel ever consider erecting a monument to the heroes of the Saraye?

The operation encouraged us to attempt a more daring endeavor: to penetrate into the city of Shchem. This time, however, chance—or the betrayal of the assisting Arab—caused "Avraham Cohen," who had been sent on the mission, to get caught and to disappear. It was a small consolation that as his car was being relieved of the explosives within, two British officers who had participated in the murderous British bombing of Rehov Ben Yehuda in Jerusalem were killed.

Revenge works in mysterious ways.

We executed another explosive operation in Haifa, the blowing up of Bet Hanajada; the importance of this operation was that it broke the cease-fire in Haifa, where Mayor Abba Hushi ruled.

Our first battle, a partial success, was fought in Abu Cabir.

One pointless operation was the blowing up of seventy empty houses in Bir-Adas, which I probably would not remember had I not opposed it, arguing that we would do better to transfer the explosives we had manufactured to Jerusalem, which day after day implored us: Send explosives! Send explosives!

But in vain.

Only after Dov's return from abroad were our first *military* units established, which began operating along the border of the "Triangle" in the Sharon and Shomron regions, since all the cracks through which we had been able to penetrate on sabotage operations had gradually been sealed. The front slowly but surely took on a military character and moved away from underground forms of warfare.

And one more operation that was valuable, more psychologically than militarily: Sheikh Munis.

Word was received that the enemy was fortifying itself north of Tel Aviv in Sheikh Munis, that they had German commanders and Iraqi officers.

A Lehi unit entered the village and introduced itself by name, which could not possibly have calmed the villagers, especially after the revenge we had taken in Abu Kishak following the murder of young Lehi members in Raanana. There, all the males had been lined up. Four were identified as those who had shown the British the location of our weaponry course, and these four were executed. Now our unit demanded of the Sheikh Munis Arabs that they either disarm or leave the village. The Arabs announced their willingness to leave, on the condition that the mayors and councilmen of the area guarantee their property.

We met with Messrs. Israel Rokach and Jacob Sapir in the home of Reb Avraham Krinitzi, the Underground's friend. The well-known argument sounded strange coming from Mr. Rokach: For political reasons we are not interested in seeing the Arabs leave the village. The only one, of course, who confronted the issue unevasively was Krinitzi. He was familiar with military matters, especially artillery (he had managed a factory producing and repairing artillery during the First World War, in Damascus). He warned of the danger that Tel Aviv's port could be bombarded from the heights of Sheikh Munis. In short, "Don't be afraid. Let them go!"

I told the two hesitant civilians that our ultimatum stood. If the Hagana would not protect Tel Aviv by disarming the Sheikh Munis Arabs, then we would go in and "put things in order." I do not know whether we had really formulated a plan to "put things in order," but we accomplished two things: The Arabs began leaving the village en masse; and the day after the meeting in Krinitzi's home, Mr. Rokach informed us that the Hagana was entering the village.

We took for ourselves an "agent's fee," a beautiful block of houses to be used for the legal Lehi camp. And the site was named: Ramat Yair (Yair Heights).

Even after all these operations, I summarize our activity on the Arab front near the coastal plain as: *without decisive historical importance*.

The operations did not spring from our fundamental beliefs; they were not acts of liberation or conquest. Inside, we knew they came only to keep us in the competition; we still existed as a separate group.

The British are still in the country.

The IZL entered into negotiations with the Hagana. We immediately announced we were ready to join the accord, on the condition that the front be united both against the Arabs and against the British who are still attacking us. And if for the standard reasons, the Hagana is not prepared to respond to British provocations, even when its members are picked up by the British and turned over to Arab gangs to be tortured and murdered, even when the British cross roadblocks to place bombs in Jewish areas—and this tolerance toward the British goes so far that the Hagana does not even dare to operate against the Arab Legion which the British support (witness, the events at Bet Naballa)—then we will offer a different condition: a united front against the Arabs, while we remain free to fight the British.

The Hagana rejected this condition, and we were forced to continue independently on both fronts.

The announcement of the British withdrawal removes the justification for ongoing operations against those who are withdrawing. At this point we are able to initiate only two types of operations: confiscations of money and arms (200,000 lira from Barclay's Bank) and escapes from prisons (through a tunnel and sewer from the Jerusalem Central Prison). But we do still provide stinging responses to provocations. And two terrible provocations bring two blood-drenched and honor-restoring responses.

The murder in Raanana: A group of boys and girls is surprised during a weaponry course. They do not have time to train or to defend themselves. The house is surrounded. Five, including the instructor, are murdered. Logically, what is the difference if a youth falls or an adult falls? But logic does not reign in such matters. The youth of Rubovitch and those murdered in Raanana (we call them the *children* of Raanana, though they long ago passed the age of childhood) adds a tear to the cup of anger, and this tear causes the blood to boil. And the enemy pays with dozens of casualties.

Haaretz reports the funeral of the Raanana dead, on the third day of Kislev:

> Close to 10 a.m. on Friday, young girls who represented themselves as Lehi messengers traversed the main streets of Tel Aviv asking store owners to close their shops during the funeral of the Raanana dead. They asked

> that the shops remain closed from 10:00 to 10:30. Almost all the store owners honored their request. But after 10:00, Hagana units appeared in the city center and they, too, went from shop to shop and demanded that the storekeepers open them immediately. For one half-hour confusion reigned in the stores. Some remained closed and some open.

That was the bouquet the Hagana sent to the funeral.

The British paid a heavy price for the Ben Yehuda bombing, too. There were also more confiscations of arms. But all these were no longer part of a regular and constant war. What is the point of fighting an enemy who has already announced his surrender? We used to say, half in jest and half-seriously: "We'll ask them to stay a little longer so we can still strike at them. We'll hold on to them."

If anyone was still capable of claiming that this was a war between the British and *Lehi*, the bombing of Ben Yehuda came and screamed from the top of the heap of houses and bodies: The enemy of Lehi is the enemy of the nation. It is the same murderer.

Faced with this single enemy in Jerusalem and Raanana, the Lehi fist again became one, the fist which had begun separating into fingers, fingers divided between the coast and capital. Meir in Jerusalem replied with death in the streets; Mazal on the coast, with the blowing up of a military train.

Blood for blood.

Only the Hagana, the force that claimed to "know how to defend," but which did not know how to defend, not the Jerusalem business district from Arabs and not Rehov Hasolel and the Jewish Agency building and Rehov Ben Yehuda from the British, only they bitterly whimper their new excuse now, with tear-inducing rhetoric: "We cannot fight on two fronts." As if they would have responded to the murder, but for the Arab front!

On this British front we stand tall, stalwart, clear, without political doubts, without ideological hesitations, without organizational difficulties, and without being afraid of a Bartholomew's Eve. When the Hagana, which supposedly fears fighting on a second front, then spares no energy and does not fear opening a second front . . . internally, within the Jewish community, and the young heads whose bodies hang *Hama'as* are split open and our members are kidnapped—

Then there is a response internally, too. Blow for blow. Kidnappings for kidnappings. I meet with Levi Skolnick in Dr. Kurtz's house in Tel Aviv to negotiate a "prisoner exchange" and a return of the Lehi documents confiscated by them and, in response, those taken by us from their Intelligence Headquarters. So this front, totally unnecessary under current circumstances according to everyone, is ended before it develops any further.

The dense fog thickens.

3. Bits of Fog

From out of this fog comes *Mivrak*,[82] a creation of the twilight, neither day nor night, a legal underground newspaper. Dr. Lubotzky is the editor in chief; he has not yet decided whether to join the General Zionists or Mapai, but meanwhile he is connected to Lehi.

I read in this paper that the "Haam Movement" was about to join the General Zionists. I had placed great hopes on its youth, one or two hundred activists in the Hagana who had made a lot of noise against a civil war.

I had met the leaders of Haam in Ramat Gan. We spoke a little about politics and political orientations and a lot about . . . the financial problems of the Haam Movement, which were forcing it to look for a new home.

After we agreed to provide monthly stipends, to help Dr. Lubotzky rent an apartment in Ramat Gan and to allow him to edit the daily paper, Lehi turned out to be no more than an alternative to the General Zionists. Why did we bother with such things?

We were thinking about a legal framework in which to operate, and we were looking for middlemen. And I erred in grasping at this middleman. Several months later Lubotzky fell under the influence of Eliezer Lowenstein,[83] and even more so under the influence of the state that was about to rise under Mapai rule, and he suddenly realized that between the IZL, General Zionists and Lehi, he would do best to choose . . . Mapai. He still wanted to be involved in decision making and suggested a joint authority. A little while later, he up and went straight to Lowenstein and his paper. Another deserter from the tragic nationalist movement. Another example of a politician with no conceptual basis.

In this midst of this fog, Friedman was holding talks with Moshe Sneh about establishing a single opposition party, to include everybody from the IZL to Hashomer Hatzair. The idea was dropped, and Friedman found consolation in Sneh's explanation:

"You, Lehi, are closer to my heart, I would feel better with you than with Ahdut Haavoda and Hashomer Hatzair, but they are a larger power . . . ." And in my heart I harbor nothing against Sneh, only this: Too bad he did not succeed in influencing Natan Friedman to leave *then* . . . he would have saved Friedman the unpleasantries of his trial and spared Lehi its upcoming crises.

Just now, in this fog, the treasure of 200,000 lira falls into our laps. Not one of us knows how to invest such a large sum of money so that it will bear profits, and we need profits to maintain the movement. *Mivrak* costs money. Arms are bought and arms are produced and the organization grows administratively.

Just now, in this fog, our enlistment suddenly increases and our Enlistment Division is on the verge of having difficulty being able to absorb all the newcomers and determine their worth. The reason for this spurt in enlistment in Lehi and the IZL (and we are more particular than the IZL about who we accept) is the draft instituted in the entire Yishuv. As they have to enlist anyway, many come to the Underground movements closer to their hearts, though as long as they did not have to, their hearts did not push them. Hisia Shapiro, who is directing our Enlistment Division, voices the suspicion that many are coming because we are not in the first line of fire, on the front. Certainly, there are a few like that. Yet hundreds of our people are very uncomfortable: An occasional operation is not enough for those who have risen from suffering and blood and who want to give their blood again and again.

Mazal (Yaacov Banai), responsible for the Combat Unit, stands before the Central Command and demands: Tell me, at least, for what should I be training the members? Underground? Partisans? Army?

And we are silent, perplexed.

Added to the fog in the country is the fog hanging over our branches abroad.

Our center is in Paris. From there, several operations have been carried out in the enemy's capital, London. Letter bombs, attempts to blow up the Colonial Ministry. Our members are transferred through various pipelines into London and are preparing operations. Once we used to say: those who fail are sent abroad. And there were such cases. But in the year 5707 our activity abroad progresses very well. Even the operations that do not succeed increase the nervous tension in London. The IZL is more successful in enlisting people abroad. Our branches deal more in operations, in searching for political connections and in securing for themselves a financial base. Yedidya is in charge of this. Alexander Aaronsohn, brother of Sarah and Aaron, provides much assistance.

Now, there, too, the fog descends. It begins with some bragging American rabbi and a provocateur-pilot who promises to bomb London. Yardur, who is responsible, falls for the temptation and into the trap. No, not exactly. He manages to get away but all the center's members are arrested and Yedidya, the gentlest of all, loses his health in this fog that enshrouds us more and more. We still hang some hopes on Michael, if he can get to Paris after his escape from Kenyan exile. But we get no break. Everything is too late. Maybe . . . if we had only had two years ago the same forces and the same means!

Maybe this "maybe" is pointless? Maybe it is like the story of the Lithuanian who taught his horse how to go hungry, and the horse had almost learned how, except that the horse suddenly died?

Our strength increased but we lost control.

In the fog, my eyes begin to search out points on which I can focus, lights according to which I can walk, according to which I can answer the many questions I am asked in the ideological courses and in letters from our members: What now? How, now?

And if the "what" is still clear to me, the "how" is not so clear.

And in this fog I see a pillar of fire: Jerusalem; and a pillar that is a dark cloud, after years of personal separation: Uri Zvi.

4. In the Pillar of Cloud

I go to him as one enters the Divine cloud.

I go to him again after years of separation. From the time *Hehazit* began to appear in the summer of 5703 (1943) until this foggy winter of 5708, I have not seen him.

It is as if I left him only yesterday. As always with him. No corridor. At least, as he always is with someone to whom his heart is open. Because he is capable of being polite and conventional and asking as others do, "How are you?" and "What do you do?" and "How are you feeling?" and so forth, when that is what is appropriate for the person to whom he is talking.

Not with me, though there is much to ask after so many years, after what has happened to me in the Underground and in prison. But I know full well that he followed it all, all that happened to me and to everyone, day after day, night after night. So I am not surprised. He already knows everything, and polite inquiries are not for us.

Before I have had a chance to say "Shalom" and hear "Shalom," before I have had a chance to look around me and see how he lives in this room in Tel Aviv, I am already in the thickest fold of the cloud and he is descending, lamenting over his father's house which is no more, and he is thundering over Jerusalem which has been betrayed, and now he is already descending with me into the innermost workings of the Lehi Underground, with the scalpel of his glance touching the weak spots as if he were inside, as if he were in contact with someone inside, but he is not. As Dr. Troy was able to smell the point of battle through my thick cast, so does Uri Zvi smell the rotten point in Lehi.

How does he do this? How?

How does he know the inferiority-complex plague has spread among us? He stands and complains again and again: You do not know who you are. Why do you feel inferior to the Palmach?

Or: What do you mean that Joe Palmachnik is "really a good man?" If he is a good man *why isn't he in Lehi*?

Or: What are these calculations: "From the perspective of our organization," and "From the general perspective"? There aren't two perspectives. If you are convinced that your framework is correct in its goals and means, then there is only one perspective: What is good for your organization is good for the people.

He sees a dark, very dark, future for Lehi.

You see—he says, opening his hand—I see it like a hand: Some of you will go left, to the Communists or to Ahdut Haavoda. Some will degenerate along different paths leading from the Underground and only a very few will remain loyal.

How does he know this? How does he know this in the winter of 5708? When I try to calm him, he himself explains how he knows: No, among the goyim it is not like this. Among the goyim a person can be a socialist or a Communist and remain a national patriot. But with us it is very dangerous. We are an exterritorial nation, uprooted. With us, a person immediately becomes cosmopolitan, immediately begins to think about saving the world, immediately begins to hate his past, the heritage of his fathers. Begins to bow before every "progressive culture" and scorn the "reactionary" Sages though he is not at all familiar with the territory of our Sages. We cannot, absolutely cannot, confuse the youth with different "isms." We must focus, not scatter, the heart.

I calm him; but I do not calm myself, for I already know from the inside that bugs are beginning to stir inside the fruit.

About our orientation, Uri Zvi says: No. I am not opposed in principle to a pro-Soviet orientation. On the contrary, I understand the motivations of true revolutionary Communists, especially if they are ready to sacrifice themselves for their beliefs. I hate only the Yevsekim and Mofasim because they pay for their Communism by betraying their people.[84] And as for Russia? *Tell me what have you gotten from them so far*?

I begin to mumble something about expressions of support, possibilities.

No. Concrete. What have you gotten so far? Nothing? So, you were sold for nothing? You are giving her all this propaganda for nothing? Every word from your mouths is worth twenty meetings of the local Communist party, Maki. Maki is hated, because they are seen as traitors, people who sold themselves. But no one thinks you sold yourselves. You are patriots; and so if you say "Amen" to Russia, it is of great worth. But at least get something in return. What you have done in the anti-British war here, Russia could not have accomplished using any other of the local groups. She should give you a lot. And if not, then you have sold yourselves for nothing and in the end, you will reach Maki's level, and Russia won't want you then, either.

Again, I calm him. I have the right to calm him, speaking for myself, because I have held talks with the representatives of various entities and I made sure that in their presence our flag was 100 percent national, we did not pay any socialist "entrance fee." But he is not referring to these other entities at all; he is warning about the internal workings of Lehi. He is not afraid for me. I am rooted in the nation's culture. But we must fear for the young. They may become pious perverts.

Only a year later did I realize that his fears were justified, when I heard, from Lehi members, that it would be best for Israel to become a republic within the Soviet Union; and also when the great "diplomat" I mentioned in Latrun blamed me, saying that because of my reactionary ideas and my mysticism the talks failed in Prague, where they saw that I was a nationalist . . . and I am therefore to blame for the failure, and I must go.

In 5708 I never even considered such possibilities, but Uri Zvi smelled them.

And lights? Are there no bright spots? No achievements?

Of course there are. Of course, from time to time they brighten his heart, his poetry, but he does not allow himself to enjoy them, and certainly he does not allow himself to inspire others with his happiness and for the same reason: We are a nervous nation. We lean toward optimism, and optimism is more dangerous than pessimism. Optimism induces sleep. And I understand the secret of Uri Zvi's sympathy for the Zionist author Brenner, the rouser, who wrote bitter novels exposing the ills of the Yishuv. It is better to rip out the flesh, even if together with the diseased flesh some healthy flesh is also rent, just do not let the decay spread. And complacency breeds decay.

Moreover, experience has shown him that the vast majority of his dark prophecies have come true. He is himself shocked today when he reads the poems he wrote in 1922 prophesying the Destruction in Europe, to the very gas chambers.

If you say: Uri, just as the dark ones came to pass, so will the prophecies of salvation, so rid yourself of the cloud that hangs over you. He answers you or perhaps he does not answer you but you know: He fears greatly the destruction of the house while it is being built, and we have had so many destructions, and the images of Datan and Aviram hover over our history from its inception. His mortification stems from the power of his love, his proper perspective, and the sharpness of all his senses.

Therefore, many find standing in his cloud and in his fire so difficult.

And look at this wonder: He shone to me from inside his dark, heavy cloud. And I began to see clearly again, out of the fog that had descended upon us.

I again lit my meager self in his fire, and I am again standing on my legs without limping, for weight and balance have been restored. And I will every once in a while see him again, when doubt enters my heart.

5. In the City of Fire

> All as one: Without Jerusalem! Without Jerusalem!
> — Do we need this "holiness?" said the unbeliever.
> — Do we need this stone, said the trader.
> It's holy to all the world . . . said the author.
> Even Birionim leaders and choice Sicarii who
> carried Jerusalem thus far—it died in their hearts.
> With my own eyes I saw the spread of betrayal
> and how rebels and dreamers disgraced their fathers.
>
> Greenberg, "Wall-Encircled Jerusalem," *Sulam*, no. 9

The prophet lashes, he does, he lashes our backs and *he* feels the pain, for the skin of many among us is too rough to feel any more pain.

The prophet lashes, and his lashing tears the skin and reveals the pus underneath.

We are ordered to stand before the mirror of our conscience and see our flesh devoid of its normal skin, its rhetorical skin, its conceited skin . . . .

I stand, as I do in this entire book, with my flesh in full view, yet in telling the story of Jerusalem I will not join the prophet in saying "it died in their hearts," because I know the many, many people—especially from the lower ranks, the masses—in whose hearts it lived, though I also know: Jerusalem no longer burned in the center of the heart, only somewhere at the edge. Therefore the scorching was not enough to take the mind off other things.

She was one point on the agenda of the Central and the High Commands. Always on the agenda but always *one* point on the agenda.

And the prophet was right in saying that *she* was the key to the whole front, militarily and politically, and she was the key to the success or failure of the Underground. We did not see this and the IZL did not see this.

When the time came and we did see . . . oh, we were very late.

Even the activity of the Lehi branch in Jerusalem, and the fact that it became the last bastion of the independent war of the Underground dedicated to the freedom of Israel, even this was not a planned and considered move on the part of the Central Command of the Fighters for the Freedom of Israel. The impetus for the development of the Jerusalem branch came with the arrival of Joshua Zetler (Meir), one of the valuable commanders who had unhesitatingly followed Yair during the split from David Raziel and who was now coincidentally given the heavy privilege of being one of the last commanders of the independent Lehi.

This was coincidental, for had it not been so, had it resulted from advance planning and had Meir been given all the assistance he requested, then the Old City of Jerusalem would have been in our hands in 5708 (1948), and together with it other wide areas of our homeland would have been opened to the armies of Israel. But with their small numbers, and with almost only their bare hands, he and the last Lehi fighters in the country were unable to break through Jerusalem's walls.

The Hagana stood at a distance and waited for an international army, and a little later under David Shaltiel's command it did its best (though certainly under orders to avoid liberating the Temple Mount), and the IZL had already accepted the Hagana's authority, and the Lehi Command was busy on the coast setting up a political party and sending a brigade to the army on the coast.

This is the story of Meir's transfer to Jerusalem, which is important because it helps explain the cold shoulder given his entire war.

I will not enter into a psychological analysis of Gera's relationship with Meir. It was always strained. Perhaps because of differences in character, perhaps because of Zetler's seniority. Upon his release from Acco Prison, we saw clearly that he was the man to direct the Operations Division; the hard years had dimmed neither his ability nor his fire. Mazal, who had directed operations until then, was a good administrator and was very organized, too organized, in fact, for a director of partisan operations requiring speed and imagination.

The tension between Friedman and Meir peaked in the chaotic days during which the order was given to dismantle the unit. I was unaware of their disagreement, except suddenly Meir stopped working. This, as the front was widening and Dov was not there and Mazal could in no way keep track in his notebook of the fast-paced events.

I pressed Gera to bring Meir back. But I realized they would not be able to work together. I suggested transferring Meir to Jerusalem, or to Haifa, which was important at the time because it was last on the British timetable for evacuation, and also because we had not yet despaired of completely destroying the oil refineries.

There was some fear that Meir's prestige as director of the Operations Division would not permit him to accept a transfer to a district command. I took upon myself the handling of this matter and went to his house (how lucky he was, he who loved children, that he was residing in the apartment of Gutta the kindergarten teacher, the first kindergarten teacher in the Zev Jabotinsky Kindergarten).

On the way from Gera to Meir I dropped the idea of Haifa and focused on Jerusalem.

Because not even I saw her as I would several months later, I did not come to him and say: "Meir, go liberate the city," but I said: "In Jerusalem there will be foreign rule, and there we will operate independently; there we will not be under the state's authority. Secondly, Meir, you have the sacred responsibility of liberating our prisoners in Jerusalem, you who have been prisoner in Jerusalem. And you must also liberate the women in Bethlehem."

Perhaps this point, the liberation of the prison inmates, was that which won over his bitter heart. He accepted. Later, when we saw the great responsibility he had been given, much greater than the liberation of prisoners (which he accomplished), he revealed to me his secret: I went to Jerusalem just to get far away from Tel Aviv. I *escaped* to Jerusalem.

This escape turned into a blessing for Jerusalem, though we should have looked at it not from the political perspective of the state's authority or lack of authority there, but rather from the perspective of the center itself, from Jerusalem's perspective, and her supreme authority. Meir and the few others who followed him, and I, who followed them, should not have escaped to Jerusalem; we should have come to her armed with the will to liberate her, with a plan to liberate her, and with the tools to liberate her, which could have been collected and requisitioned from where we had scattered them along the coast.

This *chance* relocation to Jerusalem, this escaping to her, or the moving by instinct and not by clear political and military design, this is Lehi's sin toward Jerusalem, a sin which must be mentioned and exposed since people find it so easy to blame the various Shaltiels for the betrayal of Jerusalem.

The Shaltiels did not betray Jerusalem, for they did not promise her anything. On the contrary, they promised her internationalization. In her hour of greatest need, when Dov Joseph's hopes for the presence of the Norwegian army faded, they sent aid to defend her, to defend the Jewish community within her. So it was that instead of our transforming Jerusalem into the Archimedean point of a Hebrew revolution she became, first from lack of perspective and finally from lack of forces, a continuation of the battle on the coast: There we had pulled the "Organized Yishuv" toward a "state," by our fighting and by our very existence. Now we pulled the Yishuv against its will toward Jerusalem. We fought its war. For without the part of Jerusalem that was kept under Israeli control in 1948 and *without Dir Yassin, the State of Israel would have had no chance to survive*.

The Underground forced "Israel" to come to Jerusalem, just as it had forced the Hagana to enter the "Struggle." And Joshua Zetler was the first to begin liberating parts of Jerusalem, with his operations in Lifta, Romema and Sheikh Bader. This comprised the liberation of the western part of Jerusalem, and thus it opened the road to relieving the siege of the city, as well as the initiation of a new military method: No more sitting in positions and defending, from now on *actual conquest of territory*.

The first successes are very encouraging and bring young Jerusalem zealots to the Lehi ranks. But instructors are lacking, arms are lacking, explosives are lacking. Meir begins to alert the coast: Our potential here is great. Send help!

Unfortunately, the headlines in *Mivrak* about Lehi operations are larger than the help. Every day I press Mazal: Send explosives. The available weapons are being used by the groups fighting in Abu Cabir, Manshieh, the Shomron.

In Jerusalem, they are starved for every single weapon.

Nonetheless, Meir decides to continue conquering and he goes with the IZL to Dir Yassin. Not to slaughter the population and chase out all the country's Arabs, but to conquer the site and chase out its Arab residents.

The operation becomes decisive. Not to the liberation of the country, but to the fortification of the state. But this time there is a novelty. In the past, operations like this one, which helped establish the state, brought curses from our state's leaders. The novelty is: For the Dir Yassin operation, Meir is cursed by . . . the leader of Lehi.

In a bitter letter, of which I learned only when I arrived in Jerusalem several months later, Friedman censured the operation for three reasons:

1. It will stigmatize us in the eyes of Soviet Russia, with which we hope to at long last establish contact.

2. It really was an overly cruel operation, and shocking insofar as it involved the murder of women, etc.

3. The cooperation with the IZL was without the approval of the Central Command.

And in conclusion, Friedman said, "if not for Ben Gurion's apology to Trans-Jordan's Abdullah, we would have publicly disavowed the operation."

Friedman did not tell me about this letter. He told me only that the operation was the fruit of Meir's feeling too "independent." Meir is already acting as an "independent Central Command," and, "without a doubt you encouraged him with your praise for the Fighters for the Freedom of Jerusalem in the internal pamphlet of Adar 5708."

The pamphlet stated that:

> The Jerusalem front—is the central front. Whoever rules in Jerusalem will also rule in the entire country. Ultimately, Jerusalem defends Tel Aviv and Haifa. We tell all our fighters: If Hebrew Jerusalem is holding its own until today, this is thanks to the Fighters for the Freedom of Israel, Lehi. We chased the enemy from Lifta, Romema, Sheikh Bader. And the fate of the Old City has yet to be determined.
>
> In light of these military accomplishments, the Central Command takes this opportunity to send its warm blessing to all those responsible for the movement in Jerusalem and to all the fighters. And when the great day comes and honors are awarded for the "Freedom of Jerusalem," they will be the first to win them. All honor to the freedom fighters in Jerusalem, the capital.

Only, the great day has not come. And if it has not come, we are more to blame than the others. At that time, though, one Lehi Central Command formally existed. But two hearts were already beating separately. One wrote the words of praise in the pamphlet and was rebuked for them. And one wrote the letter of condemnation with its three reasons.

And therefore the aid for which Meir was begging was not sent. Therefore, he stood with a small group of people on the roof of death near the Old City's wall on May 14. And if Dov and his company who were wandering aimlessly in the Shomron had been with him, then the whole city would have been in our hands; and we would not have needed to plead in vain for help from the Hagana and the IZL, and we would not have needed to wait afterward for a joint attack, an attack that was really nothing more than a deception, coming as it did three hours before the cease-fire was to take effect. If Meir was forced to surrender to Shaltiel's authority in Jerusalem, this was because we on the coast had already surrendered to the state's authority in spirit before we did so in body. We gave up on the path of Lehi and took up the path of "defending the state."

Though we were destined and able to conquer the Temple Mount and reach Shchem, we sent the best Fighters for the Freedom of Israel to take the Iraqi flag for Kibbutz Negba, and Uja al Chfir for . . . a demilitarized zone of the United Nations. Instead of drawing others after us, we followed others.

We betrayed Yair's path then. We betrayed Jerusalem then.

She waited for us.

And Meir called on shortwave and by messenger: Send Dov and his men to Jerusalem. Send me another few Bren guns. Send!!

And we were already sitting with Levi Skolnick and Israel Galili and Yitzhak Sadeh discussing the details of Lehi's surrender, or, in kinder language: The details of the elimination of separatism, by means of Lehi's entry into the Israel Defense Forces.

For We Were Too Patriotic

1. Dialectics of an Anonymous Jew

The Irgun Zvai Leumi called up most of its forces and opened an offensive in Jaffa.

Dov informed us that IZL headquarters suggested that we, too, participate in the attack. Dov burned to do so. But there was no enthusiasm in the Lehi Command. I personally did not believe that the attack would succeed; and since I described it as an "exhibitionist operation" in *Mivrak* and in our broadcasts, therefore today I must salute the blood spilled in the operation, bow my head and ask that I be forgiven.

That Natan Friedman opposed such cooperation with the IZL goes without saying. He received authoritative information from the Hagana leaders that the Hagana was about to lay siege to Jaffa and force it to surrender without a fight (today we know what that would have meant: Jaffa would still be Arab today, right in our country's bustling center). Natan Friedman was then in the throes of his great friendship with Moshe Sneh and they held weekly meetings, after every one of which Natan returned with new compliments for us from Sneh, and new plans for the establishment of a new united fighters party, etc., etc., etc., and under such circumstances, he said, there was no point in "sullying" our name by cooperating with the IZL. Our agents abroad, in our Paris and Prague branches, also informed us every once in a while of signs of sympathy on the left. Once it was even hinted that finally, the instructions were going to come from the Communist Information Bureau (Comminform) to support us; so obviously, getting too close to the IZL would not be helpful.

Dov did not understand high diplomacy; he was burning to join the fray. Only with the first successes, and the first heavy casualties, did our consciences become—at least mine did—befuddled. But my confusion, my wish to participate, was only on an emotional and superficially intellectual level. In hindsight, I still see things differently. Two considerations weighed against conquering Jaffa. One occurred to me only later. I did not think of it during the attack, but only after I understood that we had betrayed Jerusalem. To liberate all of Jerusalem, we would have needed not even half the men who conquered Jaffa; and with a third of the arms used for the conquest of Jaffa, we could have liberated Jerusalem's Old City.

But at the time, the Underground was not focused on Jerusalem. This is the truth and it must be told. We allocated percentages of our members and weapons for Jerusalem. The IZL allocated percentages of its members and weapons for Jerusalem. We sent a lot of food to Jerusalem. The IZL also sent food. But not real fighting forces with serious weapons.

As for Jaffa—there would have been nothing to fear. The conquest of Jerusalem would have solved the problem of Jaffa and the problem of many other fronts. But if the so-called "greatest commanders of the generation" who were serving in the IZL did not understand this, then how was a military ignoramus like me to understand?

I was surprised when another argument against the conquest of Jaffa was brought to my attention, during the days of the Jaffa battle itself. At a meeting of a group of sympathizers before whom I sometimes used to lecture, one of the older men, a long-time Revisionist, phrased the question thus: "Why does the Underground have to pluck the chestnuts from the fire for Ben Gurion? Why is Lehi sending its members to Abu Cabir and the IZL going to Manshieh or the heart of Jaffa? You are spilling your blood for Ben Gurion."

So, I asked in response, should we rely on the Hagana? The Hagana, which has gloried all these years in being ready for the Arab front, has by its renewed restraint brought about this disgraceful situation in which Jaffa is threatening Greater Tel Aviv. Every day, sniping and casualties. Rehov Herzl is paralyzed. Residents are fleeing. This is a disgrace. And the Hagana is helpless.

That's exactly it, insisted the man. For once—the Yishuv will learn what the Hagana really is. For once—this Yishuv will suffer. It will suffer and give many lives, until it is sick of this administration and this Hagana. The blood will keep flowing and you, the Lehi and IZL, must stand far, far away! Don't lift a finger. Your hearts may break—but don't lift a finger, until the Jews come to you and fall to their knees before the youths of Lehi and beg: "Save us! Put an end to the disgrace and the murder." And only then give your conditions and go. Then you will be guaranteed that others won't waste what you win with your blood. Let the Arabs enter Rehov Allenby and then the Jews will run looking for Begin and Friedman.

This was the marvelous dialectical reasoning behind that surprising suggestion not to participate in the defense of Tel Aviv and the conquest of Jaffa.

If I remembered the name of that man, I would immortalize him in this, my book, which is dealing so much with this topic of the internal Jewish relations during the War for Freedom. If after the book's publication he chooses to remind me, I will end the injustice of this revolutionary thinker's continued anonymity;

even though I did not agree with him then and even though I am still not convinced that he was correct in this particular case, as I told him at that meeting:

You are correct from a revolutionary-dialectical perspective, but all dialectics of this sort are valid only for their appropriate material, and I am doubtful that they are valid for this material, for our people. We have the example of the Diaspora. A lot is said about the heroism of the ghettoes. But not much is said about the lateness of this heroism, of the Warsaw Ghetto and Vilna Ghetto uprisings. Why did the Jews wait until they remained so few in number? Why was the revolt delayed? The answer is well known, and cruel: After every transport, after every "action," those who remained consoled themselves that now the beast of prey has satisfied itself. Those who remained were, it seemed to them, inscribed for life—and those who remained agreed and were happy to live at the expense of those who were taken. This is a horrible truth, but it is the truth. And now to us, here: How can you be sure, sir, that when we withdraw from our positions as you suggest, and allow the Arabs to penetrate Rehov Allenby, how can you be sure that the Jews of nearby Sheinkin and Hess and Pinsker Streets will come? Perhaps they will hope that at the price of Rehov Allenby's Jews, they will be saved? And afterward, they will come to the same conclusion about the Jews of Rehov Ben Yehuda? How do you know that there is such a border, that when the enemy crosses it, the people's trust in the Agency administration will waver and they will offer the Underground power, so as to gain freedom? If I knew where this border lay, and I knew that it did not lay, as it did in the ghettoes, beyond despair, then I would agree to this cruel method. But because I am not sure that there is such a logical border, we have no choice but to be patriots.

Thus I argued before the complainant. And I convinced . . . myself. In the course of the coming *Altalena* Affair, when Ben Gurion had his forces shoot and kill IZL men, this Jew must have laughed bitterly at my patriotism.

But at that time, we all sinned with our patriotism.

The IZL and Lehi announced again: We have no desire for power.

We did not know that no one believed us. Because Mapai was really unable to believe us. In a meeting with me, Lowenstein went round and round and again and again returned to the question: Why do you not want to accept our authority *immediately* (this was in March 1948)?

I promised him that there was only one reason. We are not confidant that Ben Gurion will actually establish a government. Lowenstein probably thought: One of two possibilities. Either these guys are very clever and they are preparing a surprise for the day British rule ends, or they are total idiots, and honestly do want Ben Gurion to establish the government and then they will salute him. All the repeated demands of the Hagana and the Yishuv's institutions for us to dismantle our organizations and lay down our arms while we were fighting on the Arab front, all these demands can only be understood in terms of their fear, which had a logical basis and—to my sorrow—no real basis, that the Underground would demand if not full power, then at least to be included as a partner in the government. And the Underground did have the arms to back up this demand; the arms could have been used directly or as blackmail.

The general populace had a similar feeling. An interesting phenomenon made itself noticeable during the months February-March-April 1948: Brand new sympathizers suddenly began appearing. Or people we knew sympathized with us on an emotional level, but who never before thought to speak of such sympathy, much less to actually meet with us, suddenly began showing up. These respectable members of society, the intelligentsia, professors, lawyers and authors, came to Lehi, the most extreme organization. They revealed that they supported us. They asked for meetings, background material, ongoing contact.

We did not catch on then. Only later when they began disappearing did we realize: They were sure the Underground was going to take power. It seemed so logical, so proper. They wanted to be on our side.

They were disappointed.

Because we were too patriotic.

Because in *Mivrak*, *Hama'as* and *Herut* we made do with offering recommendations to Mapai, with pressuring them so they would dare, so they would establish the state, the government, so they would not practice restraint, so they would not give up Jerusalem. We gave them the authority they did not deserve; only we who ruled in 5707 had the right to inherit the reigns of the withdrawn British government. But we in the IZL and Lehi were so unrevolutionary, so far from the desire for power and far from putting everything into perspective, that we failed to see that we were obligated to act as revolutionaries not for power's sake, but for the sake of continuing the War for Freedom, for the sake of realizing our goals, for the sake of doing away with the partition, for the sake of saving Jerusalem.

Apparently, we lacked roots deep enough for a revolutionary world-view with a clear goal and clear means. We could not free ourselves from the fundamental Zionist principle of saving Jews and from sanctifying the concept of a "state."

In the bloody war fought against British rule we had been so happy when we saw a Jew like Gruenbaum who *opposed informing*. And we had been so happy when the Palmach supported the "Struggle." And we had looked to Ben Gurion for help against Weizmann and Hashomer Hatzair. And in the winter of 5708 we stood like good children, morning and night, in print and on radio, and we begged: Ben Gurion, establish the state, we will recognize you, we will disarm ourselves in front of you—we will not remind you of past sins.

We were happy as children when we walked the streets of Tel Aviv and Petach Tikva and found that there were no more English here, no foreigners. What more could we want?

I come not to praise myself, but to criticize myself, when I say: I have no desire to rule. When I used to repeat: "I don't care who will govern in a country freed from foreign rule, we are not interested in governing," this was both honesty and a crime. If a revolution has a purpose, then one is obligated to want to keep it going and to bear responsibility even after total victory, and certainly after only partial victory. We were happy as children over the gates being opened to immigration and over Jewish independence, and we lacked the revolutionary strength to be cruel toward the understandable enthusiasm of the masses, in order to complete the work and ensure the future. This was our failure. And we did not understand that once we let go of the initiative, all our demands became irrelevant.

As the demands for our dissolution increased, as the negotiations progressed, we were obligated, both the Underground organizations, to play a role in governing, assuming that circumstances did not permit us to take total control, not even by force. We could have moved to territory not under their control, we could have moved to Jerusalem. Then we could have done in Jerusalem what a "separatist" Polish general did in Vilna in 1920. He conquered Vilna without the permission of the Warsaw government, and the League of Nations was forced to recognize the fact. We, who were students of Poland, where Marshal Pilsudski had organized this general's action, forgot all this.

So instead, we stood on the sidelines as the Provisional Council was established, comprising representatives of various and sundry movements—some of which even opposed Israeli statehood and, it goes without saying, some of which had collaborated with the British enemy (and now the Underground was actually demanding that these people be given the leadership of the council/state!). The council included representatives of the "Nationalist Movement"—who had stood by during the Underground war. Everyone, everyone was represented on this council except those whose blood had created it. With what were we busy?

With negotiations over . . . how many Israeli army battalion, company and platoon commanders would come from our ranks. As if we really were not *political* liberation movements, as if we resembled Chinese warlords with private armies, nothing more.

The truth is we were extremely political movements with specific political goals and different world-views from those to whom we gave control over our soldiers and followers.

The truth is that from a moral-political perspective, the entire government should have been in our hands.

The truth is that our strength was no less than that of our opponents. Together, the IZL and Lehi numbered about four or five thousand fighters. What did the others have scattered all over the country? Today it is no military secret; on the contrary, we should publicize and stress it, for it is sign and proof of the heroism of all our youth: a few thousand Palmach fighters. Everything else was the fictitious Hagana, which was not and which never had been anything substantial.

And we negotiated with them over battalion commanders. The IZL was more impertinent and even demanded a representative on the General Staff.

And they could not believe it. Up to the last minute, they could not believe it. They could not believe that we had given them all our arms. They could not believe what they were seeing, what they were hearing. And because they were intelligent merchants, they pretended that they deserved it all and they demanded more. And they began to set conditions.

And they drew one last conclusion from this weakness of ours:

Altalena.

Meanwhile, we had helped them by influencing public opinion in favor of daring to proclaim a state.

We were very happy.

And Begin delivered his fine speech, expansive of mind and heart. The same night the state was declared.

And we issued a statement a little less patriotic in tone but not essentially different.

On May 15, the state was established, the Arab invasion began, and the defensive flag of Tel Hai was raised high, a heroic flag but defensive, and it was waved above everyone's head, even above ours, we who had thought to become the center of Hebrew desire and thought, moving from a Zionism that defends and saves to an offensive, liberating revolution, without apologetic complexes, without looking to the goyish calendar, without a Tel Hai ideology. The external process which had begun with the announcement of the British withdrawal came to an internal conclusion with the proclamation of the state and the unconditional surrender of the Underground. The surrender of revolutionaries to reformists.

For we were very patriotic.

For we were too "patriotic."

2. A Birthday Present

Personal joy probably played some part in the patriotism.

Many gates were opened.

The gates of prisons and detention camps in Eretz Israel and abroad were opened for those who had been locked away for years. The gates of homes opened for returning husbands, sons, fathers.

A single remnant of my family also arrived, my wife's brother, of the Waschitz family, whose branches in this country include one (Dr. Ephraim Waschitz) who is a Revisionist leader, and one who is in Hashomer Hatzair. The new arrival is my brother-in-law, the one survivor from over there, one of the passengers on the *Exodus*.

How can I not be happy?

And finally:

To be with my family again.

May 15 is Batya's birthday.

I say half-jokingly and half-seriously: This State of Israel is my gift to you for your birthday.

And she answers seriously: "This gift was bought with your suffering and ours."

And I add a note about fate:

"See how lucky you are. My birthday according to the Gentile calendar is November 11, and all Poland celebrated it every year as Polish Independence Day. And your birthday—will be on Israeli Independence Day."

Except that the Hebrew date became our Independence Day, and I had no reason to be jealous.

On that Friday, the day independence is declared, I move my family to my apartment. Together, and not secretly. My daughter, who has grown accustomed to secret meetings, loosens her hidden chains and calls out loudly, very loudly, "Daddy. Daddy! Daddy!!"

And she asks: "Am I allowed to *show* you yet, Daddy?"

Only several weeks ago we sat down to a half-secret Passover seder, and when I demanded of her, the five year old, that she return the hidden Afikoman matzoh, and I threatened to bring the police, she knew how to take advantage of the situation and with her finger she threatened: "*You*, you'd better watch out for the police."

From now on, child, I do not have to fear the police. Now it is our police. Our state.

The gates of love between father and daughter were opened. For the first time I go outside with her, hand in hand in daylight.

3. No Longer without Names, No Longer without Uniforms

Now, all the arguments we had used to justify our dissent were taken from us.

A state was proclaimed. A government established. An army. I am still deriding the addition of the word "Hagana" (Defense) to "Army" (the "Israel Defense Forces"), but this is not sufficient reason for us not to accept its authority as we have promised. We made no conditions for our accepting, not the entirety of our land, not Jerusalem, not a say in governing. Nothing. We suddenly became formalists: A "state," "government" and "army" and we are ready to dissolve. We are ready to dissolve organizationally because we have already dissolved in spirit, the organizational dissolution would not have been possible without the preceding spiritual dissolution.

The negotiations conducted by the IZL before us did not differ in any practical sense from ours. They offered more men, gave more weapons and demanded more command posts and a representative on the army's General Staff. We began our negotiations late and we also shortened them. The "deal" was closed in seven or eight days.

There were internal circumstances, within our ranks, which encouraged us to do this:

1. Our members, fighters in nature, were unable to loiter with nothing to do while every day casualties were falling on the defensive fronts. When Dov returned from Italy he set up two platoons in the Shomron and, by agreement with the local Hagana commander, took part in guarding the area. But hundreds of others were walking around feeling they were shirking their duty. The lone operations in Manshieh and Abu Cabir were not enough to satisfy their will to fight.

2. This continued lack of activity really did bring some draft evaders into our ranks, who were able to carry Lehi identity cards, which kept them out of the general draft. We certainly were not interested in having such people among us.

3. The recent growth of our apparatus began to consume huge sums, and the 200,000 lira from Barclay's Bank was running out. Some months our budget reached 30,000 lira. And then we had the costs of our increased production of explosives and the manufacturing of Sten guns.

4. Though we followed the IZL in concluding an agreement with the Hagana, we preceded them in preparing to become a legal party. Our hearts and minds were already in offices and party platforms, not in the Underground.

The proclamation of the state and the establishment of the army realized the formalistic conditions we had set: "We will accept only the authority of Hebrew rule."

Dr. Kurtz, who works in the main induction center, becomes the "best man" and mediates the meetings, which are held in his house. At first, Israel Galili represents the Defense Ministry, later Levi Skolnick does. Apparently the plan to oust Galili had already been hatched, or perhaps they sent Skolnick because they feared Galili of Mapam would conspire together with the Lehi representatives.

Such fear was of course baseless, despite Natan Friedman's hopes, despite his radio broadcast expressing admiration for Galili after Galili was fired by the Defense Ministry and despite the expressions of support for us and our soldiers by Yitzhak Sadeh, the "Old Man" of the Palmach and the commander of the Eighth Brigade, to which our men were—not coincidentally—attached.

Before us was the problem of how the Lehi members would be drafted. In Lehi pamphlets and in oral explanations, I promised our members that the draft would be individual. We will enlist as individual citizens of the state and not as a movement. The main reason: There is no need to publicly reveal all the men who are members of the Underground.

I used this argument in meetings of the secretariat and the Central Command. Other arguments were: We should not reveal our numbers. They are much lower than those of the IZL. The IZL will form five or six divisions, which is a big display of strength. We will with difficulty form one division. Also, and I think it was Michael who argued this (he returned to the country from exile in Africa at the same time the state was being proclaimed), the laws of statistics indicate that the number of losses is smaller when people are dispersed than when they are together. If we join in units, perhaps an entire unit will be wiped out in battle; and we are few enough as it is, and as of yet still without reserve forces.

The arguments seemed persuasive. The secretariat decided accordingly. On this point we had almost nothing to negotiate with the Defense Ministry. We would inform them of the dissolution of Lehi; they would issue an order to enlist. We would deliver our arms.

But two or three days after the decision, Mazal appeared and with several of the "responsible" people from Lehi, suggested reversing the decision because:

The men who fought together through the Underground years do not want to separate. They want to continue the war together. They fear being strangers, and alone.

Someone also mentions: It will be easier to exert influence if we are together, not scattered.

Other reasons were also put forth. I do not know whether there were more, which they did not talk about.

I remained alone in my opposition to mass enlistment. My fellow members of the Central Command accepted the opinion of the local commanders.

In so doing they put another seal of approval on a lack of good political sense. For if dissolution and recognition of the state and its army has already been decided upon, then we must behave toward them as *loyal citizens*, but as individuals. If we are still a *group*, then we must set political conditions.

But we with the fog still inside our heads, we walked the foggy middle road.

And we argued with Galili and Skolnick over the number of platoons we would be given and the number of deferments we would be given in order to establish a party and a youth movement. We were given fifty deferments after Skolnick, like a petty peddler in the marketplace, asked to lower the number by at least five. We were not given command of a brigade; this was left to the military authorities, who would consider our candidates on an individual basis.

Thus sat the leaders of Lehi before the leaders of the collaborators, and so they negotiated while the British legacy was being divided and the Vision dismantled.

And even before the conclusion of the negotiations, we tell Galili about a large amount of bombs in our possession; and we immediately turn them over.

And we speak of the weapons belonging to Dov's two platoons; we turn them over, too. What remains—and of this we do not speak—we will transfer to Jerusalem. We will also send to Jerusalem that which is about to arrive in Haifa's port, if we succeed in getting it out of the port without any trouble. Skolnick tries to convince us the dissolution and disarming apply to Jerusalem, too, but we repeat our argument:

Please. Announce the annexation of Jerusalem and we will dissolve there, too.

This was the same sort of argument we applied on the coast: self-destructive and patriotic. Had we continued to be an independent liberation movement, taking the initiative, as Yair had prepared us to be, rather than an *oppositionist* organization pressuring opponents, forcing *them* to act, then we would have made the condition to conquer Jerusalem, not to annex her. We would have set conditions of principle, not of formalities. But we had become national reformists, and we were no longer revolutionaries.

At this point, we were no longer Lehi. And Skolnick was able to ride on our backs and snap the whip of authority, which we had so derided in the past.

There were yet more foolish difficulties between the two sides about those fifty deferments. We demanded them "blank." They demanded names, addresses and photographs, a demand to which we were very sensitive because of our days underground. A compromise was reached with the help of Dr. Avniel, a friend of the Underground and director of the Yishuv's induction center.

The main part of the negotiations was concluded in seven days. When I had last met Galili, after the cessation of the "Struggle," it seemed much more plausible that the Underground would one day dictate terms to the Hagana, which had betrayed the "Struggle."

After the negotiations over matters of principle came the practical stage of induction. And like a drowning man who grabs at a reed, we still grabbed at . . . Yitzhak Sadeh. A hope that flickered in our eyes like a fire.

Sadeh is assembling a new brigade, the Eighth, and now he asks to speak to somebody from the Lehi Command. Who was it who once said that to meetings with people to the right of Golda Meyerson, Natan Friedman sends me? Ah! I myself said this to Natan. But it is not true. For I met the Communist Mikunis, too, and non-Jewish leftist groups. And now, Sadeh. Natan gave himself a "monopoly" only on Moshe Sneh . . . .

To tell the truth, I found meeting Sadeh a more pleasant experience than meeting Galili or Skolnick. Galili is deceptive and Jesuitical. Skolnick is sometimes a grain merchant, sometimes a marketplace peddler, as if all the "On the other hand"s and "If you say"s from the Talmud and Responsia flowed into one body.

Yitzhak Sadeh, in contrast, is straightforward despite his dandy beard. Even I, who am incapable of deceit and who talk endlessly, cannot compete with his stream of words and the amount of secrets which can be gleaned from him. This is not the reason I find him pleasant, but rather because I do not feel that he is engaging in deception or purposely lying, as the others are. Or perhaps it is the

Hasidic streak in him that creates the friendly atmosphere.

When he asks me: So, Scheib, when will we finally unite? I know that this is not a socialist party member speaking, but a *fighter*. Because he asks this question at the time Galili is being ousted from the Defense Ministry and the Palmach is beginning to be liquidated, and because I have previously heard him rail against Ben Gurion, the man "responsible for this liquidation who is also responsible for the deaths of thousands of soldiers" because "he is an ignoramus and a simpleton in military matters, and he takes such power for himself" and he is the man "responsible for the failures" on front A and front B and "Jerusalem could have been in our hands already . . . ," because I heard Sadeh say all these things, I make to him and his disciple Yigal Allon, the commander of the Palmach, who is also present during our conversation, a simple and far-reaching proposal: We will establish a unified command for the three fighting groups, the Palmach, the IZL and the Lehi—all the others are as of yet only worthless cannon fodder, while the war depends on these three—and we will issue an ultimatum that this man who you think is obstructing our redemption must quit within 24 hours. The people know who are fighting, who are giving their blood, who are doing the defending. The entire nation, excepting the hacks of a certain party, will take the side of the fighters.

True, I did not have power of attorney, not from the IZL and not even from Lehi, to make this revolutionary proposal. Today I am not sure that they would have gone along with the idea, which means that then I was sticking my head out. What will I do with my proposal if these two men, who control the Palmach, say yes?

The Lord of all the counterrevolutionaries in the world came to my aid.

"No," Sadeh said, frightened, "you don't issue ultimatums and you don't overthrow governments over the firing of an officer. An opportunity will yet come."

Today I know, of course, that for them this opportunity will never come. Galili's words —"Do not belittle budgets"— ring in my ears to this day, but for some reason during that conversation with Sadeh and Allon, the soldiers, I did not hear the ringing. My ears were filled with the voices of blood, the blood of Palmachniks in the hills around Jerusalem, and the voices of blazing youth: "To Amman! To Shchem!" For the blood of the ancients, the desires of the ancients, the heroism of the ancients had stirred within them. Drunk with these voices, I believed for a short while that Galili did not exist, and the budget did not exist, and that I was sitting only with fighters, and the beard is not worn to appear dandy, and the Hebrew honesty in Yigal Allon's face is not under the supervision of some guy named Meir Yaari, and some guy named Hazan, and he is not a captive of sophists and fantasists and Arab-savers, and during this interlude I did not believe that these very people would soon joyfully execute an order, given by the "liquidator" Sadeh had condemned, to sink the *Altalena* and shoot at and murder Hebrew fighting soldiers, patriots who had given their blood to expel the British. At the time, I did not see this in them; and therefore, I erred in making this proposal to them, to these men.

Sadeh made a counterproposal. The Underground members in Jerusalem should join the Palmach.

(We are still independent in Jerusalem. The Palmach's Command is fighting for control of the Jerusalem front; our joining them will bolster the effort.)

I am prepared to agree to this proposal on condition that we unite in order to liberate Jerusalem. I ask: Will you liberate her under all circumstances or will you wait for instructions from the Provisional Government?

No, of course Sadeh cannot promise me that they will finally set out to free Jerusalem. He cannot fulfill the promises he made to me when the Palmach was still the backbone of the army, so how can he make such a promise after the Palmach has already been ousted from the army's General Staff?

This whole conversation with Sadeh came about partly because of Jerusalem. One of our boys was taking a car full of *food* to our camp in Jerusalem and he was stopped outside Hulda. He was turned back but started out again, when he was shot by Palmach members. I came to Sadeh to ask, "Can this be?" He expressed doubt that it could be, but during the conversation Yigal Allon came in and confirmed: Yes, it can be. There is an order not to permit your men to travel to Jerusalem. And an army is an army.

Yes. Right. An army is an army. If so—I answer Sadeh—if the Palmach is not ready to take independent action in Jerusalem to free the city, then why should we join the Palmach? Why should we join the army?

Now Sadeh begins to draw from socialist-revolutionary-ideological wellsprings, but this is no longer of any interest to me and nothing comes of either his or my proposals.

By this time he is already no more than a brigade commander. Nor do I bear him any grudge today that he did not keep his word, that his brigade did not rise to conquer Jerusalem in accordance with the map he drew for me.

I explain our situation to him (this was before Lehi's induction into the army): We have Dov's companies, our best men, and we are deciding whether to send them to the Defense Forces of the army or to transfer them to Jerusalem despite the difficult conditions on the road.

Sadeh promises that his brigade is being assembled almost only in order to fight on the Jerusalem front, and he gives me details of the plan, saying he places his hopes for the brigade on the offensive battalion, and that our men will certainly make up the core of this battalion. Even afterward, he continued to praise the Lehi units and commanders. All this notwithstanding, I do not blame him that the Lehi fighters' desires to free Jerusalem were not realized. Primarily because I blame us, that we were naive and that we dropped the initiative, and I blame myself for not standing by my original proposal to send Dov and his companies to Jerusalem rather than to the army.

So why should I rely on others, who were never rebels?

Of all possible paths, we chose the worst, the most nonpolitical, the most unproductive.

All that we gathered in blood and in suffering and in right-thinking during all those years since Yair rebelled and set out on his independent war to realize the vision of a Kingdom in Jerusalem—all this fell apart on the day we gathered, all of us together, to give the notice of induction to the seven or eight hundred Lehi Fighters for the Freedom of Israel, the notice of induction for the *Defense* of Israel.

And Jerusalem was waiting.

4. Ramat Yair

The fire will brand our faces
Our eyes like the sun of Givon
The shadow of our flag like the wings of eagles
Will strike fear into the Arabs of Zion.

From above, our skies will rest
On our heads—like the hand of God
And we'll weep with joy like children
And we'll kiss the dust of our land.

It will come, it will come, the greatest of days!
Its shoulders—purple majesty
The blue sky of Zion—its headrest.
And the sun—a crown of gold.

It will come, it will come, the greatest of days!
The lifter of burdens, the redeeming.
The straightener of the bent, the freer of the chained
The Day of Freedom in *Malkhut Israel*.

From Yair's *Book of Songs*

The great day did not come.

We did not feel the merciful hand of God on our shoulders. We did not weep joyfully like children.

On the Sabbath that was 20 Iyar 5708, or May 29, 1948, we stood in Ramat Yair (formerly called Sheikh Munis) for the first and last military inspection-parade of Lehi, and we saw below us Tel Aviv and Jaffa, and they were free, and we saw the port of Tel Aviv, and it was free, and in a few days it was to receive our exiled prisoners returning from Kenya, and we saw each other, hundreds of Lehi members seeing comrades-in-arms for the first time in daylight, our flag unfurled, our faces in the open, our guns firing in memory of Yair and in memory of all those who fell for the Freedom of Israel.

The day has come.

But it is not great, and its shoulders are not draped in purple majesty.

Two weeks earlier, our fighters cleaved, clung to the walls of Jerusalem to conquer her and they did not conquer her, for they were few, they were twenty or thirty, and we are seven or eight hundred bodies at the ready here, and the walls are there. And there, Yankele's blood is not yet dry, on the rooftop where he pleaded: Send help, cover, cover and we'll break through!

The evening before the first and last Lehi inspection, news came of the Destruction. The Old City fell. Temple Mount was abandoned and we are standing here in Ramat Sheikh Munis and naming it Ramat Yair. There the Kotel, the Western Wall, has died and here we stand, the Lehi Central Command, dismantling the living Kotel built with our bodies, whose cement is our blood.

Dismantling.

Speeches are spoken, proclamations are proclaimed, oaths are sworn, and the Lehi-Kotel is dismantled . . . .

Which has withstood the winds of gallows. Which has withstood the hail of gunfire. Which has withstood the spit of mockery. Which has withstood the whip of the torturer.

Now it is coming apart.

Without tears.

No tears for the Destruction and no tears of joy.

Therefore, we three members of the Lehi Central Command find it so difficult to leave this room in which we have been sitting for these long hours, while they have been coming and gathering, coming and gathering from Tel Aviv, and from the south, and from the Sharon, and the Shomron, and from Haifa—from everywhere but Jerusalem, colored purple with our blood—the Fighters for the Freedom of Israel coming to a farewell meeting, to an inspection-induction into the Israel Defense Forces. Into Israel.

It is so difficult for us to go out to them, to those lining up on the hill, line by line.

It was not difficult for us to go to them in the orchards at night, it was not difficult to recline with them in prison dungeons and to sing, but it is very difficult to go to them like this, here, and for such a parting.

This is not how we had seen the greatest of days, and we had not imagined it here in Sheikh Munis, even if a large banner is posted at the entrance: Ramat Yair.

The three of us are therefore sitting with neither sorrow nor splendor.

Not one of us, therefore, wants to be the one to speak to the assembly. Each of us suggests one of the others, each gives reasons why the other should speak and not he. I am not one to avoid speaking. But today I try to convince Michael Yizernitsky that he must have his say. He has just returned a few days ago from Paris, where he had fled after his escape from Kenya. He is full of the excitement of returning to his homeland. Among us, he has seniority. He put together the organizational core after Shevat 5702 (February 1942); he collected the first men one by one; he most resembles an underground man in appearance and mannerism; he should deliver the words of greeting and parting.

But he steadfastly refuses.

We decide: no speeches.

I will read a eulogy to the Fighters for the Freedom of Israel who fell.

Gera will read the Command's manifesto.

So we go to the inspection.

A strange inspection of the deepest underground. The sun blurs the sparks in the eyes, which have turned to us, the Central Command of Lehi.

No more. No more darkness out of which the precious enlightening eyes shone. No more calm voice pouring steel confidence.

Even the fog in which we had lived since the British proclamation of withdrawal has melted away. Now, everything is clear.

There is no reason for the parade to sing *Hayalim Almonim* (Soldiers without Names) as it does. No magic of the past, no whoop of victory. Not even in our imagination can we raise the image of Yair from under the ground and stand him here by our side, at our head, receiving a parade such as this: Fighters for the Freedom of Israel joining the Israel Defense Forces . . . .

No. It would not be.

The proof: The thought enters not one heart out of all of those standing in line: "Too bad he could not be here."

When the great day about which he sang does come, then we will be sad that he and all the fighters who fell for the sake of the day's splendor are not there to see it.

But in this inspection in Ramat Yair there is no angry tension, no joyous tension, not even sorrowful tension.

Troops—Attention!

Mazal, responsible for the Combat Unit and most recently the organizational secretary, turns the inspection over to the Central Command.

Inspection? Parade?

Yes, the *Sternists* are standing in orderly rows.

Very strange.

Avraham Amper taught us—Friedman, Begin and me—to stand in a row in Vilna.

I do not know whether much of that education remains with me. I do not know whether I am standing properly at attention. My heart is not at attention.

The parade of hearts in the underground was more precise. All the hearts of all the Fighters for the Freedom of Israel beat at the same pace. Relentlessly. Relentlessly. Relentlessly. Relentlessly.

Attention!—Only in death.

Now they are all standing around us. I recognize only a small number. Fifty, maybe sixty, with whom I worked, or who participated in ideological courses. Yet I recognize all of them. Membership in Lehi is an obvious distinguishing mark. Membership in Lehi means a brand of fire has been seared into the blood and soul of a person.

"And this fire," I conclude my eulogy, "will burn enemies. This fire will blaze in the heart of the Third Temple in the heart of Jerusalem in the heart of the Kingdom of Israel."

I still believe that this fire will be carried by these rows, and I do not yet believe that before me and by my side are standing those who will extinguish this fire.

Even before we fell apart we were certainly aware of our personal faults. But we stood, all of us, under the banner of Lehi. Soldiers without uniforms. The idea purified all the dross, pushed it deep into distant corners. All faces glowed in the light of the Vision of a Free Israel, even unpleasant faces, wrinkled faces and blistered faces. The light shone from the cave of blood and in it we appeared bright, loving, flaming with one fire, and all shadows disappeared. The one man who told me, "Listen, I am decadent (in simple language: rotten) and not interested in all this messianic talk," went to Jerusalem and became one of our best commanders fighting for that which is most mystical in Judaism, for Temple Mount. And only after the Underground had dissolved did he return to his decadence.

And one whose tongue was a real turbine, spinning without rest words to convince and influence sympathizers and writers, or foolish words of gossip and slander and incitement, yet who sat in Bethlehem Prison for refusing to purchase her freedom with even one word, just one word for her to speak and be free; but suddenly her turbine fell silent. She could spin every word in the world except for this one word the enemy wants to hear, even if they tear her limb from limb.

And one who left his farm in the Sharon, and one who left his university studies, and one who was thrown out of her prosperous family home because she had joined the Underground and one who writes thank-you letters to the Central Command for the Lehi Vision, which lifted him from the streets and from criminal activity.

Every one a small world, and all the stopped-shut worlds suddenly open into one heart, one love, from the Central Command member to the newspaper boy who has just been bar-mitzvahed, from the intellectual with a diploma to the typically rude and abrasive sergeant major (though any money or property in his trustworthy hands is in very trustworthy hands), from the blasphemer to the fellow from Mea Shearim with long, long earlocks who tosses grenades into enemy fortresses in Jerusalem on the Sabbath; he tosses a grenade and sings, "The Lord's right hand triumphs," tosses a grenade and sings, "The Lord's right hand does valiantly!" and he rides on the Holy Sabbath night with a Torah scroll in his hands and explosives on his shoulders; but after the operation, he refuses to return by car, he walks back, because conquering is a commandment that overrides the Sabbath, but returning is not. And one Marxist by birth and education whose mouth still mutters economic formulas but in whose blood the fire of desire for *Malkhut Jerusalem* has already been ignited.

The inspection and parade of Lehi hearts.

A little longer and the inspection will end. A little longer and the flag will be lowered, the flag of the one Vision, the Holy Vision, the Vision of *Malkhut Israel* over which singing blood was poured, over which the song of blood was sung.

Troops! Dis-missed!

Dismissed from Vision's command, going to a camp of the Israel Defense Forces.

An army of defense, heroic defense, defense of the state whose conquests will also be forced upon her, in defensive wars, as she is subject to external forces unlike us, who were subject to Vision, we who dictated peace and war.

Dis-missed!! orders Mazal.

We stand on the roof and see how the rows disperse, how the assembly comes apart and we do not yet realize that the assembly of hearts is also coming apart, and we do not yet realize that the charm will also depart, and each and every one's faults will suddenly come to the fore and we will wonder in surprise: How was it possible? How could we not have known him? And we will long twice as much for the force of that Vision, which suppressed impure forces, which raised the sparks of holiness in each and every one. The Vision slipped and the sparks of holiness were extinguished and men triumphed over angels.

In the ideological course—at which I apparently failed greatly—I used to refer to Rabbi Kook's metaphor about Noah's ark:

Every man can be considered Noah's ark. The ship is built on different levels, on two, three levels. And various forces are there, pure and impure animals, birds and beasts of prey. But, if Noah the righteous man rules on board, then the ark brings salvation and redemption to all.

I used this example in speaking of Marxism, Darwinism or Freudianism in the ark of our world-view. Of course economic factors exist, deep sexual desires exist, man bears within some characteristics of the ape, but the Vision, the idea must rule within man, provide for his needs as Noah provided for the needs of every living creature on the ark and, if not, then the lion will ravage him, the dark forces will rule. But if Noah the righteous, the Vision, the idea, rules firmly, then the ark will sail through any flood and rainbows of splendor will appear, and the dove of peace.

Thus the Vision of the War for Freedom ruled on the ark called Lehi with its large, multi-colored and much variegated populace. And the ark split many waters, crossed much blood and withstood all.

Now we are standing on the roof of the "palace" in Sheikh Munis which we call Ramat Yair, and we watch and wonder: Are we lifting our soldiers in holiness, or lowering them? Will they return—those who return—as members of Lehi, or not?

Lehi troops! Dis-missed!!

And in the Israel Defense Forces they will all be just like they were in Lehi. Zealous and loyal. They will give their blood in defense; with their blood they will conquer Iraq Sueidin and Uja al Chfir, and their blood will bubble on the ground of Hebron, and their blood will be swallowed by an area to be named Neve Yair (though the joining of these two words, Neve [pasture] and Yair is an oxymoron).

We are parting from them. And in parting from them we are parting from all the human dignity that grew from their blood and suffering.

One more time we shake these hands, look into these eyes. Dov, Danny, Yoad, Yoram. So great and so simple. We take leave of them as company and platoon commanders.

Companies? Platoons? In Lehi?

So strange. Officers. We never dreamed or spoke in Lehi of commissions.

Will they withstand this test, too?

Group by group they leave Ramat Yair. Who will remain here? Little Edith will spin, a tremendous dynamo, the attempts at a youth movement.

The site will be yet used as a base to help Jerusalem, and I will rush here with Kurtz and the defense minister's adjutant to enlist Lehi jeeps for the opening of a road to Jerusalem. And of all the jeeps only one will be found fit for use and Yanai is its driver, and we will meet him on the road and tell him: "There's no time, Yanai! Return, immediately." And he will head back, and in the entire country, only one other jeep will be requisitioned at that time, and these two jeeps will open the "Burma Road" and Yanai will be the first to bring ammunition to a besieged Jerusalem.

And I will leave from this site in my "escape to" Jerusalem, only to be returned by the Palmach which will find me unfit to enter Jerusalem.

And here we will discuss an election platform for the Lehi party.

Lehi officers . . . Lehi party . . . .Very strange.

On that day, 20 Iyar 5708, as we stood in Ramat Yair, we felt very strange. Though we did not know exactly why it was strange.

Dis-missed!

And I return home (home!) and that night I write in my personal notebook: Poppa.

Today, 20 Iyar, is the anniversary of your death. This time I have not forgotten, though I did not go as I usually do to synagogue to recite Kaddish. Today I parted from the Underground and today I eulogized heroes of Israel. You taught me from earliest childhood to love Israel's heroes. You read with me from *The Nation's Heroes* and *Recollections of the House of David*. Today I stood with the nation's heroes, the living and the dead. And I included your soul among them, Poppa.

negotiating—okay, keep bargaining. But the moment the order to fire was given, and the intention to sink the ship made clear, one's holiest and wisest obligation was to respond with fire and unload the arms by force. One can go further and argue that even if there had been no original intention to rebel against Ben Gurion's regime, such an intention was justified after Ben Gurion issued the order to murder those on the ship. When such an order is given, the moral and civil foundation upon which a government rests is undermined.

But even if one is in no way willing to accept this revolutionary conclusion, even if one is really the kind of "patriot" we all were in the fog that shrouded our minds and hearts, even if one is not thinking of himself and his own organization, but rather only of the precious and desperately needed weapons for the defensive war against the invaders, even then, especially then, one is obligated to rescue the arms come what may, even by force.

If our minds had been working as they should have been during those hours, or actually during the days since the dispute over the ship began, then we could have launched a quick, sharp maneuver by land and by sea and forcefully unloaded the arms. At the worst, both sides would have suffered losses and not just one side, ours. Afterward, if one wanted to be a great "patriot," he could leave the arms on the beach and walk away, thereby saving in one action the state, the Mapai government and the arms, while winning for himself the wreath of a "patriotism" that is far above the normal revolutionary. The principle "civil war—never" may not be so appropriate for a serious revolutionary movement convinced that its path and only its path will save the nation and the homeland. But even if the principle is appropriate, it depends on a fundamental condition: that both sides accept it. If one side refuses to stop before the border called: Shedding brothers' blood, while the other side declares day and night: "Anything but a civil war," and "we do not seek power," then not only is the latter side not preventing bloodshed, but just the opposite: It is inviting bloodshed.

If the artillery commanders knew that Begin was going to respond in kind, they would never have dared to give the order to fire. They would not have dared, because they would have known that they risked sinking together with their "power" in the seesaw ship called the State of Israel, if a civil war really were to break out. And they would not have dared to fire had they known that their blood might also flow this time, and quite a lot of it, considering the large amount of arms on the ship and the great sympathy on shore. They bombarded the ship because they had been repeatedly promised from its deck: We will not return fire.

I dare suppose that if the ship had opened fire, then even if the Palmach heroes had not immediately fled, the abilities of the negotiators—the Pinkases, the Rokaches, the Gruenbaums—to broker a deal would have gained, as they would have been negotiating between two warring sides, instead of between one side murdering a second side, which restrains itself out of supreme patriotism. I am not daring enough to suppose that then the road would have been opened for the Underground to join the governing coalition, though I have no doubt that chances are greater for a coalition between two battling sides than for a coalition between a victorious murderer and a restrained, surrendering murder victim. I will say that if Ben Gurion was unwilling to include Underground members in any national coalition (actually—thank God for this), it was not because he was afraid of them but because he was not at all afraid of the self-restrained people of the *Altalena*. The self-restraint of the "Seesaw" (let's call the ship by its translation) gave Ben Gurion more power than any vote.

That in the verbal dispute with Ben Gurion about his earlier agreement to allow the ship to unload its cargo the IZL had factual proof of its claims, logical proof, moral rectitude, and it demonstrated supreme patriotism—nothing helped. Nothing helped: *The masses were with the victorious cannons*. Out of fear, out of admiration for forcefulness and strength, or out of . . . pity for the vanquished. Because ultimately, pity has an effect opposite that which the one arousing pity assumes it will have.

Thus we reached the third crime of that day: the crime of weeping.

Begin's voice spoke from out of every window and every café, the same voice that only a few weeks earlier, on the day before independence was declared, had expressed strength and generosity. Now the voice was broken. And the public is interested in the arguments and evidence less than it is shocked by this fact: The Commander of the Irgun Zvai Leumi is weeping publicly.

Many men and women, boys and girls, wept with him. Just the opposite of what they should have been told to do. The soldiers of the IZL and the IZL sympathizers and Jews everywhere waited for a short announcement forged of steel. Tears flowed instead. The tears flowed from the heart and from the blood, and they will be forgiven by all those who wept with Begin that night. On that night the Commander of the Irgun Zvai Leumi was obligated to weep, to weep over many things, *privately*, but that night he was obligated to strengthen hearts, not to break them, not to soften them. "We are broken," one of the IZL commanders told me the next day when I went to IZL headquarters to see Menachem, "broken."

And I am still not sure *when* Ben Gurion won his great victory: the moment the fire flowed from his artillery or the moment the tears flowed from the eyes of the vanquished. The murderers washed their hands with these tears and said, "Indeed, it was not pleasant, but it was worth it." For they are not at all sensitive. They are very cruel, and very knowledgeable about tactics, and they know the nation's sheeplike spirit. They know that these tears, these warm, boiling tears, melted the ice which had formed in people's hearts, the ice of fear and the ice of hatred. It was melted and it flowed, melted and flowed, on and on, into the nearby sea, to the black boat that will bear the remains of the burnt weapons, together with the remains of the broken strength, together with the remains of the hatred.

Psychologists may try to explain this phenomenon of mass psychology, but the phenomenon is a fact. Weeping shocks but accomplishes nothing. Laughter is much more potent than weeping. And Menachem never learned *the powerful laughter that causes enemies to tremble*; he never learned this laughter, though his hero Jabotinsky taught it. During Begin's speech, I felt and said and said again: Jabotinsky would not have responded by weeping. Under no circumstances. He was made of true steel. And there is no way Menachem will be able to claim: Rosh Betar stood behind me and gave me the order: "Cry!" And if Begin had listened with all his soul to the spirit of Rosh Betar, he would certainly have heard, if not a voice condemning such patriotism, then at least a strong, deep voice: "Bite your lip and be silent, till the day comes . . . ."

Altalena should have been a lever, as Jabotinsky originally thought. Under the artillery bombardment it became a seesaw, with a broken body. Ben Gurion was unable to take its soul. Its soul was lost with Begin's weeping.

Only after the heavy smoke cleared from the skies of Tel Aviv, only after our hearts calmed following the shock of the explosion and the shock of the tears, only after we were able to consider the whole affair in its entirety, was something else discovered no less deep and no less shocking than all the above, but on a completely different plain, something that preceded these events in Tel Aviv but that shares, somewhere in the depths, the same roots as all the events that followed it. Only from the speech and from that which was written afterward did we learn of the order that had been sent to France to delay the ship's sailing. And this is emphasized over and over and repeated again and again in Begin's book, *The Revolt*, for he is a man of truth and will not deny it. He will not deny the mistakes he made, should he recognize them; obviously he has less reason to deny the mistakes he made that he does not recognize as mistakes.

Begin admits that he issued an order to delay the arrival of what the IZL called these "arms of salvation," not even under Ben Gurion's instructions, but as his own decision: "Whatever our attitude to the truce might be, I explained to my comrades, we are not entitled to bear the responsibility for the possible consequences of a breach."

This confession is a unique document. It was made in order to prove that not only did Begin not want to rebel, but that the ship only sailed after instructions came from the government's Defense Ministry to bring it as quickly as possible. But Begin unintentionally reveals to us how the Underground had degenerated with amazing speed from a proud, vigorous liberation movement to a sort of innocent lamb afraid to break a U.N. order, afraid to take responsibility for bringing arms, "arms of salvation," until after instructions are received from the government and the Defense Ministry—that is to say, from those who only yesterday and who again tomorrow we repeatedly accuse of defeatism and surrender. Only after they give permission, does the Commander of the Irgun Zvai Leumi say:

"We thanked God that the government understood the situation, weighed what had to be weighed and disregarded what in the circumstances it was forbidden to take into account. At once a coded message went out to the *Altalena* where as we later learnt, it aroused even greater joy. Instead of 'Keep away' it was now 'Full steam ahead.'"

Begin's behavior resembles in every way his behavior in the King David Hotel matter. There Begin laid the responsibility for the great and decisive operation on the shoulders of Sneh, and here, too, he places the crown of courage and the political and military wisdom to act against U.N. instructions on Ben Gurion's head. So Ben Gurion appears steadfast not only regarding internal relations, he also appears courageous and steadfast regarding foreign entities and the United Nations, and again Ben Gurion is able to sit and read of and enjoy the weeping of his enemy, and the laurels he has surprisingly received from Begin, when Begin portrays himself as not courageous enough to break the cease-fire even when it comes to arms of salvation.

What happened? How did the ravaging lion become a good, innocent lamb? How can he fear to take responsibility, he who yesterday took full and much more difficult responsibility when he hanged British sergeants? What lies at the root of this change?

I would not have included this analysis of the *Altalena* affair in this book if it did not serve as an additional proof of the basic root of the tragedy: the incompleteness of the national revolutionary theory. An incompleteness which led to self-abasement before the state and before its formal manifestations, even though its content is the same as yesterday, even though its presidents are yesterday's "collaborators." The formalist approach creates the kind of patriotism that obligates one to stand at attention while a thief sings the national anthem during a robbery. Only this can explain a "holier than the Pope" attitude and a fear to take responsibility for breaking a cease-fire ordered by the United Nations.

The IZL Commander's telegram to France is a shocking document which attests to the early and speedy, very speedy, collapse of the Underground. It collapsed in body and soul. This should not have happened even with the establishment of the State of Israel.

And I refer not only to the IZL. The same is true for Lehi. But the Lehi's own "*Altalena* affair," even though its roots grew in this period, lies beyond it, and should be part of a *Second Tithe*.

3. Not-Lenin

The next day I went to see Menachem. I do not remember whether I went with the knowledge of our Central Command. I run to Menachem before going to see the still-burning ship. I have no further interest in the ship. I run to save the living, I run to save the power. I do not enjoy funerals and in cemeteries I like to walk alone, alone, calmly.

I reach the IZL's fenced-in, fortified headquarters. Even the guards outside are falling apart. It is evident in everything. Near the roadblock, a tall officer approaches me and asks in a broken voice if the time to unite has not come yet. He is broken and, I know, not by Ben Gurion.

Menachem's voice is broken and it is no wonder. After such a speech the wonder is that he is still able to speak at all.

I have not come to offer comfort. I have not come to preach. I have come to ask: What next? And when he answers as he does, with fatalistic words and tone, I make my proposal.

We do not owe allegiance to this kind of "government." We should take advantage of this murderous affair and with all our men open a road to Jerusalem. Jerusalem is in danger, in Jerusalem there is still foreign rule. The authority of "the state" does not include Jerusalem. Here we are superfluous and foreign. Our place is there.

Menachem does not believe it is possible to break through, though perhaps it would be worthwhile; Menachem suggests uniting our forces in Jerusalem and proclaiming a “Free Judea” there. He asks Avraham (Haim Landau): How many men do we have in Jerusalem?—Seven hundred. To me: And you?—Three hundred. Together, one thousand men—this would be a force.

I propose that the united force take immediate action against the Arab strong points as far as Ramallah (according to a plan that Meir had devised). But Menachem, when it comes to Jerusalem, ironically leans toward ensuring administrative control of the city itself. I argue for early outward conquests, which will raise our prestige in the city now being shelled, and also increase our self-sufficiency in food, in case Israel decides to lay siege to the city (we discuss this possibility).

I am speaking in complete seriousness. But very quickly I see that Menachem is hesitant. Is it any wonder? His soldiers were slaughtered yesterday before his eyes. Is it any wonder? He has just finished weeping with a broken heart and has not yet healed that heart. Menachem says he will consult with his Command; we will discuss it further.

Suddenly word comes that Military Police are approaching the site. And this is at a time of mass arrests, accompanied by acts of brutality, in many places throughout the country.

What will happen here? I ask.

Here we will defend ourselves.

Yes? So what are you doing here? They’ll finish what they did not succeed in doing yesterday. They’ll murder you.

Perhaps. But I will stay with the last of my soldiers.

Here he is. Here he is: the same noble Menachem. Here he is: the last romantic among the world’s freedom fighters. Here he is: the man who wanted to return to Nazi-occupied Warsaw, the man who did not want the stain of desertion on his name.

Menachem, what kind of heroism is this? This is running from battle. Menachem, Lenin would not have acted this way. Lenin hid in a forest far from any fire and from there he directed the revolution and won.

Perhaps—and his voice is broken to pieces—but I have decided not to leave my soldiers.

Is this beautiful? Of course. It is a continuation of his remaining on the *Altalena*’s deck. They had to carry him off the ship against his will. The subject is worthy of a glorious epic. Greatness of spirit has not passed from the world. Menachem is one of its last representatives. But do we need material for epics or leaders to direct the Hebrew revolution?

I get out of there and only say to Avraham, over and over, "Take him from here, take him from here! Take him by force!"

I do not know whether he spirited him away. I do know that the Military Police did not go there.

Apparently, they somewhere-out-there realized that whatever they might do to him would be less than he had already done to himself.

Only after I left them did I go to the shore. I climbed onto a roof on Rehov Jonah Hanavi and I saw the dying *Altalena*, and I saw the residents of Tel Aviv returning to the areas they had evacuated.

And smoke, a great deal of smoke, at first very black, very thick, rising and spreading, spreading, and it too fades.

There is not even any smoke left.

4. All That Night in Bnei Brak

Without talking about it, without having a need to talk about it, we knew, all of us in Lehi, from the top down, from those who sympathized with the IZL to those who did not, that Ben Gurion's attack on the *Altalena* was not an action against the IZL, but against the Underground. It is an old score being settled. By chance, the IZL happened to be the target. Natan's heart bleeds with the blood of Avraham "Abrasha" Stavsky; Natan had loved him. His good friend Samuel Merlin was also wounded. But in truth we are all bleeding; we are all wounded, and we are all ashamed of the tears.

On the morning of the day of the *Altalena*, we gather in a beachfront apartment; and we, the three members of the Central Command, along with the most responsible of our officers now in the Israel Defense Forces, discuss the steps we must take.

At some point in the course of those days, I wrote an article for *Mivrak* titled "Without an Oath," which reflected my views. The topic: the oath of allegiance every soldier must take to the army. I recalled the whispered Hebrew *beli neder* (without taking an oath) one should add whenever he promises something, even when he promises with the intention to fulfill his promise. Who knows what turns fate will take? Therefore, it is best to promise and to whisper at the same time, "without an oath." Was a French soldier obligated to obey Petain's orders just to fulfill the oath he had taken? No. There are circumstances that involve values more important than simple obeisance. If a government is not faithful to a state, it is forbidden to be faithful to a government.

But during the discussion of the various sharp steps that were proposed, we did not speak about the formal side, only of the practical. At least we *spoke* of practicalities; what went on in the hearts of the military officers who were present, I do not know; in any case, neither Dov nor Mazal, who make the decisions in our units, raised any problems based on a need for obeisance to army orders.

Everyone realizes we must act. We cannot stand idly by this blood. Our members in the camp are fuming. We have received a promise from Yitzhak Sadeh's Staff that Lehi members will not be used in any action against the IZL. Indeed, very nice on the army's part. But, the army officers had added, they will be watching us.

I make the extreme proposal. I want to exploit the situation to correct the damage we have done, the sin we heave committed toward Jerusalem. I propose that our members simply leave the base, get into cars and transfer to Jerusalem. Meir presses from there, unrelentingly, by messenger and in broadcasts: Men and explosives, men and explosives. If he had Uzi and Dov and Yoad and Danny, he would be doing great things.

Today is the opportunity, I argue. Dov can lead two or three hundred men to Jerusalem.

There is no opposition, in principle. We discuss the problem of arms. On base, we can easily take control of a few cars and leave. Our officers appear a bit confused, but the Central Command is unanimously in favor of the proposal. The officers will return to the Tel Litvinsky Base and we will meet at night in Bnei Brak.

At night, Tel Aviv is aflame and afraid. The three of us Central Command members try to make our way out of the city and get nearer to Tel Litvinsky. All the roads are blockaded; thousands of residents of Ramat Gan and other suburbs are stuck in Tel Aviv, unable to go home. The army has blocked the roads. The massive crowds push for hours before the army is forced to open the routes.

We went to Bnei Brak. At the edge of Bnei Brak, on the road to Tel Litvinsky, is a detached house in which Gideon lives.

During the final months of 5707, I lived in the home of Gideon and Carny. (Carny! Whoever gave her that name knew her spirit and knew what Jabotinsky meant by the character Carny in his novel *Samson*. This is a daughter of Israel who is soft and proud, silken yet steeled when necessary.) Gideon has one hundred and one jobs—the extra one being the preservation of every piece of paper for the archives; we originally showed no understanding of the historical value of this job, but he understood and simply did it.

We had not scheduled the Central Command's meeting with Lehi's army officers for Gideon's house because of the archives, of course, but rather because the house is near Tel Litvinsky and the surrounding area is quiet. But the Lehi Archives is a fitting place to hold this meeting, during which Lehi's downfall will become so apparent. In this house, Lehi could have saved itself from the slide down the slope of the year 5708 (1948). Here the fate of the movement swung: up, down, up, down. And finally the fate was decreed: to descend.

Tense and tired, we waited almost till the light of morning for our men to come from the base. Finally: They are coming.

But not as we had thought. Not by the hundreds and not armed and not in armored vehicles. They are coming, the few officers, and they are coming to tell us: We were too late. Our men are being watched by dozens of eyes. Their guns have been taken from them. Without guns, it will be impossible to break through to Jerusalem. Dov still offers comfort: Perhaps he will be able to take advantage of a training session with his platoon to simply move them all to Jerusalem. His voice does not inspire us to believe that he will be able to do so.

Some time later, Dov is part of a delegation meeting with Ben Gurion. When the Tall Blond, the scourge of the British, is introduced to Ben Gurion, the latter asks him: Are you ready to execute any order given to you by the commander (meaning Moshe Dayan) of the regiment you want to join? Dov replies: Yes, in accordance with my conscience.

What was in Dov's and Mazal's conscience that long night in Bnei Brak and Tel Litvinsky? Did they weigh their loyalty to the army, the brigade, the regiment against the possibilities in Jerusalem? Did they realize what the two of them could have done together with the dynamic third, Meir, what this trio could have done for her, for Jerusalem, with five hundred Lehi members? Did they consider that with one assault they could have taken the Old City and cleansed the northern and eastern parts of the city of enemy strongholds, as Meir had done in the west with his small group? To do—and afterward, if necessary, to stand before a military court for desertion, or for falling in the Jerusalem front, as Uzi the Redhead will have to stand, Uzi who simply left the army and went to Jerusalem and died for her.

Which is more important, Dov, Uja al Chfir or Temple Mount, which is more important? Did you weigh this? You did not weigh then, nor did Mazal weigh that night. Had you weighed, had you known, you would have decided as members of Lehi and you would have decided the fate of Jerusalem.

The night paled, and we paled with exhaustion from the tension. Jerusalem trembled that night from the falling shells, and she trembled as she kept watch:

Will Dov and his platoon come?

Dov is no more. But Mazal (Yaacov Banai) is alive and he knows and maybe someone else knows, too: Who caused Jerusalem to wait in vain that night? Who caused the Lehi fire to die that night?

The night passed.

The Lehi Central Command is tired. We return to the city.

Heavy smoke. Smoke over the city. Smoke in the eyes. Our hearts smolder.

The members of Lehi did not desert, they did not mutiny. They did not leave the army. The IZL regiments returned to the army.

Altalena is not a lever. It is a seesaw.

Neither is the "state" a lever. It is a seesaw.

For even the Underground ceased to be a lever. Just a seesaw.

Three Border Incidents

1. Facing Yesterday: Refuge in Jerusalem

After all these events, I get up and escape to Jerusalem.

I am fed up with the Lehi *office* at 2 Rehov Pinsker, in which we sit and prepare ourselves for elections and public service. Our hearts are not with us.

Michael, still attempting self-delusion, continues to hold individual meetings as in days past, as in nights past, in one of the Underground's apartments.

Gera is tired, very tired and he, too, escapes. He escapes to recuperate on Mt. Carmel.

But I escape to Jerusalem.

What will become of the daily newspaper, *Mivrak*? Eliahu Amikam accepts the burden. I will send the main articles in our broadcasts from Jerusalem.

Our independent broadcast on the coast has already been eliminated, Geula Cohen's voice has been silenced, the voice which once caused air, darkness and hearts to tremble in the Tel Aviv night. Geula is still editing the youth paper, *Hazit Hanoar*. She is trying to fan the fire. And her heart is not in it.[85]

Before my escape to Jerusalem, we hold Lehi's first public meeting. Not about the party and not about elections. I call our first public meeting on the subject: "For a Free Jerusalem."

We appear before the public for the first time in the Habima Theater.

Who are we? On the serious, very serious stage are a picture of Yair, a map of Jerusalem, and youth with flags. In the serious, very serious auditorium is a very large crowd. Eliahu Amikam opens and he is so sad and so quiet, like a Jerusalem night. Every word he utters is heavy and deep, like a Jerusalem stone.

The oldest Underground veteran, Judah Leb Schneerson, of Hebron, of Jerusalem, sounds the cry of the starving Jerusalem.

He is followed by Joshua Zetler, "Meir," the Lehi commander in Jerusalem, the commander of the last Underground outpost—who uses the map to tell the story of the battles in Jerusalem; the story of the liberation of Western Jerusalem; the story of Gush Etzion and—in contrast—Dir Yassin; and the perfidious conclusion: the story of the Hagana's Shaltiel in Jerusalem, the story of the bluff, the final assault on the Old City three hours before the cease-fire took effect—and with only the Lehi and IZL sent to actually fight.

I was the fourth speaker. The blood of Yankele was rumbling in me, he who died on the roof of death because he was given no assistance when he tried to scale the walls, and the blood of the *Altalena* from earlier this week.

Fortunately, I ascended from the Underground to appear before the people in the name of Jerusalem. And fortunately, those whose emotions ascended to the stage with me remained with me, and remained loyal to Jerusalem during the difficult days which were to pass over Lehi. And the rest—were missing.

At the time we still had a transmitter able to operate, and our guards patrolled the grounds of Habima; just in case . . . who knows . . . .

*

Till the blood of the *Altalena* dried.

Till even those who arrived on the *Altalena* enlisted in the Israel Defense Forces.

Till even the echoes of the Habima meeting were heard no more.

Till I became fed up with the coast and the office and the newspaper and even with my articles about abandoned Jerusalem. I rose and escaped to Jerusalem. Escaped to Jerusalem.

We *escaped* there. We should have gone to redeem her. So that she would redeem us—from the shame of the coast, the pain of *Altalena*s, hollow politics, programmatic debates, ill-at-ease consciences . . . . So that she would redeem me from Yair's eyes which gaze at us at night and ask: Is this all? So that she would redeem me from Uri Zvi's dark face which asks: Is this all? Is the Underground not guilty of treason?

I escape to her. So that she should be a refuge for my heart, my conscience. So that she, being shelled, should shed light on the fog which has settled on our minds.

I escape to her. And, one by one, the members of Lehi escape to her. Ephraim, the living spirit of Lehi's religious unit in the army, occasionally escapes to her. "Old Danny" cannot stand spending his furloughs on the coast, and he escapes to her. Many, many others, too. I am the only member of the leadership to leave the leadership and the party.

The rumor spreads. There is still a Lehi in Jerusalem.

And everyone who longs for Lehi takes the Burma Road to Jerusalem. As they would go to their mother. And she is a refuge.

We escape to her. She redeems us.

*

There is, however, a turn on the road to Jerusalem at Saris.

The Palmach's Harel regiment is stationed at Saris.

They are guarding the entrance to Jerusalem. Guarding with their blood against Arab armies.

And guarding in their foolishness against . . . members of Lehi. To keep them out of Jerusalem.

I am riding in a jeep and with me is Jimmy, injured in the Jerusalem fighting.

Before Saris, a Palmach jeep passes us, and inside is one of the Palmach members who used to be a regular at the Casit or Pinati coffeehouses, a professional or semiprofessional worker for Hagana Intelligence. She is very sociable and her eyes glisten with hate and hardness. We would have passed before her, except we stopped to help a stalled car. The Palmach jeep passed us. And this woman points to our jeep. A few minutes later a guard from the regiment posted at Saris appears.

We are ordered to turn back. We cannot enter Jerusalem. Why?

Orders from above.

I ask for the regimental commander. He comes. Young and pleasant, Tzvika is his name. He knows me from Latrun.

Mother's milk still on his lips and he is ready to spill his blood here at the entrance to Jerusalem.

Still, he is very sorry, but we must turn back.

Why?

Orders.

I try this: Call Palmach headquarters, call Yitzhak Sadeh and tell him that I am going to Jerusalem and would like him to give an order to allow me to enter.

They go. They discuss. Tzvika is perplexed, quite perplexed. The others are, too. Only she, the Palmachnik, stands with her hands in her pant's pocket, her eyes flashing all around, while they, the men, the commanders, their deputies, sturdy, strong fighters, they lower their eyes from hers.

We arrived at three o'clock in the afternoon. Now it is four, five, six. They tell us they will take Jimmy, whose leg is in a cast, to Jerusalem. We, who are left, the driver and I, decide to stay. We send Jimmy to tell Meir what is happening here. That he should come with some armed men and escort us in. We will wait.

Seven o'clock. Eight. Nine.

Cars pass. Without inspections. Without delays. U.N. cars. Perhaps a man named Bernadotte passed, too; I was not paying attention. I saw only the U.N. flag. There was no reaction from any of the Tzvikas or the social butterfly. The United Nations? Let them pass. Let them drive. Let them spy. Let them investigate. Let them order cease-fires! But Scheib must turn back.

I will not turn back. I am waiting for the response to Jimmy's message.

Slowly, slowly, a Palmach group finds the courage to approach. A debate begins. One Hebrew Communist expresses support for us. A debate. Suddenly someone comes from the command post and forbids conversation with us. Only by chance does one person tell us that they did not take Jimmy to the Lehi base in Jerusalem. They are holding him somewhere until we leave.

Ten o'clock. Eleven.

A vehicle arrives from Jerusalem. Some officers get out. Who is approaching me and saying "Shalom"? Ah! It's Dan Ram. Yes, Dan Ram himself, without quotation marks, the prototype for all the "Dan Ram"s, all the good old boys.

Did they bring him from Jerusalem on purpose or by accident? I do not know. He approaches and tries to mumble something.

I have nothing to talk to you about, Dan.

And the Palmach's coffeehouse spy stands, inciting: You see he wants us to arrest him. He wants to turn this into a political affair.

They guard us so that we cannot move. Midnight. One in the morning.

At 2 a.m. I decide to turn back. An ambulance escorts us to throw some light on Burma Road.

The next day I am in Jerusalem.

Very simply. In a car with an English sign: "Press," with three English-speaking journalists and me, wearing a brimmed hat and dark glasses. The guards at Saris approach. My escorts speak to them in English. A guard answers: "Okay."

Two hours later I broadcast in our Jerusalem program:

Shalom to you, Officer Tzvika of Saris!

The pain is agonizing, and the shame. I am ashamed for them, for these men of Israel. As if they were not other people, but as if I were in their bodies, turning a member of Lehi back from entering Jerusalem, sending members of the United Nations and every English speaker to Jerusalem. I am the turned back, and I am he who turns back, and I am ashamed, and I feel the pain.

And my victory, that I am speaking in Lehi's Jerusalem broadcast, is a victory that bleeds blood of shame.

*

Now, it is good to be in Lehi's Jerusalem base.

It is good to be here even though there are no more battles. It is good even though the young men are beginning to ask and ask and ask: What next? If we have not succeeded till now, how will we succeed in breaching the walls now?

And the tragedy when our arms cache explodes on the base, and four die, including Ariella, the wonderful Bren operator?

And those U.N. officers, U.N. supervisors who are more and more plentiful, and those British and Belgian consuls who are charged with maintaining the "status quo" in Jerusalem?

Nonetheless, it is good to be in Jerusalem. Inside an armed base, a base full of desire and full of pain. Even the questions are good, because they come from pain, from longing, and they go beyond, beyond the walls. And it is good to be once again with the Birion family, in Dr. Yevin's basement. Only one hole has been added to it in the recent shelling, though the hunger has grown, and the fire, too. And the Lehi broadcasts from Jerusalem transmit this fire from Yevin's heart.

It is good to visit that basement once again, as on the day I first came to Jerusalem.

*

The night of Tisha B'Av arrives.[86]

All night the white, green and red streaks flare from Mt. Zion toward the walls and beyond, and from beyond the walls toward Mt. Zion. All night the rockets shriek. All night.

My room's window in the Lehi base in the Talbieh neighborhood faces Mt. Zion.

My heart dreams: Maybe? Maybe tonight they will break through?

My heart deceives itself: There has never been a night as furious as this. Maybe they will break through tonight? Moshe Dayan said...Moshe Dayan hinted....

Maybe?

If they had any sense of history. Oh, if!! On this night, the anniversary of the First Destruction, the anniversary of the Second Destruction, if on this night they break through and make an opening in the walls and arrive . . . . And they do have the strength to do so, it is within their capability! They have enough arms, there are enough men, and there is Jerusalem yearning, ready for such a night of terror, provided that they break through, provided they come.

To it. To the bereaved, to the abandoned, to the Kotel, the Western Wall.

To break through and to engulf everything in fire. Everything. She fell in fire and she will rise in fire. Once and forever. To destroy everything there, all the lies and hypocrisy that have been sanctified there. To cleanse. Cleanse. Cleanse.

On this night.

If they only had a sense of history.

All that night I trembled in the chill of the Jerusalem night, in a window opposite Mt. Zion, all that night I was feverish with the heat of thought:

If they only heard the weeping of this night since then, since the Destruction.

If the Kotel would only move this night. With everything, everything there.

Let it move.

*

The night passed. The day whitened, became very white, like me, probably from tiredness.

And the Jews of Jerusalem grew tired of hunger and suffering; and mothers, of fearing for their children.

Only the faces of the U.N. supervisors appeared well, very well.

For they are the lords of the land and the lords of the city, for Joshua Bin Nun is not commanding the armies of the land, and when they tell the army of Israel to stand—it stands.

And they set the borders here.

Now all they care about is Jerusalem. For every child in the city knows: If fighting starts, nothing will stop the army of Israel from passing over the walls; and after the walls, the Temple Mount; and afterward there will be no more border, not in Ramallah, not in Shchem, not on the Jordan River. Jerusalem is the last line of foreign rule in this country.

They are working hard, the consuls and supervisors.

And Hillel, good old Hillel from the Lehi base, all wrinkled and shrunken, his face like a parchment with folds upon folds and his beard a yellow-white, Hillel whose son died when the arms cache exploded, his only son, and he, the father, gathered, gathered the limbs of his son and the limbs of the other fighters, saying, "The Lord giveth and the Lord taketh away, may the name of the Lord be blessed forever." A wonderful Jerusalem character, who tied his whole life to Lehi, who offered himself to us over many years by transferring and hiding arms caches during British rule, and who now offered the blood of his only son.

This elderly Hillel sits in the Lehi base in Talbieh and holds a Book of Psalms, his eyes full of love and confidence and his whole self a prayer:

> Why do nations rage and peoples meditate vanity,
> the kings of the earth raise themselves up
> and *counts* take counsel together

against the Lord and against his anointed?
Let us break asunder from their bonds . . . . (Ps. 2)

We will break, Hillel, we will break asunder. Lehi still lives in Jerusalem. And Hillel presses my hands and his cloudy eyes flash like that night's rockets.

There were many more fine members of Lehi in Jerusalem in those days, and truly all their deeds cannot be recorded in the book of *The First Tithe*, but they shall surely be recorded in the chronicles of the Kingdom of Jerusalem, which shall rise.

2. An Obscure Incident: "Hazit Hamoledet"

What is this? An epilogue? A prologue?[87]

3. A Third Incident, Facing Tomorrow: Underground in Israel

The first autumnal rain.

It always comes as a surprise.

In the year 5709 (1948) it came early, surprisingly.

As always, it is hard and brief and cutting and deep and loving and laughing.

Like that staunch member of Lehi who sat with me in my apartment underground in Israel in the fall of 5709. He is dark and deep and his laughter is brief and cutting.

Like the first welcome rain.

But he is only a brief visitor, and he was only with me once.

As it must be with the first rain.

I am alone most days in this apartment on the bank of the Yarkon River in northern Tel Aviv. There is an Underground but there are no deeds, not even a newspaper. We maintain weak contact. For what? Natan is in Acco Prison, already broken to pieces, irreparably. The others are confused and evasive. Links in a chain, hanging in the air.

The apartment is good and safe. For I have a good neighbor. From behind my closed shutters I see my neighbor, Army Chief of Staff Yaacov Dori, coming and going. And beyond the Yarkon's treetops I can see the Sheikh Munis Military Prison, in which dozens of Lehi members are under arrest.

But my window's shutters no longer knock on windy, rainy nights.

And though many things sadden me, my spirit is not beset by the rain or wind.

I remain calm even on the windy, rainy nights of the early winter that descended upon Israel in the year 5709.

The wind whistles against the windowpane, the rain lashes diagonally: one day, one night, two days, another night.

I am calm and strong.

The rain here is not like the rain of Polish autumns that dissolved our souls when we were still young. The rain with which the memoirs of one Russian revolutionary open and close, *Flames* by Bzezovski. This book entered the spirits of many literature students in Poland. It entered mine and did not induce rot, as the rain rotted and the disappointments rotted the soul of the book's hero, the hero of the revolutionary underground in Russia. What terrible rain falls there. It ages the spirit, wears it out, dissolves it without leaving a trace of anything solid. Everything rots in it. The trees, ground, house, people, war. Everything.

And you, our land, are blessed in that your rains do not rot the trees and the people.

To me, you are blessed. You are blessed that you are rocky, that you are soft in the welcome rain and rocky all at once. And even memories do not decay when they are in your bosom.

There will be no rot here. Let there be no rot in you. In you and in me.

The rain strikes. I will even step outside on a dark night and absorb the good lashes, I will absorb them and rejoice in them. I will step out because somewhere on Nordau Boulevard the meetings are being held again, the underground meetings, and I must strengthen the blocks, the blocks of Lehi, which may crumble.

And to return. To return to the room and find a precious visitor. A youth, one who did not age in that foggy year and did not age on the day the state was established and did not age on that day in Jerusalem.

He has just now escaped from Jaffa Prison.

He is very strong. On one of those nights of hard rain I sit with him, with Mordecai Shalev, whose alias is Solomon, and we penetrate beyond the rain and the darkness to see: How hath this happened to Lehi?

And we see: Only plants with weak roots do not withstand wind and rain.

And we conclude: We must dig deeper, we must place our people's roots deeper in their culture, give them roots to feel that which is really deep, deepen their roots in a complete world-view.

And even the idea of Jacob's ladder was floated and rose during those rainy nights, an idea which would soon become our banner, central to our philosophy, and the name of our new *Sulam* (Ladder) journal. And together we edit Yair's *Book of Songs*, and we draw vitality from Uri Zvi Greenberg's wellsprings, through pipes which have not been broken, which have not been sabotaged, for their source is both deep and high, and we drink from the wellsprings of Jerusalem, water from the wells of our forefathers, and rain, too, the good hard rain. We drink from these wellsprings so that we should be blessed, and that our spirits may be rocky and soft, cruel and good, like the God of Israel who sits on the seat of judgment on the day of judgment and on the seat of mercy on the day of love, and like this land, which is ours . . . .

Like Jerusalem, which is ours . . . .

And like Momma and Poppa, who are in my blood.

From first rain to last, cycles, cycles: From the period of our Fathers stretching from the Euphrates to Egypt, from the heroic periods of the Judges and Kings, and the beautiful periods of the Prophets and Sages, to the new periods of the Fighters for the Freedom of Israel.

The heavenly Jerusalem.

And the earthly Jerusalem.

And meanwhile the rain strikes my shutters.

Strike.

Date: 5 Tamuz 5710 (June 20, 1950), the third day of the week, in which we read the Torah portion: "If he does not purify himself on the third day—then on the seventh day he shall not be clean."

That Which I Love

Memoirs: their form requires a subjective point of view. Things therefore appear differently from the way they would if they were given a historical form. Not all the people and not all the deeds that deserve to be mentioned, favorably or otherwise, are mentioned.

And naturally, the focus is on the person who remembers.

Memory naturally follows the heart. So I have followed my heart and brought near that which is close to me, and I hope I will not be judged harshly for this.

I hope I will not be judged by those with tender ears, for the many squeaky doors that I have made squeak in the book. From the first squeak in Rosh Betar's ears to the last squeak in the ears of yesterday's and hopefully tomorrow's friends-brothers-fighters.

They are obligatory squeaks, for they come to warn of plagues in the house. Put up with seven deceptions if you must, but not self-deception. Much has happened since that squeak in Warsaw. Terrible and great things have happened. This is not a time to lubricate doors with pure olive oil.

And I hope I will not be judged for the reproofs with which I have reproved my comrades, those I love. I have not preached to enemies. I have tried to understand opponents. But I have only reproved the closest, those who may have erred but did not betray.

For there is hope for the errant.

For this day shall we stand in Nov.[88]

For we have not yet finished bringing our tithes. And we cannot stand on the great mountain and say as our forefathers said after bringing their tithes:

> Gaze from Your holy abode, from the heavens . . . .
> I have removed the hallowed things from my home . . . .
> I have not strayed from Your commandments
> and I have not forgotten.

We have not removed.

We have strayed.
We have forgotten.
And the edifying reflection?
Reflect.
And know, know well:

God will not descend upon our Mountain again, and He will not gaze from His holy abode, if we do not ascend the Mountain ourselves and establish His holy abode on earth.

Notes

1. Much of this biographical data is from Ada Yevin's biography of Eldad, *Sambatyon*, published by Bet El press in Israel in 1995 (in Hebrew).
2. **Background**: A very and perhaps overly concise background to the story told by Eldad would be: The Jews always longed to return to Zion. Theodor Herzl created a political movement called Zionism in 1896. His heirs to the movement focused more on "practical" facts on the ground. During World War I, England wrested Eretz Israel (Palestine) from the Turks; England had promised the country to the Jews (the "Balfour Declaration") but reneged, gave large parts of Eretz Israel to the Arabs and limited or barred Jewish immigration and land ownership (these British policies were announced in documents known as "White Papers"). A minority of Zionists sought overall political solutions and encouraged military initiatives and sovereign attitudes among the Jews. These leaders included Vladimir Jabotinsky, Abba Ahimeir, and Avraham Stern (also known as Yair, who founded the Lehi Underground). Most Zionist establishment leaders, especially the labor movement leaders and socialists, opposed efforts to force the British from Eretz Israel. These leaders included Chaim Weizmann, David Ben Gurion, and Golda Meyerson (Meir). They had the support of labor movement or left-wing newspapers such as *Davar*, *Al Hamishmar*, and *Haaretz*, which are often cited by Eldad in *The First Tithe*. In the 1930s and 1940s, those who wanted to fight the British coalesced into the underground armies the Irgun Zvai Leumi (IZL) and Lehi. But even the IZL ceased anti-British activity shortly after World War II broke out, until 1944, and encouraged its members to enlist in the British war effort against the Germans. Eldad is critical of the IZL for this reason. Those who before, during and after the war were pro-British or who, at the most, wanted to pressure England (sometimes by means of what they called a "Struggle") to remain in Eretz Israel but adopt a kinder policy toward the Jews, were found in the Hagana militia and its offshoot the Palmach, and in the political offices of the Jewish Agency and Vaad Leumi. The Hagana and Palmach, under the direction of Weizmann, Ben Gurion and others, occasionally hunted the members of the Underground and turned them over to the British (such times were known as the "Season"); at other times the Hagana cooperated with the IZL and Lehi (this was known as the United Resistance movement). When the State of Israel was established in May 1948, Ben Gurion became prime minister and Weizmann, president. Members of the IZL and Lehi were marginalized by the labor leaders who held power, until IZL Commander Menachem Begin won the premiership in 1977, and Lehi leader Yitzhak Shamir became premier when Begin resigned in 1983.
3. **Lehi**, full name: Lohamei Herut Israel (Fighters for the Freedom of Israel), original name: Irgun Zvai Leumi B'Israel, an underground movement founded by Avraham Stern in 1940, sometimes known as the Stern Group or, pejoratively, the Stern Gang.
4. **Betar**, a city southwest of Jerusalem, the last stronghold of Bar Kochba's revolt against the Romans, ultimately destroyed by the Romans in 135; also a Revisionist youth movement founded by Aharon Propes in 1923 and built up by Jabotinsky, a main source of future members of the IZL and Lehi Undergrounds.

   Modi'in, a city in central Israel, where in 167 BCE the Maccabean military revolt began that culminated in the establishment of the Hasmonean dynasty, a victory celebrated in the holiday of Hanukkah.
5. **Hebrew months of the lunar calendar**: Tishrei (September-October), Mar Heshvan (October-

November), Kislev (November-December), Tevet (December-January), Shevat (January-February), Adar (February-March), Nisan (March-April), Iyar (April-May), Sivan (May-June), Tamuz (June-July), Av (July-August), and Elul (August-September).

6. **Ibn Ezra** (1092-1167), Jewish thinker, author of a commentary on the Bible.
7. **Revisionist Party and movement**, founded by Jabotinsky in 1923 (officially, April 1925) as an alternative to the establishment Zionist parties that accepted the British White Paper's removal of Trans-Jordan from the Jewish homeland.
8. **Goy** (plural: goyim), the Hebrew word for nation, in post-biblical use usually (and in *The First Tithe*, always) refers to Gentiles.
9. **Stavsky, Avraham** (1906-1948), Betar member accused of murdering Chaim Arlosoroff in 1933. The trials held by the British were shams. Prosecution witnesses colluded with police, blatant perjury took place, vital defense evidence was ignored or suppressed. The accused were acquitted on appeal. But the "Arlosoroff Affair," as it came to be known, had already degenerated into something far worse than a trial. Labor leaders transformed the affair first into a blood libel—accusing all Revisionists of being bloodthirsty fascists—and then into a witch-hunt—persecuting Revisionists, expelling them from workplaces, denying them other rights. The affair is one of the darkest chapters in Zionist history. Stavsky devoted the years following his acquittal to organizing the "illegal" immigration of Jewish refugees to British-controlled Eretz Israel. In 1948 he was killed in the course of another dark chapter in Zionist history: Stavsky was shot as he brought desperately needed weapons to the newly born State of Israel, on board the *Altalena* ship.
10. **IZL**, full name: Irgun Zvai Leumi (Hebrew for National Military Organization), known as the Irgun, an underground army founded in Eretz Israel in 1931, halted anti-British activity at the beginning of World War II, declared a "Revolt" against England in 1944, active till the founding of Israel in 1948, headed by Menachem Begin 1944-1948.
11. **Jabotinsky, Vladimir Zev** (1880-1940), Russian playwright and journalist, founded the Jewish Legion in World War I, founded the Hagana in 1920, imprisoned by the British in Jerusalem and Acco, organized Betar and sometimes referred to by his organizational title: "Rosh Betar," exiled from Eretz Israel by the British in 1929, warned of an impending Holocaust, urged Jews to flee from Europe to Eretz Israel, the Supreme Commander of the IZL.
12. **Begin, Menahem** (1913-1992), member of Betar in Poland, Commander in Chief of the IZL 1944-1948, member of Knesset, prime minister 1977-1983.
13. **Ahimeir, Dr. Abba** (1897-1962), journalist, teacher, founder (with Uri Zvi Greenberg and Y. H. Yevin) of Brit Habirionim, imprisoned in 1930s for incitement to rebellion, afterward assisted IZL.

    Greenberg, Uri Zvi (1896-1981), "the poet of the redemption," in 1921 predicted the Holocaust, in 1930s and 1940s inspired youths to join Hagana, IZL and Lehi.

    Yevin, Dr. Yehoshua H. (1891-1970), journalist, aided the IZL and Lehi, especially by writing broadsides, newspaper articles and radio broadcasts.
14. **Yellin-Mor (Friedman), Natan** (1913-1980), (nom de guerre: "Gera") member of Betar, one of three members of the Lehi Central Command, responsible for foreign contacts and diplomacy, arrested after the assassination of U.N. mediator Count Bernadotte in 1948, freed from prison after he was elected to the first Knesset, moved leftward in his political views.
15. **Rosh Betar** (Hebrew for Leader of Betar), the title held by Jabotinsky in the Betar movement.
16. **Levin, Rabbi Arye** (1885-1969), the "father of the prisoners," rabbi who visited and aided

imprisoned fighters.

17. **Stern, Avraham** ("Yair") (1907-1942), member of IZL High Command, in charge of illegal immigration and establishing IZL cells in Poland, imprisoned, founded Lehi (the "Stern Group"), wrote *Principles of Rebirth*, poetry and songs, murdered by the British on February 12, 1942.
18. **Aliya** (Hebrew for immigration to Eretz Israel). The British outlawed or severely limited Jewish immigration to Eretz Israel, blockading the shores and deporting or imprisoning Jewish refugees who were considered "illegal" immigrants. Jabotinsky encouraged Jewish youth, especially from Europe, to immigrate by any means possible, and the Revisionists thus helped some forty thousand Jews to escape from Europe, mostly by boat, and mostly before but also during the Holocaust. The Hagana began participating in "illegal" immigration in 1944 and brought close to five thousand Jews to Israel by the end of the year. Another seventy thousand came by the time Israel was established in 1948. An additional twelve thousand immigrated "illegally" by land routes from Europe and Arab countries. Eldad's reference to "independent" aliya is to the organization of mass aliya from Europe by the Revisionists, instead of waiting to receive a few British-approved immigration certificates from the Labor Zionist establishment.
19. **Acco**, also called Acre, a coastal city north of Haifa housing a Crusader fortress used by the British as a prison. From 1938-1947 the British hanged members of the IZL in this prison. On May 4, 1947, the IZL attacked the prison and freed over 250 inmates.
20. **White Paper**(s), three reports issued by the British detailing their policy in Eretz Israel. The first in 1922 removed Trans-Jordan (the area now known as Jordan) from the territory of the Jewish homeland; the second in 1930 ordered limits on Jewish immigration and settlement; the third, issued on May 17, 1939, further limited Jewish immigration (which was to be banned altogether in five years) and land ownership and worked to preserve an Arab majority in a future state.
21. **Granek, Yaacov** (also known as Dov the Blond, or simply as the "Tall Blond") (1923-1948), member of Betar and IZL in Poland, volunteered for Polish army in 1939, fought in the Polish defense of Warsaw, taken POW and escaped, made aliya in 1941, became one of Lehi's most famous fighters, the commanding officer of Eldad's escape in June 1946, also deputy commander of the joint IZL-Lehi bombing of Jerusalem's Criminal Investigations Department, and commander of Lehi's destruction of nine British aircraft at the Kfar Sirkin airfield and the bombing of Intelligence headquarters in Jaffa. Granek was sent by Lehi to coordinate its activity in Italy; he returned and was killed in December 1948 fighting in Uja al Chfir as a captain in the Israeli army. Eldad's references to him are always positive, except after the sinking of the *Altalena*, when Granek remained with the Israeli army rather than follow Eldad's advice to leave for Jerusalem.

    Ashbel, Michael (1922-1947), member of Betar and IZL in Poland, joined IZL in Eretz Israel, participated in attacks on Lod airfield and Intelligence headquarters in Jaffa, arrested and sentenced to death after being injured in attack on Sarafand army base, sentence commuted, shot and killed during breakout from Acco Prison. While in prison, Ashbel authored what became one of the most popular underground songs, "On the Barricades."

    Gruner, Dov (1912-1947), member of IZL, served in the British army, afterward injured in an IZL raid on the Ramat Gan police station, hanged by the British after refusing to ask for clemency.

    Amper, Avraham (1916-1942), member of Betar and IZL in Poland, Lehi in Eretz Israel, murdered by the British in an apartment at 30 Rehov Dizengoff in Tel Aviv.
22. ***Struma***, a ship carrying Jewish refugees from Europe, torpedoed on February 24, 1942, on its

way to Eretz Israel, leaving only one survivor and 768 dead.

23. ***Rehov***, Hebrew word for street.
24. **Kotel**, the Western Wall of the Temple Mount (the biblical Mount Moriah) in Jerusalem, formerly known as the Wailing Wall.
25. **Baal Shem Tov** (1698-1760), the title of Rabbi Israel Ben Eliezer, founder of modern Hasidism.
26. **Raziel, David** (1910-1941), Commander in Chief of the IZL 1938-1941, leader of reprisal attacks on Arab terrorists in 1930s, killed on a British sabotage mission to Iraq in 1941.
27. **Sabra**, an Israeli born in Eretz Israel.
28. See note 20.
29. **MacDonald letter**, a letter sent by Ramsay MacDonald to Chaim Weizmann in February 1931 making clear that the British would make Jewish immigration and land ownership conditional on their effect on local Arabs.
30. **Lubotzky (Eliav), Dr. Benjamin** (1909-1974), Zionist-Revisionist journalist and editor, his relations with the Revisionist movement were often acrimonious. From 1943-1944 he headed the Haam movement. Lubotzky was also an editor of a daily newspaper, *Mivrak*, co-published by Haam and Lehi in late 1947 and 1948. (In Israel he edited a Labor Party newspaper and became an official of the Foreign Ministry.)

    Levenberg, Zalman (1909-1983), journalist, member of the editorial board of *Hamashkif*, supported enlistment in the British army. He enlisted as well, and eventually participated in the struggle of the soldiers to fly the Jewish flag. Later, worked at the Israeli daily, *Maariv*.
31. **Yael Street** in Tel Aviv, Lehi mined 8 Rehov Yael on January 20, 1942, in an attempt to eliminate high-ranking British detectives. Instead, Jewish policemen were killed, and though the British officer who had hanged Shlomo Ben Yosef also died, the attack only increased the public's antagonism toward Lehi.
32. **Dizengoff Street** in Tel Aviv, at 30 Rehov Dizengoff, British detectives surprised members of Lehi on January 27, 1942, and shot them in bed or with their hands up. Avraham Amper and Zelig Jack died, Moshe Svorai and Yaacov Levstein recovered and were sentenced to life in prison.

    Mizrachi Bet Street in Tel Aviv, at number 8 Rehov Mizrachi Bet, Avraham Stern was murdered by British detectives on February 12, 1942. The street is now known as Rehov Stern.
33. ***Mitnaged***, a term used, especially in the nineteenth century, to describe religious Ashkenazic Jews who oppose the Hasidic movement. *Mitnagedim* had or have a more studious, less emotional, approach to religion.
34. **Jack, Zelig** (1915-1942), member of Betar, IZL, and, from 1940, Lehi; murdered by British at 30 Dizengoff Street on January 27, 1942.

    Svorai, Moshe (1914-), member of Brit Habirionim, participated in the downing of the Nazi flag from Jerusalem's German Consulate, imprisoned, then a member of the IZL in the 1930s, an organizer of revolutionary nationalist cells in Polish Betar, joined Lehi, arrested, escaped from Mizra Detention Camp, briefly Lehi's Tel Aviv coordinator, Intelligence Chief, and a member of the Lehi Command led by Avraham Stern, wounded in the British massacre at 30 Dizengoff Street, sentenced to life, escaped from the Jerusalem Central Prison by tunnel.

    Levstein, Yaacov (1917-1985), the real name of Yaacov Eliav, also known as "Yashke," member of the IZL in the 1930s, later of Lehi, demolitions expert, escaped from Jerusalem Central Prison at Christmastime when working on the electric lights of the warden's Christmas tree.
35. **Svorai, Tova** (1916-), member of Betar in 1930, IZL in 1937, Lehi in 1940, wife of Moshe

Svorai, sheltered Avraham Stern until the morning he was murdered in February 1942, imprisoned for four and a half years in Bethlehem Prison.

36. **Shapiro, Hisia** (1922-2004), member of Betar, IZL and then Lehi; Avraham Stern's "contact."
37. **Cohen, Joshua** (1922-1986), at 14, enlisted in the Nationalist Hagana (forerunner to the IZL); at 15, in the IZL; at 17, in Lehi. Cohen kept Lehi alive after Avraham Stern's murder, was exiled to Africa in 1944, and after his return to Israel assassinated Bernadotte in Jerusalem in 1948.
38. **Ahad Haam** (1856-1927), pen name of Usher Ginzburg, favored creation of a "spiritual center" in Eretz Israel and opposed Herzl's political Zionism.
39. **Gordon, Aharon David** (1856-1922), a Zionist thinker opposed to Herzlian political Zionism, he idolized manual labor and agriculture. The Gordonia youth movement, based on his teachings, sent its members to agricultural kibbutzim.
40. **Bergson Group**, headed by Hillel Kook (1915-2001, also known as "Peter Bergson"), active in the United States after 1940, promoted rescue efforts for European Jewry, foundation of a Jewish army during the war, "illegal" immigration of Jews to Eretz Israel, and support for the IZL.
41. **Shamir (Yizernitsky), Yitzhak** (1915-), member of IZL, member of Central Command of Lehi from 1942, exiled to and incarcerated in Africa in 1946, escaped to France in 1947; later, a Mossad agent, Speaker of Israeli Knesset, foreign minister and prime minister.
42. ***Altalena***, originally Jabotinsky's pen name; later, the name of a boat filled with arms and ammunition brought by the IZL to Eretz Israel in June 1948, sunk by order of David Ben Gurion; sixteen Irgunists were killed by the Israeli army's shelling and gunfire.
43. **Ahdut Haavoda**, a party founded by Ben Gurion in 1919 that merged with Hapoel Hatzair in 1930 to found Mapai. In 1944 an activist part of Mapai (called Faction B or Faction Bet) split under that name, remaining independent until 1946 when it united with the left-wing Poalei Zion. This "activist" part of the labor movement in Eretz Israel is what Eldad refers to in *The First Tithe*. (In 1948 it merged with Hashomer Hatzair to form the Mapam Party, but split off again in 1954. By 1968 it had merged with Mapai again and became part of the Israeli Labor Party.) From 1944 until January 1946 the party published a weekly newspaper, *Hatenuah L'ahdut Haavoda*, which was usually referred to simply as *L'ahdut Haavoda*.
44. ***Haaretz***, a daily newspaper of the Left.
45. **Ramat Hakovesh**, a kibbutz surrounded and attacked by the British in November 1943 in a search for weapons; the kibbutz's men were arrested and beaten, and one killed.
46. **Morrison Plan**, submitted by the British on July 24, 1946, calling for semi-autonomous Jewish and Arab states under British control, leading either to a partition of Eretz Israel or a binational state.
47. **Wedgwood, Colonel Josiah** (1872-1943), Labor member of British Parliament and cabinet, known for his independent stances on many issues, including supporting Zionism. In 1942, a member of the House of Lords.
48. **The Jewish Brigade**, a brigade with five thousand Jewish volunteers from Eretz Israel that fought the Germans as part of the British army, from late 1944. Tens of thousands of Jewish volunteers from Eretz Israel had enlisted in the British army since 1940, but the British delayed granting Jewish requests to serve under their own flag until September 1944.
49. **Bar-Giora, Moshe** (1920-1945), member of IZL in Poland, illegal immigrant to Eretz Israel, joined Lehi, escaped from prison in 1943, killed in a Lehi attack on the oil refineries. See note 34 for his escape with **Levstein**.
50. **Schneerson, Judah Leb** ("Grandpa") (1892-1971), member of Brit Habirionim, IZL and Lehi.

51. **Yavne'el**, where Menahem Luntz and Shabtai Druker were killed in a shootout with the British on April 6, 1944.
52. **Yunichman, Shimshon** (1907-1961), Betar officer, Revisionist party official.
53. **Chilevitz, Yaacov** (1913-?), a traitor in the IZL; in March 1944 he gave the British the names and addresses of 79 Irgunists, almost fifty of whom were immediately arrested; he was paid by the British and spirited out of the country.
54. **Zetler, Joshua** (1917-), (nom de guerre: "Meir") joined Hagana at 14, then the Nationalist Hagana, IZL, and Lehi, escaped from Acco Prison in 1947, commanded Lehi's units in Jerusalem in 1948.
55. ***Davar***, a daily newspaper, the organ of the Histadrut, the national labor union.
56. **Hakim, Eliahu** (1925-1945), joined IZL at 15, Lehi soon after, in 1942 enlisted in the British army, in 1944 went underground as a member of Lehi, assassinated British Minister of State for the Middle East Lord Moyne in Cairo in 1944, hanged with Eliahu Bet-Zuri by the British.
    Bet-Zuri, Eliahu (1922-1945), member of the IZL in 1937, joined Lehi in 1942, assassinated Lord Moyne in Cairo in 1944, hanged by the British.
    Feinstein, Meir (1927-1947), member of IZL, injured in IZL's attack on the Jerusalem railroad station, sentenced to death, blew himself up with Moshe Barazani in the death row cell of the Jerusalem Central Prison the night before the British planned to hang them.
    Barazani, Moshe (1926-1947), member of Lehi, found with a hand grenade in Jerusalem, sentenced to death in a trial lasting 90 minutes, blew himself up with Irgunist Meir Feinstein before the British could hang them.
57. "**Struggle**," in Hebrew: *Maavak*, was the form of anti-British activity supported (sometimes) by the Hagana. The activists called for a general struggle, while Hashomer Hatzair and the more moderates called for a "Linked Struggle," i.e., a limited fight linked only to immigration, settlement and defending arms held by Jews. Both viewed the struggle as a means of pressuring England to adopt a more favorable policy, rather than an attempt to end British rule.
58. **Galili, Israel** (1911-1986), Hagana Chief of Staff 1946-1948, later a member of Knesset from the Mapam Party and a cabinet minister.
59. **Bevin, Ernest** (1881-1951), British foreign minister after 1945 with a reputation for anti-Semitism, opposed to Jewish statehood, even opposed the idea of granting 100,000 immigration certificates to Holocaust survivors. Because his anti-Semitic policies made it impossible for Jewish leaders to reach any kind of compromise with England, Eldad ironically notes that he acted as an agent of the Underground.
60. **Landau, Haim** (1916-1981), (nom de guerre: "Avraham") IZL Chief of Staff 1945-1948, member of the first Knesset, one of the founders of the Herut Party, later a cabinet minister.
61. **Ram, Dan** (1916-2007), one of the founders of Kibbutz Hanita in 1938, Hagana fighter, IDF Intelligence officer. (A lifetime socialist, he later supported retaining the territories Israel won in 1967 but eventually supported Ariel Sharon's unilateral withdrawal from Gaza.)
62. See note 43.
63. **Bet Hadar**, a well-protected British headquarters in Tel Aviv. The IZL planned to enter by tunnel and blow it up; a Hagana sapper lost his life dismantling the IZL explosives.
64. **Yagur**, a kibbutz near Haifa, raided by the British on June 29, 1946 ("Black Sabbath"). Yagur's residents tried to hold off the British but all Yagur's men were arrested and the arms cache confiscated.
65. **Sneh, Dr. Moshe** (1909-1972), a leader of the Hagana, Vaad Leumi and Jewish Agency. In

Israel he became a member of Knesset, first representing the Mapam Party and later the Communist Party.

66. **Fuld, Bracha** (1927-1946), member of Hagana shot to death at her Tel Aviv post by the British.
67. **Eliezrov, Rabbi Dov** (1908-1997), a rabbi in Jerusalem who traveled to the detention camp in Latrun. Rabbi Eliezrov made the trip when doing so was not as easy as it is today. Eldad mentions that he appeared only for prayer services, but Eldad may not have known that the British confined him to his distant barracks at other times. Nonetheless, the rabbi thought it imperative to make the journey every week. In hindsight, Rabbi Eliezrov considered this the greatest privilege of his life. He held the post of rabbi of the Katamon neighborhood of Jerusalem until his death. At one point he called for his student Rabbi Mordechai Greenberg (later the head of the Kerem BeYavneh seminary) and said: "You are like a son to me. Make sure there are no titles after my name on my tombstone. Only this: That I was a rabbi who went every week to Latrun to be with the prisoners."
68. **Lubianiker, Pinchas** (1904-1976), changed his name to Lavon, member of Mapai, served as Israeli minister of defense in the 1950s.
69. **Sarona**, a Templar village adjacent to Tel Aviv, which the British turned into a police camp. Lehi succeeded in entering the tightly guarded area and blowing part of it up on April 25, 1947. Today the area is known as the Kirya, housing Israeli government and army offices.
70. **Commanders**: Indeed, even what the history books call (and what is translated here as) the "Central Command," is actually, in Hebrew, just the *Mercaz*: the Center.
71. **Urim and Thumim**, parts of the sacred breastplate worn by the High Priest of Israel, used for purposes of divination.
72. "**Mazal**," nom de guerre of Yaacov Banai (1920-), operations officer of Lehi.
73. **Applebaum, Haim** ("Elimelech") (1925-1947), member of Lehi, deputy commander of Lehi's attack on the rail works, killed in breakout from Acco Prison.
74. **Aliya Hadasha Party** (New Immigration Party), a party of the 1940s opposed to Jewish statehood, favoring the continuation of British rule in Eretz Israel. One of its representatives was Pinchas Rosenblitt, who shortened his family name to Rosen and served as a cabinet minister in the first Israeli government.
75. **"These Are the Things Enjoyed,"** referring to a section of the Talmud recited as part of the morning prayers: "These are the things of which a man enjoys the fruits in this world, while the principal remains for him in the next world, these are they: honoring father and mother, practicing kindness, going early to the house of study both in the morning and evening, offering hospitality to strangers, visiting the ill, providing for the needs of a bride, escorting the dead to the grave, pondering prayer, and making peace between people; and the study of Torah is equal to them all."
76. **Haviv, Avshalom** (1926-1947), member of IZL, captured during the Acco Prison escape, hanged by the British.
77. **Alkochi, Mordechai** (1925-1947), member of IZL, found with a whip on a night British soldiers had been whipped elsewhere, hanged by the British in Acco Prison.
78. **Ben Yehuda Street** in Jerusalem, a main artery in the city center, the site of a British and Arab terrorist bombing on February 22, 1948, which left 52 Jews dead and hundreds injured.
79. **Mikunis, Shmuel** (1903-1982), secretary of Palestine Communist Party from 1939, and Israel Communist Party until 1974, member of Israeli Knesset 1949-1973.
80. **Dimitrov, Georgi** (1882-1949), Bulgarian Communist leader, premier of Bulgaria from

1946-1949. Helped Lehi make contact with Soviet leaders and facilitated aliya of Bulgarian Jews to Israel.

81. **Trans-Jordan**, a state on the east bank of the Jordan River founded in 1946 on territory cut from Palestine by order of the British White Paper of 1922.
82. ***Mivrak***, a daily newspaper published by Lehi and Haam from December 1947 to September 1948. Dr. Lubotzky was the first editor, followed by Eliahu Amikam. Eldad was one of its writers.
83. **Lowenstein, Eliezer** (1902-1975), changed his name to Livna, editor of the Hagana-backed newspaper *Eshnav* 1942-1947, later a member of Knesset representing Mapai.
84. **Yevsekim**, members of the Yevsektsiya, the Soviet Communist Party's Jewish Section, which tried to suppress Judaism.
    Mofasim, members of the Socialist Workers Party in Eretz Israel, which supported the Arabs who rioted and killed Jews.
85. **Cohen, Geula** (1925-   ), member of Lehi from 1943, was Lehi's radio announcer, sentenced in 1946 to nine years in prison, escaped in 1947.
86. **Tisha B'Av**, Hebrew for the ninth day of the month of Av, the anniversary of the destruction of the First Temple in 586 BCE and the Second Temple in 70 CE, marked by mourning, fasting and prayer.
87. **Hazit Hamoledet**, a cover name for Lehi. U. N. mediator Count Folke Bernadotte was in Israel trying to remove Haifa, the Negev, Ramle, Lod, Jerusalem and other areas from the Jewish state. He was assassinated on September 17, 1948, in Jerusalem; a group calling itself "Hazit Hamoledet" took responsibility.
88. **Nov**, biblical city of priests. A prophecy of redemption in Isaiah 10:32 refers to "…today he shall stand in Nov."